South Asia's Christians

OXFORD STUDIES IN WORLD CHRISTIANITY

Series Editor
Lamin Sanneh, Yale University

Editorial Board
Edith L. Blumhoffer, Wheaton College
Jonathan Bonk, Boston University School of Theology
John Carman, Harvard University
Joel Carpenter, Calvin College
Adela Collins, Yale University
Robert Frykenberg, University of Wisconsin–Madison
Michael Glerup, Center for Early African Christianity
Todd Hartch, Eastern Kentucky University
Philip Jenkins, Pennsylvania State University
Nelson Jennings, Overseas Ministries Studies Center
Dana Robert, Boston University School of Theology
Patrick Ryan, SJ, Fordham University
Fiona Vernal, University of Connecticut, Storrs
Andrew F. Walls, University of Aberdeen

DISCIPLES OF ALL NATIONS
Pillars of World Christianity
Lamin Sanneh

TO THE ENDS OF THE EARTH
Pentecostalism and the Transformation of World Christianity
Allan Heaton Anderson

THE REBIRTH OF LATIN AMERICAN CHRISTIANITY
Todd Hartch

SOUTH ASIA'S CHRISTIANS
Between Hindu and Muslim
Chandra Mallampalli

South Asia's Christians

Between Hindu and Muslim

CHANDRA MALLAMPALLI

OXFORD
UNIVERSITY PRESS

Oxford University Press is a department of the University of Oxford. It furthers the University's objective of excellence in research, scholarship, and education by publishing worldwide. Oxford is a registered trade mark of Oxford University Press in the UK and certain other countries.

Published in the United States of America by Oxford University Press
198 Madison Avenue, New York, NY 10016, United States of America.

© Oxford University Press 2023

All rights reserved. No part of this publication may be reproduced, stored in a retrieval system, or transmitted, in any form or by any means, without the prior permission in writing of Oxford University Press, or as expressly permitted by law, by license, or under terms agreed with the appropriate reproduction rights organization. Inquiries concerning reproduction outside the scope of the above should be sent to the Rights Department, Oxford University Press, at the address above.

You must not circulate this work in any other form
and you must impose this same condition on any acquirer.

Library of Congress Cataloging-in-Publication Data
Names: Mallampalli, Chandra, 1965– author.
Title: South Asia's Christians : between Hindu and Muslim / Mallampalli, Chandra.
Description: New York, NY, United States of America: Oxford University Press, 2023. |
Series: Oxford studies in world Christianity | Includes bibliographical references and index.
Identifiers: LCCN 2022032609 (print) | LCCN 2022032610 (ebook) |
ISBN 9780190608910 (paperback) | ISBN 9780190608903 (hardback) |
ISBN 9780190608934 (epub)
Subjects: LCSH: Christianity—South Asia. | South Asia—Church history.
Classification: LCC BR1143 .M35 2023 (print) | LCC BR1143 (ebook) |
DDC 275—dc23/eng/20221108
LC record available at https://lccn.loc.gov/2022032609
LC ebook record available at https://lccn.loc.gov/2022032610

DOI: 10.1093/oso/9780190608903.001.0001

1 3 5 7 9 8 6 4 2

Paperback printed by Marquis, Canada
Hardback printed by Bridgeport National Bindery, Inc., United States of America

For Robert Eric Frykenberg

Contents

List of Figures and Tables	ix
Introducing the Oxford Series	xi
Preface	xv
Introduction	1
1. The Thomas Christians: Paradoxes of Being Pre-European	17
2. Jesuits and the Emperor Akbar, 1580–3	40
3. Cultural Accommodation and Difference in South Indian Catholicism	62
4. Early European Encounters with India's Hindus and Muslims	89
5. The Argumentative Protestant: Religious Exchanges Under British Rule	117
6. Upper Caste Converts to Protestantism	144
7. Mass Conversion Among Dalits and Tribals: Rupture, Continuity, or Uplift?	162
8. Nationalist Politics and the Minoritization of Christians	189
9. Dalits and Social Liberation	214
10. Pentecostalism, Conversion, and Violence in India	240
Conclusion	262
Notes	267
Glossary	313
Bibliography	317
Index	339

List of Figures and Tables

Figure 1.1	The Apostle Thomas distributes the treasure of King Gundaphar to the poor, with the recipient represented as an African.	21
Figure 1.2	Map of India, Persia, and Arabia.	25
Figure 2.1	Akbar in conversation with representatives of other religions.	41
Figure 2.2	Akbar's visit to the Jesuits.	44
Figure 2.3	Akbar receives a deputation of Jesuits who give him a Bible as a gift, 1576.	52
Figure 3.1	Francis Xavier calls the children of Goa to church, 1542.	66
Figure 3.2	A shrine to Francis Xavier, garlanded in the manner of a Hindu shrine.	72
Figure 4.1	Map of the Indian Ocean.	91
Figure 4.2	The Legendary Prester John in an engraving by Luca Ciamberlano, c.1599.	93
Figure 4.3	Sketch of the Portuguese arrival in India.	96
Figure 5.1	Baptist mission premises at Serampore, 1812.	124
Figure 5.2	Carey's Bengali translation of the New Testament.	125
Figure 6.1	"Pandita Ramabai & her gifted daughter Manoramabai," undated.	154
Figure 7.1	Indigenous preachers with villagers in Medapalli, c.1885–95.	169
Figure 7.2	Map of northeast India.	173
Figure 8.1	The American missionary and doctor Ida Scudder with Gandhi.	190
Figure 8.2	Gandhi and Jinnah having a difference of opinion.	198
Figure 8.3	Map showing the partition of India.	200
Figure 8.4	An image depicting the new Christian identity of Chuhras.	202
Figure 9.1	*Jesus and the Cosmic Drum* by Jyoti Sahi.	230
Figure 9.2	*Jesus the Dalit Man of Sorrows* by Jyoti Sahi.	233
Table 0.1	Christian populations in South Asia.	4
Table 10.1	Pentecostals/Charismatics in India 1970–2020.	250

Introducing the Oxford Series

Lamin Sanneh

Among the many breathtaking developments in the post-World War II and the subsequent postcolonial eras, few are more striking than the worldwide Christian resurgence. With unflagging momentum, Christianity has become, or is fast becoming, the principal religion of the peoples of the world. Primal societies that once stood well outside the main orbit of the faith have become major centers of Christian impact, while Europe and North America, once considered the religion's heartlands, are in noticeable recession. We seem to be in the middle of massive cultural shifts and realignments whose implications are only now beginning to become clear. Aware that Europe's energies at the time were absorbed in war, Archbishop William Temple presciently observed in 1944 that this global feature of the religion was "the new fact of our time." An impressive picture now meets our eyes: the growing numbers and the geographical scope of that growth, the cross-cultural patterns of encounter, the variety and diversity of cultures affected, the structural and antistructural nature of the changes involved, the kaleidoscope of cultures often manifested in familiar and unfamiliar variations on the canon, the wide spectrum of theological views and ecclesiastical traditions represented, the ideas of authority and styles of leadership that have been developed, the process of acute indigenization that fosters liturgical renewal, the production of new religious art, music, hymns, songs, and prayers—all these are part of Christianity's stunningly diverse profile.

These unprecedented developments cast a revealing light on the serial nature of Christian origins, expansion, and subsequent attrition. They fit into the cycles of retreat and advance, of contraction and expansion, and of waning and awakening that have characterized the religion since its birth, though they are now revealed to us with particular force. The pattern of contrasting development is occurring simultaneously in various societies across the world. The religion is now in the twilight of its Western phase and at the beginning of its formative non-Western impact. Christianity has not ceased to be a Western religion, but its future as a world religion is now being formed and shaped at the hands and in the minds of its non-Western adherents. Rather than a cause for unsettling gloom, for Christians this new situation is a reason for guarded hope.

Today students of the subject can stand in the middle of the recession of Christianity in its accustomed heartland while witnessing its resurgence in areas long considered receding missionary lands, but that is the situation today. In 1950 some 80 percent of the world's Christians lived in the northern hemisphere in Europe and North America. By 2005 the vast majority of Christians lived in the southern hemisphere in Asia, Africa, and Latin America. In 1900 at the outset of colonial rule there were just under nine million Christians in Africa, of whom the vast majority were Ethiopian Orthodox or Coptic. In 1960, at the end of the colonial period the number of Christians had increased to about sixty million, with Catholics and Protestants making up fifty million, and the other ten million divided between the Ethiopian Orthodox and Coptic churches. By 2005, the African Christian population had increased to roughly 393 million, which is just below 50 percent of Africa's population.

It is estimated that there are just over two billion Christians worldwide, making Christianity among the world's fastest growing religions. In terms of the languages and ethnic groups affected, as well as the variety of churches and movements involved, Christianity is also the most diverse and pluralist religion in the world. More people pray and worship in more languages and with more differences in styles of worship in Christianity than in any other religion. Well over 2,000 of the world's languages are embraced by Christianity through Bible translation, prayer, liturgy, hymns, and literature. Over 90 percent of the languages have a grammar and a dictionary at all only because the Western missionary movement provided them, thus pioneering the largest, most diverse, and most vigorous movement of cultural renewal in history. At the same time, the post-Western Christian resurgence is occurring in societies already set in currents of indigenous religious pluralism. In addition to firsthand familiarity with at least one other religion, most new Christians speak at the minimum two languages. It is not the way a Christian in the secular West has been used to looking at the religion, but it is now the only way.

Increasingly and in growing numbers, Third World churches are appearing in the towns and cities of the West, while Third World missionaries are also arriving to serve in churches in Europe and North America. This suggests the commencement of the process of the re-evangelization of a secularized West by orthodox Christians of former missionized countries. It is sobering to reflect on the implications and political impact of such a sharp cultural encounter. The empty churches of the West are being filled with mounting numbers of non-Western Christians whose orthodox religious views will pose a radical challenge to the secular liberal status quo, while institutions of liberal theological education are busy redefining themselves to preempt a cultural collision with the post-Western Christian resurgence. Orthodox Christian groups in the West are meanwhile positioning themselves to effect a complex strategic alliance with the new resurgence.

Mainline denominations have already felt the force of this shift. In the Roman Catholic Church the structural adjustment of Vatican II has allowed the new wind of change to sweep through the church (if at times it has been impeded), producing movements in several different directions and across the world. The New Catholic Catechism reflects the change in language, mood, and style, and the rapid creation of bishops and cardinals in the non-Western church, accompanied by a steady stream of papal encyclicals, testifies to the fresh momentum of post-Western Christianity. The papacy has been not only an observer of the change but also an active promoter of it, and, in the particular case of Pius XII, the source of a well-tempered preparation for it. Similarly, churches and denominations comprised in the Protestant ecumenical movement have felt jostled in unexpected, uncomfortable ways by the sudden entrance into their ranks of new Third World churches. The worldwide Anglican Communion has been reeling under pressure from the organized and concerted Third World reaction to the consecration and installation of a practicing gay bishop by the Episcopal Church USA. The other Protestant churches with sizable Third World memberships have paused to reflect on the implications for them of such a culture clash. Not since the Reformation has there been such a shake-up of authority in the Western church, with unrehearsed implications for the West's cultural preeminence.

In the meantime, the number of mainline Protestant missionaries is decreasing, while Evangelical missionary numbers are increasing steadily, complemented by a rising tide of African, Asian, and other Third World missionaries, including more than 10,000 from South Korea alone. In 1950, Christians in South Korea numbered barely half a million; by 2007, they numbered some thirteen million, and are among the most prosperous and mobile of people anywhere. It is likely that churches in South Korea rather than churches in the West will play a key role on the new Christian frontier about to open in China, which might well become a dominant axis of the religion, with hard-to-imagine implications for the rest of the world.

These facts and developments afford a unique opportunity and challenge for cross-cultural study of the asymmetry of the turnover and serial impact of Christianity, where a dip here is followed by a bounce there. The intersection of the path of decline in the West with the upward swing of momentum of post-Western Christianity makes the subject a compelling and deeply rewarding one for comparative study and critical reflection.

The new reality brought about by the shift in the center of gravity of Christianity from the northern to the southern hemisphere provides the context for the volumes in this series, which are designed to bring the fruits of new research and reflection to the attention of the educated, non-specialist reader. The first volume offers a panoramic survey of the field, exploring the sources to uncover the nature and scope of Christianity's worldwide multicultural impact. The agents, methods, and means of expansion will be investigated closely in order to clarify the pattern and forms as well as issues of appropriation and inculturation. The cultural anticipations that allowed the religion to take root in diverse settings under vastly different historical and political circumstances will be assessed for how they shaped the reception of Christianity. Similarly, Christianity's intercontinental range as well as its encounter with other religions, including Islam, elicited challenges for the religion in the course of its worldwide expansion. These challenges will be examined.

The subsequent volumes will be devoted to specific themes and regions within the general subject of Christianity's development as a world religion. While each volume is conceived and written individually, together the volumes are united in their focus on post-Western developments in Christianity and in the elaborations, variations, continuities, and divergences with the originating Western forms of the religion.

Preface

This book is the product of decades of engagement with the history of Christianity in South Asia. I wrote it at the behest of Professor Lamin Sanneh as the South Asia contribution to his edited Oxford Series on World Christianity. Sanneh wanted a volume that targets an educated general audience more than specialists in the field. He also mentioned that the book should engage timely questions relating to Christian experience in South Asia. *South Asia's Christians* discusses issues arising from Syrian, Roman Catholic, and Protestant Christianity and draws from a wider literature on South Asian history. In accordance with Sanneh's vision, I trust that the book will be of interest to many audiences and that readers will find that its thematic focus on interreligious encounters provides a captivating lens for examining Christians. Sanneh's untimely death in 2019 prevented him from seeing this contribution to his series; but hopefully my engagement with his ideas in several chapters will duly honor his immense contributions to the study of World Christianity and the development of my own research and reflection.

Research for this book was made possible by funds from the Fletcher Jones Foundation Chair at Westmont College. I am also grateful to Harvard Divinity School for appointing me a Yang Visiting Scholar of World Christianity during the 2021–2 academic year. Conversations with scholars at Harvard's Center for the Study of World Religions and with students in my seminars have helped me refine the arguments and angles adopted in these chapters. I am grateful for the supportive staff at Harvard's Divinity School, Lamont, and Widener Libraries. A collaboration grant from the Consortium of Christian Colleges and Universities (CCCU) offered additional support for research. I thank Pepperdine University's Dyron Daughrity for his energetic partnership in the CCCU grant project.

Many notable scholars of South Asia deserve my sincerest thanks for taking time from their demanding schedules to read and comment on chapters of this book. These include Benjamin Cohen, Deepra Dandekar, Richard Eaton, Joel Lee, Joy Pachuau, Prasannan Parthasarathi, Nathaniel Roberts, John Webster, Felix Wilfred, and Richard Young. I am grateful to the readers for Oxford University Press for their hugely helpful feedback. A hearty thanks is owed to Judith Forshaw for her meticulous copyediting of this text and to Theo Calderara and Chelsea Hogue for managing the production of the book so efficiently. Felix Wilfred and Patrick Gnana hosted stimulating conversations at Chennai relating to Asian Christianity, which inspired many aspects of this project. Gudrun Lowner assisted me in acquiring illustrations. Three research assistants at Westmont College—Kyndal Vogt, Addie Michaelian, and Carolyn Deal—provided valuable assistance. A research scholar at Harvard, Akhil Thomas, assisted me with photographs and maps. My colleagues in the history department at Westmont College supported my leave to complete this book and deserve my sincerest thanks. Our office secretary, Ruby Jeanne Shelton, has been a constant source of support and assistance over many years.

This book is dedicated to Robert Eric Frykenberg. He deserves credit like none other for bridging the study of Christian conversion in India, the history of modern India, and the burgeoning field of World Christianity. While a graduate student at University of Wisconsin–Madison, I served as Frykenberg's research assistant for his project "Christianity in India Since 1500." The project introduced me to scholars who made outstanding contributions to the field: Michael Bergunder, Jeffrey Cox, John Carman, Susan Billington Harper, Dennis Hudson, Indira Peterson, Geoffrey Oddie, John Webster, Richard Young, and many others. I am also grateful to Frykenberg for introducing me as a graduate student to other pioneers of the study of World Christianity such as Lamin Sanneh, Andrew Walls, Dana Robert, and Brian Stanley. The study of South Asian Christianity is currently being advanced by cutting edge scholarship at the highest levels, much of which has worked its way into these pages.

Introduction

On a balmy evening in the north Indian city of Jaipur, my students and I were enjoying the view of this historic Rajput city from a hotel rooftop. I chose this venue for my lecture on "India After Independence (1947)." How would the government of this young nation hold such a large and diverse population together—Hindus, Muslims, Christians, Sikhs, and Buddhists, not to mention differences of language, caste, and region? Was this project destined for failure or would India provide a great lesson for the rest of the world about accommodating diversity? Seventy years into India's life as an independent nation, such questions continue to weigh heavily on the minds of many. A surge in religious nationalism and heightened minority vulnerability threaten the very foundations of India's democracy. As I lectured, I tried to address the gravity of the situation while taking in the richness of our surroundings.

Across the city, we could hear the devotional practices of India's two dominant religious traditions. From the minarets of Jaipur's mosques, evening calls to prayer (*azaan*) declared the greatness of Allah and the tenets of the Muslim faith contained in the *Kalimahs* (concise Islamic creeds). As they radiated throughout the city, the recitations of *azaan* seemed to merge into a single austere chorus carrying some variations of intonation and volume. Against this steady hum, Hindus celebrated their festival of *Dussehra*, which in Jaipur commemorates events in the Hindu epic *Ramayana*. The divine king Rama slays the ten-headed demon king Ravana, who abducted Sita, Rama's wife. These events are celebrated with great pomp through dramatic reenactments (*Ram Leela*) of Rama's triumph. They culminate in the burning of effigies of Rama's enemies and the explosion of firecrackers.

It eventually occurred to me that I should stop lecturing and simply let the streets of Jaipur do the talking. What could my academic voice possibly add to this moment when local residents were making their faith traditions so audible? The longstanding coexistence and shared experiences of Hindus and Muslims are among the greatest legacies of the Indian subcontinent and make India such a fascinating place to study. At the same time, one cannot ignore how this interwoven heritage eventually came undone. Under British rule, rising polarization and antipathy between Hindus and Muslims led to competing demands for territory and influence and eruptions of violence. These developments led ultimately to the bloodstained partitioning of the subcontinent, which produced the separate states of India and Pakistan. As the sounds of *azaan* merged with those of *Dussehra*, they called forth two histories—one of interreligious coexistence, the other of communal discord and violence. Which one would prevail?

Had I completed my lecture on that rooftop, I would have drawn attention to a third religious community numbering far fewer than Hindus and Muslims, but adding a vital component to the subcontinent's history. South Asia's Christians, the main subjects of this book, have profoundly shaped and been shaped by the Hindu and Muslim environments in which they thrived. The cross-cultural and interreligious interactions of these Christians are the most defining feature of their history and form the heart of what this book is about. The three main Christian traditions of South Asia—Syrian Christian, Roman Catholic, and Protestant—have participated in the region's diverse social tapestry in various ways. At times, Christian interaction involved overt hostility toward Hindus and Muslims, as in the case of the Portuguese in western India during the sixteenth century. Converting others within this colonial context consisted of extracting souls from their original cultural milieu and assimilating them into a community of foreigners. This colonial model, however, is neither the only nor the dominant form of Christian engagement in South Asia.

South Asian Christianity could never be confined to a tiny community of foreigners. Its trajectory was always marked by migratory and boundary-crossing tendencies. The Thomas Christians of the south Indian state of Kerala trace their origins to the missionary endeavors of Jesus's apostle Thomas. These Christians predate by centuries the arrival of Muslims and Europeans to the subcontinent. The Thomas Christians (later called Syrian Christians) were not agents of imperialism but victims of it, first under the Portuguese, then under the British. Thomas Christian communities were deeply rooted in a landscape shared with Hindus and Muslims. The same co-participation can be observed in many Roman Catholic and Protestant communities. Foreign missionaries may have laid the groundwork for their emergence, but there came a point when local actors, practices, and beliefs played more important roles in the lives of Christian congregations. What was originally a missionary religion eventually rooted itself within local contexts, often in forms that were quite different from those the missionaries had anticipated. Indeed, a recurring theme of this book is the huge gap between missionary expectations and the forms of Christianity that ultimately prevailed in South Asia.

This story of a global religion becoming local is not unique to South Asia's Christians. It is part of a much larger transformation of the world's Christian population from being almost entirely European or North American to being predominantly African, Asian, or Latin American. Over the past several decades, surging Christian numbers in the Global South have taken the spotlight away from the historically dominant—but now declining—Christian presence in Western nations. This "demographic shift" has given rise to new centers of Christian vitality and a changing ethnic complexion of the Church.[1] A relatively silent element in discussions of this emerging World Christianity, however, is South Asia. Why would a region totaling a quarter of the world's population be so easily overlooked?

A huge factor relates to a preoccupation with Christian numbers. Roughly thirty African nations now have Christian majorities; and countries such as Brazil, Argentina, and South Korea are notable for their megachurches and rapid Christian growth. Quite understandably, they factor prominently in World Christianity literature. In South Asian countries, Christians comprise a small percentage of the population (see Table 0.1), but their stories teach us vital lessons about interreligious encounters and the experiences of marginal people such as Dalits (formerly called "untouchables") and tribals—themes that factor prominently in these chapters.

The term "South Asia" refers to the southern region of Asia. It consists of the Indian subcontinent, lands that extend westward toward Afghanistan, those located south of today's border with China, and those extending east toward Myanmar. Today, it includes the nation-states of India, Pakistan, Bangladesh, Nepal, Bhutan, Myanmar, and Sri Lanka. This book tells stories arising from many South Asian contexts, but mostly from what is now called India, and includes time periods that precede the drawing of national borders.

With a population of 1.4 billion, India, the largest nation of South Asia, captures attention as the world's largest democracy and as a nation experiencing rapid growth in certain sectors of its economy. Far less attention is paid to its Christians, who account for less than 3 percent of its population. Images of South Asian Christians that often circulate in global media are those of a beleaguered minority suffering violence at the hands of militants, whether under blasphemy laws in Muslim-majority states or by Hindu extremists who oppose Christian conversions.

Paradoxically, the growth of Christianity in the Global South has coincided in India with the rise of militant Hindu nationalism. For decades, a coalition of organizations known as the Sangh Parivar (or Saffron Brotherhood) has advanced its agenda of *Hindutva*—literally, the pursuit of Hindu-ness in all aspects of national life. The *Hindutva* agenda has placed India's secular democracy under severe stress and has heightened the vulnerability of many Christians and Muslims. The Sangh Parivar portrays adherents of these two religions as non-Indian or foreign, despite centuries of integration into the cultural fabric of the subcontinent. Hindu nationalists have long portrayed Christian conversion as an act of deracination and denationalization. They have introduced anti-conversion laws in several states and have launched campaigns to reconvert Christians and Muslims to Hinduism.[2]

Table 0.1 Christian populations in South Asia.

Country	Christian population	Percentage of total population
India	27,819,588	2.3
Sri Lanka	1,552,161	7.4
Bangladesh	447,009	0.31
Pakistan	1,300,000	1.59
Myanmar	3,172,479	6.3
Nepal	375,699	1.4
Bhutan	8,000–30,000	0.5–3.6

Note: These figures are drawn from official census reports of the respective governments and relevant databases from 2010 to the present.*

*"Religion Census 2011," All India Religion Census Data, https://www.census2011.co.in/religion.php; "C-1 Population by Religious Community: 2011," Office of the Registrar General and Census Commissioner, Ministry of Home Affairs, Government of India, https://www.censusindia.gov.in/2011census/C-01/DDW00C-01%20MDDS.XLS; "2018 Report on International Religious Freedom: Sri Lanka," p. 2, US Department of State, Office of International Religious Freedom, https://www.state.gov/wp-content/uploads/2019/05/SRI-LANKA-2018-INTERNATIONAL-RELIGIOUS-FREEDOM-REPORT.pdf; "Census of Population and Housing: 2012. Religion," Department of Census and Statistics, Sri Lanka, http://www.statistics.gov.lk/PopHouSat/CPH2012Visualization/htdocs/index.php?usecase=indicator&action=Map&indId=10&Legend=2; "Age–Sex Composition of Bangladesh Population. Population Monogram: Volume 9," p. 28, Bangladesh Bureau of Statistics (2015), http://203.112.218.65:8008/WebTestApplication/userfiles/Image/PopMonographs/Volume-9_Age-Sex.pdf; "Population by Religion," p. 1, Pakistan Bureau of Statistics (2017), https://www.pbs.gov.pk/sites/default/files/tables/POPULATION%20BY%20RELIGION.pdf; "2018 Report on International Religious Freedom: Pakistan," p. 4, US Department of State, Office of International Religious Freedom, https://www.state.gov/wp-content/uploads/2019/05/PAKISTAN-2018-INTERNATIONAL-RELIGIOUS-FREEDOM-REPORT.pdf; "The 2014 Myanmar Population and Housing Census. The Union Report: Religion. Census Report Volume 2-C," p. 3, Department of Population, Ministry of Labor, Immigration and Population, https://myanmar.unfpa.org/sites/default/files/pub-pdf/UNION_2C_Religion_EN.pdf; "National Population and Housing Census 2011," p. 4, National Planning Commission Secretariat, Central Bureau of Statistics, Government of Nepal, https://unstats.un.org/unsd/demographic/sources/census/wphc/Nepal/Nepal-Census-2011-Vol1.pdf. The US State Department lists the total Christian population of Bhutan as between 8,000 and 30,000; Open Doors USA lists the number of Christians as 30,000 and 3.6 percent of the total population; a 2010 Pew Research report lists the percentage of Christians as 0.5 percent. "2019 Report on International Religious Freedom: Bhutan," p. 2, US Department of State, Office of International Religious Freedom, https://www.state.gov/wp-content/uploads/2020/06/BHUTAN-2019-INTERNATIONAL-RELIGIOUS-FREEDOM-REPORT.pdf; "Table: Religious Composition by Religion by Country," p. 1, Pew Research (2010), https://assets.pewresearch.org/wp-content/uploads/sites/11/2012/12/globalReligion-tables.pdf.

At stake in this crucial moment of India's history is the very future of an eclectic and integrative political life symbolized in the *mahachakra* (the "great wheel," also known as the *dharmachakra*, the "wheel of *dharma*" or righteous order) found on the flag of India. The spokes of the wheel attach the center of political authority to diverse communities through reciprocal bonds of allegiance and trust. Historically, such bonds have integrated communities of various creeds, castes, and languages into overarching political systems. India's secular, liberal democracy, with its protections for religious minorities, may be viewed as the most recent iteration of the *mahachakra*. Will this democracy survive or will it give way to an agenda keen on eradicating dissent and diversity? This book locates Christians within this multifaceted, interactive history. It does so against nationalistic currents that are advancing the *Hindutva* agenda and its alternative reading of the past.[3]

Locating South Asia's Christians

Between Sanskritic, Persianate, and Arabic Worlds

An important factor that distinguishes South Asian from African or Latin American Christianity is the overarching influence of three classical languages—Sanskrit, Persian, and Arabic—which connected India to Arabia, Persia and Central Asia, and Southeast Asia. In ancient times, a Sanskrit-based courtly culture expanded from India to the elite circles of Burma, the Khmer country, and the plains of Java. Epic Sanskrit literature such as the *Ramayana* and *Mahabharata* and *puranic* texts contained stories that spread through a variety of media.[4] Popular devotional movements in India (or *bhakti* movements) sometimes absorbed and sometimes resisted the influence of Sanskrit.

During the eighth century, Islam reached the shores of western India through trade. Later, Turko-Mongol rulers known as the Mughals would employ Persian as their administrative language. Itinerant orders of Muslims, known as Sufis, propagated their mystical and populist variety of Islam in India, producing a rich corpus of prayers, songs, poetry, and literature in Persian. The arrival of Islam accelerated the diffusion of Persianate and Arabic traditions in South and Southeast Asia, and these intersected with networks of Sanskritic influence. The Muslim communities that dotted India's west coast prayed in the direction of Mecca and recited the Qur'an in Arabic.[5] Many Muslims of South Asia speak Urdu, a language related to Hindi but written with the Persian script and deriving many words from Persian and Arabic.

Over time, Sanskrit, Arabic, and Persian would form the basis of elite traditions commonly referred to as "Hindu" and "Muslim." Such religious labels, however, can be misleading. The classical languages had spread to different regions of Asia well before there were clearly established Hindu and Muslim "communities" to speak of. By the nineteenth century, Persian and Arabic became more strongly associated with Islam and Sanskrit with Hinduism. And yet, for much of the subcontinent's history, these languages drew people of diverse backgrounds into dynamic and creative encounters with each other and often enriched South Asia's many vernacular languages.

What Is "Interaction"?

As Christianity took root in South Asia, a robust interaction with Sanskritic, Persianate, and Arabic traditions followed. The term "interaction" can refer to many types of encounters between Christians and others. One might be inclined to think of interaction purely as dialogue, and dialogue as a conversation between two or more equal parties. For the purposes of this book, interaction is dialogical, but it does not presume equality, agreement, or mutual understanding. The following chapters showcase three domains of interaction: *knowledge production*, *debate*, and *conversion*. European writings (knowledge production) about Hindus and Muslims are discussed in Chapter 4 as instances of interaction that had far-reaching implications. They arose from attempts to grapple with the otherness of South Asian society and often involved the input of local informers. At the same time, they often reveal misunderstandings arising from prejudice, preconceived notions, and imperial interests. Apologetic encounters or debates between Christians and others are discussed in Chapter 5 as events that transformed identities. These exchanges are more easily recognized as interactive, however contentious and lopsided they often were. Conversion is rarely recognized as a form of interaction: It tends to be seen as a form of extraction (from one community into another). Chapters 6 and 7 describe the very real sense in which both individual and mass conversions became sites of interaction between old and new ideas, practices, and relationships.

What we find in South Asia is a rather poignant separation of the knowledge-producing legacy of Christian missionaries from that of actual conversion. Missionaries amassed information about "other religions" hoping to convert elites to their faith and thereby influence the masses. It was not the elites, however, who converted, but mostly marginalized Dalit and tribal peoples, largely independent of the knowledge systems produced by missionaries.[6] This dynamic is captured by a metaphor involving soda bottles. In the playgrounds of days past, people cast rings onto a cluster of soda bottles in hopes of landing as many rings as possible onto one bottleneck or another. Most rings, however, landed on the ground. The bottles are religions—Hindu, Muslim, Christian, and others—while the displaced rings are subaltern (non-elite) people who were not accommodated by any particular bottle.[7] Missionaries and their South Asian interlocutors played an important role in shaping "the bottles" through scholarship and printed books, interreligious debates, and pamphlet wars. As much as these "religions" competed for the allegiance of Dalits, it was never easy to locate Dalits within any given religious community. They often absorbed elements of multiple traditions and were not readily admitted or shaped by any particular community. This sense of identity limbo—sometimes described by terms such as hybridity, fluidity, or syncretism—is not eradicated upon conversion to Christianity, but is an enduring aspect of the experience of oppressed and marginalized peoples.[8]

One factor that may explain this rift between missionary knowledge and conversion is literacy. The small social networks in which printed Christian knowledge circulated or public religious debates were staged were far removed from the illiterate masses who ended up comprising the vast majority of South Asia's Christians. The masses became Christian largely through their own initiatives, in response to indigenous catechists who conveyed biblical teachings to them orally. These Christian converts are marginal to Hindu and Muslim communities, but, as discussed in Chapters 9 and 10, they are also marginal to many established Christian communities despite their conversion.

The Thomas Christians and Persian Christianity

The Thomas Christians are the only Christians of India whose origins cannot be linked in any way to European influence. They trace their origins to Jesus's apostle Thomas, who they believe visited India in 52 CE and established a church there. Some aspects of the Thomas tradition can be linked to an ancient text known as *The Acts of Thomas*, which describes the apostle's missionary endeavors in India. From the third century on, through trade, migration, and exchanges of ecclesiastical personnel, the lives of the Thomas Christians and Persian Christians became intertwined. Gradually, the Thomas Christians fell under the oversight of the Church of the East, whose capital was at Sasanian Ctesiphon.

The ties of Thomas Christians to the Church of the East did not make them any less anchored in south Indian society. Chapter 1 describes how their interactions with Persian Christians went hand in hand with their rootedness in local traditions. In fact, these Christian encounters between South Asia and West Asia foreshadow a more extensive Indo-Persian mingling that unfolded during the era of Islamic expansion. As a community that lived along India's Malabar Coast (southwest India), the Thomas Christians were involved through trade and religion with societies on the other side of the Arabian Sea. Their engagement with the peoples of West Asia accompanied their coexistence with Hindu and Muslim neighbors in the coastal region of southwest India now called Kerala—a dual participation that continues to the present day.

Catholic Interactions

As European Christians navigated the world of the Indian Ocean, experiences of their recent past shaped their perceptions of Hindus and Muslims in India. Back home on the Iberian Peninsula, the Catholic Inquisition had led the Church to confront heretics and purge their lands of Jews and Muslims. Portuguese Catholics introduced the same Inquisition in Goa in 1560 in order to advance their faith and justify violence and discrimination against Hindus and Muslims.

The Jesuit missions to the court of the Mughal emperor Jalal al-Din Muhammad Akbar (1542–1605), the topic of Chapter 2, provide the earliest and most detailed accounts of European encounters with the Mughals (the Islamicate Empire that ruled India for several centuries). Jesuit priests learned Persian in order to communicate not only with Akbar, but also with his courtiers and resident clerics. Their ultimate aim was to persuade the emperor to embrace Christianity, but their attacks on the Qur'an earned them the fury of Muslims residing at Akbar's court. The emperor himself, known for his religious tolerance, restrained these Muslims from beating the Jesuits when they insulted the Prophet Muhammad. But how far would his tolerance extend? Lengthy conversations that never resulted in Akbar's conversion ultimately disappointed the Jesuits. Still, they left behind a revealing account of their exchanges within this Indo-Persian domain.

Roman Catholics would adopt various strategies for advancing their faith and establishing a lasting presence in south India. Chapter 3 describes how Catholics became incorporated into a cultural fabric shared with Hindus and Muslims. At times, it was the patronage of local kings that made their integration into Indian society possible. In other instances, Catholics employed a deliberate strategy of cultural accommodation made famous by the Italian Jesuit Roberto de Nobili (1577–1656). What we find in the history of Catholicism, however, are instances of blending in as well as those of differentiation—patterns observable across many traditions of South Asia.

Protestant Interactions

Protestants shared with Jesuits a commitment to accumulating knowledge about other religions for missionary purposes. This sometimes led to the belief that they could win converts by winning arguments. During the seventeenth century, when Europeans gained access to the lucrative trade of the Indian Ocean, Protestant chaplains and travelers devoted themselves to studying Hindu traditions and documenting their findings. Chapter 4 describes how commerce and colonialism opened doors for Europeans—from the Leiden-trained

Abraham Rogerius to the German Pietist Bartholomeus Ziegenbalg—to examine Indian religions from the standpoint of their Christian beliefs. Ziegenbalg's Tranquebar mission left a lasting impact not only on Indian converts, but also on the experiences of Christian indentured laborers who migrated to the plantations of Burma, Penang, or Singapore.

During the following century, British missionaries assumed the roles as knowledge producers and translators of scripture. William Carey (1761–1834), the English Baptist missionary and professor of Sanskrit, was ardently committed to Bible translation and linguistics. Carey and successive missionaries collected manuscripts, translated the Bible into Sanskrit and several spoken languages, composed dictionaries and grammars, produced ethnographies, and wrote extensively about the beliefs and cultural practices of Indians. The Anglican missionary Henry Martyn (1781–1812) produced translations of the scriptures in Arabic, Persian, and Urdu. Based on his experiences in Iran and India, he produced his *Controversial Tracts on Christianity and Mohammedanism* (published in 1824). These were widely read by learned Muslims (members of the *ulama*) in India and laid the foundations for debates between Christians and Muslims. Scottish Evangelicals such as Alexander Duff (1806–78) and John Wilson (1804–75) believed in combining education with evangelism to influence the upper castes of Bombay and Calcutta.

Despite the heavy emphasis Europeans placed on knowledge and argumentation, their efforts to convert the elites to Christianity were largely unsuccessful. More often, they helped solidify Hindu, Muslim, Parsi, and Jewish identities and inclined members of these traditions to repudiate Christianity. Chapters 5 and 6 draw attention to missionary endeavors among the elites, which involved strident defenses of the Bible and refutations of other sacred texts. Converts from upper castes were few and far between, but they often drew praise or ostracism in the public sphere. The life of the high caste Hindu convert Pandita Ramabai Dongre (1858–1922) illustrates how a Brahmin convert could gain notoriety across global Christian networks while being shunned by Hindu elites in western India for her conversion.

Dalit and Tribal Experience

Most converts to Christianity came from social classes who were far less learned than Ramabai and her Maratha Brahmin compatriots. They came from Dalit and tribal communities, who tended to live on the margins of Sanskritic, Arabic, and Persianate high traditions. Dalits fell beneath and beyond the four main rankings (or *varnas*) of Hindu society. Upper castes considered Dalits to be "polluted" and forced them to live in separate neighborhoods. Dalit hereditary occupations were believed to have placed them in contact with substances that were ritually unclean: for example, human corpses, excrement or garbage, or carrion. Tribal peoples were deemed to be uncivilized and marginalized from Hindu and Muslim civilization. Both colonial officials and members of upper castes considered tribals to be "primitive" peoples because they were largely unshaped by norms of the dominant classes.

During the nineteenth and early twentieth centuries, Dalits and tribals became Christian through mass conversions. Their passages into the Christian fold raise questions about to which religious "community," if any, they had originally belonged and their motives for pursuing baptism. When they became Christian, they did not simply replicate practices or beliefs of elite Christian circles; rather, they revealed some combination of the old and the new. Their simultaneous involvement in the life of the Church and in village or tribal life made their identities layered and multifaceted. Dalit and tribal Christian theology continue to play an important role in formulating beliefs that arise from experiences of oppression and marginality and the quest for dignity.[9]

By the twentieth century, the congregations of South Asia's churches consisted mainly of those who were largely indifferent to missionary apologetics but responsive to the emancipatory possibility they saw in the Christian religion. Chapters 8, 9, and 10 describe the multiple personalities associated with the emerging churches of South Asia: namely, foreign missionaries, Indian Christian elites, and society's outcastes. During the early twentieth century, winds of decolonization signaled an end of the era of foreign missionaries. As they withdrew, Indian Christian elites assumed more leadership over the younger churches and tried to Indianize Christianity by accommodating themselves to "national culture."[10]

For Dalits, however, Indianizing Christianity meant Hinduizing it, a project they saw as reinforcing their subjugation. They felt oppressed not only by upper caste Hindus, but also by upper caste Christians who presided over their churches. Some Dalit Christians cultivated a greater sense of identity, voice, and self-determination by producing distinctively Dalit hymns, poetry, or theology. Others joined the ranks of those who grew disillusioned with older, established church structures. As discussed in Chapter 9, they would find empowerment, belonging, and renewal in Pentecostal and Charismatic movements. In recent decades, these movements have formed the cutting edge of both South Asian and World Christianity.

Christians and South Asian History

Christians are vital to the study of South Asia's history in three principal ways. First, during premodern times, they highlight the participation of South Asia in a world beyond itself. This is clearly the case with the Thomas Christians and their ties to West Asia. Their interactions with Persian merchants, migrants, and ecclesiastical personnel resemble the interaction on a much larger scale between India's Muslims and a Persianate world and Hindus with a Sanskritic world. Similar interactions with outsiders are evident in the Roman Catholic and Protestant communities of a later period. Through contacts with missionaries and transnational flows of people and ideas, they, too, maintained ties with other lands. Rather than making Christians a foreign or exogenous community, these ties reflect the Indian subcontinent's longstanding global connections.

The global, however, never displaced the local. Some scholars emphasize how Christians share with Hindus and Muslims a common cultural ethos. In the absence of rigid boundaries, they visit each other's shrines and participate reciprocally in each other's festivals.[11] This co-participation is a very real dimension of the Syrian Christian and Roman Catholic presence in south India. At the same time, we must not overlook instances where Christians have asserted clearer religious boundaries and have developed a distinctive consciousness through revival movements, theology, or exposure to global Christian networks.

Second, Christians refashioned India's longstanding traditions of public debate. The historian C. A. Bayly speaks of an Indian ecumene, a sphere of public engagement where members of different social classes debated doctrines and notions of the godly society. Both Jesuit and Protestant missionaries reshaped the Indian ecumene by introducing their own understandings of what a "religion" should look like (for example, a sacred book, coherent doctrines, and a concrete community) and new methods for presenting their ideas before audiences. Their printed texts and public preaching elicited spirited responses from persons of other faiths and sparked a new self-awareness among them. A new competitive economy of "religions" captivated the public imagination. During the nineteenth century, when Hindus, Muslims, Parsis, and Buddhists defended their identities in public, they entered a domain being refashioned by new technologies and forms of knowledge introduced by Christian missionaries.

South Asian converts, however, would not necessarily embrace the views or methods of foreign missionaries, and did not share their social status. An important aspect of their history relates to how they were compelled to redefine their place in postcolonial societies as "minorities." Upon conversion, some Christians gained access to worldwide networks of knowledge, education, religious media, and denominational resources. But since the vast majority were from Dalit or tribal backgrounds, the claim that these populations were immediately grafted into global networks of wealth and opportunity is highly dubious. The conversion of illiterate masses to Christianity constituted the greatest disruption to both Jesuit and Protestant notions of religious boundaries and orderliness. Dalits and tribals were indifferent to missionary argumentation and to their massive tomes about "other religions." The unmanageability of Dalit converts and their identities not only places them *between Hindu and Muslim* but also at the margins of organized Christianity in South Asia.

Finally, Christians are significant to South Asian history as both catalysts of nationalism and the "other" of nationalism. In South Asia, Christianity never became the reigning belief system that missionaries had once hoped for; instead, it became a small minority religion in states dominated by Muslims, Hindus, and Buddhists (as discussed in Chapter 8). A vision that began with universal claims and transformative aspirations triggered anticolonial nationalisms that portrayed Christians as foreigners. Today's *Hindutva* activists build upon a long history of defining a Hindu nation in opposition to a Muslim and a Christian other. Their idea of a Hindu nation includes practically anyone who is not Muslim or Christian. Those whom Europeans had formerly and erroneously lumped together as "Gentiles" appear to have become by default the "Hindu majority" of modern India.[12]

The distinction between majority and minority religions finds meaning chiefly within the context of the modern nation-state. This national framework risks portraying religious communities as monoliths and ignoring how issues of gender, caste, race, and wealth can play more prominent roles than "religion" in defining one's place in society. In South Asia, a low caste, dark-skinned Christian woman occupies an entirely different social space from a high caste, fair-skinned Christian man. They are not equally "vulnerable minorities," but the national framework of majority versus minority makes it appear that way. The Syrian Christians of Kerala belong to a "minority religion," but they wield enormous influence as landowners and share more in common with upper caste Hindus than with Dalit Christians.[13] Whether by blending in or by keeping apart, Christians of all social classes have had to respond to the politics of their national contexts in order to ensure their survival and flourishing.

South Asia and World Christianity

It is widely assumed that Christian converts in South Asia became "brown sahibs" who mimicked the customs and habits of Europeans. Besides learning the language of the colonizers, some converts adopted foreign names, wore Western clothing, or intermarried with members of the ruling race. They also derived laws of marriage and inheritance from the colonial societies that drew them into their fold.[14] This model of "conversion as assimilation" has inclined many to regard Christian missionaries as the "handmaidens of imperialism," converts as extensions of Western Christianity, and Christian conversion as a form of acquiescence to white supremacy.[15]

The problem with this model is that it projects the experience of small enclaves of colonial Christianity onto the Christian population as a whole. Just as cricket originated in England and eventually became a genuinely South Asian sport, Christianity underwent a similar transformation through which it became a genuinely South Asian religion.[16] The colonial model fails to recognize the ways in which generations of Christians adhered to their own regional languages, cuisines, customs, and ways of living out their faith.[17] This sense of local agency and *difference* from the foreign missionary is vital for understanding the experience of Christians in Africa, Asia, or Latin America. The difference arises from the ways in which Asians or Africans reached for the Christian message and shaped it according to their unique histories, beliefs, and cultural assumptions. The main story, as the historian Lamin Sanneh observes, was not about the missionary's "discovery of indigenous peoples, but of the indigenous discovery of Christianity."[18]

The World Christianity Paradigm

The growth of Christianity in the Global South makes it more difficult than ever to portray Christianity as a Western religion with mere offshoots in the non-Western world. Historians such as Andrew Walls and Lamin Sanneh have argued that, as Asian, African, and Latin American societies became increasingly Christian, those of Europe and North America underwent a great recession in their Christian identity.[19] Drawing heavily upon their study of African Christianity, Walls and Sanneh presented an alternative to the colonial model—a "World Christianity paradigm"—for understanding the growth of non-Western Christianity.

Central to their argument—which has its share of critics—is the role of Bible translation and the active agency of Africans in the conversion process. European missionaries relied heavily on Africans to teach them the nuances of local languages and how to translate biblical vocabulary into African mother tongues. The reliance upon Africans to teach, translate, preach, and baptize altered the power equation in ways that made missionaries the students and Africans the teachers.[20] As African Christians absorbed and refashioned characteristics of local spirituality, they defied missionary expectations and notions of orthopraxy. The result was not simply a translated Bible, but a translated religion.

For Sanneh and Walls, Christian pluralism is a good thing. As the gospel is translated into various mother tongues, it yields different varieties of Christianity across many contexts. In theological terms, these are moments when the gospel incarnates itself into local experience, just as the eternal Logos became incarnate in the person of Jesus Christ.[21] One of the effects of translation is the decentering of European Christian forms. No micromanagement on the part of foreign missionaries was ever able to contain the proliferation of Christian forms and practices arising from translation. According to Walls, the nineteenth-century missionary movement was not a straightjacket but a "detonator."[22] The use of this metaphor acknowledges the groundwork laid by foreign missionaries, but attributes Christian growth to the active participation of indigenous peoples in developing church practices, theologies, and forms of worship.

The prominent roles of local catechists, evangelists, and Bible translators helped make Christianity a translated religion in South Asia. They were central to large-scale conversion movements that gave rise to highly indigenous forms of Christianity. These include Tamil, Malayalam, Kannada, and Telugu-speaking churches in south India; churches established among Mizos, Nagas, Assamese, and other tribes of northeast India; or those established among Santal, Oraon, or Gond tribes of the mainland. These movements were predominantly marked by the agency, interests, and aspirations of South Asians, not foreign missionaries.

In India, Hindu nationalists are staging a popular debate about conversion in which the very idea of a translated faith or of an "indigenous discovery of Christianity" merits no consideration. Chapter 9 describes how the debate is largely centered on the notion of "inducement." Hindu nationalists portray foreign missionaries and their affiliates as the only real agents of change. They allegedly induce India's poor to leave the Hindu fold by offering them jobs, humanitarian aid, education, or access to other resources of the West. *Hindutva* activists have responded with campaigns to retain the poor within what they consider to be the domain of the Hindu religion. Anti-conversion laws and attempts to "reconvert" Christians or Muslims to Hinduism (*Ghar Wapsi*) count among their strategies. Frameworks that portray converts as passive recipients of inducements or as offspring of colonialism make it impossible to appreciate their agency and imagination in their appropriations of the Christian gospel.

Critics of the World Christianity Paradigm

A number of scholars have challenged the World Christianity paradigm. The emphasis on translatability tends to marginalize foreign missionaries and make local actors the key agents of Christianization. Critics, however, maintain that global forces, emanating largely from American capital, continue to influence Christian growth and experience in Africa, Asia, and Latin America.[23] Instead of regarding Christianity in these regions as arising in scattered, autonomous communities, these scholars emphasize the enduring hand of more affluent Western societies in steering Christian growth and forms of Christian expression in the Global South.[24] Their emphasis resembles the "inducement" argument leveled by Hindu nationalists, but is more refined. American or European financing of Pentecostal churches in India, Nigeria, or Zimbabwe and the worldwide television broadcasting of American Pentecostal preaching—a topic addressed in Chapter 10—contribute to this belief in the new role of the West in shaping Christian growth elsewhere. Unlike the *Hindutva* focus on inducement, however, this critique does not preclude local agency or cultural variation.

Another criticism of the World Christianity paradigm concerns the relevance of translation to South Asian contexts. The emphasis on translatability portrays culture as a stable entity into which the Christian message incarnates itself, when in fact culture is a multifaceted, moving target. In societies shaped by caste distinctions, into whose language or culture is the gospel translated—that of elites or of laboring classes? When translation privileged upper castes, or when the aim of "Indianizing" Christianity privileged Sanskritic culture, it reinforced the separation of Dalit from elite Christian circles, something discussed in Chapter 9.

Sanneh maintains that the embrace of African mother tongues in Bible translation was a source of cultural pride and nationalism among converts. "Armed with a written vernacular scripture," he writes, "converts to Christianity invariably called into question the legitimacy of all schemes of foreign domination—cultural, political, and religious."[25] In India, missionary translation projects and printing presses contributed to regional print cultures and linguistic nationalisms among Bengalis, Marathas, Telugus, Tamils, and others.[26] This linguistic devotionalism (as it is also called) was a gateway into Indian nationalism, but it was not the sole province of Christian converts; it was, in fact, primarily championed by upper caste Hindus or Muslim elites.[27] In India, translation, education, and print culture were venues where Christians, once again, were catalysts of nationalism, but also the "other" of nationalism, marginalized by the very forces their activities helped unleash.

For other critics, the emphasis on translation and local appropriation "runs the risk of becoming an exoticizing reification of the local, a fetishistic commitment to regional particularity, regardless of whether this is in fact how Christians choose to define themselves and their activities."[28] Some Pentecostal groups in Nigeria openly repudiate their local pantheon as demonic and deploy what Chad Bauman calls the "rhetoric of rupture."[29] As discussed in Chapter 10, this rhetoric stresses the radical break of Pentecostal converts from local practices. Newer perspectives seek to restore a sense of cohesion, transcendence, and unity to the study of World Christianity. They call for the recognition of "common threads and transnational connections that knit together Christians across the world."[30]

How can the study of World Christianity avoid the twin perils of overemphasizing local experiences and particularities, on the one hand, and passing over them, on the other, in search of unity and coherence? One path forward is to recognize how Christian growth beyond the West has created multiple centers of Christian activity that are in contact with each other through transnational networks and global media. The historian Klaus Koschorke has advanced a "polycentric" approach, which draws attention to multiple bases and actors in the worldwide Church. Their nodes influence each other across continents in multidirectional ways. Case studies from many contexts are brought into conversation with each other so as to recognize them as "part of a greater whole."[31] Koschorke's polycentrism suggests that, to some extent, we can harmonize the different approaches to World Christianity. Studies that focus on cultural particularity and those that trace transnational connections each perform valuable work and need not militate against the other. The goal should be to examine Christian particularities without embracing misguided notions of local autonomy (or insularity), and to examine the transnational without presuming Western hegemony.

Stories of local or regional expressions of Christianity are not dead ends that displace an appreciation of the global; rather, they may be seen as a series of checkpoints in our efforts to understand the Church universal. Before taking on the global, we need to pay our dues at the checkpoints of translation, local agency, and appropriation. These checkpoints call us to grapple with the messiness of what happens on the ground. They institute pauses, when we listen to alternative stories and trajectories of Christian experience. They allow us to interrogate the missionary idiom of "backsliding" or "reversion," which all too easily equates localizing processes with departures from orthodoxy or portrays them as being uniquely non-Western.

Finally, the checkpoints ensure that we do not marginalize Christian experiences that differ from those arising from Western church history.[32] These include assertions of differences by converts of all social classes. Dalit mass converts in the villages reveal such differences, as do high caste converts such as Ramabai. When Ramabai entered the Christian fold, she did not absorb every cultural, political, or theological assumption of those Westerners who attempted to convert her. On the contrary, she developed a layered consciousness, which integrated her knowledge of Sanskritic texts, experiences as a feminist reformer, and exposure to worldwide Pentecostal networks. The experiences of village Christians from lower castes similarly reflect multiple circles of belonging.[33]

1
The Thomas Christians
Paradoxes of Being Pre-European

The oldest Christian tradition of South Asia, the Mar Thoma Syrian Church, traces its origins to Jesus's apostle Thomas. Thomas is believed to have traveled to India around 52 CE, where he converted many locals, including some south Indian Brahmins, and was martyred at Mylapore (outside of Madras). In the New Testament, Thomas is the disciple who doubted Jesus's resurrection (hence the label "Doubting Thomas") until he could examine for himself the crucifixion wounds of his risen Lord. In John's gospel, it was Thomas who asked Jesus how the disciples could know the way that Jesus was going. Jesus responded that he himself is "the way" (John 14:5–6). Those wishing to defend the exclusive claims of Christianity—of Christ being the only way—often cite Jesus's response to Thomas in this passage.

Ironically, Thomas is also the disciple who was sent to India, a land of extraordinary religious diversity. Some of the great minds of India, from Akbar to Gandhi, promoted a belief in "many paths" or many sources of truth. Only this capacious vision, they believed, would hold the diverse elements of the Indian Empire together. The ancient Christian tradition tied to Thomas's legacy sustains this tension between India's diversity and the tradition's exclusiveness. Theirs, however, was more of a social and ritual exclusiveness than one of belief. Throughout their history, they balanced an interest in blending into their diverse surroundings with the desire to retain a high degree of separation based on the distinctiveness of their rites and their claims to high caste status.

The origin of the Thomas Christians predates the arrival of Europeans in South Asia. In the present day, when Hindu nationalists label Indian Christians as belonging to a "foreign religion," the existence of a Christian tradition dating back millennia carries special significance. From the early sixteenth century, the Portuguese, Dutch, Danish, British, and French penetrated the coasts of South Asia for trade and conquest. Riding the tailwinds of their ventures, missionaries introduced various forms of Christianity. The Thomas Christians, however, are known to have been in India long before this period of European imperialism. They thrived as a community since the third century—or even earlier, if the historicity of Thomas's mission to India is accepted. Far from being agents of European imperialism or reaping its benefits, the Thomas Christians would eventually bear the brunt of it, initially at the hands of Portuguese Catholics and eventually under British Evangelical influence.

In the context of rising Hindu nationalism, pointing to the Indianness of the Thomas Christians makes good sense. At the same time, it risks diminishing the importance of their transnational connections and hybrid cultural heritage. This chapter describes how the Thomas Christians flourished within Indo-Persian networks of cultural and commercial exchange, long before India's Muslims did the same thing. From their beginnings, the Thomas Christians maintained strong ties through trade and religion to the "Eastern" Christians of Persia and those of Alexandria; as such, they belong to a larger history of interaction between peoples of the Indian subcontinent and those of West Asia. For a time, their ecclesiastical language was Pahlavi (archaic Persian), an inference drawn from the discovery of Pahlavi-inscribed crosses in south India and Pahlavi signatures. Their liturgy and sacraments, however, were in Syriac.[1] The Thomas Christians might aptly be described as a highly *glocal* community. They maintained links to a wider—non-European—world and yet were anchored in south Indian localities.

The story of the Thomas Christians is central to that of Indian Christianity and provides important insights into India's history more broadly. It is impossible to appreciate India's past without recognizing how people, ideas, and goods have circulated across the Arabian Sea, the Bay of Bengal, and the Silk Road, have landed on Indian soil, and have enriched its social tapestry. The Thomas Christians provide an intriguing lens for examining this interconnected history, but their legacy is marked by certain paradoxes: They are rooted in south India's ancient history and yet are linked to other lands. They blend in with India's diversity while functioning as an exclusive, high caste community that has closed its doors to Dalits and other outsiders. They trace their heritage to one of Jesus's living disciples and yet were branded as "Nestorian" heretics by the Portuguese. Protestant Indians may point to the ancient roots of the Thomas Christians in order to defend the Indianness of Christianity, but the same Protestants may be quick to dismiss them as belonging to a lifeless tradition steeped in ritual, hierarchy, and false teachings.

This chapter examines these paradoxes first by examining the pre-European heritage of the Thomas Christians. This includes the legend of St. Thomas itself and what this legend reveals about the community's self-understanding. The chapter proceeds with a discussion of the community's ties to Persian merchants and to the Church of the East. It then discusses how Portuguese Catholics and British Evangelicals attempted to westernize the Thomas Christians. British missionaries introduced social reforms that had a direct bearing on gendered practices, such as women wearing breast cloths. The chapter concludes with a discussion of contemporary developments in the south Indian state of Kerala,[2] including the enduring legacy of migration between Kerala and Arab countries. Many of these migrants to Gulf countries are Hindu; many others are known to have embraced Pentecostalism; and some have returned to Kerala having become more stridently Muslim. From the days of Doubting Thomas to the present, Christians of Kerala thus find themselves straddling different worlds and eventually locating themselves *between Hindu and Muslim*.

The Acts of Thomas

Accounts of Thomas's evangelistic activities in India are not derived from the New Testament. They are based on oral traditions and on an apocryphal text (one that was not included in the canonical Bible) known as *The Acts of Thomas*. Rendered in both Syriac and Greek, this third-century text details key events in the apostolic ministry of "Judas Thomas," as he was called, also known as "Judas the twin." The *Acts* portrays Judas Thomas as the twin brother of Jesus and narrates his travels in highly entertaining and extraordinary ways.[3] This "twinning" motif in the *Acts* arises from Platonist ideals of identification with the divine and becomes a metaphor for the companionship of Thomas and Jesus and, more broadly, for the idea of gaining salvation through a new self-understanding arising from intimate acquaintance (*gnosis*) with the divine.[4] The text's sensational accounts make it difficult to determine whether to treat the *Acts* as historical or as a collection of amusing stories intended to impart life lessons or spiritual truths. The stories reveal the text's Gnostic orientation; Gnosticism was a philosophical tradition that extolled a spirit–matter dualism (the spirit was good while matter was evil), and, as such, it denigrated the pleasures of eating, sexuality, and material comfort in the hope of liberating the soul from these trappings. Devotees of Gnosticism are believed to gain access to a secret spiritual knowledge or *gnosis*. During the second century, the church fathers declared Gnosticism a heresy.

Accounts of Thomas's mission to India are also contained in oral traditions. Stories about Thomas were disseminated by Christian traders traveling between Persia and India and were passed down among Christian communities in south India. *The Acts of Thomas*, though, provides its own unique account of the origins of the Thomas Christians, with some details lining up with historical circumstances from the first century. This does not validate all the information contained in the *Acts*, but it lends a degree of plausibility to the belief that Thomas did travel to India.

The first two chapters of the *Acts* describe aspects of Thomas's journey to India. After Jesus had commanded his disciples to "go into all the world and preach the gospel," the disciples cast lots to determine who would go where. The task of preaching to India fell to a reluctant Thomas. "I have not strength enough for this, because I am weak," he declared. "I am a Hebrew: how can I teach the Indians?"[5] So reluctant was Thomas to go to India that Jesus had to sell him as a slave to Habban, an agent of the Indian king, Gundaphar (spelled variously). It so happened that Gundaphar was looking for a carpenter to build his palace and Thomas possessed precisely those skills. After Jesus completed the sales transaction, a resigned Thomas eventually set sail with Habban to India. Their boat initially stopped at a place called Sandaruk in Syriac, or Andropolis in Greek. Much speculation surrounds the identity of this city. Some believe it was located on the east coast of India in what is currently the south Indian state of Andhra Pradesh (based in part on the phonetic similarity between "S-andar-uk," "Andro-polis," and "Andhra"). Others believe that it was located on the western Malabar Coast, where the Thomas Christians would eventually flourish as a community.[6]

In Sandaruk, Thomas and Habban attended the wedding of the king's only daughter. It was in the context of this wedding that the *Acts* narrates some rather sensational events that cast light on Thomas's ascetic virtues (those associated with severe self-discipline and denial of bodily pleasure). Thomas refuses the wedding food and drink that are offered to him, stating "for something that is better than eating and drinking I have come hither."[7] As he was anointing his head with wedding oil, a cupbearer approached Thomas and slapped him in the face. Thomas declared that God would forgive him for this deed in the afterlife, but, in the present, he would see a dog dragging the hand that struck him. Shortly thereafter, a lion attacked the cupbearer and dismembered his body. A black dog carried off his hand. Thomas then began to sing a song in Hebrew. As he did so, he drew the attention of a young Jewish flute girl. She was delighted to hear someone singing in her own language and was also attracted to Thomas. When she left Thomas and played her flute for other guests, "she still kept looking at him, and loved him as a countryman of hers; and in his looks he was more beautiful than all those who were there."[8] Upon seeing the dog walking away with the cupbearer's hand, the flute girl declared her belief in Thomas's apostleship and became his first convert.

Later, Jesus himself appears in the bridal chamber. Since he and Thomas are twins, the bride and groom are unable to tell the difference. After clarifying his identity, Jesus instructs the couple to "preserve themselves from this filthy intercourse" in order to become "pure temples," freed from the "bitter sorrow" associated with raising children.[9] This stands in stark contrast to the Jesus of the New Testament who welcomed children and said that the kingdom of God belongs to those who become like them (Matt. 19:13–15). In the *Acts*, Jesus persuades the bride to become celibate and she gladly agrees. She declares to her parents that she will partake of a heavenly wedding feast with her eternal bridegroom. Upon hearing this, her father—the king—was outraged and offered a reward for the capture of the "sorcerer" Thomas. His men encountered the flute girl at the inn where Thomas was staying. By this time, she and some other young people had learned that Thomas had fled to Gundaphar's kingdom. Having been influenced by Thomas's teachings, they followed him and eventually were united with him.

When Thomas reached Gundaphar's kingdom in India, the king took him to the outskirts of the city to describe the dimensions and style of the palace he wanted Thomas to build. Thomas received a generous advance payment and agreed to begin construction in the winter. When Gundaphar left him, Thomas used the funds to attend to the needs of orphans, widows, and those afflicted with various diseases. Later, when Gundaphar made inquiries about the status of the palace construction, locals told him that Thomas had not built a palace; instead, he was going about the cities and villages spreading the good news and performing miracles on behalf of the poor and afflicted. The locals highlighted Thomas's life of self-denial and charity and professed their belief that he was an "Apostle of the new God" (see Figure 1.1).[10]

The outraged king eventually confronted Thomas directly and insisted that he show him the palace. Thomas responded that the king could see it only in the afterlife. The king immediately imprisoned Thomas and contemplated the kind of death he should suffer. It was at this point that the story shifts to the king's brother, Gad, who had just died of an illness. While in heaven he

Figure 1.1 The Apostle Thomas (center left, bottom row) distributes the treasure of King Gundaphar to the poor, with the recipient represented as an African. Depiction of the legend of St. Thomas at the Church of Notre Dame, Semur-en-Auxois, France.

Source: Hickey & Robertson, Houston/Lauros-Giraudon, Paris. From "The Image of the Black in Western Art" project, Hutchins Center for African and African American Research, Harvard University.

was able to see the palace that Thomas had constructed for his brother. So enamored was Gad by the palace that he found a way to reenter his body to tell his brother what he had seen. He told the king about the palace and tried to persuade him to sell half of it to him. The king was unwilling to do so, but he became a believer in Thomas's gospel. The story concludes with an account of Thomas anointing new believers with oil, baptizing them, and administering the Eucharist.

The last few chapters of the *Acts* concern Thomas's travels to other regions of India. After appointing a deacon to continue his work in Gundaphar's kingdom, Thomas traveled to the domain of the king of Misdaeus, which, according to tradition, was located in Madras (on the southeast coast of India).[11] As he had done in Sandaruk and in Gundaphar's realm, Thomas preached celibacy among the people of Misdaeus. Some influential women embraced his teachings, were converted, and thereafter renounced sexual relations. This development earned Thomas the wrath of the king, Mazdai, who accused Thomas of misleading the people and ordered his soldiers to "go up on this mountain and stab him."[12] The soldiers took Thomas to a mountain outside of the city, where they pierced him with their spears. Thomas ended his mission in India with the same words he had declared when he touched the wounds of the risen Jesus: "My Lord and my God."[13]

Several aspects of the *Acts* make it a text that is particularly well suited to the Indian context despite its Syrian origins. The first relates to the matter–spirit dualism of Gnosticism. Stories in the *Acts* highlight the denigration or denial of the body and the glorification of celibacy. During ancient times, a world-renouncing ethic circulated in Syria, which placed a strong emphasis on celibacy.[14] This resonated with Sanskritic ideals of the world renouncer who overcomes physical desire and worldly attachments to prepare for *moksha* or liberation. This common thread of world renunciation aligns itself in interesting ways with the identification of Thomas as the twin brother of Jesus. The twinship of Thomas and Jesus is a metaphor for the believer's process of identifying himself or herself with the divine. Knowledge (*gnosis*) of the self leads to union with the divine.[15] This resembles the concept of *tat tvam asi* in Vedāntic thought, by which the individual identifies with the Absolute through self-realization. The ascetic ideals in the *Acts* also resonate with the Jain tradition in India, founded by the saint Mahavira (sixth century BCE). Mahavira, a contemporary of the Buddha, is said to have achieved *moksha* through the mortification of his body and extensive meditation. During the twentieth century, if Gandhi had read the *Acts*, he would have appreciated its emphasis on celibacy and its critique of materialism. These tenets were central not only to his personal life (he had taken a vow of celibacy, or *brahmacharya*) but also to his belief in how India should obtain home rule or *swaraj*.

Another theme running through the text concerns the imagery of "black" and "fair." In one instance, the text uses the image of "fairness" to describe the Church as the bride of Christ. In others, fairness connotes the loveliness of a woman. By contrast, evil is portrayed with "blackness," as in the following prayer, where Thomas denounces the devil: "Oh you who has many shapes and appears as you wish, but your black color never changes because it is your nature!"[16] The dog that ran off with the hand of the cupbearer who had slapped Thomas is similarly described as black. This dualism between light and darkness was central to the religion of Zoroastrianism, which originated in Persia. It also resonates with the notion of *varna* in Sanskrit, which literally can mean "color" or "rank" and is commonly associated with the fourfold caste order. Fair skin in India has long been idealized as a marker of Aryan roots, whereas dark skin is disparaged as a feature of the Dravidian peoples of south India.

The resonance between these motifs in the *Acts* and Indian traditions is not presented here as evidence for the historicity of Thomas's work in India; it merely serves to show how the text—and the oral traditions built around it—could become popular among India's Thomas Christians. Many of these Christians moved back and forth between Persian and Hindu societies as they engaged in trade, and the themes of dualism and asceticism are prevalent within both societies.

Other aspects of the *Acts*, however, do line up with history. Ancient coins discovered in 1834 in Afghanistan include the name Gundaphar and are dated to the first century. A stone tablet discovered in Peshawar (in today's Pakistan) contains an inscription that refers to the reign of the king Gundaphar. This inscription also dates back to the early first century, the time when Thomas would have made his journey.[17] This alone does not prove the historicity of Thomas's visit to India, but it does make a compelling case for the reign of a king named Gundaphar. Adding plausibility to the Thomas legend is evidence of considerable seafaring traffic between the ports of Egypt (part of the Roman Empire), the Persian Gulf, and India. Strabo, the Ancient Greek geographer, reported that as many as 120 ships a year sailed from Egypt to India via the Red Sea. Merchants used their knowledge of the monsoon winds to navigate across the Arabian Sea to reach India.

The *Acts* describes Thomas's journey as having occurred by sea. Gundaphar's kingdom, however, is in northwest India near the current Afghan border and so Thomas would have reached it via overland trade routes. People have tried to resolve this inconsistency in two ways. South Indian local traditions maintain that Thomas arrived by sea at the Malabar Coast. Around 52 CE, Thomas first landed at the southwestern port of Muziris (most likely present-day Kodungallur). He made thousands of converts and founded seven churches, each bearing a "cross of St. Thomas."[18] This narrative concludes with a depiction of Thomas's martyrdom and largely ignores any reference to his work in northwest India, in Gundaphar's realm.

The second perspective addresses the inconsistency by postulating that Thomas made two trips to India, with the first taking him to Gundaphar's kingdom. He arrived by way of an overland trade route that connected exchange centers of the Roman Empire with what are currently the borders of India and China.[19] After completing his evangelistic activities in Gundaphar's kingdom, Thomas returned to Jerusalem to attend the First Council of Jerusalem, described in the *Acts*. He then sailed back to India by crossing the Persian Gulf and the Arabian Sea. This scenario does not align itself neatly with the account presented in the *Acts*, but it corresponds with actual maritime and overland trade routes used extensively during Thomas's day.[20]

Persian Connections

So how did the Thomas Christians come to be referred to as the Syrian Christians? If they had developed this connection to Syriac rites, theology, and hierarchy, in what sense can we regard this tradition as indigenous?[21] Such questions gain significance primarily during the era of the modern nation-state, when people are presumed to be citizens of one country or another. During the era of large empires, boundaries were far more porous and people moved more seamlessly between, say, Arabia, Persia, and India (see Figure 1.2).

The community that traces its origins to St. Thomas has always contained a mixture of indigenous converts and Christians who migrated to India during periods of extensive trade. The songs, poems, and other oral traditions of the Thomas Christians maintain that Thomas also converted some Brahmins in Kerala. His evangelistic activity led to the establishment of seven Christian settlements: Cranganore (Muziris), Kollam, Palayur (Palur), Parur (Kottakayil), Kokkamangalam, Niranam, and Nilakkal (Chayal). An ancient text drawn from the Sangam literature of Tamil Nadu refers to Brahmins residing within the Chera kingdom, where Thomas had purportedly come to spread his message.[22] The existence of a Brahmin community in the Chera kingdom aligns with a belief in the Brahmin roots of the Thomas Christians. The majority of the population during the first century would have been adherents of Buddhism or Jainism, two traditions that opposed caste distinctions and Brahminical authority. Hence, some of the first members of the Thomas tradition may indeed have been Brahmins, but they were Brahmins who lacked the social capital they would enjoy later. The influx of Nambudiri Brahmins from the eighth century onward more formally instituted Sanskritic norms in the region and the dissemination of these norms coincided with more formal observances of caste distinctions.

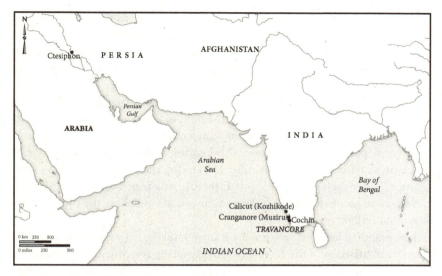

Figure 1.2 Map of India, Persia, and Arabia.

These early converts formed what might be viewed as the nucleus of the Thomas Christian community. Added to this original cluster, though, were migrants from Persia and Alexandrian Egypt, two regions with sizable numbers of Christians. The high demand for spices in Roman maritime trade brought them into regular contact with India's Malabar Coast, known for its rich supply of pepper. Trade between the Indian port of Muziris and Egyptian Alexandria made Christians of both regions aware of each other. Writings of the early church father Eusebius describe a visit to India toward the end of the second century by Pantaenus, the Christian scholar who headed the theological school at Alexandria. The Thomas Christians had sent a delegation to Alexandria to ask the bishop to send Pantaenus to India for discussions with Indian Christians on various matters of doctrine.

In Eusebius's account of this visit, he attributes the origins of India's Christian community to the mission of Bartholomew, not Thomas. This, of course, contradicts the account provided in the *Acts* and the historical memory of the Thomas Christians themselves. Still, Eusebius represents an outsider perspective, noting a mission to India by one of the original apostles. The visit of Pantaenus also serves to underscore the significant interactions of India's Christians with those of West Asia. Because of these interactions, information about an Indian Christian community spread throughout the Mediterranean. In the end, the story that predominated in accounts of the church fathers (from the third to the seventh century) was that of Thomas's, not Bartholomew's, apostolic mission to India.[23]

Even more far-reaching than the Alexandrian connection were the ties between the Thomas Christians and Persia. Scholars commonly associate Persian influence in India with Islam, especially under Mughal rule. What is far less recognized is the huge impact of Persian Christianity on the fledgling Indian Church during centuries predating the arrival of Islam. Since the first century, the rulers of Parthian Persia (modern-day Iran and Iraq) had adhered to policies of religious toleration, which allowed Christians to thrive as a minority community in Persian lands. They were heavily concentrated in Edessa, the capital of a small principality called Osrhoene. This became an important center of trade, scholarly activity, and Christian culture.[24] During the second half of the third century, under the reign of Shahpur I, the Christians of Persia established an ecclesiastical hierarchy whose bishop was based at Ctesiphon, the capital of the Sassanid Persian Empire.

Longstanding tensions between the Romans and the Persians weighed heavily upon the Christians of the East. This was especially the case after Constantine was converted in 303 CE and extended legal backing to the Christian religion. What emerged was a "Roman Christianity" associated with the West and various Eastern or "Oriental" Christian traditions—including Coptic, Armenian, and Ethiopian Christians—who fell beyond the purview of Roman or papal authority. As the Persian emperor Shahpur II grew more suspicious of a Christianized Rome, he began to persecute the Christians of his own land, regarding them as being aligned with the Roman enemy. Many Persian Christians fled to other parts of Asia. Since they were loyal to the Church of the East based at Ctesiphon and not the hierarchy at Rome, these Christians assumed a different theological identity.

The Church at Rome had branded Eastern Christians as "Nestorian" heretics. This designation goes back to a fifth-century dispute between Cyril, the Patriarch of Alexandria, and Nestorius, the Patriarch at Constantinople, over the divine and human natures of Christ. Nestorius stressed the importance of Christ's humanity and believed that a proper understanding of Christ should not subsume his humanity in his divinity. He maintained that, in Christ, two distinct natures were united in one person (*parsopa* in Syriac, *prosopon* in Greek). Instead of referring to Mary as the "mother of God," he preferred to call her the "mother of Christ." This earned him the vitriol of Cyril, who insisted that Jesus was a *hypostasis*, a unified being who is both God and human.[25] Insistence on this hairsplitting distinction reflected the factionalism and hubris that drove theological disputes of the day. It explains why Rome refused to recognize the legitimacy and orthodoxy of Persian Christians and the Thomas tradition of India and why the latter did not extend their allegiance to the Roman popes. The tendency of imperial Christianity to brand as heretics those who wished to preserve the autonomy and distinctiveness of their local traditions is evident in the story of the Thomas

Christians. The Portuguese "Nestorianized" them for political, commercial, and cultural reasons, not purely theological ones.[26]

It was in the context of Christian persecution in Persia that in 345 CE a merchant named Thomas of Cana led a migration of seventy-two Persian Christian families to Muziris, on India's Malabar Coast. This influx of migrants, numbering as many as 400 people, included church personnel such as priests, deacons, and a bishop.[27] By this time, the Christians of Malabar had become fragmented and leaderless and were declining in number. The arrival of these Persian families and their clerics boosted their morale and drew them into the orbit of the Persian church hierarchy. Over time, however, there arose a distinction between the Christians who traced their lineage to the apostle Thomas, the "Northists," and those who traced their lineage to the migrating Persian families, the "Southists."[28] By the early fifth century, the archbishop of Rewardashir in Fars (located on the sea route to India from the northern shore of the Persian Gulf) was given jurisdiction over the churches of India,[29] a development that appears to have created tension with the metropolitan based at Ctesiphon. This eastward shift of the ecclesiastical center corresponded to a period of increasing Persian influence in the affairs of the Thomas Christians.

Over the next several centuries, two developments profoundly and paradoxically shaped the identity of the Thomas Christians: their steady integration into south Indian society and their deepening ties to Persia. During this period, the kings of Malabar welcomed foreign traders for the wealth they could bring to the region. Local kings became great patrons of Thomas of Cana and these migrant families and extended them privileges such as the right to use palanquins (a form of escort often used by royalty), to ride elephants, and to clear forests for the purposes of settlement and the cultivation of spices.[30] They even endowed them with the status of Brahmins, an honor that gained significance as increasing numbers of Brahmins migrated to the region. The ritual services of Brahmins provided cultural capital that legitimized the regimes of the south Indian kings.

Ties to Persia were strengthened as the Thomas Christians accepted the authority of the archbishop at Rewardashir and adopted the rites and theology of the Church of the East. Waves of migrants from West Asia flocked to south India and joined the ranks of its already existing Christian community. This community, a mixture of native converts and migrants, was now supported by a more formal and transnational ecclesiastical structure. Nine stone crosses discovered along the Malabar and Goan coasts and in Sri Lanka contain inscriptions in Pahlavi dating as far back as the sixth century.[31] These crosses indicate the strength of the Indo-Persian connection that accompanied the growth of an Indian Church, and, when coupled with other textual evidence describing the movement of personnel between Persia and India, they reveal the extent to which the Thomas Christians had become dependent on the Persian hierarchy.[32]

The Persian Christian hierarchy did not advance its cause in India through violence and imperialism. This distinguishes the Persians from the Portuguese, who came later. The Thomas Christians actively sought out the Persian hierarchy and were eager to come under its oversight. By the time the Portuguese had arrived in Calicut, the Thomas Christians had become dependent on the theology, rites, and hierarchy of the Church of the East. As late as 1490, a delegation of Indians traveled east to meet with the patriarch, Mar Simeon, and asked him to send bishops back with them to India. The bishops he dispatched later reported that they had encountered in India roughly "thirty thousand families of Christians, our co-religionists."[33] They described locations in Malabar where these families resided, their places of worship, and the "idol-worshiping pagans" who lived in the port city of Calicut. Their involvement in south India further cemented the bond between the Thomas Christians and the patriarch in Persia.

Hindu, Christian, and Muslim

The explosive growth of Islam in the seventh and eighth centuries had a huge impact on the Church in Persia and the Christians of India. During the Prophet Muhammad's own lifetime (570–632 CE), most of the Bedouin tribes of the Arabian Peninsula were converted to Islam. Two successive dynasties ruled an expanding Islamic Empire: the Ummayads (661–750 CE) and the Abbasids (750–1258 CE). Islam spread westward across North Africa and into the Iberian Peninsula. Muslim armies also conquered Sassanid Persia in an eastward movement that destabilized Christian ecclesiastical networks across the Persian Gulf. When the Abbasids established their capital at Baghdad, the Church of the East was forced to consolidate further west, once again at Ctesiphon. No longer did the archbishop at Rewardashir oversee the churches of India; that task became the province of the archbishop of the Syriac Church.

Islamization also brought waves of Muslim migrants to the Malabar Coast, not for conquest but for trade. They constructed mosques and madrassas and established themselves as a vibrant coastal trading community in south India. These Muslims learned Malayalam, the predominant language of the region, and accommodated themselves to their surroundings. The Malayalam-speaking Muslims of Kerala came to be referred to as the "Mappilas." In the centuries preceding the arrival of the Portuguese, the Mappilas, like the Thomas Christians, were heavily invested in the spice trade across the Arabian Sea. The two communities maintained remarkably peaceful relations with each other, despite their shared interest in the maritime spice trade. The rise of Portuguese power on the Malabar Coast, however, adversely impacted Mappila access to trade and led them to embrace a more militant religious ideology centered on jihad and martyrdom for the faith (*shahid*).[34]

In order to carry on their trade and control different parts of the coast, Mappilas and Thomas Christians needed the backing of local Hindu rajas or kings. In terms of vocation, the Thomas Christians drew upon both Brahminical and Kshatriya caste markers: Besides being successful traders, they also became warriors. They provided Hindu rajas with skilled fighters in exchange for protection and for the honors the rajas bestowed on their community. Muslim and Christian communities enjoyed relative autonomy under one of the Hindu dynasties that ruled Malabar, the Zamorins.[35] Hindus, Muslims, and Christians thus enjoyed what has been called a "golden age" of toleration, and it was to everyone's advantage to cooperate in commercial ventures rather than compete. The involvement of south India's Muslims and Christians in the spice trade was global in its scope, knitting together trade centers in China, Europe, India, and the Middle East.[36] This collaborative relationship extended into the realm of religion, with Hindus, Muslims, and Christians sharing a degree of reciprocity in their visits to the shrines, churches, and temples of the different faiths.

As some Thomas Christians appropriated the identity of Brahmins, they adopted various Brahminical customs, and others gradually followed. Indeed, land ownership and claiming descent from the first Brahmins converted by St. Thomas became defining criteria for membership in this community.[37] Their Brahmin customs included the wearing of the sacred thread (*poonal*) by men, the wearing of white garments by women (*chatta* and *thuni*), the observance of birth and death rituals, and funeral feasts (*sradham*).[38] They also assumed a pattern of ethnic exclusiveness, which was rooted in rules of purity and pollution and reflective of high caste traditions. This necessarily entailed the shunning of certain groups as untouchables and the exploitation of their labor on their lands. Finally, their churches adopted architectural motifs from Hindu temples. This continued until the arrival of the Portuguese and their campaign to reform the Thomas Christians (discussed below).

As the Thomas Christians (or "Syrian Christians," as they came to be called) strove to maintain their high caste status, they eschewed any form of evangelizing that would compel them to share common spaces with members of lower castes. Their exclusive tradition prided itself on claims to a lineage traceable to Brahmins and in maintaining customs that signified their caste pedigree. In many respects, they had more in common with upper caste Hindus than with the masses of Christians who came from low caste, Dalit, and tribal backgrounds. They displayed their high caste status to others through their dress and their observance of laws of purity. Such bodily observances stood at the intersection of race, caste, and gender.

The tradition of wearing white clothes became prevalent among the Thomas Christians. This can be traced to sacred texts and customary observances of Nambudiri Brahmins, a landowning aristocratic caste that lived along India's southwest coast. These white clothes became a hallmark of Nambudiris as well as of upper caste Nayars of Kerala and the Syrian Christians. They not only signified caste status, according to Sonja Thomas, but also Aryan racial status.[39] The powerful racial ideas that arose in India came to associate Aryan status with fairer skin, and both white clothes and fair skin became markers of identity for Syrian Christians, distinguishing them from lower-ranking and darker-skinned "Dravidian" peoples.[40]

The Thomas Christians became a community that was "Hindu in culture, Christian in faith, and Syrian in polity, rituals and doctrines."[41] By the early modern period, they were occupying social spaces enjoyed by prestigious Malabar castes such as the Nambudiri Brahmins and Nayars. Many adopted strict vegetarian diets, like the Brahmins. Their families observed prohibitions on inter-dining and intermarriage with people from other castes, as did other high caste Hindu families. In this manner, they adopted key components of south Indian society—namely, the systems of honor and status that marked their high status and their backing by south Indian kings.

The arrival of the Portuguese on the shores of south India in 1498 disrupted this ethos of peaceful coexistence that had been in place for centuries. When the explorer Vasco da Gama reached the port of Calicut on 20 May, he sent ashore an exiled convict, a *degredado*, to make first contact with the locals. He met with two Muslims from Tunis who could speak Castilian and Genoese. When these men asked the *degredado* why the ship had come, he responded with the widely cited words, "We came to seek Christians and spices."[42] In other words, he conveyed the interest of the Portuguese in accessing India's lucrative spice trade and finding a lost kingdom of Christians in the East (headed by a mythical king named Prester John, who is discussed in Chapter 4). Word of the existence of these Christians had been circulating across the Mediterranean for centuries. Now, the Portuguese could encounter them firsthand.

The relationship the Portuguese developed with the local population was anything but collaborative. The Portuguese disrupted the remarkably cosmopolitan character of Malabar's port cities, where local rajas extended religious toleration to Jews, Christians, and Muslims for the sake of promoting prosperity through trade.[43] Instead of working alongside locals toward common ends, the Portuguese used their power to control the ports along the Malabar Coast, dominate the spice trade, and impose Catholicism on the local inhabitants. Fresh in their minds were violent campaigns against Muslims and Jews during the Spanish *Reconquista* and the impulse to purge their lands of heretics under the auspices of the Catholic Inquisition. The Portuguese brought this crusading mentality with them to India and it shaped their involvements with the Muslims, Jews, Christians, and Hindus of Malabar.

Westernization

Latin Versus Syriac

It eventually occurred to the Portuguese that they were encountering Christians with an entirely distinct ecclesiastical network and history from their own. The Portuguese initially approached the Thomas Christians as potential allies and coreligionists.[44] They made overtures to local authorities to enhance the social privileges of the Thomas Christians and to restore their deteriorating churches. They also became aware of the warrior skills of the Thomas Christians and hoped that they could add them to the ranks of their own military.[45] As the Portuguese became more aware of their theological and sacramental differences, however, relationships soured. Portuguese friars entered the Thomas Christians' churches and insisted that they perform mass according to the Latin, not Syriac, rite. They accused them of being "pestilential Nestorian heretics" and declared their baptisms invalid.[46] The label "Nestorian" not only branded Thomas Christians as heretics but also conveyed the prejudice against them on account of their different rites and religious customs.[47] In letters these friars sent to the pope and to the king of Portugal, they essentially outlined a long-term plan of Latinizing the practices of the Thomas Christians and of bringing them under papal authority. Because the Portuguese friars' church was backed by a king and an army, this was cultural imperialism in its purest form. The Portuguese implemented their Latinizing plan with zeal and rigor.

By the second half of the sixteenth century, the Portuguese had made Goa their ecclesiastical center and a launching point for missionary endeavors in India, China, and Japan. Under the royal patronage or *Padroado Real* that the papacy had extended to the Portuguese crown, Portuguese authorities were given a mandate to advance Catholicism in Eastern lands. This included the right to appoint clerical offices within their overseas colonies. With backing from the crown, Jesuit priests pressured the Thomas Christians to change their theology and rituals and to embrace the sole authority of the Roman pope. They insisted that they refer to Mary as the mother of God (*Theotokos*), not the mother of Christ, and also wanted them to embrace the use of images of the saints. Under the influence of Muslims and Jews in south India, and in an effort to differentiate themselves from their Hindu neighbors, the Thomas Christians had repudiated any form of image veneration. The Jesuits also introduced practices such as confession to a priest, confirmation, and extreme unction (anointing the sick with oil).

When a bishop of the Thomas Christians, Mar Joseph, evaded these reforms, a Jesuit missionary accused him of heresy and challenged him to a public disputation. The Portuguese sent Mar Joseph to appear before the church authorities at Cochin (Kochi) and later to Goa, where he was pressured into retracting his "erroneous" teachings. This sparked a revolt by 2,000 Thomas Christian soldiers. Despite their fierce defense of their bishop, the Portuguese eventually sent Mar Joseph back to Lisbon to be tried for heresy.[48] There, however, he was able to say the right things, convince the authorities of his orthodoxy, and clear his name before he died.

These theological issues were intimately tied to the commercial and political interests of the Portuguese in Malabar. According to the historian Pius Malekandathil, the branding of local Christians as "Nestorian heretics" and attempts to Latinize them were part of a larger Portuguese strategy to dominate the spice trade. Whereas the Portuguese controlled the coasts, the Thomas Christians occupied hinterland regions that were essential for spice cultivation. The Portuguese believed that, by assimilating the Thomas Christians, they could lay claim to their spice-producing centers.[49] In order to thwart Portuguese penetration into their domains, for a time the Thomas Christians rerouted their trade to the eastern Coromandel Coast. By the 1550s, Portuguese strategies had become even more aggressive. They intercepted vessels carrying East Syrian bishops coming to Malabar in order to sever their ties to the Thomas Christians. In so doing, they hoped to isolate the Thomas Christians from important trading centers in the Persian Gulf.

An equally disruptive move on the part of the Portuguese was their attempt to undermine the ties between the Thomas Christians and local Hindu rajas. The rajas had long provided an invaluable source of patronage, status, and trading rights for the Thomas Christians. Under this patronage, Christians had assimilated themselves culturally by embracing local customs and enjoying high status within the caste order. By the late sixteenth century, the raja of Cochin suspected that the Portuguese were keen to undercut his authority by making the Thomas Christians loyal to Rome. For a time, the raja tried to prevent the Thomas Christians from obeying the Portuguese archbishop, Alexis de Menezes, but ultimately Menezes flexed his political muscles to intimidate the raja. In a direct meeting, Menezes insulted Hindu deities and made threats of damnation.[50] Portuguese hostility toward Malabar's Hindu institutions, as we shall see, was more severe than their treatment of the Thomas Christians.

The Synod of Diamper

Mar Abraham, the archdeacon of the Thomas Christians, eventually became more subservient to the Catholic Church. He was forced to sign a document that disavowed Nestorianism and designated his own patriarch an illegitimate heretic.[51] The Latinization of the Thomas Christians culminated in 1599 at the Synod of Diamper. Under the lead of Menezes, the synod set out a body of doctrines that the Thomas Christians had to accept. Many of the synod's decrees were aimed at confronting the "errors" of Nestorianism, while others centered on the Roman hierarchy. Equating the legacy of Thomas with that of Peter, whom Roman Catholics believe founded the one true Church, was strictly prohibited.[52] Other decrees opposed the accommodation of the Thomas Christians to local Hindu customs and beliefs. Immediately after the synod, the Portuguese destroyed a huge supply of documents in Syriac and Malayalam that were kept in archives in the city of Angamali. In doing so, they eliminated vital sources of historical memory that had shaped the collective consciousness and identity of the Thomas Christians.[53]

The Thomas Christians responded to the demands of the Synod of Diamper with both acquiescence and resistance. According to a report from 1622, at least a third of them remained loyal to their own archdeacon instead of the Roman archbishop. The other two-thirds, however, aligned themselves with Rome[54] and became known as Syrian Catholics or the *Pazhayakur*. On January 3, 1653, a revolt solidified fault lines between the factions. An assembly of Syrian Christians (as they were now called) gathered at a church near Cochin, took hold of a long rope attached to its cross, later known as the Coonan Cross, and took a solemn oath that they would not submit to the authority of the Jesuits or to the Catholic archbishop at Goa.[55] Those who broke away from Rome by taking the Coonan Cross oath came to be known as the *Puthenkur* (the new group) and later were called the Jacobites. By 1664, a new Syrian bishop—Mar Gregorios—arrived and laid the foundations for the Syrian Orthodox Church of Kerala. Following this initial split, the division between Syrian Catholics and Syrian Orthodox Christians yielded many offshoots—a situation that has persisted to the present day.[56]

British Reforms

The Portuguese were not the only Europeans who tried to westernize the Syrian Christians. Two centuries after the Synod of Diamper, the British East India Company was rising to power and making inroads into Travancore and Cochin. These were the two princely states where Syrian Christians were most concentrated. Missionaries of the Anglican Church Missionary Society (CMS) and the Non-Conformist (non-Anglican or non-state church) London Missionary Society (LMS) worked closely with East India Company officials to reform the Syrian Christians. Just as the Portuguese had wanted to make them more Catholic, the British wanted to make them more Protestant. Among the pillars of Protestantism was first and foremost the authority of the Bible and the need to translate it into vernacular languages. In Europe, translating the Bible liberated the text from its captivity to Latin and the monopoly of the Roman Catholic hierarchy. In India, missionaries believed that translation would emancipate lay converts from their reliance on priests and an ecclesiastical language that only priests could understand.

By the time the British had arrived in Travancore, the Syrian Christians had transitioned from being a prosperous and highly esteemed community to being somewhat disenfranchised. The rajas of Travancore and Cochin had funded their armies by dominating the production of pepper, timber, and cardamom in the hinterland. They used the revenue to employ European mercenaries and large numbers of Syrian Christians, who excelled as warriors. Syrian Christian families were recipients of land grants and enjoyed high caste status. They participated alongside elite Hindu families in prestigious festival processions in which their honors were put on public display.[57] This state of integration and enfranchisement changed dramatically when the Muslim ruler of Mysore, Tipu Sultan, defeated the armies of Cochin and Malabar toward the end of the eighteenth century. Tipu's advances in Malabar prompted the British to play a more dominant role in the region, and, by the end of the century, the British had defeated Tipu Sultan's Mysore. Thereafter, Malabar was made a part of the Madras Presidency while Travancore and Cochin became dependent princely states. British intervention in these regions steadily diminished the power of local rajas and marginalized the Syrian Christians.

The condition of the Syrian Christians became a matter of growing concern for British Evangelical travelers of the period. They viewed them not as recipients of patronage and empowerment under local rajas, but as victims of Hindu oppression. They believed that their fellow Christians had fallen from greatness and were in need of rejuvenation and reform at the hands of the British.[58] In 1806, the High Church Anglican Claudius Buchanan met with the *Metran* (short form of "metropolitan," later "bishop") of the Syrian (then the *Jacoba* or Jacobite) Church. Buchanan aspired to vastly expand Anglicanism in India[59] and expressed his hope of ultimately uniting the Syrian with the Anglican establishment. Fully aware of what the Portuguese had done to them, the *Metran* remained silent. He was more pleased, however, with Buchanan's promise to construct a seminary for the Syrian Christians to train their *kattanars* (pastors or priests) and with the possibility of enjoying the patronage of the East India Company. Would such patronage, however, bring unwanted interference?

From 1810 to 1819, Colonel John Munro served as the British Resident in Travancore and Cochin. The British employed the role of a "resident" in their system of indirect rule by which they governed India's princely states (as distinct from the directly ruled provinces). Residents played an advisory role in the administration of these states but also extended princes a degree of local sovereignty. Munro, a committed Evangelical, had close ties to missionaries of the Church Missionary Society (CMS) and the London Missionary Society (LMS) and recruited missionaries from these societies to work in Travancore. The missionaries made it their aim to reform the Syrian Christians, bringing their theology and practices into line with their own. By the beginning of the nineteenth century, an Evangelical revival extending across the Atlantic (the "Second Great Awakening") had increasingly shaped the missionaries' aspirations and ambitions in India. Like the Portuguese, who were influenced by their Inquisition, Evangelicals, influenced by their revival, brought reformist zeal to their interactions with the Syrian Christians.

Missionaries working with Munro had originally intended to preserve the integrity and distinctiveness of the Syrian (Jacobite) tradition. Munro created a trust fund to support a number of projects relating to the refinement of their tradition. With his cohort of missionaries, he established a seminary at Kottayam whose aim was to "instruct the [*kattanars*] and officiating priests . . . in a competent knowledge of the Syrian language in which they are at present too generally deficient."[60] As a Protestant, he also promoted vernacular Bible translation. He entrusted the CMS missionary Benjamin Bailey with the task of overseeing the translation of the Bible into Malayalam in order to make the teaching of the scriptures accessible to those who could not read or understand Syriac. Bailey worked with local translators from various caste backgrounds toward this end. Bailey also established a printing press. The Syrian Christians were quite receptive to the founding of the seminary (also called "Syrian College") and to the production of a Bible in their mother tongue.

Munro was also responsible for promoting reforms that impinged upon the practices of converts from an untouchable caste then known as the Shanars. By the turn of the nineteenth century, many Shanars converted to Christianity (thereafter they became known as "Nadars," a less pejorative designation). Shanars had made their living by climbing palmyra trees to extract its intoxicating sap, known as toddy; because of their contact with this polluting substance, they were stigmatized as untouchables and prohibited from coming into contact with upper castes. Upper castes required them to maintain bodily practices that made their untouchability visible, thus reinforcing the basis of their separation: For instance, they prohibited Shanars from wearing shoes or gold ornaments, from using umbrellas, and from building homes for themselves that were more than one story high.[61] Shanars who violated these prohibitions were vulnerable to acts of violence inflicted by upper castes.

Among the more controversial identity markers was the requirement that Shanar women leave their breasts uncovered as a sign of deference to members of Syrian Christian, Nambudiri Brahmin, and Nayar communities. Since Shanar women also had to work in the fields (they were not restricted to the home, as were upper caste women), their exposure also signified their sexual availability to upper caste men.[62] In 1812, Munro issued an order that permitted female Christian converts from this community to "cover their bosoms as obtained among Christians in other countries."[63] Two years later, this order was followed by a circular from the government of Travancore permitting the women to wear jackets similar to those worn by Syrian Christian and Muslim Mappila women. These orders were radical for their day because they confronted a bodily practice that differentiated an untouchable from an upper caste or Syrian Christian woman.

Members of the upper castes objected to this "Breast Cloth Movement" because it challenged the social order they hoped to maintain by means of policing Dalit bodies. Syrian Christians similarly opposed measures taken to upgrade the status of Dalit castes and defended practices that reinforced their social subordination. They wanted Dalit converts to continue to be designated by what were often pejorative caste names. They also tried to oppose the enrollment of low caste converts in the Syrian College at Kottayam.[64]

Despite tensions triggered by social reforms, a degree of affinity developed over several decades between CMS missionaries and Syrian Christians in the realm of religious reform. Under the leadership of a scholar-priest at Syrian College named Abraham Malpan, the reformists tried to vernacularize the rites, prayers, and liturgy of the Syrian Church and abolish prayers to the saints or to the Virgin Mary. Following Protestant practices, they placed greater emphasis on the centrality of the sermon and altered the manner in which the Eucharist was administered and interpreted. They also objected to the burning of candles and other ritual observances that the Syrians had performed for centuries.[65] These reforms, however, were met with resistance; once again, the tradition underwent a split whereby some took the path of becoming a reformed Syrian Church, whereas others more stridently adhered to their ancient tradition. After the official separation of the Syrian Christians from the CMS, heated disputes relating to church property ensued, requiring years of arbitration.

Conclusion

The story of the Thomas Christians contains many layers, each addressing a unique aspect of their engagement with others. The oral and written traditions that describe the apostle's visit to India reveal not only the historical consciousness of this ancient community but also the scope of their interactions with a wider world. In its enchanting account of Thomas's voyage to India, *The Acts of Thomas* links the affairs of first-century Palestine to northwest and southern India. The networks of Christians moving back and forth between Persia,

Alexandria, and Muziris underscore the transnational engagement of this community dating from the third century. The flourishing of the Thomas Christians across the hinterland regions of today's Kerala speaks to their involvement in the spice trade and their development as warriors. These skill sets, along with their appropriation of Brahmin status, earned them the patronage of south Indian kings. Under this patronage, the Thomas Christians were incorporated into south India's multi-ethnic and multireligious tapestry.

This pre-European slice of their history stands in stark contrast to what followed. The Portuguese and the British subjected the Thomas Christians to a rigorous program of westernization. Backed by their respective political regimes, they pressured the Syrian Christians to align their beliefs and practices with the religion of the ruling power. This pressure led to splits within the community, with some assuming the path of reform and others adhering to their ancient heritage. Despite these external pressures, the Syrian Christians managed to root themselves within a multireligious landscape in which they enjoyed an elevated social position. As aloof as Syrian Christians may have been relative to people they considered beneath them, they participated in a common sacred landscape with Hindu and Muslim communities in Kerala and they have continued their commitment to coexistence to the present day.[66]

Several developments in postcolonial India represent important continuities with what has been described in this chapter. After India achieved independence in 1947, the princely states of Travancore and Cochin, along with Malabar, merged to form the state of Kerala. One of the unique features of Kerala has been the communist government that has ruled the state for much of its history. In 1957, a newly elected chief minister, E. M. S. Namboodiripad, a communist intellectual and a Brahmin, inaugurated an era of communist-led regimes in Kerala. Kerala's communism operated within the parameters of the Indian constitution and its principles of democracy. It aggressively promoted agricultural reforms and restrictions on landownership and rents while also supporting capitalist development by encouraging entrepreneurs to establish factories in the state.[67] All the while, the communist governments of Kerala respected the state's multireligious ethos. For decades, Kerala has maintained a literacy rate above 90 percent and it is among the more developed states in India. The state's prosperity relates to a combination of factors: entrepreneurial activity, rich agricultural lands known for their production of spices and other cash crops, and trade and migration to and from Gulf countries. At the same time, the state has the highest suicide rate in India, rampant alcoholism, and persistent inequalities associated with caste, gender, and class.[68]

Kerala's geographical access to Arab societies has resulted in a long history of interaction between its own Muslim population and those Gulf countries such as Kuwait, Bahrain, and the United Arab Emirates. The prospect of gainful employment in these oil-rich countries has attracted scores of Indian migrants from Kerala. In recent years, Muslim revivalist movements such as the Arabian-based Wahhabis and the Salafis have taken root in Kerala and other south Indian states. These movements promote more conservative and "pure" forms of Islam modeled after what is practiced in Saudi Arabia or what was practiced in the Salaf, or the early "golden age" of Islam. Some have maintained that revivalist Islam in south India is a reaction to militant Hindu nationalism and its othering of India's Muslims; others attribute such movements to the exposure of Indian Muslims to Arab societies during their terms as contract workers. From this perspective, "petrodollars" from oil-rich countries are the driving force behind Muslim revivalism. According to Javed Anand, general secretary of Muslims for Secular Democracy and coeditor of the left-leaning *Communalism Combat*, "Saudi Arabia pumped millions of petrodollars into the madrassas and mosques of the subcontinent to propagate the Wahhabi theology."[69] Clearly, Kerala's communism has not resulted in a decline in religion; rather, it has accompanied the rise of new religious movements.

Migrants from Kerala to Arab states come from many religious traditions. According to the 2011 census, 56 percent of Kerala's population are Hindus, 26.5 percent Muslims, and 16.6 percent Christians. Most migrants to Arab states from Kerala, however, are Muslim (43 percent), followed by Hindu (26.5 percent) and Christian (25.1 percent).[70] Members of Kerala's rapidly growing Pentecostal churches enter into short-term labor contracts in places such as Kuwait or Bahrain. According to theologian Stanley John, churches established among these "temporary economic migrants" form a vital component of the story of Kerala Christianity and of World Christianity more broadly.

Kerala's Pentecostal churches play an important role in meeting the various needs of the migrant population in Gulf countries. Migrant workers account for as much as 70 percent of the labor sector in Kuwait. They arrive under the auspices of the *kafala* system, whereby residence in the country is linked to a particular employer and employment contract. The transient lives of employment migrants and the restricted terms of their employment contracts produce constant feelings of displacement and intense longing for what they call home.[71] This in-betweenness is central to processes of transnationalism in our globalized world, and, in the case of Kuwait, produces a need for a sense of belonging and various forms of pastoral care.

Global Pentecostal networks are well suited to address the needs of temporary economic migrants. They tend to be adaptive to many contexts, indifferent to caste or class differences, and capable of employing their transnational networks to make contact with mobile peoples. Like migrant workers, Pentecostal pastors from Kerala relocate to Kuwait on a rotational basis with the aim of meeting the practical, spiritual, and social needs of migrant laborers. They establish small groups, promote Pentecostal worship styles, and engage in forms of outreach that appeal to laborers.[72] Instead of regarding these developments strictly as products of twenty-first-century globalization, they can perhaps be better viewed against a broader canvas. These present-day connections reenact a deeper history of religious patronage that linked the Malabar Coast to Persian societies, Nestorianism, and cross-cultural trade.

2
Jesuits and the Emperor Akbar, 1580–3

A widely printed portrait of life within the Mughal Empire depicts the emperor Jalal-al-Din Muhammad Akbar (1542–1605) engaged in interfaith dialogue with various guests at his *Ibadat-khana*, or House of Worship (see Figure 2.1).

Two Jesuit priests are seated to Akbar's right dressed in dark blue clerical robes and caps. Other participants likely include members of Muslim, Jain, Parsi, or Hindu sects. According to one observer, the scene depicts the Jesuit priests poised "in attitudes of intense seriousness" while other participants "lean forward and gesticulate in eager argument."[1] Regardless of how one interprets the dynamics of this portrait—for instance, whether one places the Jesuits at the center or the margins of the encounter—the scene represents an important moment in the early history of Jesuit missions to Asia. As guests of the imperial court, Jesuits used the platform that Akbar provided for them to explain the doctrines of their faith and refute the beliefs of others.

Jesuits tried to make a convert of the emperor in the hope that he would open his entire domain to Christianity. As representatives of the Portuguese Empire, these Jesuits gained access to the highest seat of power within the Mughal Empire, which ruled India for roughly 300 years (1526–1857). Strictly speaking, the Mughals were "Muslim" rulers, but they did not impose Islam upon their Indian subjects.[2] As the third Mughal emperor, Akbar distinguished himself by his unique approach to religious diversity. His aim in hosting his famous interreligious dialogues was to discover the shared truths of all religions and fashion from them a universal religion, his *Din-i-Ilahi*, or Religion of God. Even though many thought that Akbar had ceased to be a Muslim, his dialogues with Jesuits provide a fascinating case study of Christian interactions within a Persianate South Asian context.

Jesuit accounts of their attempts to Christianize Akbar demonstrate that their methods were not merely culturally adaptive; they were also confrontational. In their discussions with Akbar and his *mullahs* (Muslim teachers), the Jesuits attacked the Qur'an, the Prophet Muhammad, and various Indian cultural practices. The exchanges certainly illustrate how interfaith encounters of this kind could generate mutual perceptions of "East and West."[3] Jesuit interactions with Akbar, however, represent more than this. After sending three official missions to the court of Akbar, the Jesuits failed in their endeavors to Christianize the emperor and his domain. Despite their best efforts, Jesuits eventually discovered

JESUITS AND THE EMPEROR AKBAR   41

Figure 2.1 Akbar in conversation with representatives of other religions. The Jesuits are robed in blue, seated to Akbar's right.
Source: Heritage Image Partnership Ltd/Alamy Stock Photo.

their place within his court: They acted not so much as agents of religious conversion than as interlocutors of the emperor and his policies, of imperial courtly life, and of Mughal campaigns.

At times, Akbar delighted the Jesuits by his willingness to discuss Christian beliefs and by displaying what they thought was a special fondness for them. Akbar and his chief courtier, Abu'l-fazl, occasionally expressed profound appreciation for Jesuit teachings and extended to the Jesuits the highest courtesy. Akbar allowed them to sit next to him at gatherings; he kissed their holy images and Bibles; and on occasion he could be seen walking with his arm around the Jesuit priests.[4] In other instances, however, their dialogues with the emperor seemed more like a monologue. The priests spoke at length to an emperor who remained aloof, preoccupied, or distracted by other interests. The Jesuits may have succeeded at times in captivating Akbar's mind, but this was a far cry from winning his soul.

Akbar and Abu'l-fazl were not en route to becoming Christians, but quite likely were accommodating Christian beliefs within the framework of *Din-i-Ilahi*. Unbeknownst to the priests, Akbar was relativizing their Catholic faith by locating it within his new cosmology. In the end, the dialogues revealed the sizable gap between the universal aspirations of the Jesuit mission and the limited spaces their religion would ultimately occupy within India's multireligious landscape and its longstanding traditions of interreligious debate.[5]

This chapter's discussion of the first Jesuit mission to Akbar's court is divided into three parts: (1) Portuguese and Mughal imperial ambitions in India; (2) Akbar's imperial persona and Jesuit perceptions of him; and (3) theological exchanges between the Jesuits, Akbar, and his *mullahs*. Throughout their time in India, Jesuits recorded their experiences in lengthy letters or memoirs which they sent back to their superior officers and European patrons.[6] Their accounts of their time in Akbar's court illustrate their roles as missionaries, cultural mediators, shapers of European perceptions of India, and agents of globalization.[7] Even though they failed to convert the emperor, the Jesuits left behind a highly revealing record of their encounters within his court and the limitations of scripture-based "reasoned debate" as a vehicle for advancing their mission.

Indo-Portuguese Meets Indo-Islamic

Jesuits arrived in India thirty years after the Portuguese conquest of the western Indian port city of Goa (1510). They began their mission as agents of Europe's Counter-Reformation. As a response to Protestant criticisms of Catholic corruption and their rapidly expanding movement, Jesuits promoted a more rigorous inward spirituality and a commitment to foreign missions. Their activities in India, however, need to be set against a wider history of Indo-Portuguese trade, conquest, and cross-cultural encounters. At the turn of the sixteenth century, Jesuits played a unique and significant role in the "Indo-Portuguese moment" of South Asian history, marked by intersecting political, ecclesiastical, and commercial activities.[8] The Portuguese found in coastal India not simply a place for missionary endeavors, but also "an intensely commercial society" that presented opportunities for acquiring wealth.[9]

As noted in Chapter 1, the conquest of Goa gave the *Estado da India* (Portuguese state in India) access to lucrative opportunities for trade, enhanced trade routes linking Atlantic ports to those of the Indian Ocean, and an ecclesiastical base for the Catholic Church in Asia.[10] However, the Portuguese were not alone in their participation in global networks. During the sixteenth century, the Mughal Empire also was extending its reach in India through conquest and trade. The Mughals controlled much of north India, from the Afghan frontier to Bengal, and promoted trade through overland and maritime routes. They gradually moved southward to control parts of India's central plateau or Deccan region. Goa, however, remained beyond Mughal control, and the Portuguese were able to use the colony as a valuable base for trade and Catholic missions with little interference from the Mughals.

The Portuguese and the Mughals were very much aware of each other's presence on the subcontinent.[11] The Jesuits appear to have felt a racial affinity with the Mughals. The priest Rudolf Acquaviva (also written Rodolfo), who headed the first Jesuit mission to Akbar's court, referred to the Mughals as "white men like us," referencing the racial features that separated both Portuguese and Mughals from the general Indian population.[12] The similarity, however, ended there. In 1573, relations became more strained when Akbar annexed the western province of Gujarat and its port city of Surat. Even though Gujarat was located roughly 500 miles to the north of Goa, Akbar's actions drew the spheres of influence of the Portuguese and the Mughals into closer proximity. The annexation gave both empires control over key ports and access to trade across the Arabian Sea; but while the Mughals dominated overland trade routes, the Portuguese held the upper hand at sea because of their superior ships. Their naval dominance allowed them to require Muslims making the hajj by sea to pay taxes when crossing via Portuguese ports and to carry a *cartaz* (a pass or license) stamped with the image of Christ and the Virgin Mary.[13] Some speculate, not unreasonably, that Akbar aspired eventually to expel the Portuguese from Goa. Upon encountering Portuguese traders in Gujarat, Akbar's chief minister is said to have regarded them as "a pack of savages."[14]

It was in this context of rising proximity and tension that Akbar, somewhat ironically, developed a sincere interest in learning about the religion of the Portuguese. Prior to 1580, when the Jesuits undertook their first official mission to his court, other Catholic priests had made a favorable impression upon Akbar. In Bengal, two Jesuits refused to administer the sacraments to Christian merchants who refused to pay taxes to the Mughal government. So impressed was Akbar by their action that he invited to his court at Fatehpur Sikri Julian Pereira, a Jesuit priest stationed at Satgaon, a port in southern Bengal. Pereira engaged in dialogues with Muslim clerics at Akbar's court, some of whom were less than cordial. Not being a very learned Jesuit, Pereira recommended that Akbar extend an invitation to priests based at the College of St. Paul in Goa.

In his *farman* (a royal invitation or decree), Akbar expressed his "kind disposition" toward the Jesuits and his desire to learn about the "Law and Gospel" of their religion from their learned priests.[15] After much deliberation, the bishops at Goa decided to send three Jesuit priests to Akbar's court, each representing a

Figure 2.2 Akbar's visit to the Jesuits.
Source: Heras Institute, Mumbai.

different nationality. Francis Henriques was a Persian from Hormuz and a convert from Islam. He was to assume the role of translator on account of his knowledge of Persian, the official language of the Mughal court. Antony Monserrate, a Spaniard from Catalonia, was responsible for producing a detailed account of their journey from Goa to Fatehpur Sikri, of Akbar's military campaign at Kabul, and of the early dialogues of the priests with Akbar. Rudolph Acquaviva was a high-born and learned Italian who was trained at Rome in theology and philosophy. When he sailed from Rome to Lisbon to become ordained, he was accompanied by Matteo Ricci, the Jesuit who had made a similar mission to the imperial court at China.[16] After arriving in Goa at the age of thirty, Acquaviva volunteered to be a part of the mission to Akbar's court. Clearly impressed by his credentials, the bishops appointed him to lead it (see Figure 2.2).[17]

Akbar's Imperial Persona

During the sixteenth century, European lands were ravaged by interreligious conflicts such as the Spanish Inquisition and the French Catholic massacre of Huguenots (Protestant minorities). In Mughal India, by contrast, Akbar was inviting members of different religious traditions to his House of Worship to engage in interfaith dialogue.[18] Among the participants were Shi'i and Sunni Muslims, Parsis, Jains, Hindus, Sikhs, and Jews. Akbar's innovative approach to religious differences has led some to place him among the great figures of world history.[19]

More recent scholarship has contextualized, if not tempered, such praise. Akbar's notion of universal tolerance was certainly preferable to bloodshed; and yet, when presiding over a predominantly non-Muslim population, some degree of religious accommodation was a political necessity. Militarized regional kingdoms were capable of waging fierce resistance to Mughal rule. In order to maintain stability and thwart rebellion, the Mughals had to find ways of incorporating local personnel and observances into the fabric of their rule. Akbar's theological framing of this toleration (his Religion of God) was his unique creation, but in key respects his accommodative policies were a continuation of those introduced by his predecessors.[20]

That being said, Akbar had to contend with the constant threat of rebellion from Muslims, at least in part because of his openness to non-Muslims and their beliefs. Many Muslims considered Akbar and his policies to be heretical. Badauni, a more orthodox courtier, believed that Akbar had abandoned the core teachings of Islam and that there "was not a trace of Islam left in him."[21] Some resented the rapport Akbar developed with the Jesuit priests and spread rumors that he was on the verge of becoming a Christian. This resulted in attempts on his life and uprisings against his regime. Monserrate noted Muslim grievances concerning their apostate king:

> It happened that he was not in the habit of saying the customary Musalman prayers at the times appointed by Muhammad, and did not observe the month's fast which is called Ramadan. He frequently made jokes at the expense of Muhammad ... All this enraged many Musalmans.[22]

In 1580, Akbar launched a campaign against his half-brother, Mirza Muhammad Hakim, who presided over the Afghan city of Kabul. Disgruntled Mughal officers in Bengal and Bihar, resentful of Akbar's religious policies and sounding the alarm of Islam in danger, had conspired to draw Mirza Muhammad Hakim to India and proclaim him the emperor.[23] With an army of 50,000 cavalry, Akbar overwhelmed Mirza Muhammad Hakim's smaller invading army and brought an end to the uprising. Monserrate, who had accompanied Akbar on his Kabul campaign, believed that the uprising reflected increasing resentment of the emperor among Muslims.[24]

In addition to his magnanimity toward non-Muslims, aspects of Akbar's imperial persona became a point of contention. He became significantly influenced by the Mahdi movement within the Shi'i tradition, which anticipated the arrival of a messianic figure at the turn of the Islamic millennium who would restore righteousness on earth.[25] At the very time when Akbar was hosting discussions at his House of Worship, the belief in the Mahdi was gaining prominence. This belief was not derived from any particular textual tradition but was informed, according to the historian Azfar Moin, by a hodgepodge of popular cultic practices: Shi'i Muslim beliefs, Sufi mysticism and holy men, astrology, and messianic concepts derived from Zoroastrianism.[26] One of the scholars employed at Akbar's court was the famous Naqshbandi Sufi Shaykh Ahmad Sirhindi (1564–1624). It was Sirhindi who popularized the notion that, at the end of the first millennium, Muslims had lost their connection to the divine, which had been mediated for a season through the Prophet Muhammad. The turn of the millennium had diminished the centrality of Muhammad by transforming him into "a purely spiritual being." Muslims were therefore "in need of a new spiritual mediator."[27] But what kind of personality would fill the vacuum in this new dispensation?

What is striking about this millennial ideology is how it declared the end of Islam as a religion just as Akbar was espousing his new Religion of God. These concurrent developments set the stage nicely for Akbar to assume a wide range of titles that signified his status as the millennial messiah. Adherents of his new Religion of God came to designate him as the "Mahdi," the "Just King," or the "Caliph of the Age," and they gave him other titles that captured his spiritual authority.[28] Akbar's chief court adviser and chronicler, Abu'l-fazl, who had been quite friendly toward the Jesuits and arranged many of their meetings with him, portrayed Akbar as an emperor endowed with cosmic powers to heal, control the weather, and cure illness.[29] His treatise on the reign of Akbar, the *Akbarnama*, describes extensively the astrological basis for his sovereignty.[30]

Akbar introduced new rituals of courtly etiquette that encouraged greater reverence for the emperor. These included the practice of prostrating oneself before Akbar with the right hand placed on the forehead. The phrase "Allahu Akbar" became a standard greeting in his court. It could literally mean "God is Great" or "God is Akbar."[31] The ambiguity, probably welcomed by Akbar, elicited strong objections from Muslims.[32] Akbar's messianic persona also gave him sweeping powers over doctrinal pronouncements in his dominion. Through a signed and sealed document, principal *ulama* (religious scholars) and lawyers of his day invested him with supreme authority in all religious matters.[33]

One might imagine that Akbar's messianic status would have posed an immediate and insurmountable hurdle for the Jesuits, especially considering their belief in Jesus as the one true messiah; or that his imperial persona would have been central to their observations about him. Curiously, the observations of Acquaviva, Henriques, and Monserrate seem largely indifferent to the fact that Akbar was regarded by some as a divine king, millennial messiah, or even an avatar or reincarnation of the Hindu deity Rama.[34] In one of his letters, Acquaviva did note how Akbar was "paying homage to creatures like the sun and the moon" and had instituted a new festival, Mehregan, a Persian feast of the autumn equinox. These observances, he noted, "scandalized" Muslims. Apparently, they did not scandalize Acquaviva; they only "confused" him, since he primarily viewed them as diverting Akbar away from Christian dialogue.[35] Acquaviva was unable to reconcile Akbar's kindness toward the Jesuits with his entanglement with these other practices. Ultimately, it was not Akbar's messianic status that bothered Acquaviva but his inconsistency, conveying initially his profound interest in the Jesuits and their beliefs, then suddenly turning cold or diverting his attention to other things.

Earning and Expending Influence

During the early months of their stay, the Jesuits believed that Akbar had developed a special fondness for them, even over his Muslim courtiers and *mullahs*. Upon their arrival at court, the priests noted Akbar's admiration for their vows of poverty, expressed in their refusal to receive his welcoming gift of "800 pieces of gold."[36] The priests insisted that all they needed during their stay was "food and clothing." Still, Akbar was determined to send them a monthly allowance "under the guise of alms" to cover their daily expenses.[37] In the Persianate imperial traditions of India, the gifting of shawls, jewels, robes of honor, turbans, and other items was a central convention of statecraft and a vital means of building bonds of trust and loyalty between the emperor and his guests.[38] The Jesuits seem to have mistaken Akbar's *noblesse oblige* for a special interest in them and an interest in becoming a Christian. Ultimately, the priests were sorely disappointed with the different path taken by Akbar.

Akbar appears to have developed a deepening trust in the Jesuits. He came to regard them as persons with whom he could speak openly about the affairs of his court and his longing for spiritual truth. At gatherings of his council, Akbar often asked the priests to sit beside him. Monserrate clearly believed that Akbar had altered the conventions of courtly etiquette in order to convey his special esteem for them:

> Once, when he was in camp, he desired another of the priests, in the middle of a crowd of his nobles, to help him fasten on his sword, which service the father performed, amidst the envy and wonder of all the courtiers. He wished the priests to be sharers of his inmost thoughts, both in good and ill-fortune ... he ordered his door keepers to grant them entrance, whenever they wished, even into the inner courtyard of the palace, where only the most distinguished nobles

had the right to entrance. He sent them food from his own table—a mark of distinction which he is said never to have conferred upon anyone before.[39]

The Jesuits believed that Akbar's favor would provide them with the platform they needed to transform his dominion spiritually. They would use their status not only to speak plainly about their beliefs, but also to attack Islam and register their disapproval of contentious cultural practices such as *sati* (whereby a Hindu widow immolates herself on the burning pyre of her husband).

Over the course of several months, the priests claimed to have earned enough of Akbar's trust to openly criticize cultural practices within his domain. They objected, for instance, to Akbar's staging of gladiatorial contests that cost participants their lives. The priests insisted that if he were so amused by games that resembled warfare, he should protect the participants by giving them dulled swords and protective helmets and armor.[40] On one occasion, Akbar invited the priests to attend a *sati*. The priests were aghast to see what they viewed as a "cruel and savage" practice. Acquaviva "publicly reprimanded the king" for conveying his approval of the practice through his attendance. When Akbar responded without the slightest hint of resentment, it reinforced the priests' sense of being held in very high esteem by him.

Having witnessed the *sati*, Monserrate assumed the role of observer and ethnographer. Women who performed *sati*, he noted, were often drugged by opium or "a soporific herb named bang" (a form of cannabis). Sometimes they were coerced:

> Sometimes they are half-drugged: and, before they lose their resolution, are hurried to the pyre with warnings, prayers and promises of eternal fame. On arriving there they cast themselves into the flames. If they hesitate, the wretched creatures are driven on to the pyre: and if they try to leap off again, are held down with poles and hooks.[41]

From this description, Monserrate returned to the matter of public perceptions of the Jesuits. Hindu nobles were "incensed," he noted, by Jesuit interference in their affairs, whereas others praised the priests for their audacity to criticize Akbar publicly.[42]

The priests privately complained to the emperor about the presence of *hijras*, a transgender or intersex community (often men dressed as women) at Fatehpur Sikri. Monserrate referred to them as "a crowd of worthless profligates." Their message to Akbar was to either exile or "burn" them:

> They declared with the greatest emphasis that they were astonished at his permitting such a class of men to live in his kingdom, let alone in his city, and

almost under his eyes. They must be banished, as though they were a deadly plague, to his most distant territories; even better, let them be burnt up by devouring flames . . . Therefore let him give orders that these libertines should never again be seen at Fattepurum.[43]

In response to their plea, Akbar simply retired from their presence, saying essentially that he would attend to the matter on another occasion. Monserrate emphasized how their "conscientious" admonishing of the emperor only increased his respect and affection for them. Akbar apparently was moved by the sincerity of the Jesuits' convictions.

The Jesuits hoped that their lessons about Christianity would be met with Akbar's rapt attention, but their sense of being flattered by the emperor's favor would eventually give way to frustration at his inability to focus. They sometimes complained that Akbar asked theological questions but did not wait for a response before posing another question.[44] Moreover, he had many princely hobbies to distract him: hunting, archery, armor, carpentry and crafts, training and riding wild horses, cock fighting, and gladiator-like games. Besides these, Akbar's "hundred wives" and fondness for opium competed for his time. Monserrate recorded one instance when the priests came to a long-awaited meeting with Akbar only to find him thoroughly inebriated by a drink made from a mixture of opium, cannabis, and arrack (a liquor made from the extract of palmyra trees).[45]

For the priests to gain an audience with Akbar, they had to go through Abu'l-fazl, his closest courtier. As stated earlier, Abu'l-fazl was sympathetic to Akbar's universal religion and his messianic persona. This is quite consistent with the rapport he developed with the Jesuits. In some instances, Abu'l-fazl became Akbar's alter ego, standing in for him when Akbar was too busy or distracted to participate in the dialogues. The reason why Abu'l-fazl was so favorably disposed toward the Jesuits might very well have been that he, too, seemed to be accommodating them in Akbar's universal religion. Monserrate stated that Abu'l-fazl virtually "spoke as a Christian" when discussing the Christian scriptures and the gospel.[46] It was never entirely clear to the Jesuits, however, whether Abu'l-fazl's openness stemmed from his genuine curiosity about their faith or from his desire to please the emperor.[47] His role appears to have been that of someone who attempted to keep each side of the triangle happy: Jesuits, who wanted Akbar's attention; Akbar, who derived a unique pleasure from learning about religion; and Muslims, who were increasingly incensed by Akbar's willingness to listen to views that were openly critical of Islam. Describing Abu'l-fazl's mediating role, Monserrate wrote:

> Concerning him the King said we should speak with him as if with H. H. [His Highness], and we came to understand the great prudence of the King, who in

order not to excite his people to rebellion, shows himself to be on their side, and in order that we should not remain without favour, has given orders that this one [Abu'l-fazl] should always be on ours. Thus he carries on being instructed and understanding the things of our faith with as little scandal of his own as possible.[48]

The fact that Jesuits do not feature at all in Abu'l-fazl's treatise the *Akbarnama* suggests that they read too much into his warm reception of them and his apparent interest in their religion. According to Acquaviva, the case for Jesus as God's son so resonated with Abu'l-fazl that he even helped the priests explain the doctrine to Akbar.[49] Unbeknownst to him, Abu'l-fazl was probably drawing from his own belief in millennial messianism to help frame and explain Jesus's incarnation. Previously, Zoroastrian and Shi'i visitors to Akbar's court had tried to win over the emperor to their faith, though unsuccessfully.[50] The Jesuits appear to have joined the ranks of those who had been misled by the universalist ideology shaping Akbar's court. Akbar's inquisitiveness made the Jesuits all too eager to imagine him on a trajectory leading ultimately to his conversion.

The Jesuits were under the impression that they had earned enough of Akbar's admiration and trust to warrant their criticisms of Islam and Indian cultural practices and their exhortations for Akbar to embrace their faith. Besides believing that they enjoyed Akbar's favor, Jesuit ties to Portuguese imperial power and valorization of Christian martyrdom also shaped their confrontational style. As they drew upon this storehouse of goodwill, they grew increasingly aware that they were depleting its reserves.

The Dialogues

Despite the many activities that amused and distracted the emperor, the priests found a window of opportunity to discuss religious matters with him—sometimes alone, sometimes in the company of his *mullahs*. What transpired were triangular interactions involving the Jesuits, a curious but easily distracted Akbar, who had been branded an apostate, and the *mullahs*, who became the voices of orthodox Islam. Since these interactions were mediated through Jesuit letters, the letters need to be examined critically. They tend to cast the priests in a highly favorable light, the *mullahs* as being unable to respond intelligently to Jesuit criticism of the Qur'an and the Prophet, and Akbar as a king who grew increasingly sympathetic to the Jesuit message, even to the point of being on the cusp of conversion. Some aspects of the triangular dynamics described in these letters are corroborated by a wider literature. These elements include Akbar's departure from Islam and his affinity for millennial messianism and other popular cultic practices. As the earliest firsthand European accounts of Akbar's life, the Jesuit letters reveal much about the religious exchanges in the House of Worship. Biased as they are, they reveal what Jesuits tended to emphasize in their encounters with the emperor and his *mullahs*.

Defending the truth of Catholicism through reasoned debate was central to the training of every Jesuit. In their colleges, they simulated controversies with mock opponents, with some students assuming the roles of "pagans" or "heretics." Others were then tasked with steering them toward Catholic orthodoxy. For decades, Jesuit theologians deployed their debating skills in Europe in public disputations with Protestants. During this time, they became well acquainted with the overarching tropes of Protestant polemics and the central critiques of Catholicism leveled by Protestant reformers.[51]

This acquaintance with European Protestantism might explain why the defense of the Bible became such a salient aspect of the Jesuits' argumentation in Akbar's court. Their defense of the Bible over the Qur'an mirrored the emphasis on scripture developed by Luther and other Protestant reformers.[52] It is difficult to gauge how much direct influence Protestant reformers had had on the Jesuits by this point, but Jesuit defenses of the Bible and their scathing criticism of the Prophet Muhammad prefigure similar rhetoric employed by Protestants such as Bartholomaeus Ziegenbalg, Henry Martyn, and Karl Gottlieb Pfander (discussed in Chapters 4 and 5).

The Jesuits gifted Akbar with the Royal Polyglot Bible of Plantyn. Translated into Hebrew, Chaldean, Latin, and Greek, the Bible came in eight volumes. They also gave him a portrait of Jesus and the Virgin Mary. Their gifts delighted Akbar. In the presence of all the Muslims in his court, he took each volume of the Polyglot Bible into his hands, one after the other, kissed it, and placed it against his head.[53] Akbar then gifted the priests with a copy of the Qur'an, a gesture that apparently offended his *mullahs* (see Figure 2.3).

The priests tried to persuade Akbar that the Gospels, unlike the Qur'an, could be "proved."[54] Rather than pointing to extra-biblical evidence, they emphasized the internal coherence of the Bible. They argued that the Bible's different components—the law, the Psalms, and the Gospels—despite being "different books" written at different times, are consistent with each other. Since even the *mullahs* acknowledged the legitimacy of the books of Moses, the Psalms, and the Gospels, by necessity they should recognize the deficiencies of the Qur'an, since the content of the Qur'an, the Jesuits claimed, not only contradicted those books but also carried internal contradictions.[55] For Monserrate, the starting point of all reasoning with the *mullahs* was establishing the truth of the Christian scriptures:

Figure 2.3 Akbar receives a deputation of Jesuits who give him a Bible as a gift, 1576.
Source: Chronicle/Alamy Stock Photo.

In general I was unhappy over our disaccord over the truth of the scriptures which is the first door in this matter. For since the dogmas of our faith are based on what God has revealed in the sacred scriptures, and human reason does not attain to it, if these are not entirely believed, for the rest it is just discussing obstinately.[56]

For any meaningful dialogue to take place, it was necessary for the priests to develop some facility in Persian. Henriques was Persian by birth but had forgotten much of his mother tongue; it apparently took him several weeks to recover some measure of facility.[57] Acquaviva, being intellectually gifted, was able to converse in Persian after three months of being tutored by Abu'l-fazl.[58] Despite the diminishing language gap, Monserrate found himself becoming impatient with the discussions. He believed that much was being lost in translation, either on account of Henriques's excessive brevity or because of the tendency of the *mullahs* to misunderstand or mistranslate his ideas.[59]

The Jesuits introduced Akbar to the moral and theological tenets of the Bible and eagerly awaited their conversations with him concerning spiritual matters.

The most contentious issues they addressed with Akbar were those concerning the divinity of Jesus, as captured in the doctrines of the incarnation (God becoming human in Jesus) and the Trinity (one God in three persons). One exchange concerning these doctrines arose when the Jesuits were instructing Akbar's thirteen-year-old son, Pahari (the nickname for Murad, Akbar's second surviving son), in their chapel. At Akbar's request, they had agreed to give Pahari regular lessons in Portuguese and in the tenets of Christianity. On one occasion, when Akbar visited during his lessons, the priests asked Pahari to recite a lesson beginning with the phrase "In the name of God." Akbar interjected, as if to demonstrate his grasp and appreciation of Christian doctrine, "and of Jesus Christ the true prophet and son of God."[60] Later, when Akbar was seated on the floor with the priests and conversing with them privately, he admitted that he could not comprehend how God could have a son.[61]

In every other respect, Akbar, according to the priests, had given them many indications that he was drawn to the Jesuits and their message of salvation. In addition to his praise of the "Christian law" (here "law" refers to "religion"), he extended his support for the Jesuits in other ways. Besides entrusting his own son to their instruction, he promised to help the Jesuits construct a church and a hospital. He also gave them permission to "baptize all who wished to become Christian."[62] And yet, he faced an insurmountable barrier to his belief in Christianity: namely, Christ's divinity. So profoundly did this issue vex Akbar that, according to the priests, it became the primary factor preventing him from declaring himself a Christian. Years later, the French priest Pierre du Jarric would lament that Akbar displayed "the common fault of the atheist, who refuses to make reason subservient to faith."[63]

As open as Akbar was with the Jesuits concerning his reservations about Jesus's divinity, he was equally open about his disbelief in Islam and his shame in his own *mullahs*. How much of this was the Jesuit gloss on Akbar and how much of it was indicative of his real departure from Islam is unclear from the letters. According to the priests, Akbar was disappointed by the inability of his *mullahs* to defend the Qur'an effectively. Their constant quarreling and confusion concerning the content of the Qur'an also frustrated him.[64] So convinced was Akbar about the ineptitude of his *mullahs* that he would interrupt or speak over them as they were responding to the Jesuits.[65] Exasperated by his *mullahs*, he once asked the Jesuits to discuss religious matters with him directly or with Abu'l-fazl. In confidence, he reportedly declared to the Jesuits that he "regard[ed] the law of the Saracens [Muslims] as worse than any other."[66]

Akbar was also aware of the tendency of the *mullahs* to become so outraged in the course of interreligious exchanges that they would resort to violence. The "dialogues" that took place in his House of Worship often resulted in ill feeling or overt hostility between members of rival sects.[67] The Jesuit priest Julian Pereira was nearly accosted by the *mullahs* when he referred to Islam as "a tissue of errors and lies."[68] Akbar intervened on his behalf by explaining to the *mullahs* that it was not unusual in a religious disputation to "hold one's views to be true, and those of his adversaries to be false."[69] Apparently, the belligerent tone of these religious exchanges agitated Akbar and hastened his departure from Islam. This was the view of Akbar's orthodox Muslim courtier Badauni:

> They cast the emperor, who was possessed of an excellent disposition, and an earnest searcher of truth, but very ignorant, a mere novice, and used to the company of infidel and base persons, into perplexity, until doubt was heaped upon doubt, and he lost all definite aim, and the straight wall of the true Law was broken.[70]

After the third theological discussion with the priests and the *mullahs*, Akbar declared that he had "had enough of argument."[71] The stage was apparently set for a different kind of contest.

The *mullahs* began to demand that the priests perform miracles to prove their case for Christianity. In particular, they challenged them to endure a "trial by ordeal" to vindicate belief in either the Bible or the Qur'an. They proposed that one priest and one of the *mullahs* enter a burning pyre. "The book which comes out safely together with its bearer, shall be judged true."[72] This proposal found a precedent in the visit of the Jesuit Julian Pereira, who, not being a very learned man, proposed trial by ordeal as an alternative to intellectual arguments. The proposal fed Akbar's own enthusiasm for public spectacle, "hands-on knowledge," and gladiatorial competition.[73] It also deflected attention away from the issue of textual knowledge, which Pereira had lacked, as did the *mullahs* relative to Acquaviva and the others.

The response of the priests to this challenge was nuanced. They wanted to avoid the appearance of cowardice, while also avoiding the sin of "putting God to the test." The Jesuit tradition considered suffering for the faith and martyrdom to be the highest ideals of any Christian disciple. As the head of the mission, Acquaviva was committed to an ascetic lifestyle; he flagellated himself with a leather belt in order to subdue his flesh and ultimately aspired to be martyred.[74] Upon being challenged to the trial by ordeal, Acquaviva asserted that he and his fellow priests would gladly enter "a thousand pyres," but that they would not presume that they would be "miraculously kept from harm."[75] He explained that, as "imperfect sinners," the Jesuits could not assume that God held them dear enough to keep them safe. Moreover, accepting the challenge would merely appease unbelievers who demanded miracles but who would not be willing to alter their beliefs even if they were to observe one. He cited instances in the New Testament when Jesus rebuked those who demanded miracles in order to believe as well as examples from Catholic history in which saints had been martyred without effecting any change in those who had opposed them.

In response to Acquaviva's reasoning, Akbar revealed his real motives for advocating the trial by ordeal. According to Monserrate, this was not to resolve his own indecision, but rather to reaffirm his affection for the priests and execute one of his clerics. Akbar explained that there was a certain Muslim cleric who, despite his religious pretenses, had been guilty of "great crimes." Akbar wanted this cleric to be the one who would enter the fire on behalf of Islam and for him to go first. How Akbar would justify absolving the Jesuit from taking his turn is unclear. Acquaviva rejected the proposal, explaining that they could not be complicit in someone else's death, even if the ruler permitted it. Akbar then proposed that the priests simply declare their willingness to undergo the ordeal, and he would persuade the cleric to enter the flames. Acquaviva replied that they could not even agree to this. Finally, Akbar suggested that the priests simply remain silent as he declared their willingness to ascend the pyre. Acquaviva rejected this proposal as simply a "roundabout" way of executing someone and a "disingenuous course in committing him to the flames."[76]

The exchanges became more heated when the Jesuits began to criticize the Prophet Muhammad. As they tried to impress upon the *mullahs* that Jesus was the divine Son of God, they declared that Muhammad must have been a false prophet for having reduced Jesus to the status of a mere prophet. Muhammad, according to the priests, must also have been an "arrogant" man, since he made claims about himself, whereas others—that is, the prophets of the Old Testament—had spoken of Christ and his coming.

In one discussion, the priests identified Muhammad not simply as a false prophet but as the Antichrist, who had attempted to falsify the Christian scriptures.[77] The notion of deception and the association of Muhammad with Satan or with the demonic was a recurring theme of Jesuit interactions with the *mullahs* and Akbar. In his confidential letter to Father Rodrigues in Rome, Acquaviva would later lament the intransigence of the *mullahs* and their fixation on the "ugly" and "diabolical" name of Muhammad, whom he also labeled an "infernal monster."[78] When he had tried to persuade them that Jesus was divine and not a mere prophet, he claimed that he had been met with the most severe objections. "One," he explained, "says '*astafarla*' [God forbid], another stops his ears, a third laughs, and another bursts into a blasphemy."[79]

As the Jesuits sustained their direct attacks against the Prophet Muhammad, the warmth and receptiveness once displayed by Akbar and Abu'l-fazl began to fade. Regardless of Akbar's mixed feelings toward the *mullahs*, an attack on Muhammad likely pushed the limits of even Akbar's tolerance. Moreover, Jesuit descriptions of Akbar and Abu'l-fazl shift from an emphasis on their overt favor toward them to their "dissimulation." All along, the Jesuits had been convinced that Akbar admired them more than his *mullahs* and that he had ceased to be a Muslim. And yet, after their attacks on Muhammad, Akbar felt obligated to share with the *mullahs* their sense of outrage. Monserrate viewed this as mere posturing:

> Finally, when there was talk of Muhammad, he pretended to regret the offence to a person so honorable (in whom he believes as much as the Pope), saying "*Ana! Ana!*" ["No! No!"] contorting his face and bending over. And according to me he said that to satisfy the mullahs of the opposition.[80]

Akbar went so far as to ask the priests to "mind [their] words." In response, the priests replied that they were obliged to speak the truth "even though they might cut off our heads."[81] Abu'l-fazl also warned the Jesuits not to speak against Muhammad. According to Monserrate, the reason he gave them was that the Jesuits were outnumbered—they had only the emperor and Abu'l-fazl on their side.

Badauni, Akbar's orthodox Muslim courtier, decried the Jesuit attacks on the Prophet. He was equally critical of Akbar for his willingness to listen to the Jesuits (along with Parsis and Brahmins) while marginalizing Muslims. Akbar, he charged, "picked and chose from anyone except a Muslim."[82] Regarding the priests, Badauni did not mince his words:

> Learned monks also from Europe who are called *Padre* and have an infallible head (Mujtahid-i-kamil) called *Papa* ... brought the Gospel, advanced proofs for the Trinity, demonstrated the title of Christianity, and made the religion of Jesus current. The attributes of the accursed Anti-Christ and his qualities were ascribed by these accursed men to his Lordship The Best of the Prophets (God bless him and his family and preserve him from all Impostors).[83]

Badauni also objected to the many Muslim customs that were abandoned by Akbar and replaced with the customs of other religions.

Legacies

After three years, the first Jesuit mission to Akbar's court failed to achieve the ultimate goal of converting the emperor. Akbar's declining interest in dialogue and the open hostility of Muslims signaled to the priests that they needed to consider returning to Goa. Akbar himself, however, did not want the Jesuits to leave. This was not because of any interest in becoming a Christian, but because of an affinity he had developed for them. At one level, Akbar appears to have been drawn to the intensity of their spiritual convictions and their capacity to feed his sporadic need for religious discussions. At the same time, Akbar, as an astute political leader, quite likely wanted to maintain contact with the Jesuits as a form of espionage.[84] Besides feeding his appetite for learning, the Jesuits could provide him with a steady flow of information about Portuguese activities in India. The priests, however, lamented what they perceived as Akbar's declining interest in their message.

By 1583, Henriques had already left for Goa, while Monserrate and Acquaviva were negotiating their return. Upon the ascension of Spain's Philip II to the throne of Portugal, Akbar was keen to send a delegation to congratulate him. Wishing also to deliver a letter to the pope, Akbar agreed to allow Monserrate to accompany the delegation to Spain, while Acquaviva remained with Akbar at Fatehpur Sikri.

Acquaviva took great pride in his confrontational style of engaging Muslims and Hindus at Fatehpur Sikri. The hostile response of the *mullahs* to his attacks reinforced his sense of suffering for his faith.[85] As Akbar's interest in dialogue declined, Acquaviva became more of a recluse, committing himself to prayer, the study of Persian, and penance. The Father Provincial at Goa had written to Akbar on three occasions requesting Acquaviva's return. In his *farman* authorizing Acquaviva's departure, Akbar stressed his deep friendship with the priest, Acquaviva's skill in teaching Akbar about the "book of Heavenly Jesus," and Akbar's desire "to have him every hour in conversation."[86] Akbar also requested that the Father Provincial send back Acquaviva and "some other Father" as soon as possible. Such was the emperor's affection for the Jesuit who had relentlessly attacked Islam, and whom Akbar had once instructed to "mind his words."

As Acquaviva narrated his bold attacks on Islam and the hostility they evoked, he hoped to earn the blessing of his Superior General, Everard Mercurian. He also hoped that his particular style of engaging other religions would ultimately earn him the martyrdom to which he aspired. Not long after his departure in 1583, one of Akbar's sons, Prince Salim, found a whip covered in blood in Acquaviva's room, which the priest had used to flagellate himself.[87] He eventually was killed by a group of Hindus at Salsette Island.

At the behest of Akbar, in 1591 the diocese of Goa sent three priests to his court, which was then at Lahore. In his letter, Akbar expressed his eagerness to learn more about Jesus from the learned priests. He described his admiration for the priests as "men retired from the world, who have left the pomps and honors of earth."[88] Akbar had learned through a priest named Leo Grimon that there were more fathers of great learning at Goa who could instruct him on religious matters. He conveyed his eagerness to compare the spiritual knowledge of the Jesuits with that of his own doctors of Islamic law:

Your Reverences will be able immediately on receiving my letter, to send some of them to my Court with all confidence, so that in disputations with my doctors I may compare their several learning and character, and see the superiority of the Fathers over my doctors, whom we call Caziques, and who by this means may be taught to know the truth.[89]

Akbar's enthusiasm for more dialogue with the Jesuits stands in stark contrast to Monserrate's and Acquaviva's descriptions of his declining interest in learning about Christianity. Perhaps the lapse of eight years had revived his interest; or perhaps there was something about periodic religious controversies that fed Akbar's intellectual passion irrespective of any intention on his part to change his views. What seems evident from his overtures to Goa—or at least from the Jesuits' rendition of them—is that Akbar knew how to appeal to their missionary zeal in order to draw them back to his court. He deployed the idiom of Christian belief and even presented himself as a potential convert to the faith. He refers, for instance, to the doctrines of the priests, through whom he "hope[d] to be restored from death to life, even as their master, Jesus Christ, who came down from heaven to earth, raised many from the dead and gave them new life."[90]

What transpired during the second mission to Akbar in 1591, however, shattered any hopes of fruitful exchange about the merits of Christianity. Father Duarte Leitão, who headed the mission, decided to abort it when it became evident to him that Akbar had become absorbed in his *Din-i-Ilahi* and had succumbed to its underlying millennial messianism. According to Leitão:

[T]he haughtiness of this barbarian had attained to such a degree that he considered himself as a prophet and a legislator saying that the period of the law of Muhammad had now come to an end and that the world is deprived of a true law and that therefore another prophet has to come, who will establish it, and that he is the one man to do it: and in this manner he behaves himself. So openly, that people worship him in public as a prophet with such shameless praises that I heard him called God, many times in public.[91]

The cult that had formed around Akbar was an insurmountable barrier to his conversion, according to Leitão and his colleague, Christoval de Vega. Akbar, they believed, had summoned them in order to legitimate, by their very presence, the establishment of his new religion. Against the wishes of their Provincial, who wanted them to remain in Lahore, Vega and Leitão returned to Goa.

Three years later, a third and final mission to Akbar's court (1595–1605) was headed by Jerome Xavier, a grand nephew of Francis Xavier, the renowned missionary to the fishermen castes of coastal India.[92] Two other priests, Emmanuel Pinheiro and Benedict de Goes, accompanied Xavier. This lengthier mission succeeded in engaging Akbar in religious exchanges, but with no more success at converting him than the previous ones. What did transpire over the span of a decade, however, was a greater sense among the priests of the political ambitions of Akbar. It was during these years that Akbar launched a military campaign into the Deccan, in which Pinheiro and Xavier accompanied him. Xavier and Goes also accompanied Akbar to Kashmir (he went there after a fire had burned down his palace at Lahore). From Kashmir, Goes wrote letters in which he staunchly advocated for a Jesuit mission to Tibet.[93]

Catholic–Mughal Fusion

The priests of the third mission had studied Persian, authored several books on theological matters, studied astronomy and geology, and proved to be a catalyst for cultural, artistic, and intellectual activity in the Mughal courts.[94] Akbar himself had employed court painters such as Kesu Das, Manohar, Basawan, and Kesu Khurd, who were influenced by European artistic motifs.[95] This commissioning of Mughal–Christian art by Akbar and his successor, Jahangir, served to enhance the legitimacy and universality of the Mughal Empire, which presided over followers of many religions. The fact that Jesus, Mary, and other New Testament figures are mentioned in the Qur'an lent some degree of legitimacy to such depictions. Still, orthodox Muslims of this period resented the magnanimous approach of the court to Catholicism, especially within a climate of Mughal–Portuguese rivalry.

Catholics employed similar fusion motifs in their art to convey their universal faith. Jesuits at Goa hired local artists and sculptors to produce artworks depicting Christian themes. Images of Jesus and the Virgin Mary or of Jesuit priests themselves were cast in Mughal motifs, which reflected architectural styles of courtly life set within the ornate borders typical of Mughal paintings. The Royal Polyglot Bible that the Jesuits had presented to Akbar contained images produced by a Flemish painter that reflected the baroque styles and humanist tastes of the European Renaissance.

Another site of Mughal–Catholic fusion was the princely state of Sardhana. Located less than 100 miles to the northeast of Delhi, Sardhana held the unusual position of being ruled by a Catholic woman, Farzana Zeb al-Nissa Begum Sombre (r. 1778–1836). She was the consort of a German Catholic mercenary, Walter Reinhardt, who had served the Mughals. For his service, the emperor granted him the *jagir* (land grant) of Sardhana. After Reinhardt died in 1778, Begum Sombre acquired the *jagir* and oversaw its land and army. She eventually converted to Catholicism and embraced the name Joanna (after Joan of Arc) Nobilis Somer.

As a Catholic woman ruler, the Begum's life retained important aspects of her Euro-Persian heritage. She maintained lasting ties to the Mughal imperial family and interacted with them according to appropriate protocols; her army came to the aid of the Mughals in various clashes with regional powers; and her name was engraved in both Roman and Persio-Arabic script on her official, imperial seal.[96] The cultural hybridity that marked her family, military, and courtly life was also reflected in the imperial architecture of her regime. She commissioned the construction of the Sardhana church, a cemetery, a *kothi* (imperial mansion), and other structures. Their aesthetics showed her commitment to global Catholicism while at the same time displaying her participation in the cosmopolitan society nurtured in this Indo-Persianate environment.[97]

Conclusion

In 1605, Akbar became seriously ill by alleged poisoning.[98] The priests tried desperately to gain access to him but were barred from entering his chamber. This may explain the disparaging tone that pervades the reflections of the priest Pierre du Jarric over questions about Akbar's religious affiliation at the hour of his death:

> He died as he had lived; for, as one knew what law he followed in his lifetime, so none knew that in which he died. This was the just judgment of God; for when he had the means of learning and recognizing the truth, he refused to make use of them. Hence he was unworthy of God's grace; so that, at this hour, none was at hand to take the bandage of unbelief from his eyes, or to offer him the means of dying in the law of Jesus Christ, the holiness of which he had so often admitted and extolled.[99]

The lack of access of the Jesuits to Akbar during his final hours may be interpreted symbolically. It suggests far more than Akbar's lack of commitment to any particular religion (including theirs). Rather, it reveals the Jesuits' limited sphere of influence in Akbar's court despite their compelling sense of access. Akbar's overtures to learn about the gospel, his warm welcome of three Jesuit missions to his court, and his apparent admiration for their religion over that of his *mullahs* could not surmount the fact that the Jesuits could not be present for Akbar at the hour of his passing.

In their zeal to convey the Christian story, the Jesuits developed a mistaken sense of their centrality to Akbar's story. Their disconnection appears to foreshadow the binary of "universal truth versus pluralism" of a later period. Just as Akbar had accommodated Christian belief within his universal religion, men such as Gandhi or Vivekananda, centuries later, would also espouse a religious universalism, of religions being different paths to the same summit. For them, Hinduism was the universal religion (*Din-i-Ilahi*) that underwrote and explained all religious differences. Gandhi's substantial engagement with Christianity resembles Akbar's and similarly disappointed missionaries who hoped that such engagement would lead to his conversion. Were these instances of narrow dogmatism confronting a more tolerant and capacious universalism? Or did they illustrate how Christian exclusivism came face to face with an equally dogmatic assertion—namely, that all religions are true and essentially the same?[100]

3
Cultural Accommodation and Difference in South Indian Catholicism

In its gripping account of the Jesuit mission to Japan during the seventeenth century, Shusako Endo's novel *Silence* explores issues of religious conversion and persecution.[1] A crucial moment in the novel arises when the young Jesuit priest, Sebastian Rodrigues, encounters his former mentor, Christovao Ferreira. Ferreira had apostatized and become a translator of Western texts for the Japanese government. In his new role, Ferreira lectured his former apprentice about his misguided notions about Christian conversion among the Japanese peasantry. He likened Japan to a swamp in which the "sapling of Christianity" is unable to take root.[2] Offended by this grim caricature, Rodrigues referred to the time when "many Japanese vied with one another to receive baptism like the Jews who gathered at the Jordan."[3] Ferreira then presented the unthinkable to Rodrigues: that the peasant converts were not worshiping Deus, the God of Portuguese Christianity, but continued to worship Dianichi (the Great Sun) beneath the guise of a new religion. Even the renowned missionary Francis Xavier, he noted, had written about this error. Through Ferreira's eyes, Japanese culture had absorbed and domesticated Catholicism to such a degree that it ceased to be the same religion brought by the Jesuits. Rodrigues, however, insisted that the peasants had become his coreligionists.[4]

The probing questions posed in *Silence* resonate with central themes in the history of south Indian Catholicism, particularly those relating to matters of cultural difference versus accommodation. Not unlike Ferreira's description of Japan as a swamp, European Orientalists have associated Hindu society with images of sponge-like absorption and honeycombing cooption.[5] In India, as in Japan, the Jesuit missionary enterprise sparked debates about the theological costs of blending in. In Japan, Ferreira maintained that the beliefs of Christian converts were indistinguishable from those of their pagan compatriots. In India, by contrast, the saplings did take root, and Catholicism became a part of what Susan Bayly calls a "shared landscape" in south India.[6] What price, though, did Jesuit cultural policies exact from both Catholic teachings and the local society they sought to inhabit?

Jesuits are widely known for their legacy of cultural adaptation (*accommodatio*). This method of spreading the gospel encouraged missionaries to embrace "nonreligious" aspects of local culture in order more easily to draw social elites to Christianity. Roberto de Nobili, the seventeenth-century missionary to the south Indian city of Madurai, assumed the attire of Brahmin pandits, wore their sacred thread, and smeared sandalwood paste on his forehead like the Shaiva devotees he was attempting to convert. His methods sparked heated controversies about the parameters of Catholic orthodoxy and the legitimacy of "going native." Most notable is the Malabarian rites controversy, in which various Catholic orders debated the legitimacy of Jesuit practices of cultural accommodation.

This chapter discusses the nature and scope of Roman Catholic adaptation to south Indian society. It interrogates a widely held assumption that Protestant and Catholic missionaries have employed fundamentally different cultural strategies in South Asia and that their churches have assumed radically different postures toward indigenous cultures. The difference purportedly stems from the disparate emphasis of "word" versus "sacrament" within each tradition: Because of their stronger emphasis on the spoken and written word (derived from their focus on the Bible), Protestant missionaries tended to apply a textual standard (sometimes termed "logocentrism") for defining Christian doctrine and practice. They went to great lengths to separate converts from their pre-Christian beliefs and cultural traditions. As a result, Protestant churches have maintained sharper communal boundaries from adherents of other Indian religions. Catholics are viewed according to a different trajectory. On account of their emphasis on sacrament, their veneration of saints, and their observance of various festivals and ritual practices, Catholics have blended to a greater degree with the devotional practices of their Indian surroundings, especially those centered on the veneration of images and performance of priestly rituals in local cult shrines.[7]

As they competed for converts and criticized each other's practices in the mission field, Catholic and Protestant missionaries were largely responsible for manufacturing this familiar dichotomy. As a way of looking at history, the contrast carries some validity; and yet several factors make the dangers of overgeneralization all too evident. First, Chapter 2 clearly documented how Jesuits in Akbar's court employed a style of religious disputation that drew sharp lines in the sand between Catholicism, Islam, and various Indian cultural practices. Moreover, they grounded their critiques of Islam in strident defenses of the Bible. In this respect, Jesuits such as Monserrate and Acquaviva foreshadowed the polemics of English Evangelicals who would arrive in India centuries later. During the nineteenth century, even the French Catholic missionary Jean-Antoine Dubois would criticize the cultural policies of the early Jesuits for being too accommodating. Dubois made a case for the fundamental incompatibility of Brahminical Hinduism and Christianity and the futility of attempts to convert the upper castes.[8] What these examples show is that: (1) Catholic approaches to Indian society can sometimes resemble those employed by Protestants; and (2) there was considerable disagreement among Catholics themselves about how to define the boundaries of Catholic identity.[9]

Careful attention also needs to be paid to the basis and rationale of Roman Catholic cultural accommodation. As tempting as it may be to attribute local expressions of Catholicism to the strategy developed by Nobili, other factors often played a more important role. South Indian kings had long extended their backing to Syrian Christian and Roman Catholic establishments just as they had patronized Hindu temples or Muslim shrines. Kingly patronage brought honor, status, and official recognition to a range of communities irrespective of religion. Such patronage arose independently from any missionary theories of cultural accommodation and was central to the incorporation of Catholics and Syrian Christians into south India's social fabric.[10] As much as any ideological commitment to accommodation, the rise and fall of political patrons shaped the cultural complexion of Indian Catholicism.[11]

In terms of their adaptation to south Indian society, Catholics located themselves between Hindu and Muslim. This involved a combination of blending in and staying apart. On the one hand, their devotional practices would eventually resemble those of Muslim trading communities and Sufi clerics who adapted to popular Hindu cult traditions. The veneration of holy men, the performance of blood sacrifices and exorcisms, and belief in miracles in the context of shrine worship were characteristics Catholics shared with Hindus and Muslims. On the other hand, we can observe among Catholics processes of differentiating themselves from their religious surroundings and from each other. This included the emergence of separate domains among the Catholic population based on competing jurisdictions served by Catholic missionary orders. It also included growing awareness of the difference between Christian and Hindu identities. The formation of these domains reflected differences of race, class, and belief and was just as important an aspect of Catholic history as tendencies toward accommodation.

Why, then, the emphasis on cultural accommodation? Part of this stems from an ideological preference among historians and anthropologists for mixture over difference and continuity over rupture.[12] Scholars of Indian Islam and Christianity tend to portray religious hybridity, mixture, or syncretism (the terms are often used interchangeably) as authentically South Asian forms of religiosity.[13] Moreover, it is believed that religious mixture has provided the basis of coexistence, which is preferable to conflict. Assertions of religious difference in the name of orthodoxy or reformist activity occupy a more marginal place in South Asian history, where they are portrayed as aspects of divisive workings of the foreign hand, the curse of colonial modernity, or less appealing stories of disruption or disintegration.[14]

In an attempt to disrupt this binary between accommodation and difference, this chapter begins by examining early Jesuit strategies of cultural accommodation vis-à-vis the work of missionaries such as Francis Xavier, Roberto de Nobili, and Constanzo Giuseppe Beschi. It then discusses the process of domain formation among Catholics in Bombay and in different parts of south India.[15] In contrast to the emphasis on cultural blending and syncretism found in the work of Susan Bayly, more recent studies describe tendencies of Catholics to form separate domains along lines of race, caste, jurisdiction, and belief. Complex and varying factors explain why Catholics have established strong communal boundaries in any given context. They relate to matters of political patronage, global connections, proximity to centers of religious authority, and the impact of print media and literacy.

Spiritual Versus Colonial Enterprises

The diocese of Goa, established in 1534, became the center of Catholic missions to the East. Its vast domain extended from the Cape of Good Hope to China. Moreover, Goa became a center for Portuguese ecclesiastical and political power in Asia. The pope extended *Padroado Real* (royal patronage) to Portuguese political authorities, thereby authorizing agents of the Portuguese Empire to build and staff churches and oversee missionary work in India—in essence, to extend Christendom to the East.[16] Because of their backing from the pope and the crown, early Catholic missions at Goa were indelibly tied to Portuguese imperial and cultural power.[17]

The fusion of missions with Portuguese imperial power brought a more aggressive, colonial expression of Christianity to the shores of India. After 1540, the Portuguese actively privileged their own Latin form of Christianity over local religions and employed aggressive methods for converting the local population to Catholicism. During the sixteenth century, Portuguese kings in Lisbon formulated as many as six laws that explicitly sanctioned the destruction of Hindu temples in Goa.[18] The Portuguese demolished temples in Goa, Bardes, and Salsette and also appropriated lands devoted to Hindu temples. They provided a variety of incentives—including provisions of rice (hence the label "rice Christians")—for converting members of poor, lower classes to Catholicism.[19] Building upon centuries of antipathy between Christians and Muslims in the Iberian Peninsula, the Portuguese also confronted Muslims further south along the Malabar Coast in order to advance their trading interests.[20] When Jesuits arrived in Goa several decades after the Portuguese conquests, they became agents of a more imperialistic religiosity, which yielded a more pronounced sense of difference between Catholicism and local religion. It was only when priests launched missions that were further away from Goa that they grew vulnerable to local forces that would shape their experience and those of their converts. It was nearly a century after they arrived in Goa that Jesuits embraced the controversial strategy of *accommodatio*, which brought them into conflict with other Catholic orders and the Vatican.

In 1542, Francis Xavier began his ten years of labor in India, which immersed him in the fishing communities of the Malabar Coast (see Figure 3.1). He spent his early months in Goa, during which time he became disillusioned by the immorality and greed of European settlers. He then accepted an invitation to work among the pearl fishers of Cape Comorin, some 560 miles to the south of Goa. His work among the lower-ranking Parava castes of this region became the hallmark of his labors in India. To characterize his work among the Paravas as leaning in the direction of either accommodation or difference is no simple affair. Xavier was keen on teaching Paravas the creeds and confessions of the faith, and on giving them a new Christian identity; but aspects of local culture inevitably survived their conversion to Catholicism. When compared with later Jesuits, who were more influenced by Nobili's methods, Xavier may be viewed as a stronger advocate of Catholic difference.

Figure 3.1 Francis Xavier calls the children of Goa to church, 1542.
Source: Chronicle/Alamy Stock Photo.

The Paravas are one among several coastal fishing communities who occupied lower caste status within south Indian society. They resided along the southernmost tip of the Coromandel Coast (southeast India), a region known for its lucrative pearl-bearing oyster beds and conch shells. Their occupations as fishers and pearl divers were considered ritually polluting, but they were useful to local kings who sought to benefit from the export of pearls, bangles (made from shells), and other handicrafts. Following the pattern of south Indian kings, the Portuguese incorporated the Paravas into their domains by extending them protection in exchange for cooperation and loyalty. The conversion of the Paravas to Christianity was inseparable from this initial process of accommodation by way of political alliance building.

Conflict between the Portuguese and seafaring Muslims provided the context for the conversion of the Paravas to Christianity. From 1527 to 1539, the Portuguese were embroiled in a maritime war with south Indian Muslim forces for control of the region's trading ports. The Muslims had formed an alliance with the Zamorin (the Hindu "sea king") of Calicut. Amid this conflict, a delegation of seventy Paravas appealed to Portuguese officials for protection against their Muslim adversaries.[21] The Portuguese were eager to make clients of this skilled community of fishermen; it is quite likely that their interventions had instigated the Paravas' rivalry with coastal Muslims in the first place. Authorities at Goa sent a group of clerics to the south who eventually baptized over 20,000 Paravas from roughly thirty villages along the coast. These conversions, as Bayly observes, should be regarded as "declarations of political alliance" more than religious conversions as these are conventionally understood.[22]

Xavier's involvement with the Paravas began ten years later. His labors not only yielded new converts; they also consolidated a Christian identity among those who had already been baptized. He was keen on ensuring that the Paravas move beyond a merely nominal faith and learn the key Catholic creeds and confessions. This proved to be an arduous task. At Cape Comorin, his Portuguese colleague Francis Mancias accompanied him. With little or no knowledge of Tamil, but joined by several Tamil-speaking assistants, they attempted to impart Christian knowledge among the Paravas as they baptized them in huge numbers. They took a special interest in baptizing infants and children, since they represented the future of the community.[23] Moving from village to village, they drilled children to recite from memory the Lord's Prayer, the Ten Commandments, and the Apostles' Creed. As they baptized Paravas, members of other caste communities, including thousands of Mukkavars from the western Pearl Fishery Coast, also sought baptism.[24] Xavier described the linguistic and conceptual challenges faced by the Paravas as they entered the new faith:

When I first came I asked them, if they knew anything about our Lord Jesus Christ? But when I came to the points of faith in detail and asked them what they thought of them, and what more they believed now than when they were Infidels, they only replied that they were Christians, but that as they are ignorant of Portuguese, they know nothing of the precepts and mysteries of our holy religion. We could not understand one another, as I spoke Castilian and they Malabar; so I picked out the most intelligent and well read of them, and then sought out with the greatest diligence men who know both languages.[25]

In other instances, Xavier described his efforts (and those of his assistants) to impart understanding about the sacraments, heaven, grace, and the death of Christ. Quite often, such endeavors were reduced to teaching the Paravas to make the sign of the cross and rote recitations in Tamil of prayers and creeds.[26] Despite the crude methods he had to employ, Xavier is said to have baptized or re-baptized as many as 15,000 Paravas during his time in south India.[27]

In order to steer converts into conformity with Christian precepts, Xavier employed caste notables. He charged these high-ranking intermediaries, known as *pattangattis*, to punish drunkenness, idol worship, adultery, and other breaches of Christian norms. By empowering them in this manner, Xavier effectively reinforced a collective caste identity among the Paravas. Just as other castes or birth groups (*jatis*) had distinguished themselves with distinctive morals and ritual practices, the Paravas were being fashioned into a distinctive group through the enforcement of Catholic dogma and morality, which were absorbed into their overall caste *dharma*, or sense of duty.[28]

Xavier's observations about the Hindus of south India were centered on idol worship and the authority of Brahmins. He noted that Brahmin priests taught in a learned tongue (Sanskrit), just as Catholics do in Latin. He spoke with one Brahmin, who disclosed that, in reality, there is only one supreme God, but that most people worship idols, which are "simply images of devils."[29] Xavier's style of interaction tended to be dialogical and argumentative, not unlike the Jesuits who attended to Akbar; and yet he noted the intellectual limitations of the Paravas, describing them as not being "people of learning." Arguments aimed at convincing them of Christian truth, he observed, needed to be "such as their minds can understand."[30] Xavier also noted the racial awareness of the Paravas. On one occasion, they asked him whether God was black or white. Because of "the Indians being black themselves," he explained, their local gods were "as black as black can be."[31] Upon asking this particular group of Paravas whether they wished to become Christian, he sensed their resistance. They alluded to the fear of others gossiping about them and of their potential loss of their livelihood if they changed their religion and way of life. Having allied themselves with a local

Hindu king, they thus stressed the potential loss of security and status, not the advantages of associating with foreigners.

Xavier's letters concerning his work among the Paravas illustrate, as historian Ines Županov observes, the tension between "Portuguese 'colonial' and Jesuit 'spiritual' conversion enterprises in Asia."[32] From the Portuguese standpoint, the conversion of low-ranking fishermen to Catholicism formed an alliance that brought mutual benefits. Whether or not the Paravas were "real" Christians was not as important as whether they bolstered the maritime trade of the *Estado da India*. However, the Jesuits were more concerned with questions of spiritual transformation. For Xavier, this transformation would best be ensured by focusing on young children and inspiring them to break from the customs and beliefs of their parents, who were more set in their ways.[33] Were the conversions "sincere" or were they merely attempts to upgrade their station in life by associating with *farangis* (a term that could mean "Franks," aliens, Westerners, or foreigners) and their material resources? Such questions would become particularly salient in the context of mass movements of conversion during the nineteenth and early twentieth centuries, but Xavier's converts were perhaps the first to earn the label "rice Christians."

After being baptized, converts often adopted Portuguese names (or Tamil versions of Portuguese names) and Western clothes.[34] Indian converts, together with mixed-race offspring of Portuguese men and their concubines, would eventually form what came to be known as the "East Indian" community. Among them, converts were often portrayed as persons who aped foreigners. "Eating meat, drinking liquor, and donning the Western dress" was a phrase often applied to them.[35] And yet, a closer examination of their outlook reveals a combination of the old and the new, and not mere assimilation into Portuguese culture.

The tension between the colonial and spiritual enterprises became more pronounced as the Jesuits expressed increasing disgust with European immorality and mistreatment of Indians. It was quite common for Portuguese officials to have sexual unions with multiple Indian women, who were often of low caste origins, and to bear children with them. Xavier's biographer, Henry Coleridge, declared European settlers to be "the worst enemies" to the work of missionaries, largely on account of their immoral lifestyles and maltreatment of low caste converts.[36] As they exploited the poor for labor or sex, Portuguese settlers, soldiers, and merchants made it difficult for missionaries to convince Indians of the virtues of their religion. On one occasion, Xavier spared no words in condemning Portuguese officials who seized several slave girls within the domain of the rajah of Travancore. He appealed to the bishop at Quilon to rescue the girls and excommunicate the perpetrators.[37] This incident and others like it reflect the gradual souring of Xavier's relations with local Portuguese authorities. Increasingly, he viewed them as being preoccupied with acquiring wealth rather than promoting the cause of the faith. Jesuits who came after Xavier shared his disillusionment with the Portuguese. Their criticism extended beyond the exploitative aspects of the colonial enterprise: They would eventually decry the European cultural packaging of Christianity and seek to move their missionary endeavors beyond *Padroado* oversight.

Despite the pervasive tendency to associate Parava and Mukkava converts with *farangi* religion and culture, powerful undercurrents of local religiosity continued to shape their experience. The extent of their transformation as Christians was never easy to measure, especially as missionaries observed in converts enduring aspects of "pagan" beliefs and practices. The cultural location of converts was never entirely clear. Were they en route to discarding their old selves and assimilating into Portuguese culture? Were they worshiping Christ within the framework of their caste heritage? Or were they, as the apostate priest of Endo's novel contended, worshiping old gods under the thin guise of the new religion?

These options raise important methodological questions, which lie at the intersection of theology and history. From the standpoint of orthodox monotheism, it is difficult to appreciate how converts to Islam or Christianity could continue to venerate local gods or goddesses or participate in other practices associated with their earlier way of life. Xavier and his assistants persistently confronted this reality among his Parava converts. Some of them continued to visit local cult shrines; others shared with non-Christian untouchables the worship of bloodtaking goddesses (*ammans*), spiritual forces, and other deities Catholic priests had identified as "demonic." In one instance, this enraged Xavier to such a degree that he threatened to exile converted Parava caste leaders (*pattangattis*) for failing to eradicate such backsliding among the converts.[38] Clearly, Xavier saw their syncretic practices as an unacceptable deviation from orthodoxy, not as contextual Christianity.

Similar patterns of worship are observable among south India's Sufi Muslim sects, whose devotional practices resembled those found among devotees of Hindu cult traditions and power divinities. Among these traditions were the supernatural powers associated with Sufi *pirs* (Muslim cult saints). Muslim devotees venerated these figures because of their powers of physical and psychic healing and their capacity to perform miracles. Their tombs became sites of pilgrimage and venues for accessing the *pirs'* miraculous powers. Motifs of Muslim devotional literature during the early modern period bore a striking resemblance to practices associated with the worship of Shiva in south Indian Hindu traditions. The *pir's* persona was tied not only to benevolent powers of healing but also to images of death and destruction, which Hindus attribute to Shiva.

The underlying basis for these forms of accommodation is not limited to the realm of "religion" but also concerns politics. South Indian religion was inextricably tied to notions of kingship, honor, and rituals of blood sacrifice associated with warrior traditions. Huge temple complexes such as those of Tirupati, Srirangam, Madurai, and Kanchi were centers of kingly power and wealth.[39] As kings attempted to consolidate their reign over a region, they often patronized its temples and patron deities. Gifts of land for the construction of temples and *maths* (schools for Hindu religious instruction; pronounced and sometimes spelled as "*mutts*") added legitimacy to their reign. The ritual services of Brahmin priests further enhanced the legitimacy of kings. As they subdued heads of minor kingdoms (*samasthanams*) and incorporated their domains, more powerful kings absorbed smaller communities and the religious institutions attached to them. Ever-expanding networks of clientage reinforced the bonds between religion and statecraft.[40] They also enhanced the honor and status of those who served religious establishments.

When Islam and Catholicism were introduced in south India, they accommodated themselves to this system of patronage and cultural myth making. Wandering religious world renouncers (*sadhus*) of Brahminical Hinduism, Muslim *fakirs* (itinerant holy men who lent inspiration to Muslim soldiery), and Jesuit ascetics participated, as Bayly has noted, in a common religious landscape. Warrior cults centered on Hindu saints (who served warrior kings) and local power divinities provided the cultural template for devotion to Sufi *pirs* and Catholic saints. These personalities often earned their reputations in service to their patron kings, but they also acquired an independent charismatic authority. Their gravitas was tied to their reputations as healers, miracle workers, and performers of exorcisms. Indeed, Francis Xavier and St. Thomas himself became objects of devotion among those whose lives had already been shaped by a propensity to venerate charismatic holy men (see Figure 3.2).[41]

After the Catholic Church canonized Xavier, Jesuit priests in India were able to portray him as a saint possessing supernatural powers who could intercede on behalf of devotees. Tombs of Catholic saints would become the focus of devotion among those seeking their healing powers, rain for crops, or fertility.[42] Legends that circulated about Xavier bore a striking resemblance to stories of Hindu gurus and Muslim holy men who embodied divine power.[43] The Paravas venerated St. Francis for his capacity to heal the sick, raise the dead, and cast out evil spirits. Aware of the popular appeal of charismatic leaders, later Jesuits produced hagiographies that cast renowned figures such as St. Thomas and Xavier in the mold of popular south Indian cult legends. As Bayly observes, this pattern must not be seen as mere imitation of local cult myths, but as an intermingling of Catholic tradition and local devotional practices.

Catholicism in Goa thus began as colonial religion, marked by aggressive proselytizing and privileging of Latin forms and ties to both commercial and political power. It was the aspiration of Jesuits to move beyond the sphere of Goa's influence that led to the forms of cultural adaptation evident in the lives

Figure 3.2 A shrine to Francis Xavier, garlanded in the manner of a Hindu shrine.
Source: Liquid Light/Alamy Stock Photo.

of Xavier's converts. Here, comparisons with the trajectory of Indian Islam are again relevant. The vast majority of conversions to Islam, as Richard Eaton has observed, did not occur by means of the sword; rather, they happened among peasant populations and in places that were far removed from the seats of Mughal imperial power.[44] What emerged in these frontier zones were not reproductions of the Islam found in Arabia or in the Mughal courts of Delhi and Agra, but a more syncretic variety of Islam disseminated among peasants by charismatic Sufi *pirs*. Similarly, it was not in Goa but in places such as Kanyakumari, Travancore, and Ramnad that Catholicism broke free of its Portuguese cultural encasement and took root in the lives of low-ranking communities of fisherman, in forms that were quite distinct from those found in Lisbon or Goa.

Accommodation on Trial

Decades before Roberto de Nobili would employ a formal strategy of cultural accommodation (*accommodatio*) among the Brahmins of Madurai, the Catholicism of Xavier's converts underwent its own process of localizing transformation. It appears to have done so through a natural process—a cultural gravity of a sort—that drew Catholicism into alignment with local beliefs and caste practices. What need was there for *accommodatio* as a missionary strategy when this blending with local culture appears to have happened naturally?

Nobili was raised in an aristocratic family in Tuscany and became a Jesuit at the age of twenty. Upon arriving in India in 1605, he worked among Xavier's poor Christian fisherfolk of coastal Tamil Nadu. One year later, he was transferred out of the territories under Portuguese control into a region within the independent Vijayanagara Empire of south India. From here, he launched his mission to the Brahmins of Madurai.

At Madurai, Nobili observed a Christian community consisting primarily of Portuguese military and commercial officials and Parava converts. For Brahmins and other upper caste people, Christians represented not only a "polluted" community of meat eaters, but also a group of *farangis* and of local converts who had embraced their customs. The missionaries who had succeeded Xavier in Madurai appear to have fully reconciled themselves to being designated as *farangis*. This is evident in the manner in which they approached prospective converts: They would ask them whether they wished to join the "*farangi kulam*" (kinship group of foreigners).[45] The perception of religious conversion as an event that incorporated Indians into a "foreign community" appears to have been central to the outlook of *Padroado* missionaries. It was an outlook for which Nobili had no patience at all.

Nobili's missionary project was centered on overcoming the sense of the foreignness of Christianity, especially among those who possessed a highly developed civilizational identity. Nobili did not employ scientific gadgetry in his evangelistic endeavors (as did Jesuits in China); instead, he made every effort to assume the persona of a *sanyasi* (world renouncer) in Madurai. The ritual and ascetic principles of a *sanyasi* represented the highest ideal of scriptural Hinduism and resonated with notions of self-denial within the Jesuit tradition. Embracing this persona gave Nobili the greatest chance of gaining an audience with, and ultimately converting, persons of rank and influence.

A portrait of Nobili portrays him seated in the lotus position, wearing a robe of a Hindu guru, and instructing a Saiva Brahmin in a room opposite the Sri Meenakshi Sundareswarar temple. In contrast to Xavier, who knew little Tamil, Nobili devoted himself to learning spoken and written Tamil as well as Sanskrit, the language of classical Hindu texts and Brahminical knowledge. He had mastered Tamil to such a degree that he was able to compose his own poems and theological treatises in the language. He also formulated a Christian vocabulary for his converts that was drawn primarily from Sanskrit. Indeed, Nobili, along with those who upheld his methods, is widely credited for initiating the tradition of European Orientalism.[46]

To his audience in Madurai, Nobili portrayed Jesus as a divine guru (spiritual teacher). This image appealed to Brahmin devotees of the Shaiva Siddhanta tradition, for whom the guru is a central figure. Nobili creatively merged Jesuit ideals of self-denial with ascetic virtues of this particular Hindu tradition. Jesus came, Nobili taught, to help humans "end desire for pleasure, power, and honors."[47] This resonated with the local belief that the divine Shiva appears to his disciples in a concealed form as a human guru—a concealment of his divine nature adapted to human eyes. In the same way, Nobili presented Jesus as God concealed and yet revealed, who came to liberate people from worldly desire.

Nobili's missionary strategy was rooted in the distinction he drew between social and religious aspects of Brahminical culture. He considered the domain of the social as fertile terrain onto which the truths of Christianity could be grafted. This is not unlike the way in which theologians of the early Church designated some aspects of culture as *adiaphora* (matters considered non-essential to faith). Since caste customs and related social distinctions arose from this highly expansive social domain in India, Nobili had no qualms about adopting Brahmin dress, diet, language, and postures in his missionary labors.

One of the more controversial aspects of Nobili's legacy was his embrace of caste—in particular, his privileging of Brahmins. To reach them he believed he needed to become one of them. But how could he pass as anything other than a *farangi*? Nobili believed that his own high-born status could actually work in his favor within south India's hierarchical society. He claimed to have hailed from a line of aristocratic Kshatriyas (India's warrior caste) from Rome and to have come to Madurai as a seeker of spiritual knowledge. In order to overcome the perception of Christians as *farangis*, Nobili presented himself as a high caste person who could mingle freely with Brahmins without polluting them in any way. He is reported to have declared: "I am not a *parangi*. I was not born in the land of *parangis*, nor was I ever connected with their race . . . I came from Rome, where my family hold the same rank as respectable rajas hold in this country."[48]

This attempt by Nobili to become an insider among the highest-ranking members of Tamil society came at a price. By gaining access to Brahminical society, he lent Christian legitimacy to their exclusionary practices. He observed a strict vegetarian diet along with other elements of a pure Brahminical lifestyle, and he resided in a Brahmin neighborhood in Madurai. He urged other *sanyasi* Jesuit missionaries to do the same. Such measures carried immediate social implications. When "*sanyasi* priests" (as Nobili and others who embraced his methods were called) administered the sacraments or conducted services for Brahmins, they ensured that no members of "polluting" castes were present. Only by doing this could Nobili ensure that his parishioners would not lose their rank by becoming Christian and receiving instruction from him.

Parava Christians who observed such accommodations objected to the privileging of Brahmins; but, in doing so, they did not call into question the very idea of caste distinctions. They claimed that Nobili's high caste converts were not, in fact, ritually superior Christians. They were ritually compromised because of the kinds of contact they had made with missionaries when taking communion.[49] Specifically, the touch of missionaries' saliva on the communion vessels, they claimed, had polluted them. Such disputes over purity, as Susan Bayly observes, signify a larger accommodation of Catholicism to south Indian caste hierarchies and social stratification.[50]

Cultural Accommodation and Its Critics

Some have argued that the Jesuit practice of *accommodatio* was an attempt to make virtue out of necessity. As Portuguese power in India declined in the seventeenth century, Catholics were unable to use state power to coerce conversions.[51] A commitment to *accommodatio* suited their new posture of weakness and vulnerability as they encountered dominant local religions. This perspective helps contextualize the emergence of *accommodatio* among the Jesuits. It fails, however, to appreciate the significant theological investment of men such as Nobili in this method and the lengths to which he went to defend it as a preferred way of advancing the faith.

During the early seventeenth century, unique political circumstances in south India complicated the efforts of Madurai missionaries to employ their principle of cultural accommodation. Simply stated, there were some contexts in which the values of the priestly Brahmin caste were not the dominant ones. Nobili's exclusive focus on Brahmins catered to high caste sensitivities but worked against the new values embodied by the Nayaka rulers of south India. The Nayakas hailed from the lower, Sudra caste; as such, they distinguished themselves by championing alternative cultural virtues. Former kings had extolled classical ideals of kingship, which draw legitimacy from Brahminical notions of *dharma* (ritual purity and duty). This reinforced king–temple relations and added weight to Brahmin ritual services. Nayakas, by contrast, had established strong links to trade and espoused the martial values of warrior elites. As traditional ties between the imperial court and the temple weakened under Nayaka kings, lower castes found more room to assert themselves.

The implications of Nayaka priorities were not as evident to Nobili as they were to one of his successors, Baltasar da Costa. After arriving on the Pearl Fishery Coast during the 1630s, this Portuguese Jesuit immersed himself initially in the community of converted Paravas. Costa was profoundly influenced by the principle of *accommodatio*; but instead of assuming the persona of a Brahmin *sanyasi*, he would eventually assume that of the *pantaram* (a Saiva priest to non-Brahmins).[52] This form of accommodation addressed powerful crosscurrents of cultural influence under Nayaka rule in which low castes could acquire social clout through lucrative trade. During the 1630s, the Brahmins of Madurai wielded enough ritual influence to make the *sanyasi* priests reluctant to associate with low-ranking Paraiyars. And yet, the loosening of traditional hierarchies and the eagerness of low castes to embrace Catholicism warranted new forms of accommodation. By piercing his ears and wearing the robes and turban of a *pantaram* priest, Costa validated the principle of *accommodatio*, but he tailored it to the Nayaka ordering of society. His writings were sharply critical of Brahmins and revealed his grasp of the unique elevation of commercial groups and warrior elites within Nayaka society.[53]

Aside from being out of step with the currents of Nayaka rule, Nobili and his methods elicited sharp opposition from other Catholics. For some, his accommodations to Indian society—seen as fundamentally religious and superstitious—amounted to an act of heresy. Among the most outspoken critics of Nobili was the Portuguese Jesuit Gonçalo Fernandes (1541–1619). Unlike Nobili, who came from an aristocratic Italian background, Fernandes was an older Portuguese ex-soldier of "dubious" education.[54] Issues of class, nationality, and education shaped the sensibilities of each man and their respective approaches to Hindu society.[55] A proud Portuguese, Fernandes was deeply committed to the methods and ideology of the Inquisition, which extolled a more combative approach to other religions. Moreover, for at least a decade Fernandes had been primarily devoted to serving Parava converts. Over time, Parava Christians, under the tutelage of missionaries, had developed their own sacred vocabulary by which they designated sacraments, rites, and saints. Fernandes decried the manner in which Nobili had dispensed with this vocabulary in an effort to be less *farangi* and more Brahmin. He regarded the methods of this younger, educated Italian to be an affront to the tireless labors of those who had preceded him.

Fernandes had no trouble with self-identifying as a *farangi*. The designation appears to have reinforced a sense of difference, which he considered vital for nurturing a Christian identity among his converts. He criticized Nobili's efforts to shed his *farangi* identity. In his view, Nobili's immersion in the lifestyle of Brahmins nurtured among them a loyalty to Nobili's person as their guru, not to the universal Church. Concerning matters pertaining to the Church and its hierarchy, Nobili's Brahmins remained isolated and indifferent. Fernandes concluded that Nobili "behaved in everything as a man of another religion" and "of a different nation and of a royal race."[56] In his efforts to diminish the difference between Brahminical society and Christianity, Nobili had effectively dissociated himself and his converts from Christian society as Fernandes understood it. Instead, Nobili had immersed himself in the customs and traditions of Brahmins, which Fernandes considered to be demonically inspired.[57]

The dispute between Fernandes and Nobili was eventually escalated to higher ranks of authority and vetted by clerics of different nationalities. The ordeal generated a series of documents concerning the theological integrity of Nobili's methods. By and large, the *Padroado* priests of Portuguese origin tended to be most critical of Nobili, whereas priests of Italian or other nationalities tended to support him. Disagreements also hinged on how priests interpreted India's caste hierarchy. "Those who supported Nobili," Županov observes, "stressed the 'political' origins of the Indian signs of social distinctions and ranking, while those against Nobili, the 'religious' origins."[58] Nobili's methods of cultural accommodation, his opponents charged, immersed him to such an extent in Brahminical society that he and his followers failed to locate themselves within the larger Church or to honor its hierarchy.

In his written responses to these charges, Nobili contended that his accusers relied excessively on the perspectives of the "Portuguese" priest Fernandes, who, in his view, "is not well-versed in Sacred Theology."[59] Nobili also pointed to the well-developed methods of accommodation among his predecessors, most notably Matteo Ricci, the missionary to imperial China, and Alessandro Valignano, the head of the Jesuit mission to the East. According to Nobili, Valignano had expressed a strong preference for non-Portuguese priests in the mission field because of their capacity to dispense with their national customs and "become all to all," something that Portuguese priests found next to impossible to do.[60]

The dispute over Nobili's mission strategy presents a captivating case study on the impact of social class and nationality upon one's opinions about cultural accommodation. Beyond that, the dispute overlooks more pervasive patterns of acculturation in Indian Catholicism, which have little to do with the minutiae of Nobili's dress and approach to Brahminical customs. Rituals of Parava Christianity enjoyed the full sanction of the *Padroado*; these included the annual festival of the Golden Car, in which thousands of devotees dragged a vehicle bearing an image of the Virgin Mary through the streets of the coastal city of Tuticorin.[61] The festival resembles similar *Rath Yatras* (chariot processions) of

Hindu communities. Nobili's methods do not explain the tendency in popular Catholicism to venerate charismatic Catholic leaders in a manner similar to the veneration of Sufi *pirs* or Hindu cult saints.

During the latter half of the seventeenth century, another Jesuit missionary, John De Britto (1647–93), made significant numbers of converts among warrior pastoralist communities of Ramnad district, namely the Maravas and Agmudaiyars. Like Xavier, De Britto oversaw mass conversions among these influential groups, similar to those that had occurred in Japan among *daimyo* lineages.[62] De Britto's success as a missionary led to his elevation, like Xavier and Nobili before him, as a charismatic guru figure possessing supernatural powers. During his life, the Sethupathi (regional ruler) of Ramnad tortured and imprisoned him because of his alleged resistance to his rule. In 1693, De Britto was beheaded and his body impaled on a stake. Thereafter, hagiographies celebrated him as a Jesuit martyr who upheld the highest ideals of the faith. At the same time, he came to be venerated, as were other warrior gods of Ramnad, as a cult figure possessing great powers to fight demonic forces; only, in De Britto's case, it was Marava Christians who sought his intercessory powers by offering prayers at his forest shrine, located in Oriyur of Ramnad district.[63]

Another example of Catholic *accommodatio* is to be found in the life of the Italian Jesuit Constanzo Giuseppe Beschi (1680–1747). Like Nobili, Beschi assumed the persona of a local sage and became known for his extraordinary commitment to indigenous knowledge production. He is responsible for producing literary works in the classical south Indian genre;[64] he also published philosophical treatises, grammars, and dictionaries and translated Tamil texts. In keeping with the Jesuit practice of engaging in disputations with adherents of other faiths, Beschi became renowned for his exchanges with Hindu scholars and *sanyasis*. As he moved from town to town, a highly ornate royal entourage accompanied him. This closely resembled the royal durbars (ceremonial processions or gatherings) of Hindu maharajas as they were carried by palanquin, dressed in their finest garments of silk and seated on tiger skins.[65] Beschi developed a close bond with the *nawab* (regional governor) of the Carnatic, Chanda Saheb. Biographers of his life disagree, however, over the gifts and privileges Beschi derived from his ties to Chanda Saheb.[66]

Beschi's work among the Tamils illustrates the creative and sometimes conflicted relationship Jesuits had with Tamil literature. On the one hand, they needed to learn Tamil and acquaint themselves with Tamil literature in order to learn rhetorical styles and local genres through which to convey Christian teachings. This required the use of local catechists. On the other hand, Jesuits believed Tamil literature to possess a style and appeal that could seduce converts into its inherent paganism. Some Jesuits prohibited converts from reading Tamil literature but allowed their catechists to do so in order to acquire pedagogical tools for propagating Christianity. Their reliance on catechists, however, left Jesuit priests feeling vulnerable of losing their authority to the catechists. Beschi appears to have surmounted this dilemma by learning literary Tamil and embracing the Tamil cultural world to an extraordinary degree.[67]

Within the Tamil-speaking village of Alapuram, the veneration of saints and the Virgin Mary merged with local devotional forms and practices. Since the days of Xavier, Jesuits priests had worked tirelessly to instill among converts a distinctively Christian understanding of creeds, sacraments, and morality. These priorities remained intact into the nineteenth century; but they could not prevent the emergence of certain forms of Catholic devotion that replicated Tamil devotional practices. At Alapuram, crowds consisting of both Hindu and Catholic devotees gathered regularly to pray to Santiyakappar, the established tutelary saint of the Paravas (who had been brought to Alapuram in the form of a banyan tree), in hopes of invoking his powers. According to the anthropologist David Mosse, Jesuit priests traveled long distances to administer sacraments and preside over the Santiyakappar festival. So prominent had the festival become that it attracted royal patronage and became a central feature of the sacred geography of the region.[68]

Quite often, cultural accommodation occurred when Jesuit ideals merged with local cult traditions. In south India, Jesuit notions of martyrdom, asceticism, and sacrifice lent themselves easily to the veneration of Catholic saints who embodied these ideals. In Ramnad, Catholics came to venerate the martyred priest St. Sebastian by building a shrine to him; this contained a statue of his pierced body tied to a blooming tree. The shrine was believed to be a miraculous source of healing and, during local outbreaks of disease, devotees carried his statue through the streets of Ramnad.[69] Saints renowned for having spent their lives in self-denying hermitage also drew the devotion of many. Such world-renouncing saints were believed to possess powers to exorcise demons because their lives of asceticism stood in stark contrast to the eroticism of the demons with which they waged war.[70] Forest shrines to hermit saints such as St. Anthony (Vanattu Antoniar) or St. Paul (the first hermit, Vanattu Cinnappar) represent a fusion of missionary moral teachings and local beliefs in spirit possession and the need for exorcism.

Catholics and Their Others

Despite a tendency to emphasize the accommodative impulses of Indian Catholicism, it is easy to overlook the fact that clear boundaries emerged between Catholics and non-Catholics, as did fractures over race, caste, and jurisdiction within Catholic domains. Moreover, clear differences separated Catholic and Hindu devotion. This makes applying the notion of "syncretism" (the blending of religious traditions and objects of worship) to the Catholic contexts of south India problematic. As Mosse observes:

> Catholics may adopt "Hindu" ritual and aesthetic forms (but not images) along with shared attitudes to sacred power; but elements from clearly distinct provenance are not mixed ... Hindus readily incorporate elements of Catholic divinity into their practice, but Hindus worshiping at Catholic shrines (or visiting them for exorcism) do not try to give Christian saints Hindu identities or bring their own ritualists to mediate.[71]

Indeed, increasingly into the nineteenth century we find Catholic domains enjoying greater degrees of control over their own affairs. This is accompanied by a greater inclination to differentiate local Catholic practices from those of "pagan society" and to streamline them with global Catholicism.[72]

The factors that influenced this process varied. Among them, ironically, was the increasing resistance to conversion. In the absence of new conversions, a stronger Catholic identity appears to have become more solidified within already existing Catholic enclaves.[73] The arrival of British Protestant missionaries in the early nineteenth century also prompted Catholics to define their identity more sharply relative to Hindu society and Protestantism.

After the outbreak of the French Revolution, Jean-Antoine Dubois (1770–1848), a French Catholic, arrived in Mysore to build on the earlier work of the Italian Jesuits. Over time, he became a staunch critic of their missionary practices. Initially, Dubois had worked with the Pondicherry mission; he went to Mysore after 1799, when the British defeated the army of its ruler, Tipu Sultan. It was primarily in Mysore that Dubois developed his views on Indian caste, the role of Brahmins, and the futility of attempting to convert the Hindus. Dubois's anti-Brahminical discourse appears to have influenced similar critiques by Protestant missionaries.

In 1823, Dubois published a series of letters in which he criticized both Catholic and Protestant missionary approaches in India. In contrast to earlier Jesuit accommodations to Brahminical tradition, Dubois critiqued the ritual and philosophical power of Brahmins. It was in their role as guardians of custom, embodied in the caste order, that Brahmins most impeded the spread of Christianity.[74] Dubois's narrative carries a somewhat paradoxical relationship with the Jesuit strategy of cultural adaptation. He credited, on the one hand, early Jesuit accommodations to local customs, but criticized, on the other, Brahmins for making such accommodation necessary. Brahmins had solidified custom by means of their knowledge, ritual authority over other castes, and access to state power.[75]

Dubois's narrations of early Jesuit encounters initially conveyed sympathy for their methods but then progressed into a polemical assault on south Indians for being addicted to their own customs. The chief culprits behind this adherence to custom were Brahmins, whom he characterized as governed by rituals, constantly asserting their authority over other classes of Indians, and immune to outside influences.[76] For Dubois, the impact of Brahminical authority and knowledge upon the spread of Christianity was clear. Brahmins infected every layer of society with caste feeling and animosity, the antithesis of Christian love. Only those who thrived beyond the pale of Brahminical influence would consider becoming Christian. Hence, converts did not hail from the more "respected" classes, but only from among those outcastes who had played the most servile and marginal roles in society.[77]

Dubois's focus on caste not only made him a critic of earlier Jesuit accommodations to caste; it also placed him in an ambiguous relationship with Protestants. He claimed that Protestants enjoyed little success in their attempts to convert Hindus because of the simplicity of their worship. His words became a common way of distinguishing Catholic and Protestant ethos in India. Protestant worship, he charged, "has no show, no pomp, no outward ceremonies capable of making a strong impression on the senses, [and because of this] it was of course disliked by a quite sensual people, and has never had any considerable success."[78] By contrast, Catholic worship has "processions, images, statues, *tirtan* or holy water, fasts, *tittys* or feasts, and prayers for the dead, invocation of saints, etc.," all of which resembled Hindu religious practices.[79] Here again, the crosscurrents of Dubois's thinking become evident: He celebrated the appeal of Catholic worship among the Hindus while decrying the power of caste observances, which help explain the Catholic–Hindu affinity in the first place.

Priests Versus Catechists

Literature by and about Catholics tends to downplay the vital role played by Indian catechists as well as the tensions that arose between catechists and the *farangi* missionaries they served. Catechists were the "native" religious intermediaries who served foreign Jesuit priests in the mission field. Many of the day-to-day tasks of teaching, preaching, translation, baptizing, and cultural mediation became the responsibility of the catechists rather than of the more theologically qualified priests whom they served. The Madurai mission, for instance, consisted of nine Jesuit priests and twenty-five catechists in 1676; by 1734, there were only ten priests and one hundred catechists.[80] This drastic increase in the indigenous staffing of the mission is downplayed in the reports that priests sent back to their European superiors. The heavy reliance of Jesuits on their Indian intermediaries, according to historian Danna Agmon, was a source of subtle resentment, if not "muted anger," among Jesuit priests.[81] Priests faced a constant irony: Catechists made the difficult task of cross-cultural evangelism possible while at the same time contributing to the priests' sense of vulnerability and resentment.

The conflicted relationship between Jesuit priests and their Indian catechists surfaced in the experience of Jean Venant Bouchet (1655–1732), who worked among the Tamils of Madurai. Like other Jesuits at Madurai, Bouchet committed himself not only to making converts, but also to producing knowledge about Indian society and religion. Bouchet, for instance, was convinced that Hindus, whom he referred to as "Gentiles," actually derived their religion from Christianity and that principal Hindu deities derived their names from key personalities of the Bible—a theme discussed in greater depth in Chapter 4.[82]

Apparently, Bouchet's devotion to such speculative theories blinded him to the rising hostility of his own catechists. A group of them reported Bouchet to the Nayaka Prince of Madurai. They accused him of failing to pay tribute to the prince and of murdering a member of another order. They also stressed that Bouchet was a *farangi*; when they so designated him before the prince, they meant it in the most demeaning and derogatory sense that could be applied to Europeans. They offered the prince a large sum of money if he would expel Bouchet and the other Jesuits from the region.[83]

The motivations of the catechists for bringing these charges are not entirely clear. According to Agmon, they appear to relate to the fact that catechists tended to receive the brunt of hostility from non-Christians for their evangelistic work. On one occasion, local enemies of the Jesuits had seized several of Bouchet's catechists and tortured them. Bouchet himself was not tortured; in fact, he was able to ingratiate himself with the local authorities. Amid rising hostility toward the missionary enterprise, Bouchet paid a personal visit to the prince and offered him and members of his court exotic European gifts. These included a large terrestrial globe, a smaller glass one, and luxury gifts from China. The disparate treatment meted out to Bouchet and his catechists contributed to this particular catechist rebellion. The episode reveals tensions that lay beneath the surface of a mission so heavily reliant upon Indian staffing. Moreover, it reveals the persistent perils of being labeled *farangi*, despite the tireless efforts of *sanyasi* Jesuits to shed this identity.

Disputes of Jurisdiction, Race, and Class

Jesuit practices of accommodation at Madurai represent one aspect of the story of Catholicism. Other key centers of Catholic power and influence included

Pondicherry, a coastal French colony located to the south of Madras and Bombay, which fell under the diocese of Goa. Within each of these venues, Catholics maintained unique ties to European imperial power and trade interests. Against such ties to Catholic empires, Pondicherry and Bombay became venues for competition between Catholic orders. They also became sites of jurisdictional controversies and differences associated with race and caste. Their stories show that Indian Catholicism was anything but monolithic, and that it often experienced turbulent relations with the local population.

During the eighteenth century, Pondicherry became a venue for disputes between Capuchins, Jesuits, and missionaries of the Missions Étrangères de Paris (MEP; Society of Foreign Missions of Paris). Quite often, intra-Catholic rivalry in India enacted politics arising from within European contexts. For instance, tensions between the Catholic majority and Huguenots (the Protestant/Calvinist minority) in France played themselves out in India as Dutch traders competed with the Compagnie des Indes Orientales (French East India Company) for access to valuable trade ports in south India. Since 1674, when Pondicherry had come under French rule, the French had made every effort to establish it as a Catholic city, not unlike what the Portuguese had done at Goa.[84]

The French project of creating a strong Catholic domain in Pondicherry was riddled with problems. Catholic religious orders and societies competed for influence. Capuchins, an offshoot of the Franciscans, were the first order to arrive in Pondicherry after it had become a French colony. After having serviced Europeans and Indian converts in the colony for roughly twenty years, the Capuchins came to regard Pondicherry as a domain entrusted to their oversight.[85] Jesuits arrived in Pondicherry in 1689; in 1691, they constructed their first church, the Église de Notre Dame de l'Immaculée Conception. A third religious body, the MEP, was a society of secular priests, not a religious order as such. They came under the authority of the *Propaganda Fide*, the missionary establishment commissioned directly by the pope.[86] With the backing of Rome and powerful French patrons, the MEP also came to Pondicherry with the intention of making converts and overseeing Catholic congregations.[87]

These three groups adopted different attitudes toward local affairs in Pondicherry. The Jesuits, who had grown in influence in the courts of Europe, tended to adopt an aggressive posture toward Pondicherry's non-Christian residents. Keen on converting the local population to Catholicism, Jesuits did not want to see in Pondicherry a platform for other religions to flourish. Capuchins and MEP missionaries, by contrast, tended to oppose the Jesuits. They sympathized with trader officials and the concessions these officials wanted to extend to Hindu laborers.[88] These divisions became most evident in conflicts concerning religious freedom for the local population.

Instituting Catholicism in Pondicherry involved the aesthetic shaping of the urban landscape along Catholic lines. This entailed the construction of ornate cathedrals, compounds for religious orders, and chapels that served the French military. By necessity, it also required that the authorities curtail certain freedoms enjoyed by Hindus. Catholic officials and missionaries contended constantly with the visible and highly public dimensions of Hindu religiosity (festivals, processions, temple construction, and music) and Hinduism's claims to space. On one occasion, Jesuits pressured local officials to eliminate a popular temple located near one of their compounds and a military fort. The French governor, François Martin, asked the Tamil worshipers to either tear down their temple or leave town. The worshipers—who consisted of cotton weavers, land laborers, domestic servants, and wealthier merchants—chose to "call Martin's bluff," assemble at the city gate, and threaten to leave.[89] If they went, it would "leave Pondicherry an empty town" and make it impossible for the French to benefit from trade in textiles and other commodities.[90] They effectively forced Martin to revoke his demands and make concessions. The effectiveness of their protests exposed the inherent contradiction between the trading interests of the French and their ambitions to make Pondicherry Catholic. Such conflicts also show how Catholicism was far from being either a monolithic political force in India or a religion that invariably blended with local religions. On the contrary, Catholicism was always beset with sharp internal differences tied to its different orders and their complex links to imperial power.

On the other side of peninsular India, the Catholic population of Bombay became splintered along the lines of race, caste, and social class. As with the Catholics of Pondicherry, Bombay's Catholics enjoyed the backing of a powerful European state. During the 1700s, however, Portuguese influence on India's west coast declined; with it, the capacity to secure Catholic institutions under the patronage of the *Padroado Real* was also reduced. When the British East India Company became the dominant power in west India after the defeat of the Marathas in 1818, Catholic congregations had to reconcile themselves to life under a Protestant power. Adding to their need for reorientation was the expanding scope of the *Propaganda Fide*, the papal missionary body that fell outside of Portuguese control. The British East India Company became increasingly determined to undermine *Padroado* control in Bombay and tended to favor *Propaganda* priests. Conflict between *Padroado* and *Propaganda* was accompanied by a fracturing of the Catholic population along lines of race and caste.

Bombay had once consisted of seven semi-autonomous islands.[91] By the early eighteenth century, the Catholic population of Salsette Island (in the northern Bassein district of Bombay) numbered roughly 37,000 and contained some twenty-five parishes. This population resulted from a combination of Portuguese settlement and aggressive missionary activity by Jesuit and Franciscan orders. As had been done in Pondicherry, authorities restricted the religious freedom of Hindu and Muslim residents: The bishop at Goa incited missionaries to destroy Hindu religious structures in Bassein, and entire villages such as Bandra and Trindade (known as Tirandaz on British maps) came under Jesuit oversight.[92]

Despite these efforts to create a soundly Catholic domain in Bombay, the Catholic population became profoundly fragmented by race and caste; they also came to be divided by *Padroado* versus *Propaganda* jurisdiction.[93] At the top of the social hierarchy were European-born Portuguese, known as *reinois*, and then the Indian-born persons of Portuguese descent, known as *casados* or *descendentes*. This class resembled the Creoles of South America and Mexico. Beneath them were the Indian converts, who continued to retain their caste distinctions. Brahmin converts, for instance, resided in separate neighborhoods from lower-ranking castes, which included the Kunbi cultivators and Koli fishermen. The lower castes also included the salt-pan workers known as the Agri and the Bhandari, who made a living extracting toddy, the intoxicating substance found in certain palm trees. The Portuguese labeled Indian converts collectively as "*naturais*."[94] Alongside the Indian converts were persons of mixed racial descent, known as "East Indians." This designation could also apply to Indian converts to Catholicism who adopted Portuguese names and assimilated into Portuguese society. Later on, the East Indian community would include the last remaining Portuguese families on Bombay Island, who had been marginalized under British rule. They retained their prejudices, however, toward the *naturais*, who vastly outnumbered them. The segregation of *descendentes* and upper caste Catholics from lower-ranking castes is part of the legacy of Portuguese colonial Catholicism. Under British rule, this racial hierarchy would be configured in new ways.

As the British expanded their influence, they enacted measures that sought to eliminate the influence of the Portuguese crown in Bombay. They tended to regard *Padroado* priests with great suspicion on account of their loyalty to Lisbon. Company administrators similarly distrusted persons of Portuguese ancestry and upper caste Indian Catholics who retained their allegiance to the archdiocese of Goa. As they enacted measures to restrict the influence of the *Padroado* priests to specific congregations in Bombay, the British, ironically, were aided by the Vatican. In 1839, a papal decree, *Multa Praeclare*, transferred the islands of Bombay and Salsette to the jurisdiction of *Propaganda Fide*.

The dual role of the British and the *Propaganda Fide* in dismantling the *Padroado* establishment had ripple effects throughout the Catholic communities of India. Churches and properties that were once under *Padroado* control appear to have been transferred overnight to the jurisdiction of the vicars apostolic (the appointed leaders of the *Propaganda Fide* in a given bishopric). These measures were met with fierce resistance by those committed to the vast network of Goan priests who had been officiating in various parts of South Asia up to this time. The transition to British rule and *Propaganda* oversight would entail the loss of jobs and ecclesiastical control once entrusted to *Padroado* priests, not to mention the huge loss of Portuguese prestige.[95] Heated disputes between rival priests and parishioners erupted throughout South Asia.

A case of intense jurisdictional conflict occurred in 1837 in the hinterland garrison city of Bellary. That year, Bellary was transferred from the jurisdiction of Goa to that of the vicar apostolic of Madras. The Madras bishop appointed an Irish Catholic priest, Patrick Doyle, to oversee the chapel at the Bellary fort. Shortly after Doyle's arrival, the newly appointed archbishop at Goa tried to bring Bellary back under his jurisdiction by sending Fulgence Perozy (who had been the priest at Bellary since 1828) to the chapel. Doyle intervened by locking up the chapel to keep Perozy out. When the case went to court, Doyle successfully proved that the East India Company had given the site of the fort chapel to the Catholics of Bellary, who had financed it with local resources.[96]

The Bellary case illustrates a preference on the part of the British to accommodate Irish Catholics over Portuguese ones, especially in connection with the servicing of Catholic members of the Indian army. In the princely state of Hyderabad, a dispute between *Padroado* and *Propaganda* factions erupted over possession of a chapel located on the grounds of a major military cantonment. Indian Catholics and Irish soldiers supported the *Padroado* and *Propaganda* respectively. Father Daniel Murphy, an Irish priest who serviced the large number of Irish troops at Secunderabad, allegedly incited members of his congregation to violence. On this particular occasion, the East India Company blamed Murphy for disrupting the peace and prohibited him from resuming his role at Secunderabad.[97]

Such instances of jurisdictional conflict represent the eclipsing of the Indo-Portuguese phase of Indian Catholicism and the transition to British rule. As Indian Catholics were weaned from Portuguese imperial patronage and cultural heritage, they faced new challenges under British rule. The British, after all, were Protestants. The advent of British rule compelled Catholics to differentiate themselves from Protestant society and thrive as a community that could not rely on the backing of the government. This defensive posture led to new ways of asserting boundaries within Catholic institutions and vis-à-vis Hindu society.

In Goa, Konkani-speaking Catholics found themselves pulled in different directions by several factors: declining Portuguese influence, British rule, and rising Indian nationalism. A narrative arose among elite Goan Catholics that Portuguese conquests had deprived them of their Indian heritage—which they conceived of as Brahmin. The key to retrieving their lost identity was to embrace their Konkani language as a gateway into regional and national belonging and to adopt the Devanagari script as the medium for all written Konkani communication. According to Jason Keith Fernandez, the embrace of the vernacular in this instance became a means for the incorporation of upper caste Catholics into a Goa dominated by Hindus, especially those from the Saraswat Brahmin caste. Left out were Catholics from laboring classes, who continued to read and write Konkani in the Roman script, a practice instituted by missionary endeavors among the Goans.[98] As with Kerala's Thomas Christians, who claim upper caste status, the politics and posturing of Goan Catholics illustrate how the Christian community is fragmented along lines of class and caste. Elite, upper caste Christians find far greater access and inclusion within Hinduized notions of nationhood than lower caste Christians, despite the fact that the latter are numerically in the majority.

Conclusion

The central issue explored in this chapter concerns the manner in which Catholicism adapted to south Indian society and shed its aura of foreignness. On the one hand, *Padroado* priests were not ashamed to welcome low caste fishermen into their *farangi kulam*. For priests who maintained loyalty to Goa (the center of Portuguese colonial power in India) conversions of low-ranking Paravas and Mukkuvars essentially drew converts into a Portuguese cultural domain. Converts adopted Western clothes, surnames, and other cultural habits. Cultural adaptation was not a priority and quite often was not desirable.

As Catholic congregations were established in regions further removed from Goa, it became more and more difficult for priests to police what they considered to be cultural backsliding. They simply could not overcome natural tendencies of converts to observe local traditions, even when those traditions were intertwined with "paganism." Moreover, Catholics welcomed the patronage they received from south Indian kings and the accommodations to local culture that resulted from this local support. In key respects, the Jesuits appear to have made a virtue out of what would be a natural tendency toward cultural accommodation in regions beyond the reach of Goa; only the Jesuits called it *accommodatio*. The impact of Nobili's mission strategy was limited to certain spheres of Jesuit experimentation with his methods. The larger observable patterns of Catholic accommodation have more to do with adaptations to local cult traditions. These adaptations are observable among Muslim communities as well.

Catholic adaptations to the Hindu religious ethos of south India continue to the present day. This is especially evident in the enthusiasm Catholics display for the Virgin Mary. In key respects, their veneration of Mary resembles and draws upon Hindu devotional practices centered on female divinities. For this reason, many Hindus are willing to participate in Catholic festivals, such as the grand chariot processions at the coastal city of Velankanni honoring Mary and Catholic saints. In a recent study, the scholar Kristin Bloomer documents instances where Catholic women claimed to be possessed by the Virgin Mary, waged war against competing spirits of the dead (*pey*), and performed healings and exorcisms as manifestations of Mary herself. The processions, possessions, and exorcisms honoring Mary, Bloomer observes, are modeled on Hindu practices.[99]

Such accommodation is a distinctive feature of Indian Catholicism, but it is not the only development that needs to be examined. Against this heritage of accommodation, it is just as important to recognize and, if possible, explain the emergence of a distinctive Catholic identity. Does the assertion of Catholic difference represent a reversal of Catholicism's localizing tendencies? For Bayly, the choice for the historian is whether to privilege a textual ideal of religion over and against the indwelt "living system of worship" that absorbs the characteristics of a given region. "The eighteenth century Javanese rice-cultivator," she observes, "with his reverence for the shrines and divinities of the Hindu–Buddhist sacred landscape was no less a true and pious Muslim than the most rigorous Arab Wahhabi."[100] Here, Bayly walks a delicate balance between describing mixtures and accommodations on the ground and making pronouncements about what constitutes a "true and pious Muslim." Historians must navigate similar terrain between notions of orthodoxy in South Asian Catholicism and the local practices that so often pushed the limits of these notions. It is also important to recognize that accommodations to local culture are not necessarily instances of interreligious harmony. Quite often, a surface-level resemblance of religious practice is accompanied by contestations of power, authority, doctrine, and sacred space.[101] If accommodation is a fact of history, so are assertions of difference.

4
Early European Encounters with India's Hindus and Muslims

During the seventeenth century, the French Protestant traveler and gem merchant Jean-Baptiste Tavernier (1605–89) made a series of voyages to Persia and India, during which he compiled observations about the peoples of these lands. He visited India during the reign of the Mughal emperor Shah Jahan (r. 1628–58). At the time, he tried to explain how a relatively small group of Muslim rulers could preside over so many Hindus (whom Europeans of his day referred to as "Gentiles" or "idolaters"):

> The idolaters of India are so numerous that for one Muhammadan there are five or six Gentiles. It is astonishing to see how this enormous multitude of men has allowed itself to be subjected by so small a number of persons, and has bent readily under the yoke of the Muhammadan Princes. But the astonishment ceases when one considers that these idolaters have no union among themselves, and that superstition has introduced so strange a diversity of opinions and customs that they never agree with one another.[1]

Tavernier was aware of sectarian and cultural differences among Muslims worldwide, but nevertheless assigned to them a unitary identity largely centered on belief in the Qur'an. He clearly did not see Hindus as bound in the same way by a common text or core doctrines. Instead, he viewed them as defined by caste distinctions, devotion to many deities, and immersion in superstitious practices such as astrology. His categories and criteria for distinguishing India's Hindus and Muslims are similar to those proposed by other European travelers, missionaries, and empire builders during the early modern period. They viewed Islam as a religion of conquest and violence, a perspective anchored in European experiences more than in firsthand encounters in India. Their views of Hindu society, however, were more open-ended because they had not encountered Hindu beliefs and practices in Europe. Their understandings were thus formed by assumptions about "Moors" or "pagans" drawn from Christian history, available textual knowledge about Indian religion and society, and direct dialogues or encounters with Indians. What emerged was a variety of ways in which Christian Europeans located themselves *between Hindu and Muslim*.

Travelers such as Tavernier produced knowledge about India's Hindus and Muslims as Europeans penetrated the world of the Indian Ocean for trade and political expansion.[2] In order to appreciate how South Asia's Christians situated themselves between Hindu and Muslim, it is important to consider the global history of interreligious encounters in which Europeans were key players. As Europeans encountered Indian society for the first time, they were compelled to locate Hindus and Muslims in their mapping of the world.[3] Their Christian universalism (whether Catholic or Protestant) had to make sense of the seemingly familiar in Indian Islam and the relatively unfamiliar in Hinduism. To do so, they drew upon their evolving geopolitics of religious difference, readings of the Bible, and understandings of early Christianity in the more familiar world of the Mediterranean. By acquainting ourselves with European writings about Hindus and Muslims and the assumptions that shaped them, we become acquainted with the template of religious difference they imported to India, a template that Indian converts had to renegotiate as they developed their own ways of relating to Hindus and Muslims.

The religious dimension of early modern European involvement in South Asia is grossly overlooked. This may stem in part from a tendency to examine missionary activity in isolation from Portuguese, Dutch, or English imperialism. This chapter examines the two aspects together not to portray missionaries as mere extensions of European empires, but to show how they passed through corridors opened by these empires and their violence. Does this make every missionary a colonialist and every convert the offspring of colonialism? Does it indelibly tie European notions of religious difference to the project of imperial dominance, as Edward Said argued in his classic work *Orientalism*?[4]

Such questions are particularly relevant when examining the life and work of Bartholomaeus Ziegenbalg, the German Pietist missionary to south India. His life is showcased in the latter part of this chapter. He worked as a missionary in the context of European expansion, but did so in ways that were non-imperial or anti-imperial. Ziegenbalg's relationships with Tamil-speaking people in the Danish colony of Tranquebar and his dedicated study of their religion illustrate how the agendas of missionaries and colonialism were not always in agreement. This is despite his strident defense of Christian beliefs and his criticism of both Islam and Hinduism.

Indian converts of German Pietists brought new sensibilities to the question of what it means to be Christian in an era of European imperialism. The Christian poet Vedanayagam Sastri defended the cultural policy adopted by Ziegenbalg and other German Pietists because it embraced Indian cultural traditions. Sastri espoused an indigenous Christianity that upheld the place of local songs, poems, drama, and—more controversially—caste distinctions in the life of the Church.

Sastri opposed what he saw as the culturally imperialist agenda of Anglican missionaries who came to India on the heels of rising British power. During the age of empire, how should the Bible be translated into Tamil (and other mother tongues) and how should Christianity be given a local cultural expression? The chapter concludes by addressing the challenges of producing an authentic "translated" faith against this history of European imperialism.

Imperial Ambitions

From the sixteenth century, Europeans and their trading companies made every effort to access lucrative trading opportunities in the Indian Ocean (see Figure 4.1). Portuguese, Dutch, and British trading companies competed for control over trading routes and influential port cities. These ambitions also sparked conflicts with local communities who resided along the coasts of Ceylon and India and who made their living through fishing or maritime trade. In western India, these communities included the Mappila Muslims, Nayaka Hindu warrior elites, Nambudiri Brahmins, and low caste fisherfolk residing in coastal and hinterland regions.

European expansion in South Asia was commercially driven and rapaciously violent, what historian Sven Beckert calls "war capitalism."[5] Rising interest in Indian textile, spice, and pearl fishing industries led the Portuguese to launch military campaigns along India's west coast to gain control over key port cities.

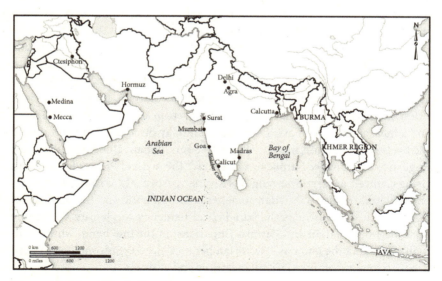

Figure 4.1 Map of the Indian Ocean.

This had the effect of suppressing Indian industries, especially by impeding access of Indian merchants to overseas markets for their goods. Later, other European trading companies engaged in their own forms of war capitalism. In 1600, Queen Elizabeth granted a royal charter to the English East India Company to conduct trade in the Far East. Shortly thereafter, Dutch and Danish East India companies launched operations in coastal India. These trading companies evolved into little states with armies and schemes for governing South Asian territories.[6] By the early 1600s, the Dutch and the British had gained the upper hand over the Portuguese by using military force to dominate the trade in Indian spices and textiles.

Finding Prester John

Christians of the Iberian Peninsula had long aspired to discover a lost Christian kingdom ruled by a legendary figure named Prester John. During the late 14th century, they imagined him to reside in Ethiopia (see Figure 4.2), but his location would also be tied to the Apostle Thomas and the lost "Nestorian" Christians of India. Rumors of this kingdom gave the Portuguese hopes of not only finding riches, but also of gaining a valuable political ally in the East. This need for an ally arose precisely at a time when Spanish and Portuguese colonial fleets were encountering new religious traditions in the Americas and in Asia respectively.[7] Finding a Christian ally in India supported aspirations to advance the cause of Christendom in the face of Muslim dominance in the Mediterranean. Adding to a sense of Catholic vulnerability was the growing Protestant movement in Europe sparked by the Reformation. Protestant reformers criticized many Catholic practices such as the centrality of sacraments, clerical hierarchy, and the veneration of images of saints. It was against this climate of a beleaguered Catholicism that a text known as *The Letters of Prester John* circulated throughout Europe. It describes a wise priest named Prester John who presided over an ideal Christian kingdom and a huge army in the East. The text was initially discovered in Latin during the twelfth century and was later translated into Italian, Dutch, German, and English to reach wider European audiences.[8] The myth of Prester John reveals rising Catholic anxiety over religious diversity, especially as Catholic empires encountered the non-Christian societies of the Atlantic and Indian Oceans. Moreover, it demonstrates the paradoxical tendency to identify a common bond between Iberian and Eastern Christians on the one hand, while eventually branding the latter as "Nestorian heretics" when confronted with their desire to retain their own clerical hierarchy and customs.[9]

Figure 4.2 The Legendary Prester John in an engraving by Luca Ciamberlano, c.1599.
Source: Harvard Art Museums/Fogg Museum, Alpheus Hyatt Purchasing Fund.

The Search for the Similar

Historians disagree over how the Prester John myth influenced Portuguese behavior upon their arrival in India. Did the myth lead them to stress similarities between Catholicism and the religious traditions of India?[10] And did this impulse cause them to see a Christian presence in places that were not Christian? Some point to the first voyage of Vasco da Gama to India; members of his entourage entered a Hindu temple in Calicut but mistook it for a church and the image inside for the Virgin Mary. In the earliest narration of this event, one of da Gama's crewmembers, Alvaro Velho, provided details about the structure of the building—which he repeatedly calls "the church"—and the customs observed by the "Christians of this country." He described the smearing of ashes on the bodies of devotees. He also noted the appearance of "saints painted on the walls of the church, wearing crowns ... painted variously, with teeth protruding an inch from the mouth, and four or five arms."[11] The historian Sanjay Subrahmanyam notes that the structure was in fact a Vaishnava temple (for devotees of Vishnu and his incarnations).[12] Why would the Catholic visitors make such an error? And why would their local interlocutors not be aware of the difference between a Hindu and a Christian place of worship, especially considering the presence of Thomas Christians in the region?

For some historians, the above example illustrates how the Prester John myth inclined the Portuguese, at least initially, to search for similarities between Catholicism and local religions. It is difficult, however, to reconcile this "search for the similar" with the hostility the Portuguese eventually directed toward both Muslims and Hindus and with their designation of the Thomas Christians as heretics.[13] Some maintain that the Portuguese approach to India shifted from a posture of tolerance (based on similarity) to one of aggression (based on the awareness of difference). The cause of that shift, however, remains vague.[14] When the Portuguese discovered the presence of the Thomas Christians, they appeared to have realized their hopes of finding a lost Christian community who shared their beliefs. It was only a matter of time, however, before they sensed their own ecclesiastical differences with this ancient community and attempted to "Latinize" them (see Chapter 1).

The Portuguese, then, either mistook Hindus for Christians or identified similarities between their beliefs and local ones. The Portuguese chronicler Tomé Pires essentially believed that Hindus were once Christian, but that they had strayed from their faith under the influence of Islam. The merchant and linguist Duarte Barbosa saw resemblances between Brahmin beliefs and the Christian doctrine of the Trinity. Others drew parallels between Hindu bathing practices and Christian baptism, or between local festivals and the celebration of Christ's birth.[15]

Eventually, the Portuguese became more hostile toward local religions. The establishment of Goa as a diocese in 1534 gave rise to aggressive measures against Hindus under the *Estado da India* (Portuguese state in India; see Chapter 3). The similarity motif, however, appears to have survived this transition; it reemerged among the Jesuits and also arose among Protestant missionaries and merchants, as we shall see. The perception of theological similarity between religious traditions does not appear to have always coincided with greater degrees of political tolerance. In some cases, the similarity motif even accompanied European war capitalism.

If the concept of similarity and the anecdote about Vasco da Gama's error do not teach us much about the basis for Portuguese religious policies, they do offer glimpses into their conceptual mapping of India and the world. Jesuit approaches to Islam were riddled with prejudices arising from their memory of the Crusades, the Spanish *Reconquista*, and the Inquisition. Early on, the Portuguese, according to historian Sanjay Subrahmanyam, appeared to have had only two classes of people on their radar: the so-called "lost" Eastern Christians, who most likely possessed deviant customs, and Muslims. "[A]nything that was not explicitly Islamic appeared, residually, to be Christian."[16] Accordingly, they divided Asia along two axes: Muslims controlled a northwest corridor leading to Arabia; Christians—their potential allies—occupied the southeast corridor, with the region of today's Kerala occupying a middle zone.[17] Only later would they realize the flaws of this geopolitical mapping, particularly its omission of various Hindu sects, whom they labeled "Gentoo."

Perceptions of Muslims

As another "religion of the book," Muslims were perceived by Jesuits as a greater threat to Christendom than so-called Gentiles.[18] Jerome Xavier, the Spanish Jesuit missionary to Akbar's court, wrote: "[W]e deal with the Moors [Muslims], who agree with us about all that concerns the nature of God; and we come into conflict with them about that which we cannot prove with reasons, but only with miracles."[19] Their antipathy toward India's Muslims was informed by centuries of conflict with Muslims in Iberia. During the *Reconquista*, Catholic armies killed or expelled Muslim and Jewish minorities in Spain and Portugal in order to consolidate Catholic power. Portuguese traders extended this combative, crusade-like mentality into their affairs in India. They competed with Muslims of the Malabar Coast for control over the lucrative pepper trade and saw their efforts to subdue and defeat Indian Muslims as part of their quest for the triumph of the true faith.[20] As the first Europeans to conduct long-term trade in India, build fortified settlements, and wage war, the Portuguese wore the hats of both trader and crusader (see Figure 4.3).

This crusader mentality elicited defensive, even militant, responses from the Mappila Muslims of South India. Portuguese assaults on their coastal enclaves incited the Mappilas to become more organized and united in a holy war against the Portuguese. One Arabic text from the 1580s exhorted Muslims to wage jihad against the "Franks," a designation, distinct from *kafir* (infidel), that drew from the Portuguese role in the Crusades during an earlier era.[21]

Control of port cities was vital to Portuguese economic success at sea. Along the Indian Ocean littoral, the Portuguese captured most of the strategic centers of trade. By the 1530s, Portuguese armadas had seized from Muslims control of prominent ports including Goa, Colombo, Melaka, Hormuz, and Diu. Their interest in the ports brought them into conflict with Muslim traders and with

Figure 4.3 Sketch of the Portuguese arrival in India.
Source: Universal Art Archive/Alamy Stock Photo.

those wishing to make the hajj across the Arabian Sea. The Portuguese believed that the seas were open to all, but this was interpreted to apply exclusively to "Christian nations" that observed Roman law. Hindus and Muslims operated beyond this law—that is, "the law of Jesus Christ"—and thus could claim no right of passage even on Asian waters.[22]

Muslims deeply resented Portuguese interference with their trade and movement across the Arabian Sea. A famous poet from Kerala, Zain al-Din, denounced the manner in which the Portuguese had attacked other ships and had violated Muslim women:

> In addition to this system of persecution, also, these Franks sallying forth in the directions of Gujerat, the Conkan, and Malabar, and towards the coast of Arabia, would there lie in wait for the purposes of intercepting vessels; in this way, they iniquitously acquired vast wealth and made numerous prisoners. For, how many women of noble birth, thus made captive, did they not incarcerate, afterwards violating their persons, for the production of Christian children.[23]

Just as the Portuguese had framed their involvement in the Indian Ocean as a Christian enterprise, Zain al-Din portrayed their violence as a means of producing Christians. The poet, however, also criticized the Hindus, especially their caste system. In his work *Tuhfat al-Mujahidin*, he described the Muslims of Kerala as a distinct community called to differentiate themselves from Hindu society. Hindus converted to Islam, he argued, in order to escape "the multitude of inconveniences" arising from the caste system.[24]

Reinventing "Gentiles"

In contrast to their approach to Muslims, which was heavily informed by Catholic–Muslim conflict in the Iberian Peninsula, Catholic attitudes to Hindu religious institutions varied. This was due to the feeling among Portuguese Catholics that no single political system unified India and, as a result, there were many Indias.[25] They designated as "Gentiles" that vast social domain of the subcontinent that was not Christian, Jewish, or Muslim—in other words, "non-Abrahamic" religions (that is, not tracing their heritage in any way to the patriarch, Abraham). Under the spell of the Prester John myth, the Portuguese initially regarded Hindus as the lost Christians, but this misunderstanding appears to have been short-lived and supplanted by heightened awareness of difference. Increasingly, Catholics drew attention to idolatry, caste distinctions (and the role of Brahmins), and belief in reincarnation as elements that separated them from India's so-called Gentiles.[26]

By designating India's non-Abrahamic religions as "Gentile," Europeans were essentially accommodating them within a framework familiar to them—one derived from first-century Jewish and Christian encounters with the Greco-Roman world. By borrowing language from this ancient context, missionaries hoped to channel the past into the present. The Portuguese became the "new Romans," Jesuits the "new apostles," and Indians the "new Gentiles," this time within the context of Asian conquests.[27] This manner of classifying the non-European Other with the amorphous category of "Gentile" was taken a step further. It became a form of cultural appropriation, more tied to cultural politics unfolding in Europe than to Indian beliefs and practices themselves. Encounters with Hindus in India provided resources for defending Catholicism against critiques from the humanists of the European Enlightenment. The triumph of Catholicism over "pagan" practices in India enhanced their case for the global relevance of their faith and its enduring relevance back home.

During the seventeenth century, an ideological climate in Europe gave rise to anticlerical sentiments and, along with them, an alternative reading of early Christianity. Some challenged the belief that the Christian gospel had prevailed over the power of demons in the pagan (Gentile) world and over oracles who were inspired by demons. Men such as Bernard Le Bovier de Fontenelle (1657–1757) and Anthony van Dale (1638–1708) argued that oracles were frauds who falsely claimed access to supernatural power. The decline of oracles was not due to the triumph of Christian belief (since demons and oracles were not "real") but to more secular factors associated with the rise of the Christian empire.[28]

It was against these intellectual headwinds that Jean Venant Bouchet presented his own observations from India. We encountered Bouchet in Chapter 3 in connection with conflicts with his Indian catechists on whom he relied heavily for the day-to-day operation of his mission. His use of Indian catechists appears to have afforded him the time to contribute to intellectual debates in Europe about the legitimacy of Catholicism. Bouchet aligned himself with those who upheld the reality of demons and oracles, and he used what he encountered firsthand in India as evidence. Unlike his predecessors, his views were not grounded in "monumental works of antiquity," but in "that which frequently occurs before our eyes in our missions in Madurai and Karnataka."[29] In other words, Bouchet believed that the prevalence of spirit possession in India not only validated the path to Christianity taken by the "spirit-possessed" pagans of the Greco-Roman world, but also set the stage for Indians' own path to Christianization.

In order to round out his argument, Bouchet had to make a broader claim about the similarity of Indian beliefs to what is found in the Bible. He claimed that the teachings of the Bible and of the apostles had somehow circulated in ancient India and influenced the beliefs of Indians. Indian beliefs about God, their creation accounts, and the names of their key deities carried vestiges of biblical influence and phonetic similarity: The goddess Sarasvati, he noted, was "Sara" of the Old Testament, just as Brahma was "Abraham." The conversion of Indians to Catholicism would return Indians to the original and true font of their religious understanding, while also answering Europeans who were challenging Catholic universalism with what they were learning about the diversity of beliefs found in other lands.[30] At a time when the likes of Voltaire were satirizing Catholic beliefs in Europe, Bouchet hoped his perspectives would enhance Catholic credibility. His cultural appropriation of Indian religion served the broader intellectual project of validating Christianity among European audiences.

Early Protestants

The Dutch

Similar approaches to Indian religions are observable among Protestants. The Dutch adventurer Jan Huygen van Linschoten (1562/3–1611) worked in Goa as a clerk for the Catholic archbishop. His employment put him in touch with the very pulse of Portuguese interests in India and their contacts with Lisbon, access that enabled him to acquire Portuguese secrets and divulge them to the Dutch.[31]

Van Linschoten also was an astute observer of Indian religion and customs. He wrote with great admiration about the customs of Brahmins, citing them as examples of high moral behavior among "the heathen." He also commented on other caste groupings from various parts of India and presented keen insights into the relationships between the various castes. He was most critical, however, of images of deities found in Hindu temples: Like other Protestant observers, van Linschoten identified the veneration of these images with idolatry and the demonic. Curiously, his critique of popular Hindu devotion (which he often referred to as "demonic superstitions") was accompanied by his recognition that the Hindus believed in a supreme divinity. His conversations with Brahmins convinced him that "idols" worshiped by Hindus played a mediating role in accessing the supreme divinity.[32]

If the 1500s saw the expansion of the Portuguese, the 1600s saw the advancement of Dutch power across the same domains. The Dutch gained control over trading posts in the Indian Ocean by conquering Portuguese forts at Melaka in 1641, Colombo and the rest of Ceylon in 1658, and the Malabar ports during the 1660s.[33] Like the Portuguese, the Dutch were keen to control the spice trade; however, unlike their pepper-mongering predecessors, the trade of the Dutch East India Company (*Verenigde Oost-Indische Compagnie* or VOC) was chiefly centered on fine spices, such as cinnamon grown in Ceylon and cloves, nutmeg, and mace acquired at strategic Indonesian ports such as Makassar or the Maluku Islands. In order to create huge profit margins, the Dutch amassed a large supply of labor through a regime of forced migration and slavery. The VOC trafficked humans between regions that fell within its spheres of sovereignty, including slaves from East Africa, the Cape of Good Hope, Persia, and Bengal. Theirs was not an empire based at a fixed capital (like Goa for the Portuguese); instead, it ranged across a "web of networks" of free and forced labor, whose movement they directed between various nodes across the Indian Ocean.[34]

Within this context of violent displacement of indigenous peoples for commercial expansion, the Dutch established settlements in which the advancement of Protestantism was prioritized. One such settlement was the island of Ceylon (Sri Lanka). There and elsewhere, the VOC's conquest of strategic ports went hand in hand with the propagation of their Dutch Reformed variety of Protestantism. Unlike the Jesuits, who somehow managed to extend their mission beyond the oversight of the *Padroado Real*, for the Dutch settlers church and state remained firmly intertwined. Under the state's mandate to propagate Protestantism, the Dutch Reformed Church transferred Catholic churches, monasteries, and schools (established by the Portuguese) to their control, and proceeded to make converts from among the Tamils and Sinhalese, the two dominant ethnic groups of Ceylon.

Immediately after expelling the Portuguese from Ceylon, the Dutch, under the leadership of the Reverend Philippus Baldaeus (1632–72), proceeded to uproot Catholicism. The coastal villages had many Catholic congregations, the fruits of missionary labors under *Padroado* oversight. The Dutch saw these congregations not only as victims of popish ritualism and aberrant Catholic teachings, but also as communities that remained politically aligned with the Portuguese. From 1658 to 1687, Dutch authorities embarked on a ruthless campaign to suppress Catholicism on the island. Baldaeus was tasked with bringing Catholic schools and parishes under the control of the Dutch Reformed Church.[35]

The Dutch prohibited Catholic priests of any nationality from working within their territories and threatened execution for anyone who harbored or concealed a Roman Catholic priest.[36] Many priests were deported to India. And yet, many converts, especially within the villages that dotted Ceylon's coasts, remained loyal to Catholicism. It was quite common for these villagers to travel further inland, into regions beyond formal Dutch control, in order to practice their Catholic religion under the oversight of their priests. Baldaeus was largely ineffective in preventing this. He and other Dutch predikants (pastors), however, made many converts of their own and established churches in the northern province of Jaffna as well as among the Sinhalese in the southern regions of the island. As Protestants who were very committed to education, the Dutch attached a school to every church and employed indigenous catechists and schoolmasters to serve under their predikants.

According to an official survey of churches and schools conducted in 1722, the number of Christians in Jaffna numbered 189,388, and there were 179,845 Sinhalese converts, administered from Colombo.[37] These figures show that Dutch missionary endeavors had yielded a substantial Christian population in Ceylon. What they are unable to measure, however, is the extent to which converts had actually conformed to the normative teachings of the Dutch Reformed Church. Many of these converts came from Hindu and Buddhist backgrounds and never fully abandoned the practices associated with their former religions. Also, layered into the identities of some of these Protestant converts were vestiges of their Roman Catholic heritage. In Sinhalese areas, the Dutch made converts from among the higher-ranking communities of Mudaliars, Muhandirams, and Majorals who had once been Catholic and had held administrative positions under the Portuguese. The complex layering of their new identities encompassed religion, vocation, caste, and social status:

> The upper hierarchy was honored with the title Don, which they retained under the Dutch, and they also had a middle Portuguese name after which followed their ancestral Sinhalese or Tamil names. Among the Sinhalese these Portuguese names took the place of surnames which they retained even after

they reverted to Buddhism. Under the Dutch these Christianized upper classes kept their offices and became members of the Reformed Church.[38]

This layering of identity reflects the waves of influence that had shaped the island's Tamil and Sinhalese populations. These influences included not only Catholic and Dutch elements, but aspects of local religions as well. The historian S. Arasaratnam likened the Christian population to an iceberg; it did not supplant Hindu or Buddhist practices, but merely submerged them beneath the strictures of one regime or another. Besides conforming to the culture of the Reformed Church, many upper caste Sinhalese and Tamil converts continued to participate in domestic rites and some forms of temple worship. So prevalent was the dual participation of converts in Christian and Hindu practices that in 1711 the Dutch had to issue an order prohibiting such participation. They whipped or imprisoned baptized Christians found to have observed Hindu ceremonies, but much of this parallel observance was impossible to police.

Lower caste converts in the villages of Jaffna sometimes participated in forms of worship centered on the miraculous powers of healers and exorcists. In this respect, they resembled many of the warrior cult traditions of south India discussed in Chapter 3. Supernatural powers, believed to be embodied in persons or objects, drew the devotion of the masses, including Christians. Viewing such devotional practices as forms of devil worship or "devil dancing," Reformed ministers resorted to edicts that imposed penalties on Christian participants, but these measures were just as ineffective among the villagers as they were among the upper castes. The incorporation of local religious practices into the lives of converts appears to have been an indelible aspect of the contextual Christianity observed in Ceylon.

Like the Jesuits who came before them, other Europeans tended to interpret Indian religion in terms of their European experience of Judaism, Islam, and Christianity—the so-called Abrahamic religions. In 1723–37, the French engraver and printer Bernard Picart, along with his Huguenot (French Protestant) colleague Jean-Frederic Bernard, produced *Cérémonies et coutumes religieuses de tous les peuples du monde*, a massive work containing images and texts concerning the religious traditions of non-European peoples. It was comparative in its scope and sought to present the various traditions of the world in an objective, non-sensational manner. The sizable section on India followed those on Judaism, Islam, and Christianity—three "religions of the book."[39] As such, Picart's compilation is one among several works of the period that juxtaposed Abrahamic religions with those of India in order to facilitate comparative analysis.

Picart had never left Europe, but one of the contributors to his compilation, a Frenchman of obscure origins named La Créquinière, boasted of having spent three to four years in India. His essay, "The Conformity of the Customs of the East

Indians with Those of the Jews, and Other Ancient Nations," draws parallels between the customs and religion of Jews and those of Indians. Previously, Catholic missionaries had compared India's religions with the pagan traditions of the Greco-Roman world. According to Subrahmanyam, what made La Créquinière's contribution unique was precisely his willingness to compare Hindu religiosity with another established and familiar religious tradition: Judaism. This appears to have emboldened Picart and Bernard to draw additional comparisons between Hindu and Judeo-Christian beliefs and practices.[40]

The English

A similar Judeo-Christian framing of Indian religion is found in the writing of Reverend Henry Lord, the English East India Company's chaplain at the west Indian port of Surat. Lord examined and interpreted Indian religion from the standpoint of the Bible. His work focuses on the religious beliefs and practices of two prominent trading communities of west India: the Banians and the Parsis. The Banians were a caste group committed to a variety of commercial activities; they worked as shopkeepers, brokers, moneychangers, and bankers and were Hindu by religion.[41] The Parsis were Persians who migrated to India after the seventh-century Arab invasion of Iran. Parsis practiced the Zoroastrian religion and entered the legal profession in Bombay and Surat in large numbers.

Lord tended to impose a Judeo-Christian framework on the material he gathered about Banian and Parsi practices and beliefs, not unlike the approach taken by the French Jesuit Bouchet. His observations about Banians are largely drawn from *puranic* texts (that is, Hindu epic literature) and they offer general observations about the ministerial functions of priests. Lord, for instance, discusses the roles of Brahma, Vishnu, and Shiva/Rudra, but narrates their activities in ways that bring to mind the great events of the Old Testament. These include the creation of the world, its destruction through the flood, and the reestablishment of civilization through the implementation of divine precepts. Lord conveys Vishnu's "descent" during a second age of restoration in ways that resonate with the story of Moses the lawgiver as well as with the Genesis accounts of creation:

> The Almighty therefore descending from heaven upon a great mountain, called Meropurbatee [Meruparvata or Mount Meru] upon the top of the same the Lord pronounced his word, and said, "Rise up Bremaw [Brahma], the first of living creatures in the second age." The earth then did render from her womb Bremaw at the voice of God, who did acknowledge and worship his Maker; and by a second and third command from the same place, raised Vystney, and Ruddery, who with no less reverence adored their Maker likewise.[42]

Lord casts the religion of the Banians and the Parsis in the idiom of biblical monotheism. Lord did not describe a society of many gods, but one in which a single creator employs various agents,[43] thereby drawing Indian religion into a comparative framework consisting of the world's principal "book religions."

The English East India Company's commitment to trade and profits placed it in a highly ambiguous relationship with Christian expansion within its overseas territories. On the one hand, Company officials wanted to avoid forms of proselytizing that would agitate the local population and diminish the Company's capacity to engage in lucrative trading ventures. On the other hand, some Company servants framed their vision for governing Indian territories in the idiom of Protestantism and formulated their ambitions in terms of advancing the cause of Christianity.[44] In practical terms, this meant that they saw in Protestantism a way to legitimize the Company's governance and vision for a just society, even as it ruled a predominantly non-Christian population. Modeled after the Israelites of the Old Testament, the Company was to be revered by Indians as a "wise and understanding nation" because of the statutes and laws it would live by and implement in its territories.[45]

The Christian framework of its governance, however, always remained distinct from any agenda to evangelize the local population. Ironically, the Company's belief in Judeo-Christian understandings of moral order and governance accompanied its official "toleration" of non-Christian religions. If officials wanted Bombay and Madras to become "new Jerusalems," they also wanted them to become cosmopolitan cities in which adherents of many religions were not antagonized and remained amenable to trade. Occasionally, they looked to the Dutch as examples of a Protestant nation engaged in Indian Ocean trade. At home, the Dutch struck a balance between adherence to Reformation ideals of godly governance and a commitment to liberty. This included the kind of religious liberty that produced cosmopolitan cities such as Amsterdam—a city, however, built from profits from the slave trade and colonial violence.[46] In the Banda islands of Indonesia, the Dutch in the early 1600's massacred local inhabitants, burned villages, and sent survivors of these massacres into indentured labor or slavery—all to secure a monopoly over the island's supply of nutmegs.[47] Such instances of war capitalism did little to alter among English traders a more favorable impression of Dutch Protestants than of Catholic Spaniards.

Josiah Child, who became the English East India Company's governor in 1681, argued that Dutch success in building its empire arose from its toleration of the Jews and other non-Christian peoples. The Spanish, by contrast, suffered decline on account of their uncompromising Catholicism and intolerance toward Jews and Muslims. The English East India Company, Child believed, occupied a "confusing middle ground" by attempting to nurture religious uniformity at home while promoting religious toleration in its overseas plantations.[48] This tendency to distinguish a Protestant English settlement committed to toleration from an oppressive Spanish settlement is evident not only in the perspectives of men such as Child, but also among philosophers such as John Locke.[49]

The Tranquebar Mission

The examples of the Portuguese, Dutch, and English during the early modern period illustrate how commercial and imperial interests in South Asia opened doors for missionary involvement. As Europeans encountered the societies of India's coasts for the first time, they attempted to locate their own Christian heritage in relation to Hindu and Muslim traditions. The imperial context of these early Christian encounters with India contributes to a prevailing sense that missionaries were the handmaidens of imperialism and that European knowledge was similarly tainted by imperial interests, a perspective put forward in Said's book, *Orientalism*. The legacy of missions in South Asia, however, is more complicated than this. For some Indians, the missionary past evokes strong feelings of resentment about racist and colonial attitudes and practices; but for others, the same history conjures feelings of appreciation, even among non-Christians.

In July 2006, residents of India's southern state of Tamil Nadu celebrated the 300-year anniversary of the arrival of the German Pietist missionary Bartholomaeus Ziegenbalg (1683?–1719) in Tranquebar.[50] Thousands of people of diverse faith traditions participated in the program and festivities. They included the chief minister, M. Karunanidhi, and other high-ranking officials.[51] Speakers celebrated Ziegenbalg's devotion to the study of the Tamil language, his contributions to book printing and print technology, and his promotion of universal education devoid of gender and caste discrimination.[52] The pervasive sense of appreciation for and ownership of Ziegenbalg's legacy across religious divides is noteworthy, especially considering the tendency to associate foreign missionaries with a history of cultural imperialism and intolerance. Ziegenbalg's commitment to language learning, translation, and producing knowledge about the religious traditions of south India seems to have struck a chord that distinguishes him from British missionaries who came a century later and tend to be remembered less favorably.

Ziegenbalg studied south Indian society rigorously in order to present the gospel most effectively. He did so as the Portuguese, Dutch, English, French, and Danes sailed the Indian Ocean in the hope of profiting from trade and colonial expansion. Within the Danish colony at Tranquebar (now called Tharangambadi), Ziegenbalg mingled with Tamil- and Telugu-speaking peoples and became an astute observer of their customs and beliefs. Here, for instance, he describes how south Indian notions of purity and pollution gave rise to a natural aversion to Europeans:

> They think of us Europeans as impure and unholy people because we eat nothing but the meat of living animals, including that of cows and oxen which they consider as a sin that deserves death. This is the reason that they do not wish to watch us eating. If a European touches them, they will immediately take a bath [to get rid of the pollution]. They are unhappy if Europeans visit them at home because they believe that our sitting and looking and our presence pollutes everything. If a European drinks from a cup, they break it immediately into pieces so that they can never use it again for drinking. They consider us [Europeans] as impure people because we eat meat [i.e., beef].[53]

These observations are part of Ziegenbalg's more comprehensive description of south Indian caste practices. Other Europeans of his day (or before him) had formed opinions about Indian society and religion, but they were not grounded in the deep relationships that Ziegenbalg cultivated with locals—a factor contributing to the celebration of his legacy among Tamils to this day.[54]

Nearly 100 years before the arrival of the first English missionaries, two German Pietists, Ziegenbalg and Heinrich Plütschau (1678–1747), arrived in the southeast seaport of Tranquebar, which had become a Danish colony. The king of Denmark, Fredrick IV, had commissioned these men to preach the gospel and establish churches among south Indians. Whereas Plütschau focused his efforts on the Portuguese population, Ziegenbalg worked among the Tamils. Their missionary approach was influenced by Pietism, a movement that placed a stronger emphasis on heartfelt devotion to Christ, as opposed to routinized traditions of established churches. Pietists wanted to renew the faith of churchgoing people by encouraging them to read the Bible in small groups, pray extemporaneously (as distinct from reciting liturgy), and learn about God's creation, not for lofty scholastic objectives, but in order to defend the faith more effectively among non-believers.[55]

When Ziegenbalg brought these Pietist sensibilities to Tranquebar, they resonated with the fervent moral commitments and devotional practices of local Tamil-speaking people. Tranquebar was a religiously diverse society located on India's Coromandel Coast. Its population consisted of low caste members of popular devotional (*bhakti*) sects, higher caste Hindus belonging to both Shaiva and Vaishnava traditions, Muslims, and European Catholics and Protestants. The fervent religiosity of Tamil Hindus impressed Ziegenbalg. He maintained that they were originally and essentially monotheists, who, over time, had departed from monotheism and had come to venerate a wide array of deities, each possessing unique powers and attributes. Ziegenbalg carefully documented not only the gods and goddesses worshiped by the Malabarians, but also the rites, fasts, austerities, and public sacrifices performed for them.[56] All of this, of course, required extensive study and grasp of Tamil texts and temple complexes as well as collaboration with local informants.

Ziegenbalg's commitment to learning was central to his missionary endeavors. To educate himself about local beliefs and practices, Ziegenbalg befriended a wide range of Tamil poets, linguists, and scholars. He also collected Tamil manuscripts of various kinds, which documented the beliefs, rituals, and traditions of Tamil peoples. During his first two years in Tranquebar, he acquired as many as 112 Tamil books, many of which were inscribed on palm leaves (*cadjan*). The passion for knowledge exhibited by Ziegenbalg and his successors would result in the acquisition of hundreds of palm leaf manuscripts, which were eventually consigned to the archives at Halle in Germany. Thanks to such efforts, these archives now preserve as many as 280 such manuscripts in Tamil, Telugu, and Malayalam.[57]

Several months into his stay in Tranquebar, Ziegenbalg described his high regard for the Tamil people:

> The Tamil people are indeed very brilliant and intelligent. They should be won with great wisdom. They have an accurate understanding about their faith just as we [European] Christians tend to have. They are more convinced of the life to come than the unbelieving [lit. atheistic] Christians. They possess numerous books which they claim to have received from their gods just as we [Christians] have received the Holy Scripture. These books contain not only several amusing stories about their deities, but also excellent things about the life to come. By contrast, they consider our Bible [lit. Word of God] uninteresting. At the same time, they live a peaceful, honorable, and virtuous life, in which they, depending on their natural powers, excel at least ten times over [the life of] the Christians.[58]

Such comments not only convey Ziegenbalg's high regard for the Tamils, but also reflect his receptivity to what Tamils had to teach him. Ultimately, the converts he was able to make did not uproot themselves from their cultural framework, but appropriated Christianity within the structures of Tamil cultural and religious practice. Instead of imposing alien cultural forms upon Tamil converts, Ziegenbalg saw the need to acquire a deep grasp of the religious and cultural milieu in order to advance his mission in south India.

A number of factors contributed to the mutual respect that Ziegenbalg maintained with the Hindus at Tranquebar. Ziegenbalg learned Tamil quickly by spending extensive time with Tamil schoolchildren and taking part in their lessons. His decision to reside in the slave quarters of Tranquebar, not the

European quarters, not only aided his language acquisition; it also reinforced perceptions among the locals that he was more aligned with *their* interests than with those of the Danish colonizers.[59]

Ziegenbalg's tense relationship with the Danish authorities enhanced his affinity with the local population, perhaps because he shared their burden of subordination. From the time of his arrival, officials of the Danish East India Company had instructed the acting governor, Johan Sigismund Hassius, to "be as discouraging as possible toward the missionaries."[60] Europeans saw in Ziegenbalg someone who defied the hierarchies of race and class observed by Danish colonists and was openly critical of their drunkenness and sexual liaisons with local women. Moreover, his Pietist approach to Christian worship conflicted with the more traditional practices of Danish chaplains. At one point, Hassius became so incensed with Ziegenbalg that he imprisoned him for four months in a dungeon in the Tranquebar fort. Such harassment at the hands of colonial officials "made the Hindus warm to Ziegenbalg."[61]

Ziegenbalg joined his commitment to knowledge and to forming relationships with Tamils with a rather confrontational approach to local traditions. His deep admiration for Tamil-speaking peoples did not prevent him from challenging their beliefs from the standpoint of the Bible. This stands out as one of the great paradoxes of Ziegenbalg's life: namely, that he could be such an ardent critic of Hindu and Muslim beliefs and yet be so well liked.[62] Ziegenbalg's criticisms of Islam and of the Prophet Muhammad find a precedent in Jesuit argumentation (for instance, in Akbar's court), but they also foreshadow the rhetoric of English Evangelicals who came to India after him.[63] This tradition of debate and argumentation also mirrored the intellectual traditions of India (discussed in Chapter 5). Representatives of various traditions—Shaiva, Vaishnava, Buddhist, Jain, and Muslim—studied each other's beliefs in order to refute them, not to understand them in a disinterested way or from pure intellectual curiosity.[64]

Roughly two thousand Muslims resided in Tranquebar and their worship took place in two mosques. Some were Tamil-speaking Maraikkayar Muslims, elite Sunni merchants and ship owners whose trading operations brought them into regular contact with Arabian ports and pilgrimage sites and with Muslims of Southeast Asia. There were also lower-ranking Labbai, also Sunnis, who included pearl divers, fishermen, land laborers, and petty traders. Sufi spiritual guides (*pirs*) modeled holiness among their disciples and taught an experiential spirituality that in some ways resembled the faith espoused by Pietists.

At Ziegenbalg's New Jerusalem Church in Tranquebar, Hindus and Muslims attended various functions to observe the performance of the liturgies. According to Ziegenbalg, they sometimes came by the hundreds. Muslims gazed at Christian beliefs and practices, just as Ziegenbalg and his colleagues would examine Muslim beliefs and practices. Both sides believed that they possessed the one true religion, an infallible sacred book, and true monotheism. Both sides repudiated idolatry of any kind and in so doing differentiated themselves from Hindus (whom Ziegenbalg referred to as "pagans"). The sanctuary of Ziegenbalg's New Jerusalem Church possessed a stone altar and pulpit but had no crucifixes or images of any kind. The main mosque at Tranquebar was similarly image-free. Despite these similarities, the differences between the two faiths emerged in the course of Ziegenbalg's exchanges with Muslims.

Ziegenbalg thought less of those Muslims he encountered than he did of Hindus. He found Hindus to be "more civil and tractable, as well as far more desirous to be instructed in better things." He regarded Muslims, by contrast, as unsophisticated, intolerant, and resistant to change.[65] Ziegenbalg documented as many as twelve theological exchanges with Muslims.[66] In Protestant fashion, he defended the Bible over the Qur'an. In one exchange, he claimed that Christians had a better understanding of Islam than Muslims did of his faith. While Muhammad was propagating his faith "with fire and sword," he argued, Christians who "escaped his fury" had provided a complete account of the Prophet. Moreover, Christians had translated the Qur'an into languages that they could understand, whereas Muslims relied on their own texts to draw conclusions about Christianity.[67]

To his credit, Ziegenbalg noted Muslim responses to his arguments. From his accounts, it is clear that Muslims were not passive recipients of Christian arguments, but responded with their own criticisms of Christianity. Muslims criticized the New Testament as a distortion of the true revelation contained in the Qur'an, and they suggested that Christians were as idolatrous as Hindus because of their belief in the Trinity.[68]

Ziegenbalg's condescension and rudeness toward Muslims is reflective of wider European attitudes and prejudice. He did not refer to Muslims as they designated themselves—as those who had surrendered to Allah (the literal meaning of Muslims)—but as "those who follow the doctrine of Muhammad."[69] In one exchange, a Sufi (those who practice a highly experiential form of Sunni Islam) asked Ziegenbalg how one can see the face of God. He observed that whereas each religion promoted outward practices that created the appearance of holiness, none succeeded at providing a glimpse of God himself. The Sufi even criticized Islamic practices such as mosque attendance, prayers, ceremonies, and austerities as being no better than Hindu customs. They were:

> fruitless pageantries, neither acceptable to God, nor profitable to ourselves; and this duly considered we make no difference between the pagan and Mahometan worship: For in this only we exercise ourselves, that if by any means and enquiries we may be rendered worthy to see the Face of God: This is the Capital

Point, in comparison to which, all other things are but mere toys in themselves, and very insignificant.[70]

The Sufi added that if he could find guides who could show him the way to this vision of the divine, he would immediately erect a church, in which Christians, Hindus, and Muslims could be instructed jointly in the most essential teaching about seeing God. Together they would abandon fruitless religious practices. This all-inclusive vision reflects a Sufi emphasis on experience over the outward practices of one religion or another and appears to have been voiced in the hope that Ziegenbalg would join him in this common pursuit. Ziegenbalg, however, responded by insisting that it was only by having a pure heart that one could see God (citing the Beatitudes in the New Testament) and that this is achieved not by human works or by outwardly washing oneself, but by the work of God as performed in the sacrificial death of Christ.[71] Such exchanges, as contentious as they may seem, demonstrate a degree of honesty and civility in coming to terms with religious differences. Moreover, they represent, according to Daniel Jeyaraj, the earliest exchanges between a Protestant missionary and South Asian Muslims.

Ziegenbalg's recorded exchanges with Hindus reflect the German Pietist use of reasoned argument to demonstrate the truth of the Bible. A recurring theme is his insistence that Hindus be able to prove the veracity of their beliefs, and his confidence in his ability to demonstrate by way of reason the truth of his own Christian beliefs. He decried the manner in which Hindus had abandoned belief in the supreme God. They had turned instead to the worship of lower deities whose quarrels with each other sprang from imperfect attributes of jealousy or vengeance, and whose earthly incarnations (*avatars*) assumed not only human form but also that of a tortoise or a boar.[72] The personalities and attributes assigned to Hindu deities and *avatars*, he maintained, only obscured the distinction between good and evil. But just as Ziegenbalg criticized the Hindu belief in *avatars*, his Hindu interlocutors took issue with the doctrines of the Trinity or the Immaculate Conception, questioning whether these did not also constitute polytheism.[73] They also raised the possibility that God had ordained different religions for different regions and peoples, a perspective for which Ziegenbalg seems to have displayed little appreciation.

The legacy of the Tranquebar mission would outlive that of Ziegenbalg, who, in 1719, died of an illness. By this time, the Danish Halle missionaries had founded a seminary and had ordained their first Indian pastor, Aaron, who was among the seminary's first graduates. Other German Pietists established churches in various parts of south India, such as the Lutheran church founded in Madras by Benjamin Schultze and the churches established by Christian Friedrich Schwartz in 1762 in Tiruchirappalli. A high caste Brahmin convert of Schwartz, Clarinda, would be instrumental in founding a church in 1785 at Palayamkottai.[74] Another student of Schwartz, Vedanayagam Pillai (who would eventually earn the honorary title Sastri), would become a renowned Tamil Christian poet and an ardent defender of the inculturation model of mission work instituted by the German Pietists. His views, which are discussed below, illustrate how an Indian could appropriate the Pietist legacy in order to defend caste distinctions within the Church.

Translatability and Tamil

How exactly did a religion that spread within a context of war capitalism become translated into one that was genuinely owned by Indians? Despite the history of European exploitation, violence, and racism, Indians became Christian. They did so not by accepting every cultural or political assumption of their European rulers, but by embracing a faith that was translated into their own language and experience.[75] The passage from European Orientalism to German Pietism to English Evangelicalism and ultimately to Tamil Christianity was neither smooth nor predictable. Against a turbulent and contested history, translation, in the fullest sense of its meaning, gave rise to non-European Christian identities.

Having examined European understandings of Indian society, we can now begin to probe how Christianity became Indianized by way of translation. This was not a purely analytical process that replaced European terms and concepts with Tamil ones. On the contrary, translation was a messy ordeal involving negotiation and contestation over the meaning of words and their social implications. Translating the Bible into an Indian language evoked controversies over which version of a mother tongue to use—the learned, literary version or the more coarse, everyday one. A similar question arose within the realm of culture and group life: Would the cultural translation of the gospel reinforce or legitimize caste distinctions, or would it work toward their eradication?

By conveying Christian belief through the medium of Tamil, by employing local catechists, informants, and translators, and by expressing the gospel through local cultural forms, the German Pietist tradition facilitated the emergence of an authentically Tamil expression of Christianity. This is not to suggest that there exists a singular, unadulterated Tamil (or Telugu, Marathi, or Kannada) culture into which Pietist Christianity had transformed itself. The churches arising from German Pietist missionary endeavors fused European traditions of Enlightenment reason, education, and Bible literacy with local, mother-tongue expressions of the faith.[76] What emerged in south India was in fact a mixture of elements. It nevertheless constituted an "indigenous discovery of Christianity" because of the active roles played by converts in the process of translating the Christian message into local idioms and in making this faith their own.

A Tamil Christian Poet

Translation sparked tensions and disagreements between missionaries and their Indian translators and between different classes of Indians. Seemingly straightforward tasks in translation became topics of great contention: for instance, how to translate the name for God or various biblical terms, whether the adoption of certain words would privilege some castes over others, or whether local cultural practices could find expression in the Church.[77] Such matters of cultural contestation played themselves out in the life of Vedanayagam Sastri (1774–1864).

Sastri, who had been raised and educated by the Pietist missionary Christian Friedrich Schwartz (1726–98), became an ardent champion of an indigenous Tamil Christianity. A precocious and talented poet hailing from the highly literate Vellalar caste, Sastri served for many years as the court poet for Serfoji II, the king of the princely state of Tanjore. As a Christian, he used his talents to convey Christian beliefs through his poetry and drama. A prime example of this was his authorship of the "Bethlehem Kuravanci," a dance drama that adapted a classical Tamil literary form (*kuravanci*) to Evangelical themes. The scholar Indira Peterson describes how this medium, anchored as it was in the motifs of Tamil drama, captivated Christian audiences. Tamil Christians of Tanjore and Tranquebar held Sastri in such high esteem that they awarded him titles such as "Evangelical poet," "the Principal Evangelical jewel," and "the monarch of the divine poets."[78]

As the influence and power of the English East India Company expanded in south India, Sastri was saddened to see the congregations established by the German Pietists come under Anglican control. By 1825, churches at Tanjore, Tranquebar, Vepery, Palayamkottai, and other places had left the umbrella of the Danish Halle mission and had come under the oversight of an Anglican missionary body known as the Society for the Propagation of the Gospel in Foreign Parts (SPG). This transition effectively made Anglicans of nearly 20,000 people who had been mostly Lutherans.[79]

The transition in leadership ushered in a different approach to local culture. Sastri strongly opposed the anglicizing tendencies of the new missionaries and found himself in a battle to defend the model of inculturation that had been implemented by the Pietists. By this time, Tamil churches had incorporated indigenous liturgical traditions, Tamil music, and Tamil poetry into worship services and had observed local festivals. Sastri decried attempts by the Anglicans—whom he labeled pejoratively the "junior missionaries"—to rid the congregations of these indigenous elements. Among the more contentious issues he disputed with the SPG missionaries were the issues of Bible translation and caste.[80]

Sastri defended the observance of caste distinctions within the churches as an aspect of the inculturation model of his Pietist forebears. Many congregations, for instance, assigned different seating and entry points for different castes and prohibited inter-caste dining and marriage. Sastri believed that such distinctions found a precedent in the Jew–Gentile distinctions of the New Testament, which, he claimed, were not eradicated upon conversion. Also, social distinctions observed by Tamil Christians were no different from the class distinctions observed within European church contexts.[81] Caste and Christianity, as we shall see, would continue to be a contentious issue within the Indian Church. The caste issue also raises important questions about the cost of notions such as translatability or inculturation. Can the worthy projects of preserving culture and opposing Western influence sanction invidious caste distinctions or other practices that are at odds with normative Christian teachings?

Trials of Translation

In addition to upholding the legitimacy of caste distinctions within the Church, Sastri opposed a particular translation of the Bible that was advanced by the SPG missionaries. He criticized its use of a less refined and more profane variety of Tamil (often referred to as *cutcherry* Tamil). This debate over the translation of the Tamil Bible—the first language into which the entire Bible had been translated in India—is yet another illustration of the challenges that accompanied Christianity's translation and local appropriation. In her history of the Tamil Bible, Hephzibah Israel, a scholar of translation studies, provides a detailed account of how Bible translation ignited cultural politics associated with matters of caste and class. Far from being a neutral or objective exercise, Bible translation gave rise to contrasting vocabulary, voicing competing notions of Tamil Christian identity.

Israel notes an important difference between the translations of the eighteenth-century German Pietists and those of the nineteenth-century Anglicans, particularly that of C. T. E. Rhenius. German Pietists certainly addressed cultural and theoretical issues of translation, but they did so while focusing on Tamil alone. The Anglican missionaries who came a century later, however, tried to standardize translation methods to be "applied broadly across *all* Indian languages."[82] Bible translation in the nineteenth century became a way to show evidence of missionary gains in the field, raise more funds, and yield more converts. The pursuit of uniformity in translation methods coincided with the pursuit of a uniform

Protestant reading community.[83] Key moments in the history of the Tamil Bible, however, would derail this agenda.

Translators grappled with the question of how words that captured key Protestant doctrines were to be rendered in Indian languages. Could words for God, atonement, or grace be translated consistently and accurately? A pervasive nineteenth-century belief was that Sanskrit was the civilizational root and source language for all Indian languages. Sanskrit was a classical, Indo-European language in which Hindu scriptures were written. Like the status that Latin had once held within the Roman Catholic tradition, Sanskrit carried a unique stamp of authority and authenticity. As such, British missionaries came to regard Sanskrit as the language from which to derive a core sacred vocabulary. If key Protestant concepts were tied to a Sanskrit root, they reasoned, the concepts could be grafted into a Tamil translation of the Bible with the best chance of retaining the intended meaning. In the process of compiling a sacred vocabulary, however, a highly grammatical and formal written register was fused with a more common, spoken language. The result was something that came to be referred quite pejoratively as "missionary Tamil" or "Christian Tamil." Reactions to this version of Tamil would come from the Dravidian movement, which espoused a devotion to "pure Tamil" and sought to liberate the language from the influence of Sanskrit.

Decision making in translation was guided by two principles that often worked in tension with each other: the desire for relevance and the desire for difference or uniqueness. Protestants wanted to avoid words they saw as too indelibly tied to "heathen" worship. But, at the same time, they did not want to use words that were so unfamiliar that they estranged the Bible from the local population.[84] Two words for God in Sanskrit, *tevan* and *paraparan*, reveal the paradoxical manner in which Sanskrit words were "baptized" into Protestant usage. The more rarely used *paraparan* referred to the supreme or transcendent God who was beyond reach; the word *tevan*, by contrast (the singular form of *tevar*), referred to the various deities of the Hindu pantheon. By the late nineteenth century, Tamil Protestants came to prefer *tevan* to *paraparan* for God. This is particularly ironic considering how Ziegenbalg had criticized Tamil Hindus for disregarding their belief in the supreme being and embracing a belief in many lower divinities. Israel uses this dispute over the proper name for God to illustrate how community interests and perceptions often took priority over purely etymological factors in determining how missionaries translated sacred words.

Vedanayagam Sastri criticized Rhenius's early nineteenth-century translation of the Tamil Bible precisely because it embraced the *cutcherry* Tamil, which mixed Tamil with other south Indian languages and wedded it to "colloquialisms, region-specific words, and low-caste registers."[85] Sastri's defense of a certain kind of Tamil for Bible translation, Israel argues, went hand in hand with his defense of caste hierarchy. Those who defended the new translation, by contrast, seemed to aspire to greater mixing between castes and a Bible with more broad-based, democratic appeal. This debate is just one instance where a case for a localized, contextual Christianity ended up legitimating caste distinctions within churches. In so doing, it undermined advocacy for a more socially transformative faith, espoused by some missionaries and members of lower castes.

Ziegenbalg represents a bridge between the early wave of Europeans who traded in South Asia (such as the Dutch, Danish, and Portuguese) and the rising influence of the English East India Company. Ziegenbalg hoped that British rule would one day help advance the cause of Protestant Christianity in India. During his fourteen years in India, he made connections with British chaplains, missionary societies, and state officials with the aim of marshaling political support for the cause of missions.[86] Ziegenbalg would not live long enough to see his hopes materialize under British rule. What he did leave behind, however, were converts and their descendants who would influence wider networks of Indians in different parts of the empire.

Protestant Indentured Servants

No discussion of Ziegenbalg's legacy would be complete without reference to the dispersion of south Indians to other parts of Asia and the establishment of churches among them. During the nineteenth century, the British relocated lower caste Tamil- and Telugu-speaking people to work as indentured servants in places such as Malaya, Ceylon, and Burma. In the Straits Settlements (Malacca, Singapore, and Penang), Tamil laborers cleared jungles and cultivated land in order to produce lucrative commodities for English traders. These included timber, coffee, rubber, tea, tobacco, and sugar. Middlemen known as *kanganies* recruited the Tamil workers, who often carried huge debts to powerful landlords. Promising them debt relief in exchange for labor, the *kanganies* lured them into an alternative life of coerced labor in other lands.[87] Tamils formed part of the human flow that fed an insatiable demand for labor in plantation economies across the Indian Ocean.

Just as Malayali Pentecostals had followed contract laborers into the diaspora to address their spiritual needs (discussed at the end of Chapter 1), European missionaries and Tamil Christians made inroads into the lives of indentured laborers in South and Southeast Asia. Large numbers of Tamils went to Burma (now Myanmar) to work in rubber plantations as indentured servants. The SPG, which was tied to the Church of England, established congregations among them and enlisted Tamil catechists to carry on the work of building up these churches. In 1878, they ordained as a deacon a catechist by the name of

Samuel Abhishekananthan, who oversaw St. Gabriel's SPG church in Rangoon. By the turn of the twentieth century, St. Gabriel's had incorporated many Telugu Christians as well and its members numbered more than a thousand.[88]

Singapore and Malaya attracted indentured laborers from China as well as south India. During the 1860s, the SPG had sent a missionary by the name of W. H. Gomes to Singapore to work among a mixed congregation of Malay, Chinese, and Tamil Christians. He held services in all three languages with the help of local catechists.[89] In 1887, a young Tamil man named G. W. Underwood, who had been educated in Ceylon by the Ceylon American mission, arrived in Singapore to build up a Tamil congregation. Underwood would eventually extend his work to Perak (Malaysia). After dying of pneumonia, he was succeeded by several Tamil evangelists who expanded the work to Tamil laborers in Penang, Ipoh, and Kuala Lumpur.[90] Methodist and Anglican mission societies were very involved in Singapore and Malaysia, but they were keen on supporting Tamils as they preached among fellow Tamils. They much preferred local evangelists from among the migrant communities—not recruits from India—to carry on the work of churches.[91] What emerged from these endeavors were networks of "regional-vernacular" identities, which shared characteristics of south India's Tamil Christians—including their social divisions—while cultivating distinctive trajectories of growth and transformation in the diaspora.[92] The diaspora Tamil Church drew upon a rich legacy anchored in Christian centers at Tranquebar and Tirunelveli, and initiated by personalities such as Ziegenbalg, Schwartz, and others.

Conclusion

From the sixteenth century onward, commercial and political interests motivated Europeans to become involved in South Asia. These worldly motivations inevitably forced them to learn about the societies they had penetrated and the religious beliefs of the residents. As the first European power that had formed a colony in South Asia, the Portuguese had to locate themselves *between Hindu and Muslim*. In their quest for the lost kingdom of the legendary Prester John, they merged homegrown assumptions about Christians and pagans with fresh experiences of religious others in India. The result was a highly contentious relationship with both Hindus and Muslims along India's western coast. As the successors to the Portuguese in India, the Dutch and the British looked at Hindu and Muslim societies through Protestant lenses. Like the Catholics, they interpreted what they observed in terms of their own cultural assumptions and experiences. Committed as Europeans may have been to understanding the religions of South Asia, they did so as their trading companies aggressively penetrated the region. A distinct tradition of Protestant Orientalism arose not in isolation from empire, but with profound connections to it. It set the stage for future missionary scholars who produced knowledge about South Asian religions in order to advance the gospel.

Ziegenbalg followed this tradition of Protestant Orientalism, but his life demonstrated how missionary practices and interests could deviate from colonial ones. His commitment to learning about south Indian society was coupled with an affinity for the lower social classes of Tranquebar (as distinct from the more affluent and influential commercial and colonial classes) and persistent conflict with Danish authorities. This inclines scholars such as Daniel Jeyaraj and Brijraj Singh to conclude that Ziegenbalg was *not* a colonialist or a racist. They draw this conclusion despite the confrontational style he brought to his encounters with Hindus and Muslims. Ziegenbalg's negative experience of Danish colonial authorities in Tranquebar was balanced by his hope that the British would be different, and that their rule would one day advance the cause of Protestant Christianity. Three hundred years later, the fact that people of all faiths would celebrate his legacy suggests that his Christian message had in some way been *translated* into Indian experience.

The translation of the Bible into Tamil and Vedanayagam Sastri's passionate defense of contextual Christianity raise poignant questions about the very notion of translatability: Does the model espoused by Sanneh and Walls, arising from African contexts (see the discussion of their work in the Introduction), apply to what is observable in South Asia? The examples provided in this chapter illustrate how missionary attitudes and methods play a key role in determining whether Christianity becomes translated or remains a religion of *farangis* (foreigners).

Methods that provide ample roles for local agents and local culture in interpreting, teaching, and propagating the gospel are more likely to facilitate translation than instances where Europeans do not want to turn over power or where they rigidly adhere to European cultural practices. Sastri's passionate defense of Pietist methods and his attacks on the "junior missionaries" underscore this point. The prominence of Tamil catechists and ministers throughout the history of Jesuit and Protestant missions and in the Tamil Christian diaspora provides clues as to how the gospel managed to cross the canyon separating European and South Asian experience. A faith that began in the context of rapacious colonialism somehow took root in the lives of elite and lowly south Indians as well as in the lives of indentured servants.

5
The Argumentative Protestant
Religious Exchanges Under British Rule

The year 2017 marked the 500-year anniversary of the Protestant Reformation. Across continents, theologians, ministers, and laypeople commemorated the watershed moment when Martin Luther leveled his trenchant critique of the Catholic Church of his day. As copies of Luther's *Ninety-five Theses* circulated to other parts of Europe, they inspired other reformers to negotiate their own breaks from Catholicism. These developments led ultimately to a historic rupture within Western Christendom. Five hundred years later, scholars disagree as to how exactly the Reformation shaped Western society. Writing from a Roman Catholic perspective, the historian Brad Gregory is critical of the Reformation. He links it to moral relativism, godless secularism, and an endless splintering of Christianity into rival denominations, each interpreting the Bible in its own way.[1] The Anglican historian Alec Ryrie credits the Reformation for giving rise to free inquiry, democracy, and the separation of church and state.[2] Ryrie also contends that the word "Protestant" is a meaningful designation that carries real analytical content. More than purely an oppositional identity designating a united front against "popery," the term concerns a particular reading of the Bible, which stresses an unmediated and unmerited experience of grace.

If reflection on the Protestant legacy in Europe can generate this degree of controversy, it is not hard to imagine similar disagreements arising beyond Europe's borders. In key respects, Protestant missionaries reproduced in India a European cultural project. In the Germanic lands of the Reformation, Lutherans, Calvinists, and a range of radical reformers defended the authority of the Bible against what they viewed as the false authority of the pope, "popish rituals," and a corrupt priesthood. Catholic–Protestant differences were sounded out in formal theological disputations (such as the famous Leipzig Debate of 1519), sermons, encyclicals, or printed tracts. Protestant reformers also defended their interpretations and translations of the Bible against those of others. In this respect, the Protestant movement in Europe was inherently argumentative and remarkably public.

India had its own argumentative tradition. The economist Amartya Sen and historian Chris Bayly both describe a longstanding tradition of public reasoning that reaches back millennia. Within forums sometimes staged by kings or heads of religious establishments, Indians openly debated religious doctrines, the nature of the godly society, gender and caste hierarchies, and the interpretation of sacred texts such as the *Ramayana* or the *Bhagavad Gita*.[3] Brahmin pandits (Hindu teachers) debated the parameters of the Hindu *dharmic* order, while low caste proponents of *bhakti*, or devotion to God, contested Brahminical authority. Muslim doctors of law interpreted the Qur'an by exercising varying degrees of independent judgment (*idjtihad*), even as Sufi orders pushed the limits of orthodox Islam by emphasizing experiential union with Allah. In this manner, the Indian ecumene, according to Bayly, "encompassed a dialogue between elite and popular culture."[4]

What happens, then, when the argumentative Protestant meets the argumentative Indian? According to Bayly, the encounter was not a congenial one. The arrival of Protestant missionaries imposed an unusual strain on the already existing traditions of debate and public reasoning that prevailed in India. Protestant missionaries not only arrived as members of the ruling race; they also came equipped with printing presses, European writings about Indian religions, and new forms of propaganda such as printed tracts. Protestant media introduced the "audience effect" into India's argumentative tradition.[5] This refers to the highly publicized nature of religious debates, the emergence of a reading public, and venues where preachers attracted audiences. Protestant rhetoric drew sharp lines in the sand. In India, it was not the Catholic establishment that weighed most heavily on the Protestant imagination (although it still did), but rather the religious beliefs and practices of Indians—their gods and goddesses, sacred texts, and caste hierarchy.

Protestant missionary work began in South Asia in the early eighteenth century, two centuries after the arrival of Catholic missions. Missionaries developed a confrontational style of interacting with India's religious traditions, an approach that combined a fervent belief in the Bible with ideas of reason and evidence derived from the European Enlightenment. Missionaries typically chose some of the most crowded venues for open-air preaching and to attack local beliefs—pilgrimage sites, bazaars, prominent temples, or mosques. A common method they adopted was to use their own knowledge of Arabic or Sanskrit to expose the ignorance of Muslims and Hindus about their sacred texts. They believed that if Muslims and Hindus were only better informed about their scriptures, they would become aware of the flaws in those texts and eventually place their faith in the Bible.

By assuming that everyone had a sacred book and could be held accountable to it, Protestants, fixated as they were on *sola scriptura*, contributed to understandings of Indian society that were largely constructed around sacred texts. The assumption, however, that Indians must abide by sacred texts just as Protestants do was a projection riddled with problems. Most Muslims in India did not understand Arabic and possessed little or no direct knowledge of the Qur'an; and, lacking any knowledge of Sanskrit, most Hindus relied on Brahmin teachers to mediate sacred literature composed in this classical language. Aided by their printing presses, missionaries nevertheless tried to expose the unreasonableness, contradictions, or moral deficiencies of other scriptures and their adherents.[6] This combination of Orientalist scholarship, defenses of the Bible through the spoken and printed word, and refutations of the beliefs of others were key aspects of the Protestant approach in India.

This chapter describes how Protestant missionaries and their zealous converts located themselves *between Hindu and Muslim* through religious debates. Their heated, public exchanges concerned the veracity of Sanskrit, Arabic, and Persian texts, but their attempts to discredit those texts—and the Hindus and Muslims who believed in them—rarely yielded the robust harvest of converts they hoped for. More often, they offended the religious feelings of others and elicited more organized forms of resistance. Indians eventually responded to missionaries with defensive reformulations of their faiths through printed texts, opinion pieces in local newspapers, and public debates. In the process, they imagined into being new collective notions of their religious identities.[7] A proliferation of elite-led counter-movements, many adopting the organizational and rhetorical strategies of missionaries, shaped an evolving public sphere. Opposition to missions became even more prominent when missionary preaching appeared to enjoy the backing of the colonial state. Arguably, such developments helped set the stage for the violence of the 1857 Rebellion.

By examining missionaries and their opponents, this chapter describes how Protestant missionaries unwittingly facilitated the paths of various religious groups toward modernity. This process not only gave rise to notions of a revitalized and coherent "Hinduism," but also played a role in making Jewish, Parsi, and Muslim communities more aware of their identities and more inclined to defend them publicly. In the process, missionaries became architects of a competitive economy of "religions" and of competing nationalisms.[8] They also helped fashion a new idiom of civilizational difference and confrontation.

The chapter begins by describing shifting colonial policies toward religion during the early nineteenth century—namely, the movement from a more conservative commitment to Orientalist learning (involving the study of Sanskrit, Arabic, and Persian) to one that afforded missionaries more opportunities for proselytizing activities. By means of public controversies over religion and cultural practices such as *sati* (the burning of widows on their husbands' funeral pyres), missionaries and colonial administrators came to regard religious texts as the key to understanding Indian society. The chapter then describes missionary encounters with Hindus, Jews, Parsis, and Muslims, which also hinged on contested interpretations of sacred texts. It concludes with reflections on the notion of "Protestantization" and its relevance to the changing religious economy in India.

A New Cultural Policy

Nabobs and Orientalism

The English East India Company underwent significant changes in its cultural policy during the early nineteenth century. Britain's Industrial Revolution, along with an Evangelical revival across the Atlantic, helped spark these changes. Prior to the arrival of British missionaries after 1813, a good number of Company officers aspired to lead the luxuriant lives of Indian princes. These "nabobs," as they were called (a colonial rendition of *nawab*, a native governor or prince), adopted Indian clothes, grew long mustachios, smoked hookahs, and were carried about in palanquins by their Indian servants. As many as 2,000 Company officers even converted to Islam.[9] Some acquired harems and parented children through their Indian concubines: These offspring were referred to as "half-castes," "East Indians," and eventually "Anglo-Indians." So profound was these nabobs' commitment to "going native" that historian William Dalrymple describes European ties to Indian society more in terms of the notions of cultural hybridity and fusion than the displacement of one culture by another.[10]

In addition to the nativist tendencies of nabobs, the Company had also adopted a cultural policy that strongly promoted training in Indian classical languages and texts. Under Warren Hastings, the first governor-general of India, the Company promoted an official "Orientalism" captured in the founding of the Asiatic Society of Bengal, which was dedicated to the study of India's classical heritage. Training in classical Sanskrit, Persian, and Arabic language and texts, along with vernaculars, became a requirement for the Company's civil servants. This emphasis on Oriental learning left little room for a Christianizing or westernizing agenda.[11]

During the first half of the nineteenth century, the era of hookah-smoking nabobs and Sanskrit philologists gradually gave way to a different cultural policy pursued by the Company. Britain's Industrial Revolution fostered universal beliefs in progress and civilization through technological and societal change. English Utilitarians were convinced that the changes occurring within their own society needed to be introduced in other parts of the Empire.[12] This led to a shift in colonial cultural policy from one that stressed religious and cultural non-interference to one that advocated the "civilizing mission" of the Company's Raj. The arrival of British missionaries after 1813 added a religious dimension to the new, transformative vision for Indian society, which contrasted starkly with the hands-off approach of Hastings.

The Pious Clause

A religious revival known as the Second Great Awakening reshaped the religious landscape in Britain and North America. Drawing upon Pietist impulses, this revival placed a stronger emphasis on a personal conversion experience and mission-minded activism as a response to Christ's salvation.[13] The growing strength of this revival would eventually bring significant numbers of Evangelicals into positions of influence within the English parliament and the Company's board of directors. Charles Grant, a prominent Evangelical official, criticized the Hastings policy as one that resulted in the "Indianization" of British civil servants—which in many respects was Hastings' objective. Instead of transforming Indian culture along Christian lines, Grant argued, civil servants had become defenders of Hinduism.[14] As parliament deliberated the renewal of the Company's charter, Evangelicals pressed for and secured the introduction of a "pious clause." This would hold the Company responsible for promoting the spiritual and moral uplift of the Indian people and would grant licenses to missionaries to propagate Christianity in India. After intense debate over the very purpose of the Company's rule in India, the voices of Evangelicals prevailed.[15]

Men such as William Wilberforce, Charles Grant, Henry Dundas, and William Carey effectively pressed their case for a stronger missionary effort in Asia. Carey pointed to the Bible's missionary mandate and demographic information about the numbers of Christians across the continents.[16] Claudius Buchanan (1766–1815), a champion of Orientalist learning and the Anglican chaplain at Calcutta, called for a dramatic expansion of the ecclesiastical establishment in India. This, he contended, would provide the best means for combating the superstition, barbarism, and impurity of Indian society.[17] After the renewal of the 1813 charter, licenses were granted to a wide range of missionaries—both Anglican and Dissenting (or non-Anglican)—to preach the gospel within Company-ruled territories. The Anglican CMS soon established outposts in north Indian cities and numerous Dissenting missions, including the Baptist Missionary Society, London Missionary Society, and Wesleyan Methodists, would join them in advancing the cause of the Christian gospel in India.

As they acquired greater political influence at home and a growing presence within India, Evangelical missionaries brought a new set of lenses for scrutinizing the Company's policies. They decried the manner in which officers of the Company, in the tradition of Indian kings, were managing the endowments of Hindu temples and officiating at popular religious festivals. Company officers had even presided over controversial traditions such as *sati* and the pulling of the huge Jagannath temple cart at Puri, which was said to have crushed devotees beneath its massive wheels. This official backing of Hinduism, they contended, was unbecoming of a "Protestant Government."[18]

Pious Tensions

It would be tempting to suppose that, because of their victory in connection to the pious clause and their expanded access to Indian territories, Evangelicals now enjoyed the unambiguous backing of the East India Company; and, as such, they were emboldened to launch a crusade against India's religions with unrestricted zeal.[19] What transpired, however, was more complicated. Missionaries proceeded to confront Hindu and Muslim beliefs through open-air preaching and the dissemination of printed tracts. The Company, however, never abandoned its interest in acting as the custodian and protector of Hinduism and Islam, the two dominant religions under its rule. They saw this cultural conservatism as necessary for fostering a stable climate for their trading operations, maintaining loyalty within the ranks of the military, and securing the collaboration and backing of Hindu and Muslim gentry. At times, the agendas of missionaries and colonial rulers converged: for instance, on the issue of English-medium instruction in mission-run schools.[20] But in many other instances, we can observe a consistent tension between the transformative aspirations of missionaries and the interest of the Company to conserve or protect Hinduism and Islam.

No controversy illustrates this tension more vividly than the debate over *sati*, a practice whereby a Hindu widow immolates herself on the funeral pyre of her deceased husband. The public debate over *sati* involved many stakeholders. Missionaries, Utilitarians, and Indian reformers called for its abolition, while orthodox Hindus and some Company officers called for its preservation in the name of religious non-interference.

The most significant aspect of this debate concerns the centrality of religious texts. By the early nineteenth century, both Orientalists and Evangelicals contributed to the belief that religious texts were the key to understanding how Indian society operated. The debate over *sati*, according to the historian Lata Mani, largely hinged on whether the practice was enjoined by the Hindu scriptures or not.[21] It was simply assumed that religious texts governed practically every aspect of the lives of Hindus, when in fact only certain members of the priestly caste, Brahmins, could read Sanskrit. Hindu scriptures became a central feature of the government's deliberations about *sati* and many other Hindu cultural practices. Indian reformers would also make scriptural reasoning central to their arguments for social reform.

The reformer Rammohan Roy (1772–1833), who had developed close ties to missionaries, opposed *sati* by arguing from Hindu scriptures. His pamphlets cited a wide range of texts, including the Vedas, Puranas, *Bhagavad Gita*, and legal treatises known as *Dharmashastras*. Deftly, he navigated these sources to refute the arguments of his pro-*sati* opponents. His reasoning also drew important distinctions between textual authority versus custom, literal versus figurative interpretations of texts, and the priority of scripture over religious rituals—distinctions that find striking parallels in European Protestantism, particularly in its repudiation of Roman Catholic ritualism. It was the arguments of reformers such as Rammohan that led the governor-general William Bentinck to outlaw *sati* in 1829.

Missionary Rhetoric and Indian Responses

The Serampore Trio

As Protestant missionaries engaged in public preaching, Bible translation, and tract distribution, they consolidated a way of talking about India that revolved around sacred texts.[22] According to Mani, missionaries employed scriptures "as a mode of comprehending India, as a means of asserting their textual knowledge over the 'ignorance' of indigenous people, and as proof of the spiritual degradation and fallen state of contemporary society."[23] William Carey, William Ward, and Joshua Marshman—widely known as the Serampore Trio—reflected this emphasis in their work in Bengal. Having arrived in India prior to 1813 (when the Company granted licenses to the missionaries), these men based themselves in Serampore, a town under Danish control located roughly sixteen miles to the north of Calcutta where an outpost of the Baptist Missionary Society was established (see Figure 5.1). To escape the scrutiny of the authorities, they involved themselves in secular activities such as horticulture, indigo manufacturing, and language instruction. Only later would they devote themselves more officially to the propagation of Christianity. And yet, even before receiving official status as missionaries, they preached openly in places where crowds tended to gather, such as roadsides, temples, and markets.

In one such instance, Carey described how he challenged a Brahmin devotee of Sarasvati, the goddess of learning. The Brahmin told Carey that the image of Sarasvati was God and not simply a powerless image. In response, Carey asked him on what authority he based his belief. When the Brahmin pointed to a *shastric* text known as the *vyakaran*, Carey recorded that he knew the text to be "only a grammar" and thus not authoritative. In a separate encounter, Carey similarly highlighted a Muslim's ignorance about the Qur'an. On this occasion, he

Figure 5.1 Baptist mission premises at Serampore, 1812.
Source: Photograph by Richard Young from the Carey Library Museum, Serampore College. Courtesy of Richard Young.

had visited a burial place where Muslims placed offerings on the tomb of the deceased. Once the conversation shifted to the topic of the Bible and the Qur'an, the Muslim asserted the divine origin of the Qur'an. It was at this point that Carey asked him whether he had ever seen or read the Qur'an, to which the Muslim replied, "No." Carey proceeded to quiz the Muslim about the contents of his sacred text:

> We asked him if he knew the beginning of every Chapter, for they all begin with these Words, "In the Name of God the Gracious and Merciful"—but he said no for it was written in Arabic, and no one could understand it—the Question now was then how can you obey it? And wherefore are you Mahometans?[24]

This style of interrogation reflects a Protestant tendency to elevate scripture over custom and ritual, something they carried over from their battles with "popish rituals" back in Europe. The Indian adherence to local customs, they contended, went hand in hand with subservience to a corrupt and conniving Brahmin priesthood.

In many respects, Carey and his colleagues conducted their work in a manner similar to Ziegenbalg. Like Ziegenbalg, they published numerous grammars of Indian languages, translated the Bible along with Indian scriptures, and

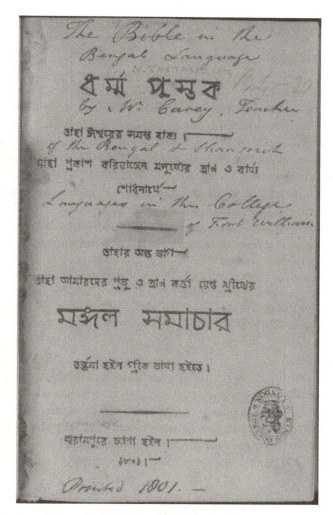

Figure 5.2 Carey's Bengali translation of the New Testament.
Source: Matteo Omied/Alamy Stock Photo.

published different kinds of literature (see Figure 5.2). They shared a similar willingness to deploy their superior understanding of Hindu or Muslim scriptures in open debates. They also shared the hope that by exposing the ignorance of Hindus and Muslims about their scriptures, they might convince audiences of the thin foundations for their beliefs and ultimately persuade them to become Christians. To a greater extent than Ziegenbalg, the Serampore Trio appear to have used textual illiteracy as a basis for their belief in the degradation of Indian society.[25]

Christian Education

In subsequent decades, more missionaries joined the ranks of those who defended the Bible against other sacred texts in the hope of converting influential classes of Indians to Christianity. Several prominent Scotsmen became champions of English-medium Christian education in India. In the tradition of the Scottish Enlightenment, they fused their Christian convictions with a commitment to rational debate. This resulted not only in a commitment to advancing Christian education in India, but also to a belief that reasoned argument could pave the way to the soul of the country. Alexander Duff (1806–78) believed that English-medium schools would attract members of India's upper castes (who hoped to qualify for government posts) and expose them to Christian teachings, and that, as these influential classes were duly Christianized, it would create an explosion within the heart of Hinduism and have a transformative impact on other social classes.

As the vision for English-medium instruction gained traction, the classical languages of Sanskrit, Arabic, and Persian were increasingly marginalized. Rammohan Roy shared the missionaries' disregard for the study of classical languages and supported education in English. It was Rammohan who brought the first class of Brahmins to the school Duff founded in Calcutta.[26] The establishment of Christian schools inspired Hindus and Muslims to establish their own schools and develop their own pedagogies for religion-based education. These schools fostered a sense of communal belonging among students and promoted reflection on what it meant to be Hindu or Muslim in the face of Western influence.[27] Decades later, educational missionaries were compelled to reevaluate their goals when it became clear that the Duff vision, rather than undermining Hinduism, had in fact fanned anti-Christian or nationalist sentiments among Hindus.

Other Scotsmen who embraced this educational model for Christian impact in India included John Muir, John Wilson, John Murray Mitchell, and William Hastie. Their schools produced a generation of Hindu students who became increasingly critical of their own beliefs and traditions. Some, such as Rammohan, became enlightened or reformist Hindus, but refused to convert to Christianity. A small number, however, did convert. Duff's educational endeavors in Calcutta, for instance, led to the conversion of Mahesh Chandra Ghosh (baptized 1832), Krishna Mohan Banerjee (1813–85), and Gopinath Nandi (baptized 1833). Two other Bengalis, Lal Behari Day (1824–92) and Michael Madhusudan Dutt (1824–73), similarly converted to Christianity within the networks aimed at shaping Indian minds with Christian knowledge. Such conversions were relatively few in number but generated disproportionate reactions. Over the span of twenty years (1832–52), government and missionary schools and colleges produced a total of only 107 converts in Bengal, but these triggered alarmist rhetoric from members of the Hindu public,[28] while converts came to be stigmatized, even within family networks.

Defending Hindu *Dharma*

What we find in subsequent decades is the emergence of a far more organized and informed response to missionary preaching by Indian adherents of other faiths. The novelty of Protestant preaching in various parts of South Asia might explain accounts such as Carey's in which listeners responded either with silence or by admitting ignorance about their scriptures. However, as missionaries established printing presses, it became possible for other kinds of religious literature, including texts produced by Hindu and Muslim apologists, to become more widely available. This, in turn, produced a public that was more informed about religious ideas, although this public consisted chiefly of literate members of upper castes. It was only a matter of time before Hindu and Muslim elites would respond more assertively to the missionary challenge, often by deploying similar strategies to denounce Christianity.

Until the 1830s in north India, Hindus do not appear to have been very vocal in their responses to missionary criticisms of their religious beliefs and practices. Their voices were largely mediated through—and perhaps distorted by—the writings of missionaries. As learned, high caste Hindus gained increased access to information and printing presses, they responded to Protestant missionaries in public debates, newspaper articles, and more theologically informed written works. Their responses not only suggested different ways of locating Christianity within a Hindu scheme of cosmic order, but also revealed different models of Hindu self-understanding. Was "Hinduism," for instance, the one true path or *dharma* among many false or inferior ones? Or was it the superstructure that explains, and in some manner accommodates, all paths within its theological framework?

The historian Geoffrey Oddie has described how Protestant missionaries contributed to emerging notions of "Hinduism" as a unified religion. Building on a substantial body of earlier scholarship, Oddie pays special attention to the writings and sermons of the Serampore missionaries, who drew upon Orientalist scholarship to confront the core tenets of "Hinduism." A significant aspect of Hindu–Christian apologetic encounters concerns the use of the Sanskrit word "*dharma*," which can describe an individual's duty as defined by caste (for instance, that of a priest or a warrior) or can refer more collectively to a righteous moral order. Early Protestant missionaries began to use the word *dharma* to refer to a religion. As Hindu pandits responded to missionary polemics, they adopted the same usage in order to contrast the Christian *dharma* with the Hindu one.

This mirroring, according to Oddie, provided the same logic by which Hindus began to appropriate the word "Hindu*ism*" to differentiate their religion from Islam or Christianity.[29] Protestant sermons tended to portray Hinduism as a unified religious system; Rammohan Roy appears to have adopted the same framework in extolling the virtues of his religion. He contrasted the "mild and liberal spirit of universal toleration, which is well-known to be a fundamental principle of Hindooism," with the open attacks on other religions by Christian missionaries.[30]

In 1839, John Muir, a Scottish civil servant with the East India Company who was both an Orientalist and an Evangelical, published an apologetic treatise entitled *Matapariksha* (Examination of Religions). In it, he drew upon his knowledge of Sanskrit and his skills in rhetoric to defend the universality of the Christian religion and to expose the shortcomings of Hindu religion. Over the next five years, his book elicited lengthy and indignant responses from several pandits from Maharashtra and Bengal; these ranged from a relativist view, which recognized Christianity as a legitimate but inferior *dharma* fit for particular peoples or regions to an absolute and thorough denunciation of Christianity as false and delusionary *dharma*.

The most irenic of the pandits went by the name of Somanatha. He placed Christians among those *mlecchas* (uncultured foreigners or persons far removed from Vedic orthodoxy) who, because of their geographical distance from Vedic knowledge and from caste traditions, were equipped with another means through which they could pursue salvation.[31] At the other end of the spectrum was the response of Nilakantha Goreh (1825–95), a Chitpavan Brahmin from Maharashtra. The Hindu god Vishnu, he maintained, had created the Christian Bible in order to inflict punishment on the wicked and keep them perpetually in ignorance of the truth. Years later, Nilakantha would be baptized a Christian, adopt the name Nehemiah, and lay the foundations for generations of theologians who attempted to adapt the Christian message to Hindu categories.[32]

Sharp opposition to Protestantism also arose among Shaiva Orthodox (or *Shaiva Siddhanta*) adherents in Tirunelveli (south India) as well as in Jaffna (a province in northern Sri Lanka). The Shaiva literati in these regions understood their relation to other religions in terms of the idea of the *mandala*, "a map whose sacred center extends outwards into peripheries bounded by a wilderness."[33] During the mid-nineteenth century, this wilderness represented a demonic realm of disorder and poverty occupied not only by Buddhists and Jains, but also by Muslims, Catholics, and Protestants.

In the Jaffna Peninsula, Tamil Saivites, led by an educated Vellalar named Arumuga Pillai (1822–79), whose honorary title was "Navalar," responded to Protestant missionaries with a large-scale revival of Shaiva Orthodoxy. This revival involved a systematic rebuttal of Protestant denunciations of the worship of Shiva. Navalar's refutations of Christianity drew upon his knowledge of the Bible, which he gained from having attended a missionary school and having assisted with the translation of the King James Bible into Tamil. In his spirited attacks on Protestants, Arumuga Navalar cited the ritual observances of the Old Testament in order to defend Shaiva temple rituals and to show how Protestants had misinterpreted their own faith. His use of the Bible to defend Shaiva practices did not alter his conviction that Christianity belonged to the realm of darkness and that Tamils needed proper instruction in Shaivism to remain in the illumined center of *dharma*.[34]

Encounters with Jews and Parsis

Members of the Jewish diaspora who settled along the west Indian coast are often overlooked in literature dealing with Protestant missionary encounters in South Asia. One case study in particular—that of the Bene Israel community of the Konkan Coast—vividly illustrates the unintended consequences of Protestant missionary activity, particularly in connection to Bible instruction. The origin of this particular population of Jews is largely unknown. For centuries, they had blended in with their cultural surroundings, functioning in almost every respect like any other Marathi-speaking *jati* (birth group) in Konkan. Until the eighteenth century, they did not self-identify as Jews, but as "Bene Israel" or *B'nai Yisrael* ("Children of Israel"). Through their contacts with the Cochin Jews during the eighteenth century, members of the Bene Israel community gradually learned the ritual and liturgy of that Jewish community. It was, however, their exposure to Protestant missionaries, according to a study by Mitch Numark, which gave them their understanding of Hebrew and the stories of the Old Testament,[35] and this linguistic and scriptural knowledge contributed to their self-identification as Jews.

As the British rose in prominence in west India, Bene Israelis migrated to Bombay city in search of new employment opportunities. They eventually settled in the "Israel quarters" of the Mandvi district of Bombay's Blacktown. It was here that the missionary John Wilson (1804–75), of the Scottish Missionary Society, founded a number of schools that were widely attended by Bene Israelis. Like Ziegenbalg and the Serampore missionaries, Wilson applied his commitment to Orientalist scholarship, his mastery of Indian languages, and his skills as an educational administrator to his efforts to impart Christian knowledge to others. His belief in the centrality of language learning in missions—both classical and vernacular—distinguishes Wilson from Duff, who championed English-medium education and knew no Indian languages. American and Anglican missionaries also established schools that educated the Bene Israel community.

For a time, missionaries and Bene Israelis appear to have developed a symbiotic relationship, with each side using the other for their own interests. Whereas missionaries hoped the knowledge of Hebrew and the Old Testament would draw Bene Israelis to recognizing Jesus as their messiah, Bene Israelis themselves became more settled and self-aware Jews through their knowledge of Hebrew. For Bene Israelis, systematic instruction in Hebrew and study of the Old Testament appear to have completed a process of discovering their heritage and "strengthened and transformed their Judaism."[36] And, upon the consolidation of their Jewish identity, Bene Israelis more openly repudiated Christianity. As Numark describes, this encounter concluded with Bene Israel Jews extricating themselves from their ties to missionaries, becoming more networked with India's Baghdadi and Cochin Jews, and rejecting Christianity.

Wilson's ambition to use knowledge and argumentation as vehicles of Christianization extended to Bombay's Parsi community. Like the Jews of India's west coast, Parsis had fled the hostility of an imperial power during the nineteenth century and had settled in places such as Surat and various parts of the Bombay presidency. Over time, they grew to be a highly prosperous, educated, and professionally advanced diaspora community. They flourished in Bombay's legal profession and as merchants. Recognizing the influence they wielded in Bombay, Wilson viewed the conversion of Parsis as carrying great strategic value.[37]

Parsi ritual practices tied to their fire temples were oriented to preserving community identity and values more than maintaining doctrinal adherence to their ancestral Zoroastrian religion and its scriptures. In his attempts to convert Parsis to Christianity, however, Wilson attacked their ancient Zoroastrian beliefs, some of which were contained in their sacred text, *Zend Avesta*. Drawing from this text and other ancient historical examples, Wilson portrayed Zoroastrianism as a violent, idolatrous, and polytheistic religion;[38] his criticisms elicited spirited rebuttals in the Parsi newspaper *Samachar* and a debate with a prominent Parsi.[39] What we find in Wilson's critiques and the Parsi rebuttals is a recurring pattern of voices talking past each other. Wilson approached Parsis with detailed scholarly arguments arising from painstaking examination of ancient texts and analysis of the European sources available to him. Much of this knowledge was largely irrelevant to the ways in which Parsis understood their identity and place within Bombay's diverse society. His criticisms of their ancestral faith offended them and prompted many to rediscover those beliefs and defend them publicly. Parsis at the time were undertaking reforms that allowed them to define their community boundaries more clearly,[40] and Wilson's apologetics added another layer to their sense of defensiveness, since now they had to protect themselves from missionary influence.

Parsis used their knowledge of the law to file a formal complaint against Wilson for his role in converting two Parsi youth to Christianity. Wilson had baptized the youth and kept them in his home to protect them from alleged threats of violence from family members. Parsis alleged that Wilson had kept the youth against their will and had used "undue and improper means . . . to convert and seduce them . . . from the faith of their ancestors and families."[41] The court, however, eventually sided with the youth when they pleaded for protection for their lives and for religious freedom. The ordeal led to yet another backlash by members of the Parsi community and an "anti-conversion memorial" signed by more than 2,000 residents of Bombay.

Wilson's apologetics appear to have radicalized members of the Parsi community who might otherwise have remained liberal, moderate, and eclectic in their ways of relating to the diverse environment of Bombay. Many resolved to withdraw their children from Wilson's schools. Both English-medium and Parsi newspapers reported extensively on Wilson's educational evangelism and the legal battles in which he became embroiled. The exchanges appear to have produced a different tone in Wilson in the years to come: He became less aggressive and more focused on sustained educational services for Bombay's youth. Like the Bene Israelis, Parsis became more self-aware as a community and Parsi scholars began to define and defend their religious beliefs in more formal ways, even reformulating Zoroastrianism as a text-based religion.[42]

Encounters with Muslims

Protestant missionary encounters with South Asia's Muslims were structurally similar to those with Hindus and Jews: Missionaries deeply committed to Orientalist knowledge were at the forefront of attempts to convert Muslims to Christianity, and they made ample use of print media, mostly pamphlets and books, to criticize Muslim beliefs. The missionaries shared a common strategy of asserting the superiority of the Bible over the Qur'an and an interest in exposing the ignorance of most Muslims about their own sacred book. Exchanges between Muslims and missionaries tapped into a classical tradition of debate in medieval Islam known as *munazara*; the staging of *munazaras* resembled the argumentative tradition described by Amartya Sen. In many respects, Protestant missionary activity among South Asian Muslims would reinvigorate and reshape this classical tradition.

One of the earliest missionaries to Muslims, Henry Martyn (1781–1812), served as a chaplain for the British army in the north Indian cities of Dinapore and Kanpur. He is responsible for translating the Bible into Urdu, Persian, and Arabic, three languages central to Islamic learning and religious practice. In

1807, he established a school in Patna, which enrolled many Muslim students. He eventually abandoned the school when rumors of students being converted to Christianity evoked opposition from families.[43] Martyn was less successful as a bazaar preacher than as a producer and translator of texts. Whether because of his own temperament or because of the constraints of his military chaplaincy, he rarely succeeded in drawing learned Muslims into debate with him about religious matters. His chief accomplishments, according to the historian Avril Powell, lay in his translations of the Bible and his publication of a number of controversial tracts (posthumously published in 1824) refuting Muslim claims about the Qur'an and the prophethood of Muhammad. Martyn's emphasis on evidence and proof, Powell notes, indicates the fusion of his Evangelical convictions with rationalism.[44] These publications eventually landed in the hands of members of the *ulama* (scholars who interpreted the Qur'an) and would open channels for formal *munazaras* between Christians and Muslims in the following decades.

One of the ironies of Martyn's early career is his own lack of knowledge about Islam, despite his commitment to working among Muslims. Perhaps even more than the Serampore missionaries, he relied extensively on those who assisted him with his translations of the Bible. These Muslim *munshis* (language teachers or clerks) placed themselves at considerable risk in assisting Europeans with Bible translation, as they could easily be branded as heretics and be shunned by Muslim society.[45] A similar fate awaited them if they converted to Christianity. One such convert, an Arab man named Nathaniel Sabat (or Jawad ibn Sabat, 1774–1827), had aided missionaries at Calcutta and Martyn at Patna with Bible translation. For a time, missionaries held great hopes in employing Sabat—as an insider to elite Muslim society (the *ashraf* class), he would be more effective than the *farangis* (foreigners), who struggled to draw audiences among Muslims. As a Christian, Sabat wrote several evangelistic tracts aimed at converting Muslims to Christ. Martyn, however, would eventually complain about Sabat's erratic temperament, even lamenting in his journal that he had become "the keeper of a lunatic."[46]

The volatile Sabat eventually renounced Christianity and published a refutation of Christianity in Arabic entitled *Sabatean Proofs of the Truth of Islamism and the Falsehood of Christianity*. The text is arguably the first formal reply of an Indian Muslim to missionaries. Years later, the *ulama* at Lucknow would refer to this work in their response to another of Martyn's converts, Abdul Masih. In Agra, Abdul Masih preached the divinity of Christ among prominent Muslim scholars. His evangelistic efforts were met with initial openness but eventual resistance. His conversion raised anxieties among Muslims that others would follow his example; some even feared that his preaching signified a more pervasive demise of Islam under British rule.[47]

As missionaries attacked Muslim belief and practice, Muslims called for religious reform and revival. During the 1820s, large crowds of Muslims in north Indian cities attended meetings of a reform movement known as the *Tariqah-i-Muhammadiyah*, which originated among the Indo-Afghan warrior networks of northern India. Muhammadiyas were followers of Syed Ahmad Barelvi (1786–1831). There is little evidence that Syed Ahmad's movement formulated its vision in response to Protestant missionaries, and yet key aspects of its theology and practice mirrored the Protestant emphasis on a sacred book, the rejection of ritual, missionary organization, and the dissemination of reformist teachings through pamphlets in Urdu (the language spoken by most north Indian Muslims).[48] Muslim reformers also employed technologies of print media, introduced by Christian missionaries, to formulate and defend their faith.[49]

Amid the transition from Mughal to British rule, Syed Ahmad called on Muslims to purify their faith by returning to the original teachings of the Qur'an. Reformers opposed any and all religious innovations (*bidat*), usually ritual observances derived from their Indian environment, including worship before the tombs of Sufi saints, genuflections extended to their religious teachers, and any practice deemed idolatrous (*shirk*).[50]

In the years preceding the outbreak of the Great Rebellion of 1857, Christian attacks on Islam contributed to rising Muslim anxiety about the demise of their religion under British rule.[51] During the 1840s and 1850s, exchanges between Muslims and Protestant missionaries intensified. A "Muhammadan Controversy" involving a German missionary, Karl Gottlieb Pfander (1803–65), related to an exchange of published statements and, in 1854, a formal debate at Agra. The different sides of this debate disputed the relative merits of the Bible and Qur'an along with Jesus and the Prophet Muhammad. In contrast to earlier critiques of Islam by missionaries, Pfander's were more sophisticated due to his deeper reading of Muslim sources and his knowledge of Arabic. During the 1820s, prior to his work in India, he had received special instruction in Islam and Arabic at Basel missionary seminary. He also had worked for ten years among Muslims and Armenians in Georgia. In addition, he had undertaken several journeys to Persia, where he had learned Persian and engaged in controversial religious exchanges with learned Muslims. By the time of his most heated exchanges with Muslims in Agra, new approaches to reading the Bible were emerging in Europe that called traditional approaches into question. As a result, Pfander was more knowledgeable about Islam than missionaries such as Henry Martyn, but he was less equipped to defend the Bible against those in India who may have kept abreast of the new trends in biblical interpretation.[52]

In 1839, the Basel mission sent Pfander to India. He eventually settled in Agra, which was a center of Muslim learning and culture. He produced Urdu versions of his books and published them with the Agra Mission Press. These books presented familiar Christian critiques of Islam concerning the prophethood of Muhammad and the validity of the Qur'an, while offering a defense of the doctrine of the Trinity. For decades, Muslims had appeared to remain silent in the face of missionary bazaar preaching and pamphleteering critical of their religion. The dissemination of Pfander's work—perhaps because of its higher degree of sophistication—appears to have been a tipping point that led to more organized deliberation and rebuttals. Their circulation in Agra evoked unusually intense opposition in the form of letters, pamphlets, and books that countered his claims. A Muslim named Ali Hasan, who worked in the appeals court in Agra, produced an 800-page volume (*Book of Questions*) that sought to refute all of Pfander's arguments.[53]

Among the most significant critics of Pfander was a high-born and learned Muslim by the name of Maulana Rahmat Allah Kairanawi (1818–91), who had served as a *munshi* for a maharaja in Delhi. Later in his life he established his own *madrasa* where he devoted himself to teaching the Qur'an. In response to Pfander, Rahmat Allah produced a number of books of his own that critiqued various aspects of Christianity; he published these in Persian, but also in Urdu, in order to reach the Muslim masses. He and his close colleagues were guided by the sense that missionaries had gained undue access to ordinary Muslims through their publicity and knowledge of Urdu. His goal was not to win arguments within a small coterie of intellectuals, but to boost the morale of a wider audience of Muslims who had been subject to a steady stream of missionary rhetoric directed against Islam. Rahmat Allah's work focused on two themes: refuting the doctrine of the Trinity; and demonstrating that the Bible had been altered over time and therefore was not divinely inspired. Rahmat Allah drew from the Athanasian Creed, which formulated the doctrine of the Trinity for Christians, in order to expose its contradictions; he also drew from European scholarship that questioned the chronology of the Bible.[54]

Eventually, Rahmat Allah concluded that the printed word was not enough to deal a blow to Pfander's arguments: He had to debate publicly with Pfander. The much publicized two-day event of 1854 drew an audience consisting of many sections of Agra's population. By some estimates, between 200 and 600 people attended. Rahmat Allah considered the event to be a huge success for the cause of Islam. Pfander was disappointed by the results, according to Powell; he appears to have been ill equipped to respond to ideas Muslims had gained from recent works in biblical criticism.[55]

The 1857 Rebellion and Its Aftermath

The religious controversies that rocked Agra and Delhi contributed to the turbulent cultural climate that preceded the 1857 Rebellion. The rebellion erupted in Meerut and moved with great speed and violence to Delhi, Kanpur, Lucknow, and Gwalior. The scale and intensity of this uprising against East India Company rule was surpassed only by the severity of colonial suppression. Delhi, a city with a population of 250,000, was nearly empty after the overwhelming counterassault of British troops. After the suppression of the rebellion, Queen Victoria issued a royal proclamation in 1858 in which she pledged the commitment of the British crown—which was now to replace the banned East India Company—to the strict policy of religious neutrality. This emphasis reveals the extent to which religious tampering and missionary proselytizing had become a dominant explanation for the rebellion.

The Muslim reformer Sir Syed Ahmed Khan (1817–98) had served as a *sheristadar* (high-ranking clerk) at Agra and later as a *munshi*. His loyalty to the British was exhibited in his active role in saving British lives during the rebellion. To his fellow Muslims, he explicitly advocated loyalty to the British and denounced jihad as a Muslim response to colonial rule. Such loyalty, however, did not include a favorable impression of missionary activity. His explanation of the causes of the rebellion singled out the public nature of missionary polemics and their backing by the government:

> The Missionaries introduced a new system of preaching. They took to printing and circulating controversial tracts, in the shape of questions and answers. Men of a different faith were spoken of in those in a most offensive and irritating way. In Hindustan these things have always been managed very differently. Every man in this country, preaches and explains his views in his own Mosque, or his own house. If any one wishes to listen to him, he can go to the Mosque, or house, and hear what he has to say. But the Missionaries' plan was exactly the opposite. They used to attend places of public resort, markets for instance, and fairs where men of different creeds were collected together, and used to begin preaching there. It was only from fear of authorities that no one bids them off about their business. In some districts, Missionaries were actually attended by Policemen from the station. And then the Missionaries did not confine themselves to explaining the doctrines of their own books. In violent and unmeasured language they attacked the followers and holy places of other creeds.[56]

Syed Ahmed Khan proceeded to describe how the Christian instruction in public schools had also offended the sentiments of Indian families. Parents sent their children to English-medium schools in order to qualify them for employment in government services, but they often received Christian instruction against their wishes.

In response to missionary activities, elite Hindus and Muslims eventually resorted to reasoned responses like that of Rahmat Allah.[57] As prominent as this model may have been among the Sunni Muslim *ashraf* class, other forms of religiosity prevailed at the grassroots level. Bombay's working classes, as the historian Nile Green has shown, were not drawn to rational systems of belief based on sacred texts; they were much more anchored in "familiar customary religious products based on miracles, rituals, and the intercession of charismatic saviours."[58] These characteristics of populist Islam were not unique to industrializing cities such as Bombay, but were also common among the rural peasantry.

Still, print media could provide a bridge between populist and "rational" defenses of Islam in the face of missionary arguments. In late nineteenth-century Bengal, another charismatic Muslim, Munshi Mohammad Meherullah (1861–1907), countered missionary propaganda in the Jessore district of eastern Bengal while calling for the reform of Islam. Meherullah resented the manner in which Evangelical missionaries were luring poor Muslims to their religion through popular preaching and humanitarian aid. His writings and powerful oratory crossed class lines. To reach illiterate Muslims, he employed in his pamphlets and speeches language that was "idiomatic, rustic, playful, indebted to genres like poems, folk songs, folk tales and parables, and in general easy to memorize and recite."[59] His written texts were read aloud. This capacity of print media to cultivate a "space of imagined belonging" among illiterate, rural Bengalis is evident in other contexts where reformist pamphlets were mediated to the masses through literate teachers.[60]

The Scotsman Versus the Bengali

One might imagine that, in the aftermath of the 1857 Rebellion, missionaries would have toned down their rhetoric and embraced a more irenic style. They did eventually move away from their caustic methods, but this transition came in phases. A development in late nineteenth-century Calcutta, a key center of rising Indian nationalism, illustrates how missionary denunciations of Hinduism continued to trigger spirited responses. A particular encounter between a Scottish Christian educator and a renowned Bengali novelist presents far more than an object lesson in missionary rhetoric. It illustrates the close relationship between Protestant influence on the one hand and elite-driven nationalism on the other. This relationship is not unique to India—it is observable in the Arab world at roughly the same time, as well as in China in the decades surrounding the Boxer Rebellion (1899–1901).[61] Within many world contexts, local elites responded to Protestant preaching and institutions with strident (if not militant) opposition to foreign influence and with aspirations for self-rule.

In Calcutta, these dynamics became racialized, especially in the context of the Ilbert Bill controversy. The Ilbert Bill was a measure that allowed Indian magistrates to preside over Europeans accused of crimes. British residents launched strident opposition to the bill, which won them a compromise in 1884: Europeans would be guaranteed a jury that was at least half European. The following year, the Indian National Congress party was founded. It became the main platform for the articulation of Indian aspirations and grievances against British rule.

It was in this racialized and increasingly political climate that another religious exchange ignited conflict and controversy, this time in the city of Calcutta. Lying at the heart of this exchange was the question of whether European scholars were better positioned to understand Hinduism than Indians who practiced the religion in their daily lives. William Hastie, the principal of the General Assembly's Institution of the Church of Scotland, had committed himself (like earlier Scotsmen such as Duff and Wilson) to shaping the minds of upper caste members of Calcutta's *bhadralok* (respectable or middle-class people). Many of them were Hindus who had received a Western education at colleges or schools established by Europeans. By influencing this class of Hindus, Hastie hoped that he could encourage them to take the lead in steering others away from popular practices associated with the veneration of images and figures of Hindu deities.

In 1882, Hastie's campaign against "Hindu idolatry" drew him into a heated exchange of letters with a prominent Bengali novelist. What triggered the controversy was a funeral ceremony held at the famous Shobhabazar Rajbari in Calcutta. In attendance were a large number of educated Hindus, members of the Kulin Brahmin caste, who were considered to be the highest of the Bengali Brahmins. Because Hastie viewed them as cultural leaders, he was outraged to learn that, in keeping with the observances of *shraddha* (a ritual offering for the deceased), these men had venerated a figure of the Hindu god Krishna (worshiped as Gopinath, lord of the milkmaids). Some of the Hindus who had participated were known for having taken a public stand against devotion to images and figures of deities. Because of this, Hastie believed that their devotion to Hindu deities was not only insincere but also set a bad example to the less enlightened Hindus in attendance. Incensed by their duplicity, Hastie decided to publish a series of lengthy letters in the Calcutta-based newspaper *The Statesman*.[62]

At first, Hastie attempted to strike an empathetic tone, conveying sympathy for the deceased and awareness that the family would want to honor him with this hugely elaborate ceremony. But after these initial courtesies, his letters became more polemical. Hastie's principal grievance concerned idol worship, particularly among less "enlightened" Indians, who venerated images of various gods and goddesses at shrines or temples. Most Indians who worshiped idols, he contended, came from communities that were largely ignorant of the more sublime aspects of Hinduism, contained in Sanskrit texts. Indeed, knowledge of Sanskrit and Sanskrit literature, Hastie observed, was far more advanced in Europe and America than it was in India.[63] Repeatedly, Hastie asserted the intellectual preeminence of European scholars of Hinduism on account of their superior grasp of Sanskrit.

As he continued to expound his understanding of Hinduism, Hastie's tone became more triumphalist. His critiques of particular Hindu deities descended into alliterative quips amounting to ridicule: He referred to the image of Krishna as "dead as a door nail . . . like old Marley" (as if the *Statesman*'s readers would appreciate the reference to Dickens), and denounced the "Shiva temple that makes one shudder," or the "merry music and mincing movements" of Krishna devotees. The worship of gods and goddesses, he contended, was contributing to Indian moral degeneracy. He devoted an entire letter to refuting the idea, put forward by Hindu apologists, that the worship of idols was necessary for "less cultivated minds" who were unable to contemplate a formless divinity.

Hastie's letters in the *Statesman* triggered a series of responses by Bankim Chandra Chatterjee, writing under the pseudonym "Ram Chandra." To fully appreciate Bankim's response, some facts about his own religious journey are helpful. For much of his adult life, Bankim was employed in the colonial bureaucracy as a deputy magistrate. His early writings convey a recurring theme of servile roles for Indian bureaucrats and their racial humiliation at the hands of Englishmen.[64] Like other members of Calcutta's *bhadrolok*, he had received a Western education. He was drawn to European skepticism and utilitarianism and used these lenses to reexamine his family's religious tradition. Bankim became increasingly critical of the culture and religion of his Brahmin parents: He no longer observed the rituals or dietary restrictions of his caste. Ten years prior to reading Hastie's letters, he had reached the conclusion that "Hindu philosophy in its entirety was a great mass of errors."[65]

By the time Bankim responded to Hastie's letters, however, his outlook had changed. No longer a harsh critic of Hindu thought, he emerged as a highly informed defender. Did Hastie's letters spark this change? In his replies to Hastie, Bankim distinguished the "husk" or non-essential, surface characteristics of Hinduism—which tended to preoccupy European scholarly interest—from the kernel of Hinduism, found in vernacular traditions. Bankim challenged Hastie to learn about Hindu beliefs by studying the original scriptures under Hindus who actually believed in them, not by reading European translations or commentaries, since Hindu believers would bring to those texts a vernacular sensitivity needed for their proper interpretation.[66] Bankim sharply criticized the knowledge that missionaries and other European Orientalists had acquired about India and Hinduism. He drew attention to the "vast mass of [traditional] and unwritten knowledge of India," captured in oral, vernacular traditions that were wholly inaccessible to Europeans and accounted for their warped understanding of the Hindu religion.[67]

This exchange between Hastie and Bankim is revealing on two counts. First, as historian Tapan Raychaudhuri observed, Bankim's response to Hastie contains his first "uncompromising avowal of faith in Hinduism."[68] It was almost as though Hastie had converted him to his own religion. Bankim's radicalization, however, followed a longer trajectory and would lead him to write the famous patriotic hymn "Vande Mataram" and become a chief architect of a more aggressive Hindu nationalism. The manner in which Bankim dug in his heels and defended what he had previously questioned—and that, too, through the medium of print—reveals a larger cultural process of Hindu identity formation that arguably was shaped by Protestant missionary activity. Second, it should be noted that Bankim responded to Hastie in very Protestant ways. His distinction between the kernel and the husk of Hinduism resembles Protestant—if not Pietist—distinctions between religious externalities and rituals versus interior or "heartfelt" belief in the gospel; and his emphasis on vernacular knowledge clearly resonates with the Evangelical emphasis on vernacular translations of the Bible and the lived experience of faith.[69] While it did not convert Bankim, Hastie's incendiary rhetoric appears to have succeeded in further consolidating his identity as a Hindu. This, as we have seen, is a recurring pattern in the encounters between missionaries and adherents of other faiths.

Into the twentieth century, Protestants with a more liberal theological orientation attempted to change the tone and content of Christian approaches to Indian religions. Scholars associated with the Indian YMCA during the early twentieth century generated this new perspective. From 1910 to 1940, scholars such as J. N. Farquhar, Kenneth Saunders, and H. A. Walter produced works on Hinduism and Buddhism that treated Indian religions far more sympathetically than did missionaries of the William Hastie variety. Employing scholars affiliated with the YMCA of India, Farquhar edited three series of books: The first, *The Religious Quest of India* (1915), presented books dealing with the great religions of Hinduism, Buddhism, Jainism, Zoroastrianism, and Islam. The second, *The Religious Life of India*, moved away from the textual emphasis of the first series and focused more on popular or folk religious practices. The final series, *The Heritage of India*, was less religious in its emphasis and drew attention to representative works of literature, philosophy, music, and art.[70]

This "Y Orientalism," according to historian Harald Fischer-Tiné, distinguished itself by moving beyond an emphasis on sacred texts to an examination of the lived practices of Indians at the grassroots level. An overarching aim of "Y Orientalists" was to communicate a more sympathetic attitude toward Indian religions. However, despite these aims, the authors of "Y Orientalism"—notably

J. N. Farquhar—essentially retained a missionary framework for their writings that was less than sympathetic to local religions. Farquhar's approach, which came to be known as "fulfillment theology," essentially viewed Hinduism and Buddhism as moving along an evolutionary trajectory. The ultimate end of this trajectory was a religion's fulfillment in Christianity, the apex religion. Leading missionary figures such as the American John R. Mott were deeply committed to the evangelization of India and did not share Farquhar's fulfillment perspective. Still, Mott was a great patron of the series and championed the use of these books for the training of missionaries.[71]

Protestantization?

Early Protestant activities in India carried unintended long-term consequences. Instead of dismantling the religious traditions they attacked in public, missionaries' polemics made other traditions stronger. This should come as no surprise. The idea that attacking the beliefs of others in public can make people more stridently committed to those beliefs is something we can observe in the polarized politics of many parts of the world. Relentless public criticism of the beliefs of others mobilizes opposition funding, counter-propaganda, and new patrons of opposing agendas. One question posed in this chapter is whether such responses, as unintended as they were, can be viewed as an aspect of Protestantism's universal history. Could it not be possible that Protestantism performed in India a type of cultural work that it had performed in Europe so well—that is, sparking "awakenings" within other traditions, which evolved into new degrees of sectarian difference, new forms of identity assertion, and new aspirations for nationhood?

Some scholars have described such organized reformulations of religious identity as instances of "Protestantization." Drawing heavily upon the work of the German sociologist Max Weber, they are not referring to an actual conversion to Protestantism, but rather to the transformation of a religious tradition along the rhetorical or conceptual lines of European Protestantism. This often involved an attempt to present one's religion as a more rational, organized set of doctrines, with a singular message of salvation, anchored in a sacred text.[72] This reformulation marginalized popular, customary, or devotional practices of illiterate people while privileging the ideas espoused by educated elites (as representatives of a "high tradition") who were well versed in their sacred texts.[73] Both Scottish missionaries and their Indian respondents participated in what was essentially a Protestant project of separating the husk from the kernel in religion. They manicured India's religions to purge them of weeds and unruly bushes so that they could resemble an idealized, European notion of what religions should be.[74]

When Muslim scholars in Bombay or Lucknow, for instance, defended Islam according to the categories and media presented by Protestants, they may be said to have been Protestantized, even in their opposition to Christianity.[75] Similarly, when Jews, Hindus, or Parsis employed the medium of print to defend their sacred texts (as Protestants did the Bible), they may be said to have adopted the persona of a "book religion" as distinct from one that is primarily lived out through local customary practices.

Another aspect of Protestantization concerns the role of choice. In contrast to those who identified with a religious tradition by virtue of having been born into it and having absorbed its norms, a Protestantized Muslim or Hindu possessed a greater sense of agency, not only in choosing his or her religion but also in refashioning it and living up to its ideals. Having entered a marketplace of religions shaped largely by Protestant missionary propaganda, such individuals represented a new role for the laity in appropriating a collective identity and defending it in public.[76]

The Protestantization thesis provides a useful lens for appreciating the wider impact of missionaries in South Asia, even when they were unsuccessful in making converts. It compels us to consider whether transformations of other religious traditions, even public opposition to Christianity, may be viewed as belonging to a universal history of Protestantism. Once we recognize some expressions of a religion as manifesting Protestantization, we are better positioned to distinguish those expressions from customary or hybrid practices that are not Protestantized. In drawing such distinctions, we are perhaps less likely to make generalizations about "other religions," especially generalizations arising from a distinctly Christian understanding of what constitutes a religion (organized beliefs, a doctrine of salvation, and a sacred text), a tendency noted by the anthropologist Talal Asad.[77]

The notion of Protestantization, however, comes at a price. What does it really mean to say that a particular religious movement bears the marks of Protestant influence? By identifying the structural resemblance of an organized religion to Protestantism, we may be tempted to portray that tradition as engaged in a form of mimicry of the colonial other and as lacking any real anchor in local traditions. During the nineteenth century, this is how some Hindu nationalists reacted to the Brahmo Samaj, the Hindu reform movement that sought to purge Hinduism of its superstitions, polytheism, and backward social practices.[78] The Muslim reformist *Tariqah-i-Muhammadiyah* preached a return to a purer form of Islam grounded in the Qur'an. Reformist preachers and their angry critics illustrate the rift between the reformed version of a religion and adherents of the non-reformed, customary, or orthodox varieties. This chapter, however, makes no claim that one is authentic and the other derivative; rather, they all belong to an evolving socioreligious environment that was profoundly impacted by Protestant missionary activity, albeit in ways that missionaries had not intended.

Toward the end of the nineteenth century, educational missionaries in India pondered why a century of missions had not yielded greater numbers of converts. Some lamented that targeting India's elites had produced just the opposite effect from what men such as Alexander Duff had intended. Principals of Christian colleges observed rising nationalist sentiments among upper caste Hindu graduates along with perspectives that were quite critical of Christianity. For some missionaries, the silver lining in such developments was that they could attribute the "reformation" of Hinduism to Protestant influence; they even suggested that this new, Christianized Hinduism was in fact the "explosion" envisioned by Duff. The Wesleyan Methodist missionary to south India W. H. Findlay summed it up aptly: Christian education had awakened Hindus from a "coma" of superstition, devotion to idols, and ceremonialism. "Our triumph," he claimed, "is that the Hindus who have, at last, begun to value religion, have a high, Christian ideal of what a religion should be."[79]

Where missionaries did not succeed in spreading Christianity in India, they did succeed in spreading a Christian understanding of religion. Nineteenth-century missionaries approached Hindus, Muslims, Parsis, Jews, and Buddhists of the subcontinent as confessional others; that is, as bearers of religious beliefs, grounded in sacred texts, who needed to be challenged and changed. Scots such as Wilson grouped the peoples they encountered in Bombay into religious systems, privileging doctrines and texts over popular practices.[80] As missionaries compiled knowledge about "other religions" and confronted them with rational arguments, non-Christians often appropriated the very identities that came under attack.

Conclusion

This arena of competing religions and civilizations became a powerful tool of missionaries for organizing the world and making it navigable for evangelism.[81] But it was only a matter of time before these imagined identities turned against them. Into the twentieth century, the emergence of Muslim, Hindu, and Buddhist nationalisms in South Asia nurtured anti-Christian sentiments among literate elites. In the postcolonial era, the same nationalisms are fanning anti-Christian violence. Today, South Asian Christians find themselves marginalized and victimized by the same religious nationalisms their European predecessors helped bring into being.

The encounters described in this chapter never resulted in large numbers of conversions—winning an argument or making people feel ignorant rarely made anyone a Christian. Neither was it the case, as William Hastie believed, that elites were the gatekeepers of the masses and that, by converting the elite class in

Christian schools, the message would trickle down to the rest. No doubt, there were some converts who, through their exposure to Christian knowledge, were inspired to become Christian: for instance, Krishna Pal, Nehemiah Goreh, Abdul Masih, Lal Behari Day, and Pandita Ramabai. These converts came from India's educated upper castes and would eventually wield considerable influence in an evolving public sphere.[82] Brahmin converts (the topic of Chapter 6), however, were few and far between.

Valuable lessons can be gleaned from the history of Protestantism within both European and South Asian contexts. In Europe, the Protestant Reformation gave rise to multiple confessional identities—for example, Lutherans, Calvinists, and Anglicans—who occupied territorial domains. In India, Protestant propaganda drew members of other faiths into the rhetorical playing field of missionaries. In their efforts to rebut missionary claims, they produced spirited defenses of Hindu, Buddhist, or Muslim beliefs and more bounded notions of their religious identities. These identities, in turn, would inspire claims to territory or independent statehood voiced through Hindu, Buddhist, or Muslim nationalism.

Dividing the world according to coherent "religions" de-historicizes difference and presumes uniformity where it does not exist. The political scientist Samuel Huntington popularized the notion of "clashing civilizations" as a way of understanding the geopolitical divisions of the post-Cold War world. Centuries before Huntington, missionaries divided the world in a similar manner in order to formulate appropriate missionary strategies.

Viewing today's world as consisting of incompatible Christian, Hindu, Muslim, or Buddhist nations encourages Christians to align themselves with what they presume to be a Judeo-Christian geopolitical domain. People of faith then seek the protective cover of this domain and regard those living beyond its borders as belonging to one "mission field" or another. This perspective fails to appreciate the transcultural, multi-ethnic, and migratory nature of Christianity, and the fact that there are now many centers of Christian presence in the world.[83] Paradigms of confrontation also diminish, as Andrew Walls has noted, "a certain vulnerability, a fragility, at the heart of Christianity," which is the vulnerability of the cross. This vulnerability, according to Walls, is intimately linked to the fact that there is no single "Christian civilization" or "Christian culture." Indeed, to assert one is to undermine the cause of the gospel.[84] Since the days of Duff and Hastie, Christians have been compelled to set aside the confrontational paradigms of the nineteenth century in order to more effectively convey their message in a pluralistic world.

6
Upper Caste Converts to Protestantism

In his inaugural lecture of April 1861, the Oxford Sanskritist Monier Monier-Williams stressed the importance of the study of Sanskrit to missionary work in India. As the "sacred and learned language of India," Sanskrit, he claimed, was not only the source of "all the spoken dialects of India," but was also the "only safe guide to the intricacies and contradictions of Hinduism, the one bond of sympathy, which, like an electric chain, connects Hindus of opposite characters in every district of India."[1] Regardless of the small numbers of people in India—usually members of high castes—who could actually read or understand Sanskrit, Monier-Williams was convinced that India's "national character is cast in a Sanskrit mold" and that a grasp of Sanskrit language and literature was the "one medium of approach to the hearts of the Hindus."[2]

For Monier-Williams, "Sanskrit" did not simply refer to the classical language, which recorded the sacred Vedas and the epic literature of ancient India; it was far more generative in its scope and meaning. In keeping with earlier Orientalist scholarship, Monier-Williams regarded Sanskrit as designating a race of people, their dialects, and their cultural institutions.[3] He devoted a significant portion of his lecture to ethnographic descriptions of the Sanskritized upper castes and their fundamental difference from low caste and untouchable communities, whom he labeled "Semi-Hindus" and "Non-Hindus" respectively.[4]

Monier-Williams observed that only a small minority of Christian converts "belong to the Hindu race properly so called." His 1861 address drew attention to the fact that hardly 3,000 of the 112,000 converts who had been made in the whole of India belonged to the "true Sanskritic race," and that the vast majority of converts had come from south India.[5] Only by learning Sanskrit, he maintained, could missionaries hope to gain access to the heart and soul of the Indian nation.

Buried in Monier-Williams's assertions are weighty assumptions about what constitutes the national culture of India and the privileging of Sanskrit (which happened to be his area of expertise). What about the importance of understanding Persian or Arabic? Or the masses of people whose lives were shaped by multiple traditions? Monier-Williams is but one example of how missionary knowledge helped consolidate certain understandings of South Asian societies.[6] However we might respond to Monier-Williams's categories or ambitions, it is difficult to deny their enduring relevance to debates about conversion in India—not only during the colonial period, but also in today's climate of Hindu nationalism (or *Hindutva*). The majority of Christians in present-day India come from Dalit (formerly known as "untouchable") and tribal communities that are considered to be the furthest removed from Sanskritic influence, although they are subject in varying degrees to processes of Sanskritization (acculturation to the beliefs and practices of Hindu upper castes). Their stories are discussed in the following chapters.

What is often overlooked in histories of Indian Christianity is that Brahmins and members of other upper castes also converted to Christianity. The earlier discussion of the Syrian Christians of Kerala provides one example of this. Stories of Brahmin conversion to Protestantism, although small in number, reveal conflicts between converts, their families, and the social structures of their day. Upper caste Christian converts occupy a unique social location between Hindu and Muslim high traditions and foreign missionary networks. Their conversion narratives are worth examining because they are less susceptible to the "rice conversion" critique so often assigned to Dalit converts. This allows us to shine a spotlight on factors other than material needs that influenced their religious conversions. Because of their literacy and knowledge of multiple religious systems, upper caste converts also recorded their passages from one religious tradition to another and the motivations that guided them.

Instances of high caste conversion were infrequent, but they carried weighty implications because of their coverage in local print media and transnational missionary publications. By converting to another religion, members of high castes risked losing their reputation, social status, and livelihood.[7] At the same time, they could make a huge impact in the evolving Indian public sphere by discussing their experiences and theology in their writing and through activism and spirited exchanges with their opponents. In many instances, books written about such converts by family members, missionaries, or other admirers amounted to hagiographies. Adulation of these so-called "trophies of grace," however, paid little attention to the intensity of their struggles as persons caught between different worlds.[8]

To illustrate the identity crises faced by converts, specifically their anxieties of being in between, this chapter presents three distinct but related discussions of high caste conversion. The first addresses more theoretical questions. Conversion is not a moment when one's consciousness is colonized by foreigners; nor is it a form of "selling out" to missionaries in order to access their resources. Instead, conversion yields a distinct form of consciousness that complicates both missionary and nationalist agendas. Drawing upon the work of the feminist historian Deepra Dandekar, this section describes a vernacular Christian tradition that arose in Maharashtra during the nineteenth century. By printing and disseminating biographies and other texts, a Brahmin Christian community brought visibility to high caste converts and their stories. Among those who rose in prominence were luminaries such as Baba Padmanji, Nehemiah Goreh, Narayan Vaman Tilak, and Pandita Ramabai.

The heart of this chapter, its second section, concerns the spiritual journey of the high caste Hindu convert Pandita Ramabai. Her life reveals a tension between her inner conscience and structures of power that sought to mold her in their own images. Throughout her life, Ramabai navigated between starkly contrasting audiences: orthodox and reformist Hindus, Anglicans, American Pentecostals, and fellow Indian Christians. Male converts who were contemporaries either befriended her or criticized her conversion; in key ways, they carved out spaces that Ramabai would refashion with her own convictions as a learned female convert. Her ability to retain a sense of identity and mission amidst the pressure applied from all sides helps us appreciate her impact across many domains.[9]

The chapter concludes by comparing the Indian Christian consciousness that arose in Maharashtra with that of Madras during the early twentieth century. In contrast to the Marathi vernacular Christianity described in Dandekar's work, the public consciousness arising in Madras was voiced by Christian elites, primarily through English-medium newspapers, against the backdrop of the politics of the day—Gandhian nationalism, non-Brahminism, and the rise of Dalit movements across south India. By examining high caste conversion in these lights, the chapter addresses some of the questions raised by Monier-Williams in his Oxford address. There was indeed an upper caste response to Protestant Christianity that produced a public discourse of a very high order, channeled through Christian print media. The effervescence of this moment, however, appears to have been short-lived. By looking at these productions in their heyday, we catch glimpses of the middle space Christian converts occupied between European Christianity on the one hand and India's Hindu and Muslim traditions on the other.

Conversion, Colonization, and Protest

Religious conversion is a complex process combining elements of the old and the new; it channels elements of the original cultural matrix of converts into a new orientation. Moreover, converts are not passive recipients of a foreign religion; they are active agents in embracing the new religion and interpreting it through their own cultural lenses. Despite an abundance of evidence that supports such findings, there remains a tendency to regard conversion crudely as a form of conquest or colonization. This informs the rhetoric of *Hindutva* activists, who portray conversion as an act of violence, a siege on the autonomous consciousness of the person (or group) being converted.[10] Within societies under British rule, it is similarly tempting to regard Christian conversion as an act of capitulating under duress to the colonizer's interests and worldview.

The anthropologist Nathaniel Roberts points out the deficiencies of this perspective. "Portrayals of conversion as a form of conquest," he argues, "are rooted ultimately in a political-moral universe in which autonomy is a paramount value."[11] This belief in an autonomous subject underlies secular, liberal societies of the West and academic disciplines such as anthropology. Within these frameworks, religious belief is understood as belonging to an interior, sovereign, and presumably authentic domain of an individual and his or her original culture. Seen from a perspective that treats one's original religion as a stable, authentic default setting, a change in one's religion is inherently inauthentic and guided by problematic motives. Since all religions are equally subjective, the decision to move from one to another must relate in some way to motives that are *not* religious. The secular, liberal orientation does not view religion as capable of making valid claims about a reality beyond that of subjective experience and a relativist notion of "culture." Such claims are reserved for science. The relegation of religion to this interior domain is itself a political act arising from the project of European liberalism. Building on arguments by Talal Asad, Roberts contends that most converts do not approach religion in this manner.[12] Based on his fieldwork among slum dwellers in Chennai and Mumbai, he observes that people convert because they believe that their adopted faith is universally true. The tools that scholars employ to understand the passage of a convert from one faith to another cannot help but be condescending and dismissive of the reality claims of converts.

Brahmin converts in nineteenth-century Maharashtra (west India) believed that they had accessed in Christianity a universal truth. Their conversion did not align them with missionary or colonial interests, but preserved important aspects of their original identities. According to Dandekar, Brahmin conversion in the former Maratha territories gave rise to a vernacular Christian literary tradition, which helped consolidate a triple identity: Brahmin, Marathi, and Christian.[13] This complex identity was being formed just as Hindu nationalists in Maharashtra and Bengal—who were mostly Brahmins—were portraying Christians as denationalized and Christianity itself as a foreign faith.

In 1818, the British defeated a powerful regional kingdom in west India known as the Marathas, who were ruled by leaders known as the *peshwas*. This event demoralized Brahmins and members of other upper castes in the region. Some responded to rising Western influence by calling for the reform of Hinduism—a strategy popularized by the Brahmo Samaj in Bengal—as a way of cleaning up one's own house, so to speak, in response to missionary critiques. For many upper caste Hindus, internal social reform presented a much preferred alternative to Christian conversion. In Bombay, the Prarthana Samaj advocated belief in one God (and the renunciation of image worship) and proposed social reforms aimed at improving the lot of women and untouchables. Amid the transition to British rule, other high caste Hindus found in Protestant Christianity a source of spiritual renewal, access to education, and inroads into the modernity brought by the British. They found conversion to Protestantism more transformative than the vision of Hindu social reform, which they considered ineffective and hypocritical.[14]

Narayan Vaman Tilak (1862–1919) was a renowned Maratha Brahmin poet and writer before becoming Christian. His path toward the Christian faith began with an encounter with a European man on a train with whom he conversed at length about Sanskrit poetry. Upon parting, the man gave him a copy of the New Testament, which Tilak read with great interest in the following months. In a series of anonymous letters and poems he submitted to the Marathi Christian periodical *Dnyanodaya*, Tilak revealed the emergence of his Christian faith.[15] His journey reflected a remarkable fusion of his Sanskritic cultural heritage and his newfound belief in Christ, with much of his outlook anchored in the devotional emphasis of Hindu *bhakti* tradition. By the time of his conversion, missionaries of the American Marathi mission had come to appreciate the richness of local *bhakti* devotional poems and literature; they had discovered, for instance, the poetry of the Hindu *bhakti* saint Tukaram (1608–50). Tilak befriended the missionary Justin Abbott, who had produced a collection of twelve volumes on poet saints of Maharashtra.[16] Like other Maratha Brahmins, Tilak was committed to social reform on behalf of women and untouchables. He demonstrated his commitment, however, by producing hundreds of *bhakti* hymns and by promoting a form of Christianity that was not wedded to European cultural norms and practices.[17]

The conflict between missionary Christianity and Hindu social reform is central to understanding the unique social location of Hindu converts such as Ramabai and those who came before her. Baba Padmanji (1831–1906) was an outspoken Christian convert in mid-nineteenth-century Maharashtra who hailed from the *twashta kasar* caste, a community of metalsmiths and jewelers. He eventually converted through his contacts with the Free Church of Scotland, but his path to Christianity took him through the Hindu reformist circles of Bombay and the surrounding area. He was involved for a time in a secret reformist society known as the Paramhansa Mandali, a precursor to Bombay's Prarthana Samaj. Padmanji's conversion stemmed from his conviction that only Christianity could liberate Indian society from the social evils associated with Hinduism.[18] He criticized the path taken by members of the Prarthana Samaj for occupying what he viewed as a noncommittal middle ground between Christianity and Hinduism. The society, he believed, lacked any grounding in a particular scripture or a theology.[19]

Padmanji authored more than 100 texts, including tracts, essays, and editorials published in *Dnyanodaya*. He also wrote books on comparative religion, such as *A Comparison of Krishna and Christ* (1867). The published output of converts such as Padmanji represented an alternative consciousness, a literary "third space" that, according to Dandekar, was neither Sanskritic (or Arabic) nor European. It was what she terms a "vernacular mission field," in which converts, mostly men, represented a new generation of leadership. They achieved a stamp of legitimacy through their writings and gained devoted followings as they increased in public stature. In fact, the devotion or *bhakti* directed toward public figures such as Padmanji became a defining feature of this vernacular mission field and was often expressed through hagiographies written about Brahmin converts.

Padmanji represents only one segment of a greater Marathi Christian tradition that made its mark through mother-tongue intellectual production. The focus of this evolving third space was the formulation of an authentically "native Christianity" through a variety of genres: biography, literature, instructive pamphlets, and polemics.[20] In this vernacular literary public sphere, many converts would make their mark, including male converts such as Nehemiah Goreh (formerly Nilakantha), Narayan Vaman Tilak, Appaji Bapuji Yardi, and Dinkar Shankar Sawarkar. As was the case in Europe's Protestant Reformation, print media became the vehicle for the emergence of a Marathi Christian reading public and community. It should be noted that the medium of print would also advance the causes of Bombay's Muslims, Sikhs, Parsis, and Hindus. Printed texts for other religions, however, did not necessarily promote rational or learned expressions of those faiths. During the same period, a populist form of Islam was promoted by cheap print hagiographies of Sufi saints, prayer booklets, and tracts extolling the miraculous powers of saints and holy men. This form of Islam gained traction in Bombay among the city's working-class Muslims.[21] The Christian vernacular mission field shared with this populist Islam the element of *bhakti* (devotion) toward leaders. Its main difference from Bombay Islam, however, was that it was constituted chiefly by Brahmin converts whose writings appealed to more educated audiences.

Pandita Ramabai rose to prominence within already existing reformist and Christian networks in Maharashtra, which she expanded by infusing her feminist consciousness into an arena thus far dominated by men. Like other Brahmin converts, Ramabai differentiated herself from both Hindu reformist and Western missionary networks and perspectives. To a degree not yet seen, she protested against the oppression of women within Hindu society and exposed how Hindu sacred texts sanctioned this oppression. Her conversion was by no means one of assimilation into Western missionary culture; on the contrary, she illustrates what Gauri Viswanathan calls "conversion as protest."[22] This perspective underscores how conversion functions as a form of cultural criticism. Against a tendency to regard religious conversion as a deeply personal experience centered upon an individual coming to faith or meeting God, Viswanathan develops the notion of conversion as a *worldly* event that challenges social structures and institutions, including the very premises of a nation. The real meaning of conversion, she argues, has less to do with accepting a new set of beliefs or assimilating into a new community and more to do with the dissent or protest it voices against oppressive systems of authority.

In making her case for "conversion as protest," Viswanathan rejects the notion that religious experience can be isolated from social and political institutions. Contrary to the myth of "autonomous religious experience" (developed in the work of the American philosopher William James), belief is "worldly" by its very nature. It is not born in a vacuum but articulates itself in relation to political authority, culture, and law. Viswanathan's interest in belief that actually *does things* renders the purely spiritual testimony (one that is indifferent to social institutions) a disappointing retreat into subjectivism. If conversion can be described independently of the political culture in which it occurs, it is because conversion in such instances is fundamentally aligned with the goals of that political culture.

William James presented a well-known description of conversion: The individual moves "from dullness to vibrancy, division to wholeness, delusion to enlightenment . . . imprisonment to freedom."[23] This story of the emancipated individual does not engage with history or with opposing societal norms precisely because of its conformity with the aims of the American polity. In North America, the conversion of individuals supports the project of creating a godly nation, built upon democratic norms. However, this congruence between individual conversion and societal norms conceals the worldliness of belief by yielding a "religious subjectivity removed from its political moorings."[24] In Ramabai's story, by contrast, conversion is accompanied by a trenchant critique of both Hindu patriarchy and missionary paternalism. What makes her story particularly compelling is her complex social location: She was a Brahmin woman and yet from an impoverished family; a reformer of Hindu society who was ultimately shunned by fellow Hindu reformers; and a Christian convert who resisted being indoctrinated, even by the Anglican sisterhood who oversaw her time in England.

Pandita Ramabai and Indian Christian Consciousness

Ramabai Dongre, better known as Pandita Ramabai (1858–1922), is best known for her unusual journey as a Brahmin convert to Christianity and her commitment to female emancipation within Hindu society. Scholars such as Meera Kosambi, Uma Chakravarty, and Robert Frykenberg have described her passage from Hinduism to Christianity and the evolution of her feminist convictions.

Ramabai's story reveals her capacity to interrogate oppressive power structures, including those prevalent within Christian institutions. In this respect, her life provides a microcosm of a key aspect of World Christianity—namely, how converts appropriate the gospel on cultural and ideological terms that are quite different from those set out by Europeans. When converts suppress the awareness of this difference and outwardly conform to the cultural idioms and perspectives of missionaries, they risk becoming proselytes, not converts.[25] The church historian Andrew Walls draws this distinction to explain how first-century Gentile converts accepted the gospel within a Hellenistic framework; this included their way of talking about Jesus as the "Christ." The Apostle Paul prohibited anyone from insisting that Gentiles had to embrace Jewish customs (especially circumcision) in order to become Christian. "The followers of Jesus," Walls emphasizes, "are not proselytes. They are converts."[26] He uses this distinction to explain how Asians, Africans, and Latin Americans have become Christian without becoming Western. As an individual anchored in Sanskritic tradition, Ramabai's constant interrogation of authority prevented her from ever becoming a proselyte. Her battles with Brahmin society appear to have provided a training ground for her questioning of Christian ecclesiastical authority in England. This differentiation yielded a unique consciousness that easily escapes the attention of those wishing to claim her as a trophy for the missionary agenda in India.

Ramabai hailed from the Chitpavan Brahmin caste of Maharashtra, a community that had produced a significant number of reformers, educators, and nationalists during the nineteenth and twentieth centuries. Her father, Anant Shastri Dongre, a native of Mangalore district, was a man of great learning who was determined to teach his wife and daughter Sanskrit language and literature. Not only was this uncommon among Brahmin families of his day, but it was also prohibited in the laws of Manu. Under her father's tutelage, Ramabai learned Sanskrit and grew in her knowledge of the Puranas, or epic literature of the Hindus. She and her family, poor as they were, traveled throughout India as *puranikas*, or teachers of the Puranas. During the course of their travels, Ramabai displayed her knowledge of these sacred texts through recitations given in temple halls, on the banks of sacred rivers, or at other auspicious venues.[27] She recited lengthy passages from the Puranas and responded to questions, posed on the spot, by drawing from texts she had memorized.

During her time in Calcutta, a wider Hindu public, which included Brahmin and European scholars of Sanskrit, became aware of her brilliance. In Calcutta she received the titles "Pandita" (female teacher or pandit) and "Sarasvati" (the goddess of learning).[28] During the 1880s, a nationwide network of social reformers became aware of Ramabai's talent and convictions. A Bengali leader of the Brahmo Samaj, Keshab Chandra Sen, encouraged her to study the Vedas and the Upanishads, ancient Sanskrit texts that laid the ritual and philosophical foundations of Hindu beliefs and practices. Other reformist men in Calcutta befriended Ramabai and invited her to lecture on the duties of women. What they did not realize, however, was that Ramabai's knowledge of Sanskrit texts would lead her to criticize Hinduism much more incisively than Hindu reformers had done before.[29]

Ramabai's elevation to the status of "goddess of learning" occurred during a season of great personal hardship. She lost her parents, older sister, and eventually her brother and husband to famine and disease. This steady stream of death and struggle became difficult to reconcile with the pious Hindu life to which she and her family had been profoundly devoted and led to disillusionment with her family's religion. Moreover, as she grew in her knowledge of Sanskrit texts and what they had to say about the status of women, her attitude toward Hinduism moved from disenchantment to revulsion. The entire corpus of sacred literature, she observed, portrayed women as "very bad, worse than demons, as unholy as untruth; and that they could not get Moksha [liberation] as men."[30]

What she read about in sacred texts appeared to play out in the lived experiences of Hindu women of both high and low castes. Their servile position within Indian households, lack of education, and experiences of cruelty at the hands of men became matters Ramabai could not ignore. As she grew more and more incensed by the plight of Hindu women, she committed herself to a life of activism and social reform. In collaboration with other high caste reformers, she founded the Arya Mahila Sabha, a women's association devoted to female education and the abolition of child marriage. In 1882, Ramabai addressed the Hunter Commission, which was assessing the state of education in British-ruled territories, and pleaded for improved facilities for female general education and improved medical education.[31] Elsewhere, she became an outspoken critic of Brahminical society, paying special attention to the status of women within the Hindu family. She detailed the systematic preference for male children, the unwillingness of even the most enlightened and reformed of Hindu men to educate their daughters, the mistreatment of women at the hands of their in-laws, and the miserable experience of Hindu widows (who are prohibited by the *shastras* from remarrying).[32]

Not surprisingly, Ramabai's forceful critique of the Hindu family was accompanied by her own longing for an alternative faith. She shared Monier-Williams's assumption that so much of Indian culture derives from Sanskritic tradition; and so, in order to challenge female oppression, she needed to challenge that tradition and ultimately embrace a new faith. In this respect, her posture resembled that of the Dalit reformer Bhimrao Ramji Ambedkar (1891–1956), whose attacks on the practice of untouchability were inseparable from his desire to leave the Hindu fold. Whereas Ambedkar advocated that all Dalits find liberation in another religion, conversion for Ramabai appears to have remained deeply personal, and not a point of generalized advocacy for all Hindu women. Upon reading a copy of Luke's Gospel and discussing it with a Baptist missionary named Isaac Allen, Ramabai stated, "Having lost all faith in my former religion, and with my heart hungering after something better, I eagerly learnt everything I could about the Christian religion and declared my intention to become a Christian."[33]

Ramabai's move to Christianity, however, did not arise from a sudden conversion experience: It resulted from many years of reflection on Christian ideas and interactions with Westerners. As proud as she was of her Indian identity, it was not her exposure to established *Indian* Christian communities—for instance, the Thomas Christians of Kerala or the Roman Catholics of Mumbai—that tipped her in the direction of Christianity, but her encounters with isolated Indian converts along with Europeans and North Americans. This does not mean that her conversion placed her on a path of assimilation into Western culture.[34] On the contrary, it was fraught with conflict, resistance, and critical engagement with Christian beliefs and practices. She was drawn to the gospel, but differentiated herself from its European encasement. According to historian Meera Kosambi, her new faith always betrayed her disdain for colonialism and her own Indian nationalism.[35]

Nowhere is her dissonance with Western Christianity more evident than in her encounters with the religious order that hosted her in Britain. In 1883, Ramabai traveled to Britain to study English with the hope of ultimately pursuing a medical career. In Wantage, England, an Anglo-Catholic mission, the Community of St. Mary the Virgin (CSMV), hosted Ramabai and her young daughter, Manorama (see Figure 6.1). Wantage was not only where she was baptized into the Christian faith, but also where a tense relationship began with Sister Geraldine, her spiritual guide, and with the Anglican Church hierarchy more broadly. Her experiences with this establishment illustrate how imperial power could strain interracial relationships and undermine the possibility for a transnational sisterhood.[36]

Ramabai's time at the CSMV was a defining moment in her spiritual journey. She committed herself to a new faith, while also critically engaging with the culture and ideologies of her mentors. At roughly the same time as she was baptized (September 1883), Ramabai experienced yet another traumatic experience. She had befriended another widow, Anandabai, who resided with her at the Wantage home. According to one source, Anandabai feared that she and Ramabai would be forced to become Christian at the CSMV. To save them both from this fate, she

Figure 6.1 "Pandita Ramabai & her gifted daughter Manoramabai," undated.
Source: Photograph by J. Paul, Bangalore. Council for World Mission Archive, SOAS Library.

attempted to strangle Ramabai in her sleep. When this failed, Anandabai committed suicide by drinking poison.[37] The episode, which appears in scattered sources but with few details, is significant because it reveals the acquaintances that had become vital to Ramabai and her recovery. Ramabai was so traumatized by the event that she was unable to write about it. She took refuge in the home of Friedrich Max Müller, the German philologist who would eventually publish *The Sacred Books of the East*, a compilation of ancient Asian religious texts. It was Max Müller, along with Sister Geraldine, who would briefly describe the event in their writings. Her fellow Marathi Brahmin convert, Nehemiah Goreh, also played an important role in comforting Ramabai after this tragic loss.

During her stay at Wantage, Ramabai would eventually subject herself to the tutelage of Geraldine and the Anglo-Catholic tradition.[38] She was also exposed to many other varieties of Christianity seeking to find expression in opposition to England's reigning Anglicanism; she recounts being overwhelmed by the sheer variety:

> Besides meeting people of the most prominent sects, the High Church, Low Church, Baptist, Methodist, Presbyterian, Friends, Unitarian, Universalist, Roman Catholic, Jews, and others, I met with Spiritualists, Theosophists, Mormons, Christian Scientists, and followers of what they call the occult religions.[39]

Encountering this vast landscape of religious difference, Ramabai began to identify commonalities between religious organizations in England and various forms of religion prevalent in India. In doing so, she used the familiar to make sense of the unfamiliar.

Geraldine, however, disapproved of Ramabai's explorations of other traditions and her constant questioning of Anglo-Catholic doctrines. In particular, she objected to Ramabai's questioning of the Athanasian Creed, an integral part of Anglican liturgy, which expounds on the doctrines of the Trinity and the divinity of Christ. The Creed also issues condemnations for those who disagree with it. Geraldine considered Ramabai's attitude to be a form of insubordination and prideful disregard for the Church's authority. She expected Ramabai, after her decision to be baptized an Anglo-Catholic, to wholeheartedly accept the religion's core doctrines. For Geraldine, the time of exploratory questioning was over:

> You say in the matter of your religion you are following God's guidance, and a little further on that it is your right to choose your own religion. Is this not a contradiction? As far as my own experience has taught me, if I am following God's guidance, I am giving up my own, having no choice of my own except to make His Will mine . . . It was when you came to England you said you were following God's guidance, and to whom did He guide you and whom did He give you as your teachers? Members of that Church whose teachings you now reject.[40]

Geraldine told Ramabai plainly that, as a mere "babe in Christ," she was in no position to "argue or lay down the law as to the prerogatives of the Catholic Church."[41] Geraldine insisted that she was not invoking the condemnatory clauses of the Creed to address Ramabai's apostasy, and yet reminded her that a childlike faith was needed to "enter the kingdom of God."[42]

In her response, Ramabai stated that she had no regrets in deciding to be baptized a Christian. She maintained, though, that her baptism did not preclude her from experiencing a life of learning and growth as a Christian, which is often accompanied by asking questions. Ramabai also distinguished the content of the Bible from that of the Athanasian Creed and questioned how much understanding of Christian doctrine could be expected of newly baptized Christians:

> I wish I knew that your Church required of a person to be quite perfect in faith, doubting nothing in the Athanasian Creed, so that he had left nothing to be learnt and inquired into the Bible after his baptism... Do all the thousands who are daily baptized in the world become quite acquainted with all your doctrines and are free from doubts? And do all ministers of God wait to baptize them until they had attained to the highest perfection of faith?[43]

Ramabai's use of such phrases as "your Church" and "your doctrines" indicates that her process of differentiating herself from the Christian culture at Wantage had reached a very advanced stage. When the sisters confronted her for her "arrogant" exercise of her own intellect, Ramabai retorted: "I have just with great efforts freed myself from the yolk of the Indian priestly tribe, so I am not at present willing to place myself under similar yoke by accepting everything that comes to the priests as authorized command of the Most High."[44]

By 1884, after only one year at the CSMV, her ties to the sisterhood had become so strained that she decided to move to Cheltenham. She took classes at Cheltenham Ladies' College and paid for them by teaching Sanskrit. At Cheltenham, she made the acquaintance of Dorothea Beale, an ardent feminist and the founder and principal of the college.

Upon her return to India, men who had once admired Ramabai for her learning castigated her because of her conversion. Liberal, reformist men criticized her decision as an act of feminine fickleness. The Hindu saint Sri Ramakrishna criticized her for her egotism in pursuing fame and visibility. His disciple Swami Vivekananda, the reformer and spokesman for a new Hinduism, lamented that Ramabai could have achieved so much had only she remained Hindu.[45] The editor of the newspaper *Indu Prakash* disparagingly commented: "[Y]ou are, after all a woman, whatever your culture and achievement may be."[46] Another writer from the same newspaper resorted to scathing ridicule:

> Pandita Ramabai was in the first instance a Hindu, then she became a Brahmo, now she has become a Christian. This shows and proves she is of unstable mind. We should not be surprised if she becomes a Muslim soon. She has only to meet a Muslim Kazi who will convince her that his religion will give her peace and salvation.[47]

Orthodox Hindus chided Ramabai even more severely than the reformers. Some charged that she had committed an unpardonable sin in converting and described her as fallen and polluted (*batleli*). Middle-class Hindus were especially grieved in no longer being able to point to Ramabai as an example of an educated woman who had remained committed to Hinduism.

Among her few supporters, the Marathi reformer Jyotirao Phule stood out. He had long been a critic of Hindu texts that consigned women and untouchables to a life of servitude, and, although he did not convert to Christianity, he developed strong convictions about human rights based on Western texts such as Thomas Paine's *Rights of Man* (1791). In his novel *Gulamgiri* (Slavery), Phule credited missionaries and the British for recognizing the human rights of lower caste peoples. It was not difficult for him to appreciate Ramabai's decision to embrace Christianity—he commended her for seeing for herself what was in these texts and believed this left her no choice but to break away from Hinduism. Phule attacked Ramabai's male critics as not being able to stomach the idea of women expressing dissenting ideas through the printed word.[48]

The chorus of voices criticizing her conversion overwhelmed Ramabai. And yet, she never took complete refuge in missionary circles. Her strength of mind would place her in the unique and lonely position of being removed from any real institutional base of support. Accounts of Ramabai's conversion usually recount her years as an itinerant *puranika*, her acclaim as a Hindu reformer, and her baptism and experiences with the Anglican establishment in England. Her time in England, however, represents only the beginning of her Christian experience. In 1886, Ramabai traveled to America to attend the graduation of a good friend of hers, Anandibai Joshi, who had completed her studies at the Woman's Medical College of Pennsylvania. During her visit to America, Ramabai was able to observe many aspects of American society, including the status of women, church life, government, and the missionary movement. She praised the elevated standing of women in America (especially compared with what she experienced in India) along with other achievements of the American polity in her travel narrative, published as *The Peoples of the United States*. Underlying Ramabai's praise of American institutions, according to Meera Kosambi, was her Indian nationalism and her critique of British colonial rule. Ramabai viewed England as an oppressive imperial force, but America as "an ideal liberating force and indirectly as a precedent for India to follow in its pursuit of political freedom and social reform."[49] She became particularly gripped by the American commitment to liberty as captured in the liberty bell in Philadelphia; in fact, she named the home in Kedgaon she would later establish for high caste Hindu women the Mukti mission, with "*mukti*" meaning "liberty."

In contrast to the colonial attitudes she experienced within Anglican circles and the elitism of Hindu reformist circles, Ramabai experienced in American

Christianity the populist and democratic impulses of fiery preachers, revivalists, and voluntary associations of the holiness movement.[50] During her time in America, she also developed a strong mutual affinity with members of female missionary societies. American women missionaries were captivated not only by Ramabai's conversion story, but also by her passion for uplifting India's women. They found in her an exotic, high caste woman who, on account of her strong Christian convictions, presented a gateway into the Indian mission field. While touring America, Ramabai insisted on wearing only saris and maintaining her vegetarian diet, which reinforced her aura of saintliness among audiences. Ramabai was pleased to discover in America more prominent roles for women in all areas of life and a strong base of support for her work among India's women. As a result of her far-reaching contacts in America, she founded the "Ramabai Association," for which she received pledges of support for her work in India among high caste widows.

This transition from England's High Church to America's populist Christianity coincided with a greater emphasis in Ramabai's life on personal experience and the work of the Holy Spirit. One might also view this as a shift from the mind to the heart in her discovery of the gospel. Frykenberg notes that this was a phase in her Christian journey most marked by *bhakti*, or personal devotion to God expressed with great emotion.[51] A range of influences in America sowed the seeds of this new orientation to faith. Clusters of trans-denominational voluntary associations had rallied in America to the mutually reinforcing causes of spiritual revival at home and in overseas missions. Revivalists such as Dwight Moody, the itinerant evangelist from Northfield, Massachusetts, and the Methodist Bishop James Thoburn were among those who traveled about the country preaching the need for revival and the Holy Spirit's power. As Ramabai mingled with the leaders of these groups, especially as she traveled along the East Coast of America, she bridged their theological perspectives and activism with networks she belonged to in India. English-language periodicals containing vivid accounts of spiritual revival worldwide found their way to Christians in India who subscribed to them.

Toward the turn of the twentieth century, before there was any official designation such as "Pentecostalism," missionary periodicals circulated accounts of various manifestations of spiritual gifts and ecstatic experiences occurring at roughly the same time in various parts of the globe—from south India and the Khasi Hills of northeast India to Azusa Street in Los Angeles and Wales in the UK.[52] Descriptions of these revivals often referenced fiery preaching and tangible manifestations of the Holy Spirit among those in attendance. Members of the congregation are said to have spontaneously uttered prophecies, spoken in tongues, undergone exorcisms, repented of their sins, and gleefully exhorted others to pursue holiness in all aspects of life. In September 1907, one periodical, *The Apostolic Faith*, published a letter that described a visitation of the Holy Spirit at Ramabai's Mukti mission. Teachers at the mission, along with 300 "native girls," experienced manifestations described at other revivals. These included:

> Trembling, shaking, loud crying and confessions, unconsciousness in ecstasy or prayer, sudden falling to the ground twisting and writhing during exorcisms, and "joy unspeakable" manifested in singing, clapping, shouting praises and dancing.[53]

The author of this account, quite likely Ramabai herself, warned readers of the dangers of suppressing the movement of the Spirit out of disdain for emotional excitement. Doing so ran the risk of bringing the revival to a complete halt. "We have learned," the author observed, "that God's ways are past finding out, as far above ours as heavens are above the earth."[54]

Christian Voices of Madras

Monier-Williams's assertions about the centrality of Sanskrit for the missionary project in India reflected a belief that guided many nineteenth-century missionaries: that converting the upper castes was the key to the conversion of India. The Marathi-speaking Christian tradition to which Ramabai belonged complicates this picture in important ways. Conversions to Protestantism among Brahmins and other literate, upper castes were not great in number, but they gave rise to a print culture that expressed a unique Christian consciousness. The conversions of people such as Padmanji and Ramabai, however, did not trickle down to reach the masses, as many missionaries hoped would happen. In fact, the third space that flourished in Maharashtra under their leadership eventually faded away. The growing strength of Hindu reform and Hindu nationalism in this region appears to have marginalized what was once a vibrant and innovative Christian imagination.[55]

In Madras, however, another community of Christian elites addressed the issues of their day through local newspapers. Unlike the tradition in Maharashtra that yielded perspectives printed in Marathi, Madras Christian elites formulated their views in English. Still, their project was very much centered on Indianizing Christianity. Madras Christian elites shared with Maratha Brahmin converts a capacity to engage regional and national developments in distinctively Christian ways. Their use of English, however, suggests that they were more integrated into Western denominational and ecumenical networks than their Marathi-speaking counterparts.

In order to demonstrate their commitment to Indian nationalism, Protestant leaders in Madras tried to shed their foreign complexion and adopt a persona more aligned with Hindu or Sanskritic culture. Three projects embodied this vision: the National Church, the Christo Samaj, and the Christian Ashram Movement. Pulney Andy (1831–1909), a retired medical practitioner in Madras, started the National Church with the aim of freeing Indian Christians from the denominational divisions of Western churches. The ideas of his National Church were voiced in a weekly paper, *Eastern Star*. During his tours of south India, another advocate of Sanskritized Christianity, Sadhu Sundar Singh (1889–1929), stressed the need to locate Indian Christianity within the framework of India's classical religious traditions. His influence, along with that of Vengal Chakkarai (1880–1958), the founding editor of the *Christian Patriot* newspaper, led to the formation of the Christo Samaj in 1916.

Christian Patriot, which ran from 1890 to 1929, claimed to represent south Indian Protestants. According to historian Klaus Koschorke, contributors to the newspaper envisioned a unique social location for Indian Christians, which steered clear of both missionary paternalism and militant Hindu nationalism.[56] Other Christians, however, accommodated themselves to a softer variety of Hindu nationalism. During the 1920s, the Christian Ashram Movement shared the vision of the Christo Samaj in promoting a more Sanskritized image of Christianity. An *ashram* was literally a place of meditation or rest and a retreat from worldliness—Gandhi had founded a number of *ashrams* in order to embody the kind of selfless political community he wanted India to become. The Christian Ashram Movement attempted to ride the wave of such aspirations.

During the 1920s, the *Guardian* newspaper became the mouthpiece for "Rethinking Christianity" in Madras. This group of theologians promoted a stronger commitment to interfaith dialogue and a greater regard for Hindu culture and traditions. The weekly newspaper *Harvest Field*, established by the Wesleyan Methodists, also aired the views of the Rethinking Christianity group and published a number of controversial articles dealing with missionary practices and Indian nationalism. At the time, the YMCA of India had become hugely significant for cultivating a spirit of patriotism and for training future church and civic leaders. Its newspaper, *Young Men of India*, was replete with articles concerning the mission of the Church, social services, and Christian civic and political involvement.[57]

Conclusion

An important aim of the emerging Christian print culture was to orient Indian Christians to national issues and draw them into the mainstream. The effectiveness of their strategies, however, is not easy to measure. We find in this period a proliferation of newspapers that offered sophisticated public discourse and raised awareness about the key issues of the day: for instance, caste, social reform, and Indian nationalism. The ability of this discourse to alter nationalist perceptions about Christians, however, was minimal. In other words, print culture had the effect of inventing an Indian Christian community (just as the historian Benedict Anderson tied print media to the origins of nationalism), but that community appears to have remained marginal to the wider society. Moreover, because elite members of upper castes constituted and steered this domain of public opinion, converts from Dalit and tribal backgrounds remained excluded. Christian elites debated among themselves what to do about members of the so-called depressed classes, while these marginal classes factored minimally at best in the newspapers of the day. This may have been due to prejudice directed against them or their low literacy rates. The next chapters describe the mass movements of conversion that contributed to a predominantly Dalit and tribal Church in India. Eventually, Dalit theology would provided a trenchant critique of the contextual or indigenous theologies of upper caste Christians, which were centered on the project of Sanskritizing Christianity.

A highly revealing trajectory from Sanskritic religion to Christianity can be seen in the life of Pandita Ramabai. Long before she became a Protestant, her life was immersed in sacred Hindu literature. Under the influence of her father, she became a teacher of Hindu *puranic* texts. However, after her conversion, and especially after her first visit to the USA, Ramabai became integrated into worldwide networks of Protestant piety. By the turn of the twentieth century, popular Pentecostalism would come to play a more central role in shaping these networks. Ramabai's movement out of Anglo-Catholicism and into Holy Spirit-centered religion may therefore be viewed as a lens for examining wider developments, including democratizing tendencies within Indian Christianity and within an emerging World Christianity. When Ramabai challenged Sister Geraldine to consider whether the masses of baptized converts were well versed in Christian doctrines, she was unwittingly signaling a new phase in the history of Christians in South Asia. Far more than the doctrinal debates staged by the Rethinking Christianity group, mass movements of conversion among Dalit and tribal communities would shape the composition and complexion of South Asian Christianity.

7
Mass Conversion Among Dalits and Tribals
Rupture, Continuity, or Uplift?

In recent years, numerous books have drawn attention to the plight of India's Dalits, those persons (formerly called "untouchables") who occupy the lowest strata of the social order because of hereditary occupations deemed "impure."[1] In her book *Ants Among Elephants*, Sujatha Gidla describes her experiences growing up in a Dalit family in the south Indian state of Andhra Pradesh. Despite managing to become highly educated, she and her family suffered many instances of stigmatization and mistreatment at the hands of village landlords, college professors, and employers.[2] Y. B. Satyanarayana's *My Father Baliah* narrates the experiences of a Dalit family in early twentieth-century Telangana (in south-central India) who made their living first as agricultural laborers and later as railway workers. Like Gidla's powerful story of social advancement in the face of oppression, Satyanarayana describes how his father was able to leave the inequalities of village life and find employment as a railway worker.[3] As an enterprise developed under British rule, the railways drew large numbers of Dalit laborers. They found in this modern environment an escape from rigid, ritual hierarchies observed in village life. Railway labor, however, would not provide Dalits with a more dignified existence in the decades following India's independence. As writer-activist Arundhati Roy has noted, the thousands of trains that run daily across the Indian subcontinent funnel human excrement directly onto the tracks through open discharge toilets. As the largest employers of manual scavengers, India's railways enlist only Dalits to clean massive amounts of trash and human excrement with no protective gloves or equipment.[4]

Hoping to escape the stigma of untouchability and to experience greater social mobility and self-respect, many Dalits converted to Christianity or Islam, two religions that do not teach caste distinctions. Gidla's family was able to become educated because of their access to schools established by Canadian missionaries. Satyanarayan's father aspired to read and write but was told that it was a sin under Hindu law for an untouchable to be educated; it was a Muslim cleric who educated him by meeting with him in a local mosque.[5] Among South Asians, it was primarily the poor, oppressed, and socially stigmatized from Dalit and tribal communities who responded enthusiastically to the appeal of Christianity, converting mostly as groups rather than as individuals.

"Mass conversions" (or "mass movements" of conversion) refer to contexts in which an entire village, caste community, or network of families made a collective decision to undertake baptism and join the Christian religion. This often involved the initiative of a village headman or patriarch on behalf of members of a tribal or caste community. Mass movements challenged the notions of individual conscience and choice that were so central to Protestant Evangelicalism, and so they consistently raised questions among missionaries about the sincerity and depth of commitment among those who converted in this way.

Converts from Dalit or tribal backgrounds were located *between Hindu and Muslim*—and sometimes Buddhist—by virtue of where they lived and their marginal status relative to these dominant traditions. It is inaccurate to presume that mass converts were extracted from clearly defined Hindu or Muslim communities; quite often, their pre-Christian beliefs and identities were ambiguous and marginal to Brahminical Hinduism or orthodox Islam. The Chuhras of the Punjab, for instance, lived within a highly complex religious environment with overlapping Hindu, Muslim, Sikh, reformist, and Christian influences.[6] Joining a different religious community was quite common and did not necessarily entail the adoption of an entirely new social identity. The Mizo and Naga tribes of northeast India resided between the Indian mainland and Southeast Asia and China. Because of their location near the frontiers of Tibet and China, they lived on the margins of Hindu, Muslim, and Buddhist societies. Therefore, when they became Christian, they solidified an already existing sense of difference from mainland Indian religious traditions.

During the nineteenth and early twentieth centuries, mass conversions often took foreign missionaries by surprise. Many had to reorient themselves to the vast socioeconomic needs accompanying the desire for baptism. Instead of presenting a silver lining to their failure to convert the upper castes, mass conversion among Dalits and tribals often left missionaries feeling ill equipped to address the sheer scale of their numbers and needs. If the elite, Sanskritized sections of society largely passed on the invitation to become Christian, a new demographic consisting of those considered ritually impure was now altering the complexion of South Asian Christianity.

Christian mass movements raised important questions about motives. Did access to schools, medical facilities, or other forms of humanitarian aid incline Dalits or tribals to seek baptism? Or did they convert for more "spiritual" reasons? As is so often the case, the answers to such questions are not simple and often depend on how words such as "spiritual" are defined.[7] Over the past century, the debate over the motives of mass conversions has wavered between those who emphasize external factors such as foreign capital, humanitarian aid, and colonial power, and those who believe that mass conversions sprang from spiritual hunger and the active agency of converts.[8] This binary is itself problematic. Why should the pursuit of a better material existence in another religion be considered unspiritual or inauthentic? Does this not create a scenario in which conversions among the poor carry a unique burden to prove authenticity while those among the more affluent are absolved of such interrogation?[9]

Another way of framing mass conversions is in terms of rupture versus continuity. Did conversion mark a radical break from the past and entry into an alternative social and cultural space? Or was conversion more gradual than is often imagined, and a process that extended earlier beliefs and practices into a new Christian identity? The anthropologist Joel Robbins describes the striking contrast between the ways in which cultural anthropologists describe conversion and the stories told by actual converts. While converts (and clergy) tend to portray conversion as a radical break from the old religion, anthropologists often emphasize continuities between preexisting beliefs and practices and the new Christian ones.[10] Robbins argues that this tendency toward continuity is problematic, because it fails to recognize the possibility of a distinctively Christian culture arising from mass conversion.

The focus on continuity makes it difficult to account for instances where converts stressed their radical break from the past and differentiated themselves from their pre-Christian beliefs and practices. They did so by adopting new names, dress, rituals, vocations, and public displays of religiosity. An emphasis on rupture also tends to align itself with those who stress the emancipatory, transformative, or developmental impact of Christianity. If one argues that Christian conversion elevated the quality of life of Dalits by extending them education or other aid, it becomes more difficult to maintain that converts remained anchored in the very social structures or beliefs that formed the basis of their oppression.[11]

This chapter presents mass conversions as events that took Protestant missionaries by surprise and radically reshaped their approaches to matters of caste and culture in India. It focuses on three contexts of mass conversion movements, with each illustrating a different theme. First, a discussion of Telugu mass conversion during a time of famine explores the motives behind conversion and its social impact among Dalit converts. Second, the chapter discusses conversion among the Nagas and Mizos of northeast India. Their stories highlight themes of rupture and continuity and questions relating to the impact of colonialism on conversion. Finally, an examination of the mass conversions of Chamars and Chuhras in the Punjab illustrates complex issues of identity in a region impacted by Hindu, Muslim, and Sikh traditions. The chapter concludes by discussing enduring controversies associated with caste and Christian identity, particularly among untouchable communities in contemporary India.

Mass Conversions in South India

Caste and Untouchability

In the traditional caste system, society is divided into four major castes or *varnas* (which literally translates as rank or color): Brahmins (priests), Kshatriyas (warriors), Vaishyas (merchants), and Sudras (service providers). The first three castes undergo rituals of initiation (*upanayana*) that are believed to constitute a second birth. Hence, they are referred to as "twice-born" (*dvija*) castes. Those who do not fall within any of the four *varnas* are referred to as *avarnas* (persons lacking *varna* or caste status). These include tribal communities (sometimes known as *adivasis*, which means "original inhabitants") who conform to different patterns of group life that are not anchored in the assumptions of Hindu caste society.

Within the fourfold division of society into these *varnas* lies a more fundamental unit of social identity known as *jati*. Within traditional societies, this sub-caste or birth group is marked by commitment to endogamous marriage and prohibitions against dining with people of other castes. In any given region, many *jatis* can be considered Brahmin or Vaishya, and there can be menial laborers of different *jatis* who are considered untouchable or *avarna* on account of occupations deemed to be polluting. During the colonial period, lowly communities such as sanitary workers, toddy tappers (who extracted liquor from palmyra palms), leather workers, and landless laborers were referred to as "untouchables." The term "pariah" also designated untouchables during this period, deriving from the word *paraiyar*, which referred to a particular community of untouchables mostly consisting of landless laborers. Highly derogatory designations were assigned to untouchable *jatis* and these communities were forced to live separately from higher-ranking communities.

Nineteenth-century developments provide a useful lens for examining shifts in missionary attitudes toward India's caste system. Early on, Protestant missionaries had reached near consensus in their opposition to caste.[12] Forced labor of "untouchables" resembled the slavery they had opposed in abolition campaigns across the Atlantic. Many came to regard caste customs and caste mentality as antithetical to Christian community and an impediment to the spread of the gospel.[13] Much of this changed with the arrival of the mass movements. As entire caste communities converted to Christianity, it became more difficult for missionaries to condemn the group principle steering these conversions. Conversion had become a collective decision, not an individual one, which was how Evangelicals were in the habit of portraying it. The persistence of caste feelings in the lives of converts did not shatter missionary aspirations for a complete rupture from a caste-oriented past, but it forced them to concede the role of group identities in decision making. Simply stated, missionaries could not be too strident in opposing caste identities while also affirming the legitimacy of mass conversions. Scrutinizing the sincerity of mass converts was one way of reconciling their discomfort with caste with their desire for the advancement of the gospel.

Motives and Outcomes

Toward the end of the nineteenth century, Tamil- and Telugu-speaking districts of south India suffered severe famines following drought, crop failure, and the death of livestock. The lack of water also led to poor sanitation and the spread of diseases such as typhoid, cholera, and smallpox. Amidst such dire need, Protestant missionary societies provided relief for members of Dalit communities; and, in the process, many were baptized as Christians. The American Baptist missionary John Clough provided a firsthand account of his work in the Telugu-speaking city of Ongole, where he claimed to have baptized as many as 9,000 people from a Dalit caste known as the Madigas. Further south, in Tamil-speaking regions, the SPG baptized 23,000 people in 1878. The American Evangelical Lutherans baptized 6,000 in North and South Arcot.[14]

Clough's account of the famine afflicting the Telugu country refers to widespread hunger (especially among Sudra and Madiga communities), dying livestock, and overwhelming needs confronting him and his catechists. At the time, the British were constructing a 500-mile canal known as the Buckingham Canal, which ran parallel to India's eastern Coromandel Coast. Many Madigas had hoped to be employed by this project, but the caste prejudice of Indian supervisors made this impossible. Clough, who had past experience as a surveyor, was able to acquire a contract to work on a segment of the canal. This allowed him to recruit Madiga laborers. Hundreds and eventually thousands of emaciated Christian Madigas flocked to his camp—referred to as a "Christian coolie camp"—and began digging. Soon, many were afflicted with cholera.[15] Clough's catechists were stretched to their limits as they distributed food, attended to the sick, and propagated Christian teachings. For Clough, this was "Christianity applied in practice on their portion of the canal."[16] Still, the hardship of the famine vastly outweighed the advantages of employment.

For the Madigas, Christian conversion enabled them to share common spaces with missionaries—in this case with Clough and his team of catechists. The scholar Chakali Chandra Sekhar notes how these became arenas where untouchables became "touchable."[17] This was clearly the case in the camp Clough established for canal construction; it was also the case in Rayalaseema, a

Telugu-speaking region where missionaries of the LMS and the SPG had led conversion movements among Madigas during the 1850s. Conversion movements created a new "contact zone" between Dalits and missionaries that fundamentally differed from their village experience.[18] Not only had village life segregated them from upper castes (by confining them to separate spaces or *palems*), but it had also made it a taboo for upper castes to touch them. The sharing of common meals and spaces for instruction and the acts of touching through handshakes, the clasping of hands in prayer, or embracing were deeply humanizing experiences for Dalit converts. They extended dignity, recognition, and comfort to those whose bodies were otherwise despised.[19]

During the months of famine relief, many people approached Clough and his catechists in the hope of being baptized. According to Clough:

> The people were knocking at the gates of the church. They made themselves heard. Letters came pouring in upon me voicing the request of groups of people—families and villages. They wanted baptism. Deputations from villages came, some a distance of sixty miles, with village elders as spokesmen. They assured me that the request of the people was sincere. Their minds were not fixed on rupees; they wanted salvation of their souls.[20]

Despite these widespread and persistent calls for baptism, Clough was hesitant to accede to their requests.

Rice Christians?

Local newspapers had raised questions about missionaries making "rice Christians." The *Madras Mail*, for instance, ran articles that questioned the admission standards for baptism and charged various missions with gross exaggeration of their numbers. An article in *Native Public Opinion* drew attention to the caste and poor social conditions of the converts, suggesting that their desire for baptism was hardly miraculous; rather, it was oriented toward increasing "creature comforts."[21]

Such criticisms made Clough cautious about creating the appearance of exploiting the situation to add numbers to his mission; but, after much deliberation, Clough proceeded to admit Madigas in large numbers for baptism. He and his catechists grouped them by family and village into three categories: those who would be subject to questions about their commitment to and grasp of Christianity; those who would be examined by Clough himself; and those who would be baptized in a local river. Clough's methods reveal the extent to which questions of sincerity weighed on him.

The sheer scale of mass conversions among downtrodden communities was greater than anyone had sought or anticipated. It compelled both missionaries and their critics to debate issues of motive. These explorations of motive, however, never moved beyond a basic facet of human decision making: When a method, device, ideology, or religion fails to deliver basic needs, people tend to reach for something else. Given the layers of social and material adversity faced by Dalits, it should come as no surprise that they would turn to any religion they perceived as more likely to address their needs.

Critics of mass movements argue that Dalits in their vulnerability were uniquely susceptible to manipulation, inducement, or opportunism by proselytizing religions. As news of the famine gained international attention, it prompted missionaries from many parts of Europe—along with Hindu and Muslim relief workers—to travel to the afflicted regions to offer aid. Should this be seen as an outpouring of compassion for famine victims, or as interreligious competition for their allegiance?

The rise of mass movements changed the way missionaries talked about caste. Earlier in the nineteenth century, when they tended to target the upper castes and conversions were few and far between, missionaries were fixated on whether caste was inherently at odds with Christianity. The main focus was whether churches should allow members of different castes to observe laws of purity and separate themselves from Dalits.[22] Mass conversions among Dalits did not entirely displace this conversation, but they redirected it toward the issue of motives and the role of churches in meeting the Dalits' social and material needs. Missionaries such as Clough tried to maintain a sense of local grounding by employing Indian catechists, while at the same time upholding the sincerity and transformative nature of conversion (see Figure 7.1). His approach stands in contrast to those who prioritized cultural continuity at the expense of social transformation.

A Twentieth-Century Example: V. S. Azariah

By the early twentieth century, mass conversions had become highly politicized. Many Indian Christians contributed to discussions of mass conversions and their implications. Among the most prominent voices of the 1930s was that of Vedanayagam Samuel Azariah. Educated in Anglican missionary schools and at Madras Christian College in south India, Azariah rose to prominence through his involvement in international missionary circles, particularly those affiliated with the YMCA. He was made a bishop in 1912 in Dornakal, a large Telugu-speaking town in what is now the state of Telangana. During the 1920s and 1930s, Azariah, referred to affectionately as *Thandrigaru* (Father), played a key

Figure 7.1 Indigenous preachers with villagers in Medapalli, *c.*1885–95.
Source: Council for World Mission/London Missionary Society Archive, SOAS Library.

role in inspiring mass movements of some 200,000 Dalit Malas and Madigas, tribals, and low caste persons in his diocese.[23] Azariah defended the Christian gospel's capacity to overcome caste divisions, while at the same time recognizing the many displays of caste prejudice that persisted within the life of the Church. He pointed to churches within his Telugu-speaking diocese in which Christians of diverse caste backgrounds sat together, received communion, and shared common meals. Such integration, he maintained, provided proof of the transformative power of Christian belief.

Azariah defended the legitimacy and authenticity of mass conversions and rejected the notion that evangelism among the poor constituted a form of exploitation for sectarian ends. In 1936, Herbert Arthur Popley, the former general secretary of the National Council of YMCAs, claimed that Christians were "exploiting the situation" of India's poor in order to grow in numbers. Azariah refuted Popley by drawing attention to instances in the Bible where people sought repentance and salvation during times of physical duress and hunger. He also emphasized the agency of Dalits in the decision to join the Church. When individuals or groups approached him to learn about the faith and seek admission, he reasoned, he could not be said to be exploiting the situation.[24]

The diverse castes, languages, and races that made up the Church brought with them different habits, perspectives, and experiences. Azariah grappled constantly with the tension between the old and the new, between the universal Church affirmed by his ecumenical involvements and the particularities of local traditions. His belief in the universal Church inspired his career-long struggle against caste divisions among Christians. Like many missionaries before him, Azariah had to draw lines that separated certain caste practices from the new morals and beliefs of the Christian faith. His diocese strictly prohibited converts from working on Sundays, despite angry reactions from their high caste employers. Converts abandoned their caste names for Christian names that often were drawn from the Bible. Notions of purity and pollution that distinguished one community from another were strongly discouraged. The diocese prohibited Madigas from consuming carrion with the aim of ridding them of the stigma of impurity.[25] At the same time, Azariah believed in retaining aspects of culture he did not consider to be at odds with Christianity. Marriage and baptismal ceremonies were adapted to suit indigenous customs and ceremonies, while his diocese also adapted Christian liturgy, hymns, and festivals to Hindu—and, in some cases, Muslim—traditions.[26]

These accommodations to local customs, however, could not prevent converts from regressing or "backsliding" into their former practices and being subject to church discipline. The historian Susan Billington Harper describes how churches imposed various censures for matters ranging from poor church attendance to apostasy, which was usually associated with the veneration of idols.[27] Through the eyes of the churches, these instances of backsliding revealed the back-and-forth movement between conversion to Christ and reversion to paganism. When seen in a less evaluative light, they display the dual participation of converts in ecclesiastical and village life, as well as the blurred religious boundaries among those who occupied the lowest levels of the social hierarchy.

Women and Mass Converts

Just as Protestant missionary societies had initially targeted elites before diverting resources to mass converts, they had also targeted elite women before conceding that they needed to work among lower caste and Dalit women. Early on, they sent female missionaries to elite households in order to share the gospel with Indian women. These women were often kept in seclusion or *purdah*, residing within separate living quarters known as the *zenana*. The seclusion of women was believed to preserve their domesticity and purity by protecting them from the gaze or advances of other men. The aim of "*zenana* missions," as they came to be called, was to reach Indian women with the gospel, thereby enacting a transformation of the family and of wider society. *Zenana* missions did not seek to ensure the equality of the genders within the life of the Church; instead, they cultivated a new and presumably more modern Christian domesticity among converted women. The notions of domesticity advanced by missionaries, according to the historian Eliza Kent, merged indigenous notions of female purity and seclusion with Victorian understandings of the home as a site of women's work and of the moral regeneration of society at large.[28]

As missionaries increasingly diverted their attention to the lower castes, they had to contend with alternative gender norms. Practices of gender seclusion and separation were not as prevalent because Dalit women often had to work in the fields alongside the men. However, missionaries sought to inculcate the same notions of domesticity among Dalit women, prioritizing modern techniques of "home management," which included literacy, sewing, buying food, cooking, and so on.[29] This brought their mission in India into alignment with the Victorian separation of the sphere of men, who worked in factories, from that of women, who cultivated home life.

Eventually, the task of reaching Indian women with the gospel was passed on to converts. Indian "Bible women," as they were called, gained access to families and women more effectively than foreign women due to their cultural and linguistic skills. They employed songs and stories from the Bible as vehicles for making contact with women and imparted knowledge of reading and writing as well. In these endeavors, the Bible represented more than a sacred text conveying the knowledge of salvation; it came to signify a source of education and literacy, something denied to many Hindu women.[30]

If conversion among Dalits and women was not ideologically committed to social liberation, it certainly carried the potential for social advancement for some women.[31] Within the context of the mass movements, converts acquired skills and knowledge that widened their options for employment and enhanced their sense of self-worth. The goal of emancipating the downtrodden from oppressive structures and ideologies, however, was not the focus of Protestant Evangelicalism, but of theological liberalism. Toward the turn of the twentieth century, new impulses in theology to transform society gave rise to the "social gospel." John Clough's second wife, Emma Rauschenbusch-Clough, was an ardent feminist and the sister of the renowned proponent of the social gospel, Walter Rauschenbusch. Her social gospel priorities found expression in the account she provided of her husband's work among the Madigas, particularly in its emphasis on the social impact of the mass movement.[32]

Mass Movements Among the Nagas and Mizos

Studies of conversion among the tribes of northeast India tend to emphasize cultural continuity. The project of "conserving" tribal culture began with British colonial activities in the region, but missionaries also committed themselves to preserving important aspects of the tribal way of life. The historian Frederick Downs describes how Christianity played an important role in preserving tribal identity in the midst of rapid socioeconomic changes toward the turn of the twentieth century. This conservative impulse even shaped government policies after independence. Each of these external actors wanted to avoid the appearance of eroding tribal culture through their involvement in the region.[33]

Residing in frontier zones of India, tribal peoples were located *between Hindu and Muslim*, and sometimes Buddhist. Rarely did northeastern tribals come under the influence of Islam (the Pangals of Manipur were an exception). Mountain ranges formed a barrier that separated the subcontinent from the Islamized regions of Central Asia to the west and the Xinjiang region of China to the east. Dense forests and rugged hill terrains had enabled tribals to set themselves apart and develop skills that would ward off intruders.[34] Their conversion to Christianity integrated them into ecclesiastical networks, while accentuating their sense of difference from urban adherents of Islam or Hinduism.[35]

Another important aspect of the peoples of northeast India is their ethnicity. Residing on the frontiers of South and Southeast Asian societies, the peoples of Nagaland, Mizoram, Meghalaya, and Assam are notable for their distinctive racial and ethnic features; they are more akin to East and Southeast Asians than to mainland Indians. Because of their location between the Indian subcontinent, China, and Southeast Asia, their territories have formed a vital buffer for the larger and more powerful regimes of China and India (see Figure 7.2). Despite their racial, cultural, and religious differences, the Government of India has therefore been keen on "protecting" tribals and their lands in order to secure this buffer zone from Chinese encroachment and influence.[36]

From Local Religion to World Religion

The mass conversion of Naga and Mizo peoples to Christianity illustrates a shift from localized, tribal religion into a world religion. Their conversion also reveals the unique challenges faced by ethnic groups residing near the frontier zones of British India. Their isolation from the cultural and religious influence of the plains appears to have motivated their interest in becoming Christian. As they became integrated into church structures, they developed a sense of participation and belonging amidst global influences that threatened their way of life.

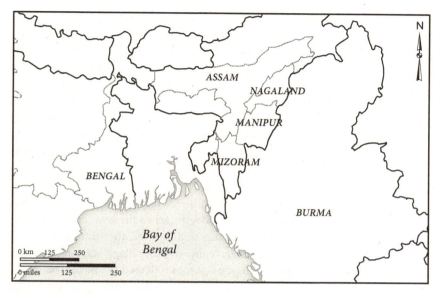

Figure 7.2 Map of northeast India.

Recent scholarship about conversion in northeast India draws upon the work of the anthropologist Robin Horton. Horton's work, based on fieldwork among the Kalabari people of Nigeria, portrays indigenous African beliefs, experience, and agency as the driving forces behind their conversion to Christianity. In other words, Christian identity is not imposed from the top down, but arises when earlier beliefs make contact with the new religion and interpret it on indigenous cultural terms. To what extent can this paradigm apply to conversion in northeast India without committing the error identified by Robbins? In other words, can we recognize the enduring relevance of older cosmologies in the lives of converts while also appreciating their production of a new and distinctive Christian culture?

Horton draws a distinction between two tiers of cosmology. The lower tier is associated with "typical traditional cosmology"[37]—people residing within a premodern locality venerate lesser spirits who address various everyday needs. The second-tier cosmology is centered on a supreme being who oversees the entire world (the macrocosm). As long as people are confined to a locality, they will venerate lesser spirits and tend to regard the supreme being as less relevant to their immediate circumstances. But as lives are integrated into a larger world through trade and the emergence of the modern nation-state, the role of the supreme being becomes more prominent. People who leave their microcosms develop a new moral code now underpinned by the supreme being.[38] Horton argues that exposure to Islam or Christianity when a group is widening its horizons can lead to a large-scale adoption of one of those world religions.

Richard Eaton, a historian of South Asia, applies Horton's model to the Nagas of northeast India. These tribes, he claims, experienced the most large-scale conversion to Christianity in the whole of Asia.[39] Their trajectory entailed a transition from localized tribal religion to a new, global faith. This coincided with their exposure to a wider world through British rule and the arrival of American Baptist missionaries. The convergence of these factors, however, does not assign primary agency to the outsider in the conversion process. On the contrary, the driving force behind conversion was the adaptive cosmology of the Nagas as their horizons expanded under British rule.

Huge mountain ranges on both sides of their villages had long isolated the Naga tribes from those of Burma (now Myanmar) to the east and the Indian state of Assam to the west. Situated in this middle zone, they developed a way of life marked by slash and burn agriculture, intervillage warfare, and the practice of headhunting. Their religious system reflected the needs that arose within their locality. The Ao Naga tribe worshiped a range of lesser spirits who wielded malevolent influences over the sky, jungle, and houses of the village. Because of this, village priests (*putirs*) had to appease the spirits through sacrifices of pigs, fowl, and cows and perform occasional exorcisms.[40] The Ao Nagas also believed in a transcendent, benevolent deity named Lungkijingba who presides over the universe but is quite removed from the day-to-day affairs of the people. This supreme deity became more relevant to the Ao Nagas as their exposure to Westerners increased through colonial expansion in the region.[41] Much of this related to the interest of the British in establishing lucrative tea plantations.[42]

Conversion Among the Nagas

Conversion among the Nagas began with individuals and moved to groups.[43] A convert from the American Baptist mission in Nowgong (now Nagaon) named Godhula and his wife Lucy befriended an Ao Naga named Subongmeren who had regularly visited the Assam Valley to trade. After learning about Christianity from the Assamese couple, Subongmeren received baptism with great enthusiasm. He then persuaded Godhula and his wife to accompany him to his Ao Naga village, Molungkimong, to share the Christian message. Using their musical talents, teaching skills, and acquired grasp of the Ao Naga language, Godhula, Lucy, and Subongmeren made nine converts and in 1872 erected a small bamboo chapel where they held services and imparted Christian instruction. This became "the nucleus of the first Naga Christian congregation."[44] However, due to hostility from local village chiefs, the young congregation had to relocate to a new village, Molungyimsen (New Molung).

Also in 1872, the American Baptist missionary Edward Winter Clark and his wife Mary arrived in Molungyimsen. Over the next two decades, they followed the pattern set by other missionaries of committing themselves to Bible translation, the creation of grammars, education, and the training of Ao Naga catechists.[45] Initially, the Nagas viewed the Clarks as white intruders and agents of British colonial power. By declaring Sunday as a day of rest, the Clarks evoked opposition from locals who considered this and other missionary strictures as a disruption of their way of life.

Despite this initial opposition, the Clarks made inroads into Ao Naga society by working with Godhula and training other catechists and by embracing key aspects of Naga cosmology. Clark and his team of local assistants made every effort to adapt the new faith to the already existing spiritual vocabulary of the Nagas. A crucial issue was the word they would use to translate "God" in their rendition of the New Testament. They rejected biblical names such as Jehovah; they even rejected the Naga name for the supreme deity, Lungkijingba. They chose instead to use the Ao word *tsungrem*, the more everyday term used to denote a spirit. This choice ran the risk of reducing the biblical conception of a universal God to a local, territorial deity in keeping with earlier Naga belief. What the translators maintained, however, was that *tsungrem* could be a generic designation for "spirit" when no specific place is attached to it. In this way, writes Eaton, missionaries were able to bring the essence of the Ao pantheon ("its 'spiritness' or '*tsungrem-ness*'") into harmony with the biblical concept of God and endow *tsungrem* "with the power and universality of the Biblical supreme deity."[46]

During the 1870s, this new village of Molungyimsen grew rapidly as more and more families relocated there. They were drawn to the cultural, educational, and economic activity that the new Christian society had stimulated. Soon, neighboring Ao Naga villages invited missionaries to visit them to bring the Christian message. The novelty of missionary intervention in this region was offset by the continuity of the new faith with indigenous cosmology.

During the 1880s and 1890s, the growth of Ao Naga Baptist Christian congregations accelerated and Christian village settlements multiplied. This period coincided with a more aggressive colonial presence in the region. The East India Company army entered the Naga Hills with an eye to securing a stronger position in this borderland region: By penetrating the Naga country, the Company would be able to bolster its commercial interests in neighboring Assam and Burma.[47] The colonial army was met with fierce resistance from the Angami Nagas, among the most powerful and skilled warriors of the region; but, after much fighting, the Company army defeated the Angami, who were forced to surrender and pay indemnities. Thereafter, the Company established a lasting military presence in Kohima.[48]

The larger story arising from the case study of the Nagas is what Lamin Sanneh calls the *indigenous discovery of Christianity*, which is distinct from the missionary discovery of the Nagas.[49] As encounters with missionaries and British colonial officers expanded the horizons of Naga cultural engagement, their cosmology became more oriented toward the worship of a higher, benevolent deity. This coincided with the affinity the Ao Nagas developed with American Baptist missionaries such as Clark, the performance of baptisms, and transformations in literacy, ways of life, and modes of worship. The vast majority of the Nagas, however, became Christian *after* the withdrawal of British forces and foreign missionaries from the region. Moreover, the rates of conversion correlate directly with the degree to which a particular group extended its local cosmology into the new Christian framework.

The Sema Nagas, whose villages converted with little or no contact with Baptist missionaries, also discovered Christianity on their own cultural terms. A study conducted by the writer J. H. Hutton noted that, from 1915 to 1920, there was only one small Christian village and several Christian families in the Sema country. By the mid-1920s, a missionary traveling through the region observed many Christian groups worshiping in private houses, apparently with no official leadership.[50] The entire village structure of the Semas, which was centered on a powerful village chief, was transformed through conversion. One colonial observer noted that the steady diminishing of the chief's authority through the British prohibition of warfare led many Semas to break from his authority and embrace Christianity.[51]

This perspective suggests that colonial rule created a vacuum that was eventually filled by Christianity. British policies and influence had eroded a cultural system oriented to tribal warfare, headhunting, and the power of chiefs. In keeping with Horton's paradigm for conversion, the Nagas' cultural horizons were expanded through exposure to the British presence in northeast India as well as to a greater British Empire. During the First World War, as the Nagas fought for the British across European heartlands, they were exposed to many aspects of Western societies. Christianity was made available to them within this context. Recognizing the timing of this encounter, however, is quite distinct from suggesting that colonial rulers coerced the Nagas into converting or that their conversions amounted to rice conversions.

From 1942 to 1950, the events of the Second World War and those tied to Indian independence severely impacted the peoples of northeast India. The Japanese invasion of Burma in 1942 created extraordinary hardship for the Burmese and a massive flow of refugees into Manipur (located to the south of Nagaland). As many as 600,000 fled Burma to escape Japanese violence and coerced labor, the majority of whom were Indian laborers who had migrated to Burma to serve on plantations. Tens of thousands died of disease or malnutrition. As Nagas were increasingly affected by the war, many sought relief and protection from the British military and providers of humanitarian aid. In the process, they grew dependent on the colonial government and outside sources of daily commodities.[52]

When the British withdrew from India in 1947, the Government of India assumed responsibility for and oversight over the lands of northeast India. Many Nagas aspired to complete autonomy from both British and Indian rule. The government suspected foreign missionaries of breeding antinational sentiments among the Naga Christians and of sponsoring separatist activities. Government scrutiny and charges brought against American Baptist missionaries led ultimately to their withdrawal from the region. Christian revival movements of the 1950s led to mass conversions among the Nagas that were led by Nagas. These conversions were now energized by the hope that Christianity would provide a new source of identity during times of political turmoil and transition.

The fact that Naga mass conversions happened after the withdrawal of Westerners from the region and that they were anchored in their distinct, local cosmology casts doubt on both coercion and inducement as explanations for their occurrence. The mass movement that swept through the Naga Hills would eventually yield a population that is 95 percent Christian. This transformation was accompanied by higher literacy rates and the abandonment of warfare as a way of life. Printing presses and schools established by the American Baptists gave rise to a print culture, which in turn laid the foundations for national consciousness among the Nagas[53] and a Naga Christian identity that provided a new framework for resisting Hindu or Muslim hegemony.[54] By becoming Christian, peoples who had already resided between Hindu and Muslim traditions further cemented their difference from these larger categories of belonging.

Despite the continuous threads of cultural identity that are evident in Naga conversion, it is also important to note the distinctive Christian culture that emerged from their conversion. Besides developing new doctrinal beliefs, which were taught in the institutions established by American Baptists, Naga Christians embraced an alternative lifestyle that signaled a clear departure from their former way of life.

Downs identifies several important aspects of this new lifestyle and notes how descriptions of a new Christian culture arise from accounts given by the Nagas. The abandonment of the use of opium and other intoxicants was central to the Nagas' new Christian identity.[55] This had important economic implications, because it cut into an important source of revenue for the British, who promoted its cultivation and sale in northeast India. Another virtue stressed in Christian communities was personal and household cleanliness, which missionaries had emphasized in response to diseases that prevailed in the region. The mandate to bathe daily created a new demand for a clean water supply and an infrastructure to secure it. Commitments to prayer, evangelism, charity, and loving one's neighbors, even those belonging to hostile tribes, also became central to the praxis of the emerging Christian culture. The development of a culture of worship centered on singing was also important to Naga Christianity.

Finally, Downs notes that, by becoming Christian, northeasterners such as the Nagas were liberated from their old cosmology in which they were "socially and psychologically enslaved by the fear of spirits." As Christians, their belief in a loving God and faith in Christ, who possessed power over demons, represented a marked change from their past.[56] These characteristics of a distinctively Christian culture address concerns raised by the anthropologist Joel Robbins about the dangers of a methodological commitment to continuity. The Nagas, and perhaps other mass converts of the northeast, present a "both-and" model of conversion in which both continuity and rupture are displayed in the lives of Christians.

Conversion Among the Mizos

A very similar trajectory to that of the Nagas is found among the Mizos of northeast India. Their land, Mizoram (literally "land of the Mizos"), was also the site of a large-scale conversion to Christianity. Their path to conversion similarly entailed the adaptation of tribal cosmology to Christian belief. This was a process that coincided with colonial expansion in the region and the broadening of Mizo spheres of engagement. In assessing the motivations and contingencies that led to the mass conversions, it is tempting to overemphasize the role of foreign missionaries. As Frykenberg has noted, their role was to put in place a basic infrastructure consisting of biblical teachings, schools, printing presses, and church practices. The waves of conversion, however, would arise only after decades of incubation and through the key roles of indigenous preachers, catechists, and translators.[57]

Toward the end of the nineteenth century, the British launched military operations in the Lushai Hills (now called Mizoram) against Mizo warriors who were conducting headhunting raids near the Assam Valley. By this time, the British had established tea plantations in Assam and were keen to protect them from the Mizos. After a series of Mizo raids and punitive British responses, the British finally subdued the Mizos. They pursued a policy of pacification that led to their occupation and, in 1895, the annexation of Mizoram.[58]

Shortly thereafter, two missionaries, James Herbert Lorrain and Frederick William Savidge, who worked for the Arthington Aborigines mission, arrived in Mizo country to preach the gospel. They committed themselves to language acquisition, establishing a school for children, and the development of a script for the orally based Mizo language. The two men had some medical training and made attending to the sick an important aspect of their work. Savidge, who had received more medical training than most missionaries, was able to treat illnesses among the Mizos with the latest Western drugs. He regarded Western medicine as a powerful vehicle in drawing the Mizos to faith in Christ. It became a test of their faith, he maintained, to see if they would be willing to abandon their sacrifices to evil spirits and place their trust in Christ, who was now coming to them through the agency of modern medical practices.[59]

In terms of their pre-Christian belief system, the Mizos possessed elements that resembled Naga cosmology. They believed in a creator and transcendent being called *Pathian* (which literally translates as "Holy Father") who factored minimally in everyday life and in the religious practices of the people. Despite the fact that he resided in a distant heaven, the Mizos prayed to *Pathian* in times of extreme distress and appeared to attribute the larger course of their lives in some measure to his providential steering.[60] Beneath *Pathian* were a variety of lesser spirits, both malevolent and benevolent, that more directly influenced the day-to-day affairs of the Mizos and were objects of sacrifice and propitiation. However, in terms of their transition to Christianity, there was a difference between the Nagas and the Mizos. Whereas the Nagas employed the word *tsungrem* (which had previously referred to lesser spirits) to designate God, the Mizos moved *Pathian* from his rather limited earlier role to being identified with Jehovah, or the God of the Bible.

During the early twentieth century, Christianity grew rapidly in Mizoram through a series of revivals. In 1905, Welsh missionaries made many converts among the Khasi, through intense evangelistic efforts. The Welsh hoped to recreate in India the revival that was occurring in Wales at the time. The conversions among the Khasi eventually spread to the Mizo Hills and resulted in several waves of conversions: From 1911 to 1921, the Mizo Christian population grew from 2,461 to 27,720.[61] Indigenous factors were key to the size and scale of Mizo revivalism: The Naga and Mizo mass movements shared the central role of indigenous catechists and preachers, an anchor in local cosmology and traditions, and a strong sense of collective imagination and participation.

Initially, missionaries had attempted to ban many activities that were central to Mizo culture, believing them to be tied to their former religion. These included drinking beer, involvement in local festivals and feasts, and what the missionaries regarded as religious chanting. The revivals among the Mizos were followed by traditionalist counter-revivals in which Mizos reclaimed many of these practices, a trajectory that missionaries interpreted as a reversion to heathenism. As Christian revivals continued into the following decades, some indigenous cultural practices—including those that had previously been banned—were brought back into the lives of Mizo Christians.[62] Dancing, chanting, the use of drums, and especially singing became central to Mizo Christian experience. In sum, "revivals became instruments of indigenization."[63] Abstinence from liquor and opium, however, would remain an important "test of sincerity" for converts and a marker of commitment for church members.[64]

In the years following the Second World War, Pentecostalism made inroads into Mizoram. Its Spirit-centered and emotionally expressive forms of worship merged with the revivalism already prevalent in the churches of this region. However, this merging of traditions evoked resentment on both sides. Pentecostals resented Presbyterian control of the churches, while local leaders appear to have pushed back against Pentecostal influence with a call to sounder doctrine and ecclesiastical traditions.

Beneath the surface of Western denominational affiliations is a highly distinctive Mizo spirituality. The historian Joy Pachuau notes the centrality of the notion of "being in the Spirit" for Mizo Christians. As tempting as it may be to regard this as a marker of global Pentecostal influence, Pachuau stresses its indigenous moorings. It is not uncommon, she writes, to see in the streets a woman "shaking uncontrollably and moving vigorously," especially in times of revival. Groups of people can be seen dancing in the streets and "entering backwards" into a private home in order to pray for a particular family.[65] In the context of Mizo Christian experience, this phenomenon of being "in the Spirit" is accompanied by a commitment to righteousness and other markers of biblical commitment; and yet, it displays continuity with notions of spirit possession that prevailed in Mizo spirituality prior to the arrival of Christianity.

It might appear that northeasterners simply inherited the denominational structures and theologies of the missionaries, the three largest establishments being the Baptists, Roman Catholics, and Presbyterians. The Baptists of American Baptist origin now fall under the Council of Baptist Churches in North East India (CBCNEI). They predominate in Nagaland, the Garo Hill district of Meghalaya, southern Mizoram, Manipur, and parts of Assam. The Presbyterian Church of India is prevalent in parts of Meghalaya, northern Mizoram, and parts of Assam and Manipur.[66] Those who travel to these regions of India can plainly see the prevalence of institutional Christianity in the lives of the people. In Mizoram, where 80 percent of the population is Christian, church attendance is built into the very fabric of social life, with the average professing Christian attending several services a week. Beneath the surface of these structures, however, is a vibrant spirituality that re-channels older beliefs and practices within the new faith.

Conversions in Northwest India

Christians of north and northwest India tend to receive less attention than those of south India, at least in part because of their smaller numbers. Northwest India is a religiously diverse region lying at the intersection of Hindu, Muslim, and Sikh traditions. This makes it difficult to create a simple narrative about conversion and the emergence of churches in the region. As a complex frontier zone, the Punjab's diversity created unique challenges for missionaries, especially as they attempted to nurture a new Christian identity among converts. Conversions among Dalits gave rise to unique questions of identity relating to caste and religion. Did converts ever really leave behind their former beliefs and ways of life? And to what religion did they belong before they converted?

Urban Conversions

Missionaries and Indian church leaders shaped a distinctive expression of Christianity across urban centers of north and northwest India. American Presbyterians worked extensively in the British Northwest Provinces. These included the Punjab and other regions that underwent a series of subdivisions (or partitions) under British rule: for instance, the Indian states of Jammu and Kashmir, Himachal Pradesh, Haryana, and other regions located near the current India–Pakistan border. In Allahabad, Presbyterians established schools staffed with Hindu and Muslim teachers who taught in both English and vernacular languages. Elsewhere, missionaries established orphanages, boarding schools, asylums for the blind and lepers, and printing presses.

According to the scholar Arun Jones, many north Indians were drawn to Christianity because of continuities between the new faith and pre-Christian devotional practices. The message preached by Methodist and Presbyterian missionaries resonated with locals because of the way in which their Christian message resembled elements of local religions. *Bhakti* movements (Hindu traditions that placed a strong emphasis on intense devotion to a personal deity) were widely noted for their rejection of caste distinctions. As they "criticized inherited orthodoxies and hierarchies, and imagined and formed new kinds of communities," Jones writes, *bhakti* movements "created a religious and sociological Thirdspace in their society."[67] By "Thirdspace," Jones refers to a place of religious experimentation, where groups can borrow from and critique dominant traditions.[68]

Jones's analysis helps us appreciate how missionary Christianity in north and northwest India located itself *between Hindu and Muslim*. The new faith entered a sacred terrain shaped by the poet saints of *bhakti* movements along with practitioners of Sufism, a form of Sunni Islam stressing mystical experience and personal devotion as the path to the divine.[69] As Indians assumed more prominent leadership roles in churches, they incorporated the spirit of local devotionalism into the life of congregations and embraced forms of music, liturgy, and theology from *bhakti* traditions. The socioreligious ethos created by *bhakti* was "used by Evangelicalism [to] provide crucial ground on which the newly arrived religion can be understood in terms that make sense in the existing religious culture."[70]

Congregations established by American Methodists or Presbyterians included converts from Hindu, Muslim, and Sikh backgrounds. Muslims in Hindi-speaking north India consisted largely of persons from low-ranking communities of weavers and cultivators. Most Muslim converts to Christianity came from those backgrounds. Sikhs belonging to the Kabirpanthi and Mazhabi communities, who were also poor, converted to Christianity under the influence of American missionaries. Both Sikhs and Muslims in the region were also significantly impacted by the lore and practices of Hindu asceticism and devotionalism. When they entered the Christian fold, therefore, their diverse sectarian influences merged with the religious culture introduced by missionaries. As with converts described in south India, these converts also faced ostracism from their families upon conversion. Because of this, they often joined "Christian villages" that were modeled after indigenous schemes and concepts of village life.[71]

Chuhra and Chamar: A Potpourri of Identities

A different set of dynamics accompanied the conversion of low caste communities of the rural northwest in a region known as the Punjab.[72] Because the communities in question were most often oppressed and impoverished Dalits, their decision to become Christian on a large scale raised a different set of questions for missionaries. As in south Indian mass movements, questions about motives abounded. How to address their substantial material needs and how to integrate them into churches also weighed heavily on the minds of missionaries. Conversion to a more egalitarian religion did not relieve Dalits of caste oppression as menial laborers; this was another issue missionaries had to address, but often did not.[73]

Low-ranking groups in the Punjab provided menial services through a variety of occupations. They were essentially divided into two groups: one associated with aspects of domestic village life; the other chiefly associated with agriculture. Among those who provided services in villages were the Nai (barbers), Dhobis (washermen), and Julahas (weavers). The agricultural laborers included the Tarkhan (carpenters), who made and repaired wooden plows and wells; the Kumhar (potters), who provided clay vessels for carrying water and for domestic use; and the Lohar (blacksmiths), who worked with plowshares and other iron tools.

The Chamars and Chuhras not only were the most numerous among the menial population, but they also were the most stigmatized of the untouchable *jatis* of the Punjab.[74] Chamars (leatherworkers), who made leather bags, whips, and bridles for animals that pulled bullock carts, were deemed polluted because of their contact with animal hides. The Chuhras were agricultural laborers or sanitary workers who also produced brooms and ropes.[75] They converted to other religions in large numbers.

The Chuhras were sweepers in urban settings but mostly land laborers in rural ones, where their livelihood depended almost entirely on village landowners who exploited their labor. Most lived in perpetual poverty because of the low wages they were paid or the small portion of the harvest they were accorded by landlords. Because of their contact with filth, their consumption of carrion, and their involvement with other "polluting" activities, they came to be regarded as an untouchable community. The label "Chuhra" was one among several designations that were freighted with highly derogatory and abusive connotations.[76] As a stigmatized untouchable community, Chuhras were forced to reside in ghettos that were far removed from the residences of "touchable" castes; they were denied access to public wells, tanks, and roads that passed through residences of "touchable" communities; and they were funneled into an oppressive system of forced labor on agricultural tracts.

Despite their low status, Chuhras navigated between the dominant religious traditions of the northwest, worshiping at Hindu, Muslim, and Sikh shrines along with those of their own deities. During the nineteenth century, Chuhras did not understand themselves to be either Hindu or Muslim, and members of those communities did not recognize Chuhras as belonging to their folds.[77] So eclectic were their day-to-day religious practices that one Presbyterian missionary noted that the "Chuhras are chameleon-like in their copying of the externals of other faiths."[78] This adaptive quality seems to have played an important role in leading the Chuhras to the Christian religion. They had always maintained a tendency to absorb the characteristics of the Hindu, Muslim, and Sikh traditions of the Punjab, in some cases identifying with one rather than another, and their songs invoked the names of figures from various faiths: Ram, Moses, Krishna, Allah, Nanak, and others.[79] It was their own agency that led them ultimately to regard the religion of missionaries as one that would address their aspirations. As one missionary noted: "It was rather they who sought us out than we who sought them."[80]

Adding yet another layer to the potpourri of religious influences on the Chuhra were cult traditions, religious lore, and reformist movements that attempted to lay claim to Chuhra heritage and identity. Hindus designated Chuhras as "Balmikis," a name deriving from Valmiki, the author of the *Ramayana*, who is believed by some to have come from lowly origins but achieved salvation by reciting the name of *Ram*. That "Balmiki" would remake—or mask—the name of their local guru, "Bala Shah," shows how the Chuhras were situated between multiple traditions, with each narrativizing their past in its own way. The influence of a legendary Sufi saint, Lal Beg, and of Sikh religion also influenced Chuhra identity well before their mass conversions to Christianity.[81]

The Chuhra Mass Movement

The Chuhra mass movement, which began in 1873, shares with other mass movements a sense of the unexpected and overwhelming scale of the baptisms and the somewhat marginal roles played by missionaries. It changed the entire complexion of the Church in northwest India from a small, highly literate urban community to a much larger population that included the rural poor and illiterate.[82] There is near consensus among historians that Chuhras were the primary initiators of their conversion to Christianity. In order to address the demand for baptism and pastoral services over vast distances, missionaries employed Indian catechists (subordinate teachers) who often were Chuhra converts. These catechists worked for missionaries, but they coordinated their efforts with village headmen. These headmen played important roles in leading members of their villages to embrace Christianity.

Some missionary reports trace the mass conversion movement of the Chuhras to the conversion of a man named Ditt, an illiterate vendor of animal hides who lived in a village in Sialkot district. After learning about Christianity from a convert from a neighboring village, Ditt was baptized by a Presbyterian missionary residing in Sialkot. Later, he made arrangements for members of his own family to be baptized; shortly thereafter, as word spread of their baptisms, larger networks of Chuhra families began seeking baptism. "News of the new religion spread by word of mouth at weddings, funerals, melas, and wherever Chuhras met for business or social reasons."[83]

As increasing numbers of these menial castes embraced Christianity, other missionary societies were drawn to the region (besides the CMS and SPG), including the Salvation Army, American Methodists, and the Belgian Capuchins, a Roman Catholic order. Inevitably, conversions compelled missionaries to come to terms with the unique circumstances of backward communities. These included cultural issues associated with dietary laws, hereditary occupations that contributed to their polluted status, multiple or hybrid identities, and the complex demands of their ties to rural landlords.[84]

In a study that compares the work of Belgian Capuchins and Anglican missionaries of the CMS, Christopher Harding examines the mass movement among the Chuhras. CMS missionaries arrived in 1850; they tended to be better staffed and maintained favorable ties with their fellow Protestant British rulers. Capuchins arrived in the Punjab in 1885. They felt estranged from the Protestant colonial administration and prided themselves on the austere means with which they labored in comparison to CMS missionaries. The two groups competed with each other for converts and were sharply critical of each other's views. What they shared in common, however, was their status as Europeans and a tendency not to hold their local catechists in very high esteem, despite their heavy reliance on them.

From 1890 to 1920, the number of baptized Christians and catechumens (young Christians preparing for baptism) among the Chuhras rose from 4,896 to 29,776. Catholic numbers increased to roughly 25,000.[85] As a whole, the size of the Christian population of the Punjab grew from 3,912 members in 1881 to 395,629 in 1931. By the late 1930s, Chuhras are reported to have comprised as much as 95 percent of the Punjab's Christian population.[86] This numerical predominance would become an important aspect of the Pakistani Christianity that would follow the 1947 partition of India (discussed in Chapter 8).

The hidden story told by these numbers concerns the role of native catechists in negotiating group decision making. They did so through local, face-to-face interactions between Indians. This is not surprising, since Indian catechists possessed knowledge of local languages, social cues—including local hierarchies and networks of influence—and the importance of maintaining good relations with families and the local community (*izzat*) in village settings.[87] Moreover, only local catechists understood the needs and sensitivities of the region's Hindus, Muslims, and Sikhs and were in a position to gauge their interest in Christianity. Despite their centrality to the mass movements, their precise roles remain vague, largely because of the lack of any direct or detailed accounts of their activities in missionary reports.

Sincerity, Communion, and Reconversion

As news of the Christian option spread by word of mouth and numbers of converts increased, missionaries had to come to terms with their new roles in nurturing congregations and addressing their humanitarian needs. Both Capuchin and CMS missionaries conceded that a quest for material advancement was at least part of what motivated Chuhras to become Christian. At times, the Capuchins lamented this. Still, missionaries seem to have accepted that, in the initial phases of conversion, motives for conversion were mixed. The more profound work of nurturing the new faith of converts would come later, perhaps generations later, after habits of belief and practice were more clearly established in congregations.[88]

Missionaries, however, were vexed by the task of producing committed, doctrinally informed Christian subjects from the mass converts. Their concern over how well converts truly grasped the new faith is illustrated in the attention paid to baptism versus the taking of communion. Missionaries tended to be more lenient in administering baptism than in serving communion. A study conducted by the Presbyterian missionary scholar to the Punjab, Hervey De Witt Griswold, noted that baptism and communion were important identity markers for mass converts. Both sacraments represented the convert's breach with "heathenism." Quoting an unnamed observer, Griswold portrayed mass converts in rather demeaning terms. He noted, for instance, how baptism marked the Chuhras as Christians "as a lumber company marks their logs."[89] If baptism marked their entry into the Christian fold, however imperfect their grasp of the gospel, the taking of communion represented a more complete consolidation of Christian identity. Griswold likened the baptism of mass converts in India to "infant baptism" in European Christian traditions. Both involved classes of people who apparently lacked the cognitive ability to grasp what they were doing—an argument strikingly similar to one made by Gandhi (discussed in Chapter 8). Just as in Europe, baptism was followed years later by a ceremonial first communion—Protestant missionaries in India instituted at least a six-month interval between baptism and the taking of communion—and during this interval, converts underwent instruction in Christian doctrine. This different weighing of baptism and communion represented the difference between a merely nominal Christian identity and a more reverential and informed one. Griswold likened the taking of communion among Chuhra converts to their practice of taking *prasad* (food devotionally offered) at Sikh gurdwaras or Balmiki shrines. In Griswold's tabulations, there were far more baptized converts across denominations than communicants.

The matter of Christian baptism and communion relates to the larger issue of nurture and instruction in the lives of converts. Missionaries and the Indian catechists working under them shared responsibility for the spiritual formation of converts in newly established churches. The roles of missionaries were marginal in the early phases of the mass movement but became more prominent as the task of recruiting and training catechists, establishing schools, and administering pastoral care increased. By 1882, the burgeoning population of converts needed more trained, literate catechists than missionaries were able to provide. Both CMS leaders and Capuchins complained of being too understaffed to meet the overwhelming demand for instruction.

In the midst of rapidly growing Christian numbers in the Punjab and in other parts of India, upper caste Hindus came to believe that their religion was under siege by foreign-induced conversions. Using this as a rallying cry, an increasingly organized Hindu public in major cities of British India launched countermovements that sought to stem the tide of conversion, especially among Dalits.

One such movement was the Arya Samaj, a Hindu reformist organization founded by a Gujarati Brahmin named Dayananda Sarasvati (1824–83) that sought to revitalize Hinduism through both inward transformation and outward campaigns of propagation. The Arya Samaj became quite active in the Punjab as well as in Gujarat and parts of south India. Internally, Dayananda Sarasvati believed that Hinduism required a greater degree of cohesiveness and clarity in terms of its identity; this would be achieved by an emphasis on the four Vedas as foundational sacred texts and by presenting Hindus with more clearly enumerated and articulated beliefs. Outwardly, Sarasvati espoused the rite of *shuddhi*, whereby those who had lost their caste by becoming polluted could be purified and rejoin their original caste (or Hindu) community. This would be a way of readmitting "outcasted" Christian and Muslim converts back into the Hindu fold.[90] Similar to *Ghar Wapsi* (reconversion) campaigns of the present day, these *shuddhi* campaigns were grounded in the belief that conversions to Christianity were insincere and induced by Westerners. High caste Hindus in the major urban centers of India came to regard conversion to Christianity and Islam as a threat to Hindu survival. The response was to advocate a strong campaign of counter-proselytization through public *shuddhi* campaigns.[91]

Conclusion

The mass conversion movements of South Asia gave rise to a Church that was predominantly Dalit and tribal. Examples from mainland and northeast India highlight several overarching features of these movements and the kinds of public reactions they elicited. First, mass conversions sparked heated debates over questions of motive or "authenticity"; the latter adds to motive a test of purity. For a conversion to be authentic, the decision must not be contaminated by worldly interests, which are unrelated to the unique claims of a religion. An authentic conversion presumes an autonomous self who freely chooses a religion and is not lured or coerced in any way by external factors.[92] Opponents of missionaries accused converts of simply trying to gain access to material resources and of having little or no interest in the content of the Christian message.

Interestingly, the views of missionaries and their critics converged around the concept of an authentic conversion. Both employed the language of sincerity or authenticity, but for very different reasons. Missionaries ranging from the Jesuit Francis Xavier to the Baptist John Clough went to great lengths to ensure that candidates for baptism were adequately knowledgeable about the tenets of the faith and would not amount to mere rice converts. Ultimately, missionaries defended the enterprise of conversion and strived to yield a harvest of converts who were motivated by spiritual factors. The same, however, cannot be said of the critics of conversions: Their main concern was not to produce authentic converts, but to contest the very idea of conversion among poor, illiterate masses. This, as Chapter 9 discusses, was the perspective of Mohandas Karamchand Gandhi.

Debates about mass movements also raise questions about their transformative impact on Dalits and tribals. Missionary accounts of their work among Dalits tend to emphasize the cultural transformation and social advancement enacted by Christian conversion. This was the case in the transformation of the toddy-tapping Shanar into the upwardly mobile, entrepreneurial Nadar documented in the work of Robert Hardgrave. In his work among Madiga leather workers, Clough required converts to abstain from eating carrion, working on Sundays, and worshiping Hindu deities. These, he claimed, struck at the very heart of "Dravidian village life," revolutionizing the Madigas' relations with their Sudra employers, meat vendors, and Brahmin leaders at temple establishments.[93] The humanitarian aid his mission provided for Madigas during the great famine of 1876–8 played a critical role in turning people, in his words, from "idols" to the God of the English and American people.[94] Local newspapers, however, portrayed these conversions as the direct result of foreign aid in a time of need.[95]

Mass conversions also highlight the role of indigenous agents in the conversion process. It was not foreign missionaries who led the mass movements: On the contrary, missionaries were often overwhelmed by the eagerness and scale with which Dalits and tribals sought baptism. Native evangelists and catechists bore the brunt of the burden as they assisted with Bible translation, propagated the faith, and provided Christian instruction for new converts. This was the case among the Mizo and Naga tribals of northeast India. Their massive transformation did not entail the effacement of their former cultural and religious frameworks; accounts of their conversions reveal continuity between their local cosmologies and their new, Christian identities. Mizo and Naga converts used local names applied to their supreme being or to the more immanent spirits to refer to the God of the Bible. This lends support to Lamin Sanneh's observations about the radical translatability of the gospel, specifically his claim that Christian expansion in the Global South is especially prevalent in those societies that preserved the indigenous name for God.[96]

8
Nationalist Politics and the Minoritization of Christians

In 1928, Mohandas K. Gandhi, the leader of India's independence movement, visited the renowned Christian Medical College of Vellore, south India. The American missionary Ida Scudder founded the college with a vision for training women nurses and doctors. The topic of Gandhi's speech was *swadeshi*—literally "of one's own country," or the doctrine of national self-reliance. Under the banner of *swadeshi*, the boycotting of foreign goods and embrace of "homespun" cloth had become central to Gandhi's campaign against British rule. While addressing the medical students, Gandhi was seated cross-legged on an elevated platform, accompanied by a few members of his entourage. To his right and seated below him was Ida Scudder, the granddaughter of John Scudder, an American medical missionary whose children had all become missionaries.[1] The shirtless Gandhi was clad only in *khadi*, or homespun cloth, and assumed the posture of a *sannyasi*, a world renouncer and a teacher of spiritual truths. Through the corners of her eyes, the apprehensive American woman looked *away* from the Mahatma (which means "great soul," as Gandhi came to be called). Perhaps she feared the impact of Gandhi's stature and charisma on her young and impressionable flock. Perhaps she thought he posed a threat to her Christian vision for this prestigious institution (see Figure 8.1).

Whatever Scudder's eyes and Gandhi's posture may have conveyed at that moment, they capture the mutual anxieties of Gandhi, foreign missionaries, and Indian Christians during the early twentieth century. At the center of their many exchanges was Gandhi's interpretation of *swadeshi*. Far from limiting its scope to economic and political self-reliance, Gandhi extended it into the realm of culture and religion. Not only should Indians break their dependence on imported goods, Western institutions, and modern technology, but they should also break their affinity for Christianity, a foreign religion.[2] The aspect of *swadeshi* that stressed "one's own religion" also became an influential aspect of the Muslim nationalism of independent Pakistan and the Buddhist nationalism of independent Burma (Myanmar) and Sri Lanka. Notions of homogeneity and majoritarianism that influenced postcolonial South Asian states made life difficult for minoritized communities such as Christians and for ethnic minorities.

Figure 8.1 The American missionary and doctor Ida Scudder with Gandhi.
Source: Copyrighted by the Scudder Foundation Association and used with permission.

As Gandhi pursued India's independence from British rule, he encountered two major fault lines that threatened the unified nation he longed for. The first of these was the division between Dalits (then called "untouchables") and upper castes. His disagreements with the Dalit leader Bhimrao Ramji Ambedkar (1891–1956) are discussed in Chapter 9. The other fault line related to Hindu–Muslim conflict and is a key focus of this chapter. By the 1930s, political parties representing the interests of Hindus and Muslims were wielding increasing influence in public life and making it more difficult for Gandhi to maintain a united front against British rule. Gandhi's relationship with Muhammad Ali Jinnah (1876–1948), the leader of the Muslim League, became another point of contention in his pursuit of home rule. Gandhi and Jinnah engaged in tireless deliberations with each other and with representatives of the British Raj to arrive at a power-sharing scheme for Hindus and Muslims. Despite the various solutions that were placed on the table, members of the Congress Party and the Muslim League ultimately opted for the creation of the two separate nation-states of India and Pakistan, with India holding a Hindu majority and Pakistan a Muslim one.

The partition of India resulted in violence, displacement, and the rape and abduction of women on an unprecedented scale. The enthusiasm for political independence was overshadowed by this collective trauma and a crisis of belonging that accompanied the birth of new nation-states. National constitutions defined the nature and rights of citizenship but could not fully address feelings of marginality, vulnerability, and dislocation among those who became minorities—or were minoritized—overnight. Minoritized groups felt an undue burden to prove their loyalty toward and membership within new nation-states. In order to find their place in lands dominated by Hindus, Muslims, or Buddhists, Christians made use of newspapers to vocalize public opinion and turned to the law to press for religious freedom. Some stressed their vernacular language or asserted their high caste status to become insiders. These, according to Jason Keith Fernandez, are among the "citizenship acts" employed by marginal groups to gain access to civil society. Christians, of course, are not a monolithic community but included members of high and low castes. Christians claiming high caste status more easily found their niche within the new nations because of their cultural proximity to social groups who came to embody the "ideal citizen subjects."[3]

This chapter begins by discussing competing notions of the very idea of "India" and the events leading to the partition of the subcontinent along religious lines. It then discusses disagreements between Gandhi and Jinnah and how Christians responded. During the colossal violence and displacement resulting from the partition, Christians found themselves located *between Hindu and Muslim*, often extending enthusiastic support for the leaders of their new governments in hopes that those governments would honor their religious freedom. The chapter concludes with reflections on the challenges faced by Christian minorities in independent South Asian nations. Whatever cover or protection Christians appear to have reaped by sharing the religion of their imperial rulers quickly evaporated after independence. As minorities within Hindu-, Muslim-, and Buddhist-majority nation-states, Christians—especially those from marginal classes—struggled to find security and status as citizens.

Competing Ideas of "India"

During the early twentieth century, three political parties—the Congress Party, Muslim League, and Hindu Mahasabha—presented competing ideas of India. Under Gandhi's leadership, the Congress Party envisioned an integrative, tolerant nation that would accommodate many religious traditions. For some Muslims and Christians, however, the Congress Party remained too Hindu. Under the banner of *swadeshi*, new forms of politics that emphasized Hindu revivalism gained a platform, even as the party espoused national unity.[4] The Maratha Brahmin Bal Gangadhar Tilak (1856–1920) turned the annual Ganesh *utsav* (a festival honoring the Hindu elephant deity, Ganesh) and festivities surrounding the seventeenth-century Maratha warrior Shivaji into tools of political mobilization. Shivaji became a symbol of Hindu masculinity and anticolonial defiance.[5] The Hindu Mahasabha defended Hindu interests against the rising assertiveness of Muslims and the growing sense that the Congress Party was too accommodating of minorities. The hardline nationalist Vinayak Damodar Savarkar (1883–1966) laid the foundations of *Hindutva* ideology in his book *Hindutva: Who Is a Hindu?* and would later be implicated in the plot to assassinate Gandhi.

Such developments led to the emergence of the Muslim League in 1906. This was a party founded to advocate for Muslim interests and safeguards in the midst of rising Hindu revivalism and a Congress Party that accommodated it. The Muslim League did not always push for a separate state for Muslims; only later would Jinnah advance his "two nation theory," which stressed the radical differences between Hindus and Muslims.

These growing fissures in the Indian polity assumed the form of religious macro-communities holding radically divergent interests. Commonalities that Muslims, Hindus, and Christians had shared with each other within a given locality, such as vocation, language, or everyday cultural practices, gradually gave way to large, collective notions of identity, whose representatives competed for influence at the national level. The emergence of this new emphasis on religious interests did not happen overnight, however; it arose in large part from colonial policies that categorized Indians according to religion. Religion-based personal laws, separate electorates for members of different religions, census categories, and religion-based quotas in government employment heightened the sense of religious difference among Indians. Such policies also increased tendencies toward communalism, the use of religious identity for political ends. Notions of a "Hindu majority" endangered by minority assertiveness and conversion, a threatened "Muslim community," or an all-India "Christian community" rallied the allegiance of large constituencies who had not thought of themselves in these terms previously. A high caste Christian or Hindu from Kerala, after all, had little in common with a Chuhra Christian or Balmiki (Hindu) from the Punjab. By the final years of the British Raj, however, representatives of the Hindu Mahasabha and Muslim League invoked these solidarities in order to advance their agendas.

Gandhi's Prioritization of Muslims

Despite his emphasis on the essential unity of all religions, all religions did not factor equally in Gandhi's political imagination. Christians had two factors working against them: First, they shared the religion of their colonial rulers, whom Gandhi was trying to push out of India; and second, they were perceived as benefiting uniquely from the material resources of foreign missionaries.

Gandhi consistently portrayed foreign missionaries as leveraging their wealth—or, as he would say, "dangling" material goods in front of India's outcastes, often in the form of humanitarian aid, in order to lure them into their religion.[6] In the era of Indian nationalism, it made little difference to Gandhi that India's oldest Christian tradition, the Thomas Christians, long predated the arrival of Europeans and that their adherents were not poor. Nor did Gandhi acknowledge that it was Indians who initiated and led mass conversions, not missionaries—who, in fact, were taken by surprise by them.

In Gandhi's day, Hindus and Muslims were India's largest religious communities, and they remain so today. Hence, there is a very real sense in which Gandhi's accommodative strategy was chiefly centered on maintaining Hindu–Muslim unity. Rarely if ever did Gandhi treat Indian Christians as a constituency that merited the same degree of consideration as Muslims. Ending British rule entailed an end to a reliance on all things Western, including Western culture and religion. Christian conversion, he felt, was denationalizing; he believed that it westernized converts and inclined them to despise Hindu traditions.[7] He found Hindu conversion to Islam to be similarly offensive, but he did not decry it as a form of Arabization, a perspective that is more prevalent in India's current political climate.

In contrast to his critical posture toward Christian conversion, Gandhi went to great lengths to validate the place of Muslims in India, despite the fact that Indian Muslims, like Christians, belonged to a transnational, proselytizing religion and were seen by Hindu nationalists as bearing the legacy of Mughal rule. At the conclusion of the First World War, after the deposing of the Ottoman sultan Abdul Hamid II, Muslims rallied to the cause of restoring the caliphate, the office that wielded symbolic authority over Muslims worldwide. Gandhi joined hands with Indian Muslims in this pan-Islamist Khilafat movement in order to woo Muslims into his own anticolonial agenda in India.[8] From this point on, Gandhi would be consistently mindful of the need to preserve Hindu–Muslim unity in his pursuit of home rule.

Protestants and Nationalism

Under British rule, Catholics and Protestants voiced their opinions about the political developments of the day through their newspapers. In the face of anticolonial nationalism, Catholic and Protestant elites contended with their growing sense of vulnerability and marginality. They responded to this marginality, however, in different ways. While Protestant elites embraced the spirit and cause of Indian nationalism as conceived by the Congress Party, Catholic elites tended to emphasize their community boundaries and fight for Catholic interests.[9]

Protestant elites attempted to align themselves with Indian nationalism by minimizing their sense of sectarian difference; some even called for the end of the Christian community as a political entity. Likening the Christian community to salt, which disappears when dissolved in water, the YMCA general secretary, Kanakarayan Tiruselvam Paul (1876–1931), encouraged Christians to dissolve themselves in service to the Indian nation. Others embraced the project of Indianizing Christianity, but in the process equated "Indian" with "Hindu." They wanted to purge the Church of its foreign complexion and reframe it in ways that reflected the religious culture of Sanskritic Hinduism.

Such impulses emerged in Indian Christian theology in the late nineteenth century and extended well into the twentieth. They included efforts of theologians such as Vengal Chakkarai (1880–1958) to produce an authentic, indigenous Christian theology by harmonizing it with Hindu philosophical thought. In his work *Jesus the Avatar*, Chakkarai employs a number of Hindu concepts, including that of *avatar* (literally, the "descent" of God into humanity) and *guru* to describe Jesus.[10] Chakkarai's contribution to the Indianization project is particularly noteworthy because of his unique path from Hinduism to Christianity. He hailed from an upper caste Hindu family (Chettiars, a prominent south Indian merchant and banking community) and received degrees in philosophy and law in Madras. He was raised on the lore of Hindu classics such as the *Ramayana* and *Mahabharata*, the observance of pilgrimages and festivals, and the veneration of *sannyasis*. As a young adult, he became an ardent nationalist, inspired by men such as B. G. Tilak and Gandhi. Upon becoming a Christian, Chakkarai tried to reconcile his Christian identity with Hindu nationalism, but the exclusionary aspects of this nationalism often called the Indianness of Muslims and Christians into question. This made his project of Indianization all the more necessary. Chakkarai eventually championed an Indian Christianity that downplayed the role of the Church as a visible entity. Instead, he advocated a personalized devotion or *bhakti*, which streamlined itself with the devotional practices of his upbringing and national culture, which he understood to be Hindu.[11]

Other attempts to indigenize Christianity can be traced back to early twentieth-century figures such as Sadhu Sundar Singh, the Sikh convert who became an itinerant Christian guru in the tradition of Hindu world renouncers. Singh is known for preaching "the water of life in an Indian cup," a phrase conveying his attempted indigenization of Christian ideas.[12] Theologians comprising what came to be known as the "Rethinking Christianity" group (discussed in Chapter 6) in Madras explored a similar project of streamlining Christianity with Hindu heritage and traditions.

Catholics and Nationalism

If Protestant elites embraced Indianization and nationalism, Catholics were more oriented toward securing their religious freedom, the autonomy of their institutions, and their cultural preservation as a minority community.[13] In this respect, their politics resembled those of Indian Muslims, who felt increasingly threatened as Indian nationalism became a Hindu nationalism. During the early twentieth century, Catholic newspapers and societies were established to articulate and defend Catholic interests. The Catholic Association of South India (also known as the Catholic Indian Association) served to bring the Catholic community's grievances to the attention of the government. These included matters relating to religious education, the employment of Catholics in government services, the question of communal electorates, and the right to observe various Catholic holidays. In 1919, the Catholic Truth Society established a branch in the southern city of Trichinopoly. Its purpose was to define religious and moral positions on various issues and to "assist Catholics in counteracting prejudices against religion."[14] In 1930, the Catholic Truth Propagation League added its voice, establishing numerous libraries and reading rooms aimed at promoting a more literate and publicly conscious Catholic laity.

As Catholics came to terms with their status as members of a minority community, within both British India and European national contexts, they sought new ways to become politically involved. Occasionally, the activities of the laity sparked conflicts with the hierarchy over the parameters of legitimate social and political involvement. The need for a united Catholic voice on public matters culminated in 1944 in the establishment of the Catholic Bishops' Conference of India. Its aim was to "facilitate common action of the hierarchy in matters affecting the common interests of Indian Catholics."[15]

Catholic newspapers linked local affairs in India to those affecting Catholics worldwide. During a turbulent interwar period, articles in the Madras-based *Catholic Leader*, the Bombay-based *Examiner*, and the Calcutta-based *Friend of India* helped Catholics navigate the fault lines between competing ideologies and international conflicts. These newspapers portrayed Catholics as being embroiled in an ideological battle with modernism and all of its derivatives: Socialism, Naziism, Communism, and, of course, Protestantism. The differentiation of Catholics from various international "others" contributed to the fashioning of a distinctive Catholic identity in India. This included Indian Catholic responses to the towering moral influence of Gandhi, and their need to weigh his influence against that of their pope.

One might imagine that the Catholic press was chiefly concerned with resisting Hindu nationalism or the emergence of Muslims as a political force in society. Far more prominent, however, was their differentiation from Indian Protestants. For the Catholic hierarchy, Protestants represented a path of moral compromise and accommodation to secular nationhood. As much as Catholic elites wanted to oppose Hinduism as a false religion and paid little attention to Muslims, they opted to avoid any frontal assault that would lead to reprisals. They saw in Protestants a softer target whose main problem was their accommodation to the political or ideological winds of the day.[16]

The Bombay-based newspaper *The Examiner*, for instance, often criticized Protestant compromises with modernism, Hindu nationalism, and secular nationhood. Protestant attempts to make Christianity appear more "Hindu" or Sanskritic in its cultural complexion demonstrated their capitulation to Hindu nationalist pressure on minorities. Editors criticized a statement produced by Protestant ministers, *The Laymen's Report on Christian Missions*, which recommended a more irenic approach to other religions and a reconsideration of the belief in Christian exclusiveness. The fact that Protestant missionaries had criticized *The Laymen's Report* even more severely than Catholics appeared irrelevant to their larger aim of presenting the Catholic Church as the guardian of the one true ancient faith.[17]

Although Protestants and Catholics voiced their opinions about nationalist politics and their growing sense of marginality, they were far less effective in preparing their constituencies for the calamitous events that accompanied the end of British rule. During the 1940s, riots between Hindus and Muslims erupted in major cities. Christians found themselves in the crossfire of communal tensions with few if any opportunities to formulate a collective response. After the conclusion of the Second World War, the sheer speed with which British and Indian leadership moved toward independence and partition made it difficult for Christians to fully comprehend the gravity and implications of the events that followed.

The Path to Partition

The vast literature describing the partition of India, which created the separate states of India and Pakistan, draws attention to Hindu–Muslim violence in the run-up to and aftermath of independence. Many scholars, however, challenge the idea that this conflict was inevitable or the result of irreconcilable religious differences. The feelings and choices of people on the ground—residing in the Punjab, Delhi, or Bengal—played just as much of a role in paving the path to partition as the so-called high politics being waged between Gandhi, Jinnah, and representatives of the British Raj. The Indian National Congress and Muslim League ultimately did not embrace the various power-sharing schemes that were proposed to hold India together and avert partition. Disagreements at the all-India level combined with local or provincial political tensions to move the needle toward the creation of separate states.

Interactions between Gandhi and Jinnah had a significant impact on Hindu–Muslim relations in places as distant as Bombay, Lahore, and Calcutta. Gandhi labored tirelessly to maintain harmony between Hindus and Muslims, but he was never able to agree with Jinnah and the Muslim League on the best path. Gandhi rejected Jinnah's proposals for Muslims for reasons similar to his rejection of B. R. Ambedkar's proposals for Dalits. Both Jinnah and Ambedkar stressed the radical *difference* of their constituencies from Hindus and the need for political safeguards. For Ambedkar, the pivotal issue was separate political representation for Dalits; for Jinnah, whom Muslims called the *Qaid-i-Azam* (Great Leader), Muslims constituted a separate nation—that is, a people with distinctive beliefs, customs, and social bonds. He most famously voiced this "two nation theory" at the 1940 Lahore session of the Muslim League:

> It is extremely difficult to appreciate why our Hindu friends fail to understand the real nature of Islam and Hinduism. They are not religions in the strict sense of the word, but are, in fact, different and distinct social orders; and it is a dream that the Hindus and Muslims can ever evolve a common nationality; and this misconception of one Indian nation has gone far beyond the limits and is the cause of more of our troubles and will lead India to destruction if we fail to revise our notions in time. The Hindus and Muslims belong to two different religious philosophies, social customs, and literature[s]. They neither intermarry nor interdine together, and indeed they belong to two different civilisations which are based mainly on conflicting ideas and conceptions. Their aspects [perspectives?] on life, and of life, are different. It is quite clear that Hindus and Mussalmans derive their inspiration from different sources of history. They have different epics, their heroes are different, and different episode[s]. Very often the hero of one is a foe of the other, and likewise their victories and defeats overlap. To yoke together two such nations under a single state, one as a numerical minority and the other as a majority, must lead to growing discontent, and final destruction of any fabric that may be so built up for the government of such a state.[18]

In this particular instance, Jinnah did not call for the creation of a separate state called "Pakistan," but he adopted a vocabulary of difference that would fuel the quest for partition from many sides. In fact, recent histories of the partition have argued persuasively that it was Hindus, not Muslims, who called most stridently for partition in the Punjab and in Bengal.[19]

Figure 8.2 Gandhi and Jinnah having a difference of opinion.
Source: History and Art Collection/Alamy Stock Photo.

Four years after Jinnah made this declaration at Lahore, he met with Gandhi to address Hindu–Muslim relations. In the "Gandhi–Jinnah talks" of 1944, Jinnah reiterated his belief in the distinctive heritage of Muslims using language that was just as emphatic as at Lahore. Jinnah drew attention to those provinces of British India in which Muslims were in the majority: namely, Bengal, the Punjab, Sindh, and the Northwest Frontier Provinces.[20] He insisted on a plan that promoted the sovereignty and autonomy of these provinces, which were located on two opposite sides of the subcontinent. He rejected Gandhi's proposal that Muslim demands be addressed *after* obtaining independence. This, Jinnah believed, would place Muslims at the mercy of a Hindu majority for which Gandhi and the Congress Party had become spokesmen, however tolerant and inclusive they claimed to be (see Figure 8.2).

Gandhi's response to Jinnah at these 1944 talks reveals much about his conception of Muslim identity in India. He did not perceive them as being any less Indian on account of their embrace of Islam. Where Jinnah emphasized difference, Gandhi minimized it:

> I can find no parallel in history for a body of converts and their descendants claiming to be a nation apart from the parent stock. If India was one nation before the advent of Islam, it must remain one in spite of a change of the faith of a very large body of her children. You do not claim to be a separate nation by right

of conquest but by reason of the acceptance of Islam. Will the two nations become one if the whole of India accepted Islam? Will Bengalis, Oriyas, Andhras, Tamilians, Maharashtrians, Gujaratis, cease to have their special characteristics if all of them become converts to Islam?[21]

Here, Gandhi acknowledged that the vast majority of India's Muslims consisted of converts and their descendants, not immigrants from other lands. They were just as "Indian" as they had been before their embrace of Islam.[22] Jinnah's insistence that Muslims constituted a separate nation was based on a longer tradition of Muslim separatism that includes the poet Muhammad Iqbal and Rahmat Ali, the Punjabi Muslim whom Jinnah had met while at Cambridge, England. It was Rahmat Ali who had coined the name "Pakistan," which at the time was an acronym designating the lands that would constitute the separate state he envisioned for South Asian Muslims.[23] Only much later would Jinnah warm to this territorial notion of Pakistan.

After several failed attempts at creating a scheme that would accommodate the demands of the Muslim League, Congress Party, and local stakeholders, the heads of each party and Lord Mountbatten, the last viceroy of India, opted for partition. By this time, Great Britain was in no position to retain control over its Indian Empire. With its military weakened by fighting in the Second World War, its prestige diminished, and its economy massively in debt to the USA and the Government of India, the British pursued as rapid an exit as possible. A boundary commissioner, Cyril Radcliffe, was tasked with drawing the border that would separate India from Pakistan. The new nation of Pakistan would be formed from Muslim-majority regions on two separate sides of the subcontinent: the western half of the Punjab and the eastern half of Bengal. Radcliffe, who had never visited India before, drew his line on the basis of outdated maps, census reports, and conflicting evidence on the ground regarding the demographic composition of the affected regions (see Figure 8.3).

A massive migration followed the announcement of the Radcliffe Line. Millions of Hindus and Sikhs residing on the Pakistan side of the border migrated to India, while millions of Muslims residing in India migrated to West and East Pakistan. The partition created the largest planned migration in world history. While some moved to the other country by choice, many more were forced to pack up and leave due to hostility from neighbors who belonged to the "majority religion." Many left properties that could never be retrieved and were later occupied and owned by migrants. As many as twelve million South Asians were displaced and more than a million killed in the communal violence triggered by the partition. Accompanying this violence was the rape and abduction of women on an unprecedented scale.[24]

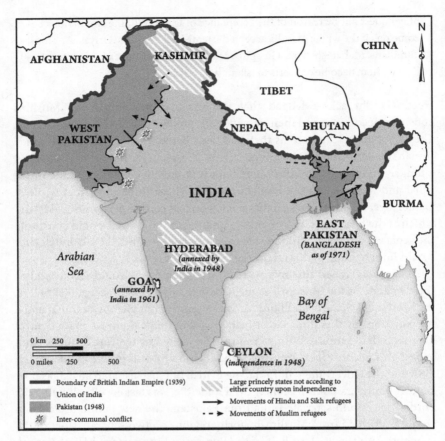

Figure 8.3 Map showing the partition of India.
Source: Licensed under CC BY-SA 3.0.

Christian Responses

Christians were affected not only by the colossal violence and displacement caused by partition, but also by the need to demonstrate their loyalty either to Pakistan or to India. Nowhere was this more evident than in the Punjab. As a region that underwent partition, the Punjab in 1947 became an epicenter of communal violence and mass migration. Chuhras and Chamars, the sanitary and agricultural laborers who had undergone mass conversions to Christianity, became either Indians or Pakistanis overnight. Moreover, they became Christian minorities in Muslim- or Hindu-majority states.

The upheaval caused by partition affected different classes of South Asians in different ways. Muslim families with financial resources or family relations on the

Pakistan side of the border had the means to migrate and thrive in their new setting. These Muslim migrants or *Muhajirs* were able to occupy abandoned lands in Pakistan if they could prove that they had held land in India. The vast majority of these migrants settled in the western or Pakistani region of the Punjab. As landholders, they tended to hire their own relatives and fellow villagers to meet their labor needs. This displaced massive numbers of Chuhras who had made their living as agricultural laborers. Out of desperation, many Chuhras migrated to cities, where they were compelled to join existing communities of urban sanitation workers (sweepers). As Christian converts, they had to endure the humiliation of joining a community that was perceived to be "polluted."[25] In Pakistan, these laborers maintained the advantages associated with the sale of products made from animal hides and their consumption of beef or mutton. In India, where cows were protected, this became more problematic.

The arrival of Chuhra migrants changed the demographics of cities such as the port of Karachi. Prior to the partition, most Christians in Karachi were of Goan Catholic or Anglo-Indian descent. During the nineteenth century, these westernized Christians had migrated to the Punjab in the hope of finding employment in the colonial army. They were employed as tailors, cooks, and servants in the army and held low-ranking government posts.[26] Reportedly, the military favored them because, like English soldiers, they consumed beef, pork, and alcoholic beverages, which were shunned by Hindus and Muslims.[27] With the influx of low-ranking and ethnically diverse converts, and with Karachi now belonging to a predominantly Muslim nation, many Goans migrated to the United Kingdom, Australia, or other Western countries that would accept them.

For Christian migrants, another problematic issue was how their respective governments would classify them. A complex variety of religious influences had shaped Chuhras prior to their becoming Christian (see Chapter 7). As missionaries withdrew from the region, it was yet to be seen which aspect of their identity would gain official recognition. In the newly established Pakistan, the term "Chuhra" was replaced with "Christian,"[28] and, as Christians, the new constitution extended them religious freedom (see Figure 8.4). For pastors, priests, and Christian educators, this was a valuable provision. Many professed their loyalty to Pakistan and their support for Jinnah's leadership because of his assurances that the rights of non-Muslims would be protected. The promise of religious freedom, however, was of little use to economically backward Christian migrants in dire need of state assistance. A very similar pattern developed in independent India for Dalit Christian converts. Because of their classification as Christians, they were denied recognition as "scheduled castes" who qualified for state assistance and quotas in education.

In Bengal, the other province through which Radcliffe had drawn his line, there were far fewer Christians and they appear to have been less directly

Figure 8.4 An image depicting the new Christian identity of Chuhras.
Source: From the 1926 PhD thesis of Herbert Johnson Strickler, Department of Sociology, University of Kansas. Scanned and provided courtesy of Arif Rahman Chughtai, Chughtai Museum, Lahore, Pakistan.

impacted by the unfolding trauma of partition. In Midnapore, a city located in West Bengal, which became part of India, Christians organized an independence celebration in which they waved Indian flags and wore Gandhi caps made of homespun cloth. A report from the American Baptist mission in Bengal and Orissa noted that events in Midnapore were not nearly as traumatizing as those in the Punjab. It described Muslims as "probably the most joyful in the whole country," because "they had obtained the division that had been their goal from the first."[29] This report's portrayal of Muslims as separatists stood in contrast with its portrayal of Gandhi as a peacemaker. It noted Gandhi's visit to Calcutta, where he had quelled Hindu–Muslim riots by fasting for several days in a Muslim quarter. Despite its celebration of relative calm in Midnapore, the report seemed oblivious to the convulsion caused by the Radcliffe Line and the flow of refugees into and out of what came to be called East Pakistan.

This particular Protestant missionary perspective also reflected an anti-Muslim bias and a prejudice against the very idea of Pakistan. It ignored the fact that the Pakistan demand was a very late development, not a "goal from the first," and that independent India possessed a huge Muslim population who did not migrate to Pakistan. By contrast, the report celebrated India as a bastion of religious diversity and freedom, ensured by Gandhian tolerance.

National Christian bodies in India were either silent before and during the events of the partition, or they limited their commentary to expressions of loyalty to one state or the other. In 1946, the National Christian Council of India, Burma, and Ceylon issued a statement pledging its commitment to offering "succour and relief to those in trouble."[30] The Council also decried the spirit of vengeance that was driving communal violence and forcing many to migrate to escape the rioting. The statement did not express any opinion on the matter of partition, but its preference for national unity was implied. It recited what had become a standard Protestant opinion that Christians "should seek no exclusive communal privileges" and expressed its desire for religious freedom.[31]

By contrast, Christian voices in western Punjab expressed their support for Jinnah and the creation of the new state. S. P. Singha, a registrar at Punjab University who was elected in 1937 to the Punjab Assembly, was a staunch supporter of Jinnah and the creation of Pakistan. He and other Christian leaders, however, objected to the partitioning of the Punjab, preferring instead that the entire province be included in Pakistan.[32] In 1942, Singha founded the All India Christian Association, whose members expressed their wholehearted support for Jinnah and his vision for Pakistan.[33] These Christians appear to have preferred to be minorities in a predominantly Muslim state than in a caste-ridden Hindu one.[34]

Pakistan's premier college, Forman Christian College in Lahore, was hugely impacted by the events of the partition. The college had been founded in 1864 by the American Presbyterian missionary Charles Forman (1821–94) in a city that was Muslim majority but had an influential class of Hindus and Sikhs as well. The college had significant numbers of Hindus and Sikhs in its student body and faculty. Prior to independence, the college community had not known whether Lahore would go to India or Pakistan, and, in the days following partition, the city was rocked by stabbings, bombings, looting, and the destruction of property. Two of the college's residence halls were converted into makeshift hospitals.[35]

Two Forman faculty, James and Miriam Benade, were eyewitnesses to the communal violence and provided a far more nuanced assessment of the situation than can be found in official statements by missionary bodies. Miriam acknowledged the unfair treatment meted out to Muslims in British India and their fear of Hindu domination. In the midst of the carnage, however, she clearly wished that the Muslim League would have taken a stand that averted partition:

[W]e recognize that there has been real need for the Muslims to rouse themselves to improve their economic and educational status and to free many of their group from the clutches of monied interests among the Hindus. We wish however that the tactics of the Muslim League revealed less a sense of inferiority and that the party could have worked to obtain rights within the context of a whole united India as envisaged by Jawaharlal Nehru and the National Congress Party, including some of the more thoughtful Muslims.[36]

In her account of the violence in Lahore, Miriam Benade described how unemployed soldiers in the Punjabi army and communal leaders actively encouraged "the rough elements of the population to set off crude bombs, to murder, and to set fire to buildings."[37]

In November 1947, the Catholic Union of India had to divide its jurisdictions along national lines. The branches of Sindh and Baluchistan, which were located in Pakistan, broke away from the union, which now focused on its dioceses in independent India. The Catholic Union declared its gratitude that, upon independence, India did not establish itself as a Hindu state but created provisions in its constitution that ensured religious freedom. In a manner that mirrored their Protestant counterparts, Catholic leaders from Madras such as M. Ruthnaswamy, C. J. Varkey, and others decried the communal violence of the day while expressing their appreciation for Gandhi's attempts to promote peace in the newly created states.[38]

Postcolonial Minoritization

Decolonization in South Asia consolidated notions of nationhood that were built around Hindu, Muslim, and Buddhist identities. As minorities within these postcolonial landscapes, Christians struggled to find their place. In recent years, they have contended with new forms of stereotyping and violence, whether under the weight of blasphemy laws in Pakistan or Bangladesh, anti-conversion laws in India, or a more assertive Buddhist nationalism in Burma (now Myanmar) and Sri Lanka. Just as Gandhi's principle of *swadeshi* legitimized the defense of Hindu heritage in India, nationalist leaders of neighboring South Asian states defended their understandings of Muslim or Buddhist heritage. This marginalized Christians and other minoritized groups who did not fit neatly within emerging religious nationalisms.

Pakistan and Bangladesh

Christians in Pakistan voice concerns about religious freedom that very much resemble those of India's Christians. The main difference is that Pakistan was established as a homeland for South Asia's Muslims. The precise role of Islam in defining state institutions, however, was yet to be seen at the time of partition. Jinnah's towering influence as a Western-educated statesman with liberal commitments gave Christians hope that, despite Pakistan's Muslim majority, they would be able to thrive as a community. His untimely death in 1948 created a huge vacuum and raised additional questions about the identity of Pakistan. Would it be a Muslim-majority state with commitments to education, the rule of law, and development, resembling other modern nation-states? Or would it become a theocratic state? If the latter, the country would essentially be run by conservative *mullahs* (scholars, teachers, or religious leaders) intent on seeing Pakistan governed by Qur'anic teachings and particular interpretations of shariah law, to the detriment of Christians, Hindus, Sikhs, and those Muslims who may not embrace the state's interpretation of Islam. If Pakistan moved too far toward secular democracy, it would undermine its raison d'être and alienate its *mullahs* and their followers. Both Jinnah and his successor, Liaquat Ali Khan, rejected the option of a theocratic Pakistan, but their preferred middle path—a democratic Pakistani state that privileged its Muslim heritage—would prove to be a difficult balance to strike.

Jinnah's death appears to have removed a vital lynchpin for a modernized Pakistan with stable and well-functioning state institutions. In the decades following independence, Pakistanis have seen their government avail itself of US Cold War funding and patronage and descend into periods of military rule. The country has fought four wars with India and numerous border skirmishes, largely related to the disputed region of Kashmir. Key leaders have been executed, assassinated, or sent into political exile. Its prime ministers have had to contend with two different visions for its future: a constitutional vision promoting participation in the international community and the protection of minority rights; and an Islamizing vision, espoused by a variety of religio-political groups. A Council of Islamic Ideology has steered the government toward a more explicitly Muslim approach to education, politics, and law. Political instability and the government's inability to address the needs of its citizens have fueled calls for further Islamization. This process has coincided with the scapegoating of religious minorities such as Christians. Pakistan's Sunni religious clerics and majority have also vilified the country's Shia minority along with members of the Ahmadi sect of Islam, which they have branded as heretical.

In the face of rising extremism, Christians in Pakistan have faced more frequent instances of violence against individuals, church congregations, and schools. Anti-Western sentiments among Islamist organizations fueled stereotypes of Pakistani Christians as extensions of Western neocolonial influence. Since the 1980s, the government's balancing act between constitutionalism and Islamization has tilted in the direction of the latter. Perhaps no aspect of this turn has drawn more international attention and ire from human rights organizations than Pakistan's blasphemy law. Blasphemy laws have become a prominent feature of the treatment of Christian minorities not only in Pakistan but also in Bangladesh, a nation formed when East Pakistan waged war against and broke away from West Pakistan in 1972 to gain its independence.

The law prohibiting blasphemy derives from Chapter 15, Section 295 of the Pakistan Penal Code. It was originally intended as a provision that would protect any group from harassment and persecution. The reasoning behind the law dates back to the colonial era, when the British prohibited speech that was likely to offend the religious feelings of others or result in communal violence, despite the fact that the British themselves had fanned communal rivalry through their divisive, religion-based laws.

The number and variety of blasphemy cases in independent Pakistan have been documented by human rights groups and Christian organizations and are too numerous to recount here. Most striking is the way in which allegations based on meager or dubious evidence can set in motion legal proceedings, community polarization, and international reactions and protests. When someone is accused of blasphemy, not only is his or her life at stake, but also those of the family and village networks. Accusers are known to distribute inflammatory pamphlets inciting villagers to take revenge. Reprisals in the form of burning and looting of property can follow mere allegations of blasphemy.[39] For this reason, the blasphemy law is not only about religion but can also be a tool for waging a personal vendetta, asserting control over land, or attacking sectarian rivals.

Since the 1980s, Pakistan has amended its blasphemy law so that it protects Islam, not minorities. The law is used to confront even the most powerless individuals, such as low caste Christian minors, who are suspected of offending Islam. The language of the amendments is vague and far-reaching, permitting spurious allegations in the manner of witch hunts. The addition of Section 295A prohibited the use of derogatory remarks "by words or by imputation, innuendo or insinuation, directly or indirectly, about persons revered in Islam." Sections 295B (which covers willful defilement of the Qur'an) and 295C (defiling the name of the Prophet) set punishments of life imprisonment or even death.[40]

In February 1995, three Christians belonging to separate villages in the city of Gujranwala were tried and sentenced to death for blasphemy: Salamat Masih, Rehmat Masih, and Manzoor Masih (Masih, meaning "messiah," is a common name adopted by Christians). In 1993, a Muslim religious teacher accused the twelve-year-old Salamat of writing anti-Islamic messages on a piece of paper and throwing it into the mosque. At the hearing of the three, an angry crowd assembled and demanded the death sentence. When the Lahore High Court granted them bail, it enraged onlookers and one of them shot Manzoor Masih dead. During the two-year proceedings, the prosecution failed to produce evidence that the other two accused had written derogatory messages concerning the Prophet Muhammad on the wall of the mosque. Attorneys for the defendants pointed out that one of the accused was a minor and the other two illiterate. The fact that one of the complainants was illiterate and therefore would have been unable to read the objectionable material did not prevent the court from issuing its death sentence. Salamat and Rehmat were hanged shortly thereafter.[41]

In 1996, twenty-five-year-old Ayub Masih was accused and eventually found guilty of having made derogatory comments about the Prophet Muhammad during a dispute with a fellow villager. His comments came in the form of discussing sympathetically Salman Rushdie's 1988 novel *The Satanic Verses*, a banned book whose author was in hiding due to the *fatwa* pronounced against him. When discussing the book, Ayub had allegedly referred to the Prophet using the casual designation "uncle." After initial charges were brought against him in Arifwala, fifteen families from his village were forced to evacuate out of fear of reprisals. Masih was imprisoned in Multan during which time he endured inhumane conditions and violence from other prisoners. A neighbor was allocated his land. After Ayub was found guilty, he was shot and injured while exiting court.[42] In protest against Ayub's conviction, a Roman Catholic bishop, John Joseph, committed suicide in front of the court building. Ayub spent years in prison at Multan in dehumanizing conditions. When his case finally came before Pakistan's Supreme Court in 2002, the justices acquitted him due to violations of his right to due process under the law, issues that were pointed out by international human rights organizations.

A more recent blasphemy case receiving international attention was that of Asia Bibi, a Pakistani farm laborer from a rural area south of Lahore. A conflict erupted between Asia, a Christian, and her Muslim co-workers when, after hours of grueling labor, she went to fetch water from the nearby well. Asia is reported to have sipped the water from a jug before handing it to her Muslim co-workers. This ignited the conflict that led them to level blasphemy charges against her. Her co-workers were repulsed by the idea of drinking from the same vessel as a Christian. They regarded this as "polluting"—a sentiment that resembles that of caste Hindus fearing contamination by Dalits. In the fiery exchange between Asia and her co-workers, the latter alleged that Asia uttered words defaming the Prophet and Islam. They reported the incident to Qari Muhammad Salaam, the man who made formal charges against her. Asia was severely beaten and her family threatened before a lower court charged her with blasphemy and sentenced her to hanging under section 295C of the blasphemy law. When, in 2018, Pakistan's Supreme Court set aside the sentence due to insufficient evidence, radicalized Muslims called for her death and politicized her trial. In 2019, Asia Bibi was able to leave Pakistan and find asylum in Canada.[43]

Others known to have been accused of blasphemy include Tahir Iqbal, a Muslim who converted to Christianity—something the judge described as a "cognizable offense involving serious implications"—and, most recently, a Hindu boy who allegedly urinated intentionally "on a carpet in the library of a Muslim madrassa, where religious books were kept."[44]

Beyond exposing egregious human rights abuses against minors, blasphemy cases can also provide a pretext for enacting caste prejudice or hatred toward the West. Accusing a Christian of blasphemy can be a way for landholding Muslims to increase their control over land or Christian laborers. Outraged by the American hand in Pakistani affairs, others might find in allegations of blasphemy a way to exert power over Pakistani Christians—local soft targets who are perceived as extensions of the "Christian West." The charge can also be directed against Muslims deemed heretical (such as the Ahmadi sect), popular writers, or intellectuals. In 1994, the feminist author Taslima Nasreen was sent into exile after being accused of blasphemy for the publication of her novel *Lajja* (*Shame*), which depicts the suffering of a Hindu family in Bangladesh at the hands of Muslim fanatics. Like Rushdie and his *Satanic Verses*, Nasreen's book was banned in Pakistan for attacking Islam and Nasreen was forced to remain in exile to avoid imprisonment for blasphemy in Bangladesh.[45]

India and Nepal

After independence in 1947, Prime Minister Jawaharlal Nehru set out to establish India as a secular, socialist democracy. A constituent assembly, chaired by none other than Ambedkar himself, staged roughly four years (1946–50) of debate and deliberation. The assembly yielded a highly progressive constitution for the new country. Article 15 prohibited discrimination on the basis of religion, race, caste, sex, or place of birth. Article 25 upheld the principle of freedom of religion. It guaranteed that "all persons are equally entitled to freedom of conscience and the right to freely profess, practice, and propagate religion subject to public order, morality and health."[46] In a land of such immense diversity and riddled with a history of caste oppression and religious strife, such guarantees held out the promise of a more equitable and humane future.

It was not long before the issue of religious conversion among the poor and oppressed again drew the attention of state officials. Immediately after independence, the government prioritized issues of economic development, and it was hoped that missionaries would advance the cause of development through education and humanitarian aid. In 1953, the Home Minister, Kailas Nath Katju, declared that missionary humanitarian aid was welcome in India, but that missionaries should not engage in proselytization. He drew attention to allegations that missionaries were proselytizing members of tribal communities within certain districts of the state of Madhya Pradesh. This concern led Katju to call for an inquiry into whether such proselytizing violated Article 25 of the constitution.

The very idea of freedom of religion was being interpreted in very different ways. For missionaries and Indian Christians, it meant the freedom to propagate religion and receive converts into the Church. For critics of conversion, it meant that certain vulnerable communities should be protected from proselytizing, especially by foreigners or foreign-funded agencies. In 1954, the government established the Christian Missionary Activities Enquiry Committee, which was headed by the retired Supreme Court Chief Justice Bhawani Shankar Niyogi. The findings of the Niyogi Report (as it came to be called) emphasized how missionaries had used humanitarian aid (especially schools, hospitals, and orphanages) as inducements for conversion.[47] The report essentially reinforced the Gandhian critique of missionary work and resulted in significant restrictions on missionary visas for decades to come. Critics of the report, however, observe how it reenacts the paternalism of the Gandhian approach by presuming that Dalits or tribals have no choice or agency in the conversion process.[48] The report also inspired the passing of an anti-conversion law in Madhya Pradesh. Seven other Indian states passed their own anti-conversion laws, some with and some without implementing rules.[49]

It is no simple matter to compare South Asia's largest country, India, with a much smaller one—namely Nepal—but the similar challenges faced by Christians in both contexts warrant the comparison. Nepal was a protectorate of Great Britain (a client state relying upon the British military for protection), but was not ruled directly like other colonies. Because of this unique arrangement, the borders of Nepal and its neighbors (Sikkim and Bhutan) were not impacted by the partition of India. Situated in the Himalayan region between India and China, Nepal possessed its own constellation of ethnic, linguistic and religious groups. Since the mid-nineteenth century, hereditary kings of the Rana dynasty ruled Nepal autocratically. In 1951, an attempt was made under King Tribhuvan Bir Bikram (1906–55) to end the Rana dynasty, convene a constituent assembly, and introduce democracy. He did not realize this dream, and, after his death, his successor, King Mahendra Bir Bikram (1920–72), restored a monarchy that lasted decades. Under the monarchy, Nepal declared itself a Hindu kingdom and its kings were required to protect its Aryan heritage and Hindu religion.[50] They presided over a population that was nearly 80 percent Hindu. The government banned Christian preaching and proselytizing and violators were subject to beatings, imprisonment, and other severe reprisals.

In 1990, democracy was again introduced in Nepal, but it was unable to be sustained without lapses into political turbulence of various kinds. Still, the higher degree of openness to change after 1990 led to many reforms and a greater acceptance of Christianity among Nepalis. The influx of evangelistic ministries holding open-air meetings, healing crusades, and other Pentecostal-style deliverance ministries led to growing Christian numbers in Nepal. In March 2008, an estimated 25,000 people gathered in the national stadium in Kathmandu for an evangelistic crusade, demonstrating the enthusiasm of many Nepalis for Pentecostal spirituality.[51] According to one study, the Christian population of Nepal grew at a rate of 10.93 percent in 2020, the fastest growth rate in the world.[52] As is the case in India, the majority of this growth has occurred among Dalit and other marginal communities.

As Christianity grew in Nepal, so did opposition to conversion. The government introduced a new constitution in 2015 that imposed additional restrictions on religious conversion and declared religious activities that lead to conversion punishable by law. Such activities include church planting, evangelistic crusades, and other open-air meetings that propagate the gospel. In 2017, the government enacted a law that criminalizes conversion along lines that resemble the blasphemy laws of Pakistan and Bangladesh. Section 9 of Criminal Code 2074 prohibits language that insults the holy places and beliefs of another religion or offends religious sentiments of other communities. It punishes such offenses with a three-year prison sentence, a fine of 30,000 rupees, and deportation for foreign missionaries after they complete their prison sentence.[53] Despite the significant growth of Christianity in Nepal since 1990, such measures contribute to a sense among Nepali Christians that they remain a persecuted community, compelled to thrive in the face of persistent opposition.

Sri Lanka and Burma

Sri Lanka was a historically Buddhist island kingdom that was not directly impacted by the events of the partition. Like Pakistan, it emerged from British rule wanting to preserve its dominant religious heritage. During the 1920s and 1930s, constitutional reforms in Sri Lanka drew Christians into the political process, to a greater degree than in India, even amidst a growing Buddhist revival movement. Christians possessed the English education needed for participation on district boards and legislative councils and in professional services.[54] The representation of Christians was more prominent at the national rather than the regional or district level, and often exceeded their actual strength in numbers. Gradually, however, Hindu and Buddhist representation in the legislature also increased. A rising group of Sinhala Buddhist propagandists began to insist on reclaiming their "rightful place" as the majority while curbing the influence of Christian and Tamil minorities. Such protective sentiments continued after 1948, when Sri Lanka gained its independence. In the interest of reforming an educational system that favored Christian schools—now seen as "alien institutions of privilege"—the government nationalized education. This resulted in the steady marginalization of Christian influence within Sri Lankan society.[55]

Independent Sri Lanka had a Tamil–Sinhala division, which resulted in an ongoing civil war. A related division was between Buddhists and non-Buddhists. The constitution expressed a commitment to protecting Buddhism while upholding the rights of minorities. This framework was designed to accommodate divisions between Tamil-speaking Hindus in the northern Jaffna Peninsula, Sinhala Buddhists, a sizable Muslim minority, and Christians. In the decades following independence, stronger ties developed between the Buddhist Sangha (the society of Buddhist monks) and the Sri Lankan state, leading to a more assertive Buddhism and a state interest in curbing the activities of Christian missionaries and NGOs. Propaganda directed against Muslims and Christians portray Buddhists as a community threatened by rising birth rates among Muslims and increased Christian numbers due to proselytizing. In 2019, the National Christian Evangelical Alliance of Sri Lanka documented ninety-four instances of attacks on churches and acts of intimidation and violence against clergy and congregations.[56] During the same year, on Easter Sunday, militant Islamists launched suicide attacks on three churches and four hotels, killing more than 250 civilians and injuring over 500. The government responded by banning several Islamic organizations. The event, however, prompted widespread retaliation against Sri Lankan Muslims, some led by Buddhist monks.

Burma similarly emerged from colonial rule riddled with ethnic and religious cleavages that consistently hampered the path to unity and stability. Burmese society consisted of many language groups, ethnicities, and religions; but British and missionary classifications played a significant role in making such differences more pronounced and more inclined toward conflict. During the nineteenth century, the British gradually consolidated their rule, first by their conquest of Lower Burma (1826–52), and later by annexing Upper Burma (1886). Scholars and ethnographers identified as many as fifty-seven tribes and races in Burma. In their quest for administrative ease, the British reduced this cultural complexity to manageable blocks. They devised policies that distinguished the "Burmese Buddhists" of the Irrawaddy Valley from migrant tribes of the north and Indian Hindu and Muslim migrant laborers. By the 1940s, the division between Europeans, Indians, Burmese, and "minorities" was firmly intact.[57]

The vast majority of Burmese Christians hailed from "minority" ethnic groups such as the Kachin, Chin, and Karen. American Baptist missionaries contributed immensely to their social and cultural transformation by giving them access to education, hospitals, Bible translations and grammars, printing presses, and other church resources. These factors enhanced the economic development of Christians relative to other groups and strengthened the bond between

Christians and the colonial government, something resented by Burmese nationalists seeking decolonization.[58]

In the years following independence in 1948, the Burmese government embarked on a project of "Burmanization," one that sharply distinguished true children of the soil from "foreigners." The project involved the expulsion of Indians from the country; this included those Indians who had served the colonial administration or army as well as laborers who, for generations, had worked on plantations.[59] Burmanization also entailed the nationalization of the Burmese language and the recovery and preservation of Buddhist heritage, which nationalists felt had been undermined by colonialism and Christian influence. Such policies imposed enormous pressure on Christian minorities to assimilate and placed severe restrictions on the operations of their churches and other institutions. The Burmese army deliberately subjected Christians to forced labor on Sundays and turned some churches into military bases. The army is also known to have forced Christians to convert to Buddhism, built pagodas on church lands, and committed acts of violence against Christian minorities.[60] The equation of Buddhism with Burmese national identity contributed to the outbreak of conflict in 2012 between Rakhine Buddhists and Rohingya Muslims. In recent years, this conflict has led the Burmese army to engage in an all-out attempt to expel or eradicate the Rohingya, a campaign resulting in the widespread killing of Rohingya, the destruction of their villages, and a massive flow of refugees into Bangladesh, actions labeled as genocide by many international human rights groups.

Conclusion

During his campaign against British rule, Gandhi called for the rejection of all things Western—goods, political institutions, values, and religion. As he and other nationalists factored religion into their notion of *swadeshi* ("of one's own country"), they marginalized classes who were unable to embody this particular idea of national culture. Gandhi's failed attempts at reaching a lasting agreement with Jinnah indicate the limitations of *swadeshi* as a framework for anticolonial resistance or nation building. Whose country is "one's own country" and who would be excluded? As it turned out, the principle of cultural and religious homogeneity (as an offshoot of *swadeshi*) would underwrite many anticolonial nationalisms of the Global South. In South Asia, it laid the foundations for Hindu-, Muslim-, and Buddhist-majority states that marginalized those rendered minorities upon independence.

Elite segments of minority communities, however, pursued paths to acceptance that were unavailable to lower castes. In Kerala, Syrian Christians, as Sonja

Thomas notes, were "privileged minorities" whose claims to Brahmin status and incorporation into the elite strata of Malayali society made them appear for all practical purposes as Hindu elites.[61] Similarly, in Goa, a region of India colonized by the Portuguese, not the British, elite Catholics strived for acceptance by emphasizing their Brahmin heritage, which they claimed was taken from them by the Portuguese conquests. In order to make a case for this heritage, Goan Catholics drew upon Orientalist knowledge that linked Konkani to Sanskrit.[62] These stories, however, are elite exceptions to a general rule that defines nationality in terms of a dominant religion and excludes Christians and Muslims from *swadeshi* religious nationalism.

The hope that South Asia would produce liberal, constitutional states whose citizens would embrace an ethos of toleration has faded in Pakistan, India, Bangladesh, Myanmar (formerly Burma), and Sri Lanka in the midst of rising religious extremism. Despite a long history of migration, conversion, and population mixtures, these nations have gravitated toward narrow definitions of citizenship anchored in notions of purity and homogeneity. On what basis would citizenship be extended to people belonging to "religions of non-Indian origin" in India, to non-Muslims or so-called heretical Muslims in Pakistan or Bangladesh, to non-Buddhists in Myanmar, to non-Malays or non-Singaporeans? Groups who had established themselves over generations in a given region—for instance, religious converts or indentured servants—were often asked to pack up and leave. Where would they go and who would receive them? Upon independence, new governments sent these "outsiders" to places where their roots had long vanished or where they never possessed any roots at all. As newly constituted "minorities," they enjoy at best a second-class citizenship. The legacy of colonialism has worked hand in hand with *swadeshi* nationalism to produce adverse conditions faced by Christians and other minorities in postcolonial South Asia.

9
Dalits and Social Liberation

During the twentieth century, Dalits began to claim Jesus for themselves. They produced poems, literature, and artwork that portrayed Jesus as a despised, marginal, and poor outcast whose body was "broken" in the manner of Dalit bodies. They also claimed Jesus as their liberator. Dalit theology arose from the experiences of those who comprised the majority of South Asia's Christian population. Why, however, was this newer Dalit theology needed for a religion that did not teach caste distinctions to begin with? Did missionaries not preach that in Christ "there is neither Jew or Gentile, slave or free, male or female" (Galatians 3:28)? Was their message not emancipatory enough to shake the very foundations of untouchability in India and challenge the oppression of women? Such questions point to a complex and layered history in which Christianity sometimes accommodated itself to local hierarchies and sometimes decentered them with its message of God's unmerited love and redemption.

This chapter examines the ways in which Christianity has interacted with entrenched social structures in India. It begins by revisiting the missionary legacy. Evangelical missionaries encountered caste hierarchies and untouchability in India at the very time when other Evangelicals were engaged in antislavery agitation in England, the islands of the Caribbean, and the American colonies. Why did they not launch in India a campaign against Dalit servitude modeled after abolition? Comparisons between the two contexts shed light on how Evangelicals understood their mandate and how emancipatory their impact really was. It also brings into sharper focus the binary between spiritual and material motives for conversion, especially among Dalits.

This discussion of the missionary legacy is followed by an examination of opposing approaches to Christian conversion taken by Gandhi and Ambedkar. Both leaders championed their own notions of social and political liberation, but it was Ambedkar's ideas, as we shall see, that won the hearts of both Dalits and Dalit converts to Christianity. Aspects of Ambedkar's legacy shaped key tropes of Dalit Christian theology, which the chapter discusses next. Disappointed by the responses of major religions to their plight, Dalits developed their own theologies to resist the oppressive structures of their day and incorporated Dalit experiences into their readings of the New Testament. As they appropriated Jesus as their liberator, many also appropriated Ambedkar as their interpreter of what liberation should look like.

The chapter concludes with an examination of affirmative action for Dalit Christians. By law, Dalits who convert to Christianity are not recognized as "scheduled castes" who qualify for state assistance or quotas in employment or education. Those who oppose this policy argue that Dalits continue to face economic deprivation and the debilitating stigma of untouchability even as Christians.[1] The persistence of caste oppression and economic need among India's Dalit Christians resembles the plight of Christians in Pakistan. Advancing their cause, however, is no simple matter. Advocates have to work against Hindu nationalist biases that have accumulated over centuries while also confronting aspects of missionary history that emphasized the transformative impact of Christianity, its antipathy for caste, and its capacity to uplift the downtrodden.

Social Liberation and the Missionary Legacy

During the first half of the nineteenth century, missionaries across many denominations shared a common opposition to India's caste system and untouchability. Most English missionaries repudiated caste with the zeal of abolitionists, in some cases drawing direct parallels between their task in India and the emancipation of African slaves.[2] For all practical purposes, Dalits in various parts of south India were treated as slaves who were owned and exploited by powerful landlords. Inspired by the abolitionist movement influencing other parts of the British Empire, missionaries of the LMS and CMS played an active role in opposing slavery in the princely states of Travancore and Cochin and in the Madras Presidency.[3] Through their advocacy and writings, these missionaries drew international attention to the matter of slavery as it pertained to landless, laboring Dalit groups in India.[4] Their advocacy led to the eventual banning of slavery in India, but the practice continued despite this. Many Dalits remained unaware of antislavery legislation that might have helped them. Beyond this, questions remained about the difference between transatlantic slavery, which had become a morally repugnant institution, and caste distinctions in India, which had broader cultural and religious connotations.

It should be noted that Protestants in the Atlantic world were not always committed to abolition or even to the conversion of African slaves. Prior to the abolition movement, Protestant slave owners had found ways of making slavery compatible with their Christian beliefs. According to the historian Katharine Gerbner, many slave owners were averse to baptizing their slaves. In fact, strong *anti-conversion* sentiments were pervasive among Protestant slave owners throughout North America and the Caribbean during the seventeenth and eighteenth centuries. During this period of what she calls "Protestant supremacy," Protestants did not want to convert slaves or even to expose them to Christian knowledge. This would undermine a crucial justification for slavery, namely the distinction between "Christian slave owners" and "heathen slaves."[5]

As slaves increasingly became Christian, largely through their own initiatives, many aspired to obtain their freedom as fellow Christians. This possibility alarmed slave owners and clergy alike and led Quaker, Anglican, and Moravian missionaries to replace "Protestant supremacy" with a new framework that made converting slaves compatible with slavery. Gerbner calls this framework "Christian slavery."[6] The notion of Christian slavery made a case for the gospel as a civilizing force in the lives of slaves without attacking the enterprise itself. Ironically, the baptism of slaves enhanced their sense of humanity but ultimately served to buttress and expand slavery.[7] Protestants could now argue that Christian slaves made better slaves. With religion no longer serving as the basis for separating master and slave, racial difference and white superiority became the dominant factors that justified slavery.[8]

For Protestant missionaries and colonial officers in British India, the resemblance between African and Dalit slavery was striking. Like African slavery, untouchability was rooted in exploitative labor relations and inhumane methods of enforcing labor demands. Just as racial difference became the basis of slavery in the Atlantic, essentialist notions of Dalit impurity and caste degradation formed the basis of their enslavement in India. Even when missionaries did not use the term "slavery" explicitly (they sometimes did), their reference to landlessness, impoverishment, and the severity of punishments placed Dalit servitude in the same category as slavery, even after laws were passed against it.[9]

As Dalit laborers became Christian through the mass movements, missionaries prioritized their "spiritual" transformation: that is, the abandonment of pre-Christian rituals, behaviors, and beliefs, and the embrace of Christian teachings and morality. Missionaries were also compelled to address malnutrition, disease, and social degradation among mass converts. Despite their awareness of the injustice meted out to Dalits, missionary priorities and limitations prevented them from launching a comprehensive campaign to end Dalit servitude in British India.[10] In key respects, their approach resembles the model of "Christian slavery." The overarching aim of their work among mass converts was to nurture in them a new Christian identity, not to liberate them from their degrading agrarian roles. Missionaries made schools, orphanages, medical facilities, and humanitarian aid available to Dalits, which in itself was quite radical. In some cases, these services resulted in greater social mobility, alternative sources of employment, and greater degrees of self-respect. Missionaries, however, never launched in India a campaign that paralleled the scale or capital investment of the abolition movement. Their acceptance of the group principle that guided the mass movements appears to have diminished the possibility of sustaining a radical, Christian critique of Dalit labor.

Missionaries were acutely aware of conflicts that arose between new converts and their landlords, who sometimes brought false charges against converts, required them to work on Sundays, and subjected them to physical harassment. The motives for landlord aggression were primarily socioeconomic, not "religious." Landlords feared that Christian conversion would incline Chuhras, Madigas, or Shanars to abandon their roles and would thereby reduce access to a cheap and steady supply of labor.[11] In some instances, children of laborers who attended Christian schools were able to find alternative sources of employment, often within the mission societies themselves. By and large, however, conversion did not alter the social structure and converts remained bound by debt obligations to moneylenders and the need to serve their landlords.

The transformative aspect of Christianity among Dalits related primarily to the abandonment of pagan beliefs, the consumption of carrion, and other lifestyle changes associated with education, dress, cleanliness, and manners. These changes gave some converts access to alternative forms of employment; but for the most part the social impact of Dalits' new Christian identity was more ambiguous and indirect. Toward the end of the nineteenth century, missionaries in Madras, responding to the abject conditions in which pariah converts labored, proposed that alternative settlements be established for them under their patronage. (Pariah was the name given to Dalits in the Madras Presidency.) The idea was met with fierce criticism by Hindus, who accused missionaries of buying converts with tracts of land and producing "inauthentic" conversions.[12]

The idea of separate settlements never gained traction and the focus of most missionaries remained on making converts and establishing churches. Advocating for a fairer, restructured landlord–laborer relationship or providing alternative sources of patronage, employment, and livelihood for converts not only required vast resources but also deviated from missionary priorities tied to the propagation of the gospel. Some converts hoped that missionaries would replace their landlords as new patrons, treat them more humanely, and provide them with an alternative infrastructure for flourishing. John Clough's employment of Madigas in his canal project offers one instance of a transformed employment space, but this was not a widespread feature of mass movements. Overwhelmed and surprised as they were by demands for baptism and humanitarian aid, missionaries would have found the very idea of refashioning India's social structure as an unfeasible and overly secular involvement.

Missionaries intervened on behalf of converts when they perceived them to be suffering religious persecution, but rarely did they call the entire system of bonded labor into question.[13] And yet, one cannot deny that the Christianization of Dalits provided a vocabulary of dignity and equality that readily translated into aspirations for liberation from caste oppression. The Christian declaration that Christ's saving work is available to all, irrespective of caste, dealt a blow to the notion that converts were irreversibly "unclean" or "polluted." It was an important step in fostering an alternative self-understanding and imagination among Dalits.

The balancing act between spiritual and material transformation has inclined some scholars to reconceive the roles of missionaries in relation to India's caste system. Instead of viewing missionaries as direct agents of radical change, Rupa Viswanath views them as having formed alliances with Dalits without necessarily challenging their station in life. What she calls the "pariah–missionary alliance" underscores initiatives taken by pariahs in enlisting the support of missionaries for their social emancipation, and it directs attention away from the emphasis missionaries placed on the radical change in belief and lifestyle that accompanied conversion. It moves us toward a model that stresses the structural basis of the alliance, grounded in the agrarian context of pariah–landlord relations.[14]

Viswanath's framework corrects unreasonable claims about the emancipatory impact of mass conversions and the tendency to couch Dalit subjugation in terms of "religion" as distinct from exploitive labor. By framing the pariah problem as a fundamentally religious one, state officials used "religious non-interference" as their excuse for maintaining the status quo.[15] At the same time, reducing the pariah–missionary relationship to an "alliance" driven purely by pariah social ambitions unduly minimizes the role of a genuinely Christian imagination being birthed among them, and the sense in which they were drawn to the gospel precisely because of its emancipatory potential. The language of an "alliance" conjures notions of utilitarian motivations that, as discussed below, resonate with the Gandhian critique of conversion being driven by material inducement.

Gandhi on Conversion

Before examining Gandhi's notion of inducement, his critique of Christian conversion needs to be seen in terms of his quest for national unity and *swadeshi*.[16] In his efforts to forge a unified and self-reliant nation, he espoused the unity and equality of all religions. This became a formula for holding India together in a common front against British rule. The great religions of the world, he believed, were different paths to the same summit. Hence, the very idea of converting someone to another religion was repugnant to him. He much preferred that people try to make a Hindu a better Hindu, a Muslim a better Muslim, and so on. Conversion should not lead to a change in religion, but should promote moral growth within the framework of one's own religion and inspire greater dedication to one's country. It was only in this sense that Gandhi believed in conversion.

In addition, Gandhi recognized the need to address the plight of Dalits. In 1932, Gandhi founded the Harijan Sevak Sangh, an organization committed to eradicating untouchability. From 1932 to 1937, he traveled to various parts of India to advance this campaign. He tried to persuade caste Hindus to change their attitudes toward Dalits, whom he had renamed "Harijans" (literally, children of Vishnu). Ultimately, he wanted Dalits to be absorbed into the Sudra caste (the lowest of the four castes) so that they would be recognized as "touchable" *savarnas*—that is, persons holding caste status as distinct from *avarnas* (who lack such status on account of their pollution). He believed this would give them access to land, education, temples, and public facilities such as wells.

Gandhi preferred to adopt persuasive rather than coercive methods for abolishing untouchability. He called upon caste Hindus to change their hearts and admit Dalits as never before into common public spaces. However, he had another aim in mind as he campaigned against untouchability. He wanted Dalits to trust the good will of reform-minded Hindus, avoid political agitation, and avoid converting to other religions. They would thus integrate themselves into the fabric of Hindu society. It was this desire to keep Dalits within Hinduism that made Gandhi such an ardent critic of Christian missionary work. Some have interpreted his renaming them "Harijans" as nothing more than a political move that designated them, for all practical purposes, as Hindus.[17] When such insistence on absorbing Dalits into Hindu caste society was accompanied by strident opposition to conversion, it placed Dalits in a "no entry, no exit" situation.[18] They could not enter Hindu society on account of their pollution and were left to the mercy and good conscience of caste Hindus, but, at the same time, they were denied the opportunity to convert to another religion.

The Stomach, the Mind, and the Cow

Against this gradualist strategy for integrating Dalits into Hindu society, Gandhi had to contend with mass conversions to Christianity. Gandhi wrote extensively about his encounters with Christian missionaries and his feelings about conversion. He viewed these conversions as instances where missionaries leveraged their material resources to lure Dalits into their religion. Repeatedly, he distinguished falsely material from genuinely spiritual motives for conversion. To demonstrate true spiritual motives, one needed to possess the intellectual facility to grasp religious doctrines. Since the vast majority of Dalits lacked such facility, he believed them to be guided by their "stomachs." Gandhi had no reservations about making such sweeping and disparaging statements:

> I do maintain that the vast majority of Harijans, and for that matter Indian humanity, cannot understand the presentation of Christianity, and that generally speaking their conversion wherever it has taken place has not been a spiritual

act in any sense of the term. They are conversions for convenience. And I have had overwhelming corroboration of the truth during my frequent and extensive wanderings.[19]

In an exchange with an American clergyman, Gandhi expressed similar sentiments: "I strongly resent these overtures to utterly ignorant men."[20] In the same exchange, Gandhi claimed that Harijans were incapable of reason, particularly with regard to "theological beliefs and categories," and that they responded to those preaching Jesus as the Son of God with "a blank stare."[21]

When Gandhi criticized conversion in this manner, he was in part responding to the attention mass movements were attracting across missionary circles. In 1933, the American Wesleyan Methodist J. Waskom Pickett published his influential study of mass movements. Pickett had spent forty-six years in India as a pastor, denominational superintendent, Methodist bishop, and editor of the magazine *Indian Witness*.[22] In *Christian Mass Movements in India*, he draws attention to the vast numbers of India's depressed classes who embraced Christianity.[23]

Pickett's aim was to use big data derived from fieldwork to shed light on the motives that drove these mass movements. The fact that he had been so deeply invested in conversion as a career missionary suggests that his study was less than scientific and more of an attempt to lend legitimacy to the enterprise. Still, his methods involved nearly 4,000 interviews of those who had converted in mass movements. Pickett grouped the motives of converts into four categories: spiritual, secular, social, and natal (being a child of a convert). After tabulating the results, he concluded that the highest percentage had converted for spiritual motives (34.8 percent), then natal (34.7 percent), social (22.4 percent), and secular (8.1 percent).[24]

Gandhi dismissed Pickett's findings as gross exaggeration and remained adamant that socioeconomic factors (that is, "secular" factors) were the driving force behind mass conversions. Elsewhere, Gandhi rejected the claim made by the American missionary John R. Mott (chairman of the International Missionary Council, which had commissioned Pickett's study) that Dalits were responding out of spiritual hunger to the Christian message. Mott tried to impress upon Gandhi that Christ had given his followers a mandate to preach and teach. "The whole Christian religion," he said, "is the religion of sharing our life, and how can we share without supplementing our lives with words?"[25]

In response to Mott's question about the place of words, Gandhi responded by emphasizing the ignorance of Dalits. He described Pulayas and Pariahs (two untouchable groups) as having "paralyzed intelligence."[26] To even attempt to convert them exploited their ignorance and was not true Christianity. Perhaps none of Gandhi's statements concerning the cognitive facilities of Dalits elicited greater consternation than his likening them to cows. "The majority of Harijans," he said, "can no more understand the presentation of Christianity than my cows."[27] Despite angry responses to this demeaning comparison, Gandhi refused to withdraw his statement; rather, he argued that, since cows were venerated in India, the comparison did not amount to an insult.

In a conversation with a Polish Roman Catholic philosopher, Gandhi went so far as to declare that conversion is "the deadliest poison that ever sapped the fountain of truth."[28] Clearly, what was at stake in the conversion of Dalits was nothing less than the future of Hinduism itself:

> Hinduism is passing through a fiery ordeal. It will perish not through individual conversion, not even through mass conversion but it will perish because of the sinful denial by the so-called *Savarna Hindus* of elementary justice to Harijans. Every threat of conversion is therefore a warning to the *Savarnas* that if they don't wake in time it may be too late.[29]

This language reveals that Gandhi's opposition to conversion was not purely philosophical; it was also communal, or tied to his interest in preserving Hinduism. For Gandhi, Hinduism would survive only if its reformers abolished untouchability. Doing so, he believed, would make it unnecessary for Dalits to separate themselves politically or religiously from Hindu society.[30] His goal, then, was to absorb Dalits within Hinduism.

Another key instance where Gandhi used the word "poison" was in connection with the proposal to grant Dalits separate political representation. At the 1932 Round Table Conference in London, Ambedkar proposed that Dalits receive a separate electorate or "communal award." This would allow them to elect their own representatives to the seats reserved for them in the assemblies. Gandhi described this proposal as "an injection of a poison that is calculated to destroy Hinduism and do no good whatever to the Depressed Classes."[31] To prevent this communal award from being extended to them, Gandhi threatened to fast to death. Unwilling to bear responsibility for Gandhi's death, Ambedkar reluctantly accepted a compromise in the form of the Poona Pact; this reserved seats for untouchables in the assemblies, but only within a general electorate (where anyone could vote for the Dalit candidates). Gandhi's rejection of legal and political solutions for the oppression of Dalits significantly diminished his credibility in their eyes and enhanced their reverence for Ambedkar.[32] To this day, Dalits recognize Ambedkar, not Gandhi, as their iconic, emancipatory leader.

Ambedkar on Conversion

Gandhi's paternalist view of the problems faced by Dalits led many to seek alternative approaches to achieve their liberation. Rather than relying on the goodwill of caste Hindus, many preferred to fight for separation and autonomy from Hindu society. Ambedkar came from the Mahar community; these were Dalit sanitation workers from the western state of Maharashtra. As someone who was actually Dalit, he believed that he was better suited to address their needs than Gandhi. In contrast to Gandhi, who believed in gradualist, noncoercive means of assimilating Dalits, Ambedkar insisted on legal and political solutions.[33] Beyond this, he called for a total rejection of Hinduism by Dalits.

Annihilating Caste

Ambedkar's radical position drew him into a direct confrontation with Gandhi. Their disagreement mainly related to their understanding of caste, or what in Sanskrit was termed *varnashrama dharma*. Gandhi's aim was to eradicate untouchability, while preserving the essential integrity of the fourfold division of labor in traditional society (priests, warriors, merchants, and service providers); he believed that people should observe the social duty into which they were born. Ambedkar, however, believed that untouchability was the inevitable byproduct of the social distinctions embodied in *varnashrama dharma*. His perspective was grounded in his concept of graded inequality, which refers to the tendency of each caste to secure its privileged status above the caste or castes below it. This constant state of one-upmanship prevented the lower castes from forming a united front against Brahminical dominance.[34] Untouchability proceeded naturally from the system of graded inequality, since members of the lowest caste needed people to step on. By this reasoning, it was impossible to preserve the *varnas* and abolish untouchability, as Gandhi envisioned. What Ambedkar called for was the total annihilation of caste, which he viewed as an essential aspect of Hinduism.

Ambedkar rebutted Gandhi's stance on Christian missionary work and conversion among the Dalits and criticized the double standard that Gandhi applied to Muslims and Christians. Members of both religions held beliefs and customs that differed from those of Hindus, and both Christians and Muslims had raised funds to support missionary projects among Dalits. The same charge of inducement that Gandhi had directed at Christians, Ambedkar believed, could just as well have been directed against Muslims. Yet Gandhi had treated Muslims far more charitably than Christians, largely for political reasons. Since Muslims far outnumbered Christians, they could easily have made themselves "a thorn in the side of Nationalism."[35]

All Religions Are Not True or the Same

Ambedkar criticized Gandhi's universalist religious beliefs even more sharply. He regarded as "utterly fallacious" Gandhi's claim that all religions are equally true and valuable. In fact, he argued, it was precisely because they were not all true that adherents of one faith may indeed have a duty to share the truth with their unenlightened neighbors. Ambedkar went to great lengths to attack Hindu caste precepts found in the laws of Manu (*Manusmriti*). He was aware that caste distinctions were observable in India's churches and Muslim communities as well, yet he maintained that the normative basis for caste found in Hinduism made it an essential aspect of the religion: "[If] Muslims and Christians start a movement for the abolition of the caste system in their respective religion, their religions would cause no obstruction. Hindus cannot destroy their caste system without destroying their religion."[36]

Ambedkar also disputed Gandhi's contention that missionaries had been providing material "bait" for conversion. He found it strange that Gandhi wanted Indians to enjoy the material services provided by missionaries while opposing conversion as a response to such services:

> It is difficult to understand why Mr. Gandhi argues that services rendered by the Missionaries are baits or temptations, and that the conversions are therefore conversions of convenience. Why is it not possible to believe that those services by Missionaries indicate that service to suffering humanity is for Christians an essential requirement of their religion? Would that be a wrong view of the process by which a person is drawn to Christianity? ...
>
> Nobody will deny to Mr. Gandhi the right to save the Untouchables for Hinduism. But in that case he should have frankly told Missions, "Stop your work, we want now to save the Untouchables and ourselves. Give us a chance!" It is a pity that he should not have adopted this honest mode of dealing with the menace of the Missionaries.[37]

Ambedkar's trenchant criticisms of Gandhi's views on conversion stem in part from his sense of indebtedness to missionaries for the shelter from Hindu tyranny they had extended to Dalits. These criticisms, however, are best understood not as a defense of missionaries or of the Christian religion as such, but as part of his repudiation of caste and of his defense of the legitimacy of conversion.

At the Yeola Conference in 1935, Ambedkar declared that Hinduism had no power to liberate Dalits and that Dalits should seek equality of status within another religion. Because they lacked the strength required to challenge Hindu tyranny, they had to secure strength "from the outside":

> [U]nless you establish close relations with some other society, unless you join some other religion, you cannot get the strength from the outside. It clearly means that you must leave your present religion and assimilate yourselves with some other society.[38]

"Conversion," he argued, "is as important to Untouchables as self-government is to India . . . there is not the slightest difference in their ultimate goal."[39] Again, in his speech at the Yeola meeting, he declared:

> I advise you to sever your connection to Hinduism and to embrace any other religion. But, in doing so, be careful in choosing the new faith and see that equality of treatment, status and opportunities will be guaranteed to you unreservedly . . . Unfortunately for me I was born a Hindu Untouchable. It was beyond my power to prevent that, but I declare that it is within my power to refuse to live under ignoble and humiliating conditions. I solemnly assure you that I will not die a Hindu.[40]

Not surprisingly, Ambedkar's bold declaration pricked up the ears of leaders of other religions. Would Ambedkar convert to Sikhism, Buddhism, Islam, or Christianity? Would he lead masses of Dalits with him? There is some indication that he seriously entertained the possibility of becoming a Christian. Pickett claimed that Ambedkar was a secret believer in Christ and that he had every intention of directing Dalits to the Church. In a letter to Thomas S. Donohugh, a member of the board of the National Christian Council's Mass Movement Study, Pickett claimed:

> The Mohammedans are making desperate efforts to capture them, the Sikhs and the Buddhists are also competing for them, but there can be little doubt that Dr. Ambedkar's own purpose is to turn his people towards Christianity. He is quoted as having said privately to several people that he is personally a firm believer in the gospel of Jesus Christ and plans to confess the Christian faith and seek admission to the Church sooner or later.[41]

Despite such optimism, Ambedkar did not choose to become a Christian or encourage the same for his fellow Mahars. In fact, his rejection of both Christianity and Islam appears to have been based in no small part on political calculations.

A mass conversion to Islam by Dalits could result in Muslim domination, while one to Christianity, he reasoned, could end up strengthening British rule.[42] Moreover, he appears to have bought in to the idea that conversion to either religion would be denationalizing. Ambedkar ultimately chose Buddhism as his alternative to Hinduism, since he found in Buddhism an egalitarian religion of Indian origin that placed a strong emphasis on reason. In 1956, following his lead, 55 percent of all the untouchables of Maharashtra embraced Buddhism; thereafter, they were referred to as neo-Buddhists. As for Christianity, Ambedkar maintained that churches too often had perpetuated caste discrimination and that the Christian community had merely replaced the dominance of caste Hindus with that of caste Christians.

Dalit Christian Theology

Asserting Difference from Hinduism

The mass movements had yielded a Church consisting of as many as 70–80 percent *avarnas* (outcastes); and yet the Church in India was led by caste elites who were doing most of the theologizing. This elitist impulse has a deep history in South Asia's Christian traditions: The Syrian Christians function as a caste community in Kerala, claiming Brahminical roots.[43] Roman Catholics since the days of Roberto de Nobili were fixated on converting the upper castes, and he and his associates claimed for themselves Brahmin status. Even the Lutheran Pietist missionaries who followed Ziegenbalg's lead adhered to theological perspectives that ended up accommodating caste distinctions within the Church.[44]

From a Dalit perspective, the attempts of Christian elites to Indianize Christianity only added to their oppression. "Indianizing" had become synonymous with Sanskritizing and Hinduizing, and such a project only reinforced the primacy of Brahminical knowledge and upper caste dominance.[45] Each of these historical instances of contextual or culturally adapted Christianity laid the foundations for traditions dominated by upper castes, even when church pews consisted primarily of low caste and Dalit peoples. The twentieth-century project of Indianizing Christianity simply added another ideological layer to what was already an elite-driven Church.

Dalit Christian theology emerged as a powerful critique of this impulse to adapt the gospel to upper caste culture. As Indian nationalism increasingly became a Hindu nationalism, it tended to invalidate or marginalize the aspirations and experiences of Dalits.[46] In response, Dalit theologians developed a theology that employed and interacted with the symbolic resources of their own communities. An important strategy was to differentiate Dalit religion from so-called Aryan, Sanskritic, or Brahminical religion. This was Ambedkar's approach, and others have since followed suit in different ways. In his book *The Confusion Called Conversion*, Ebenezer Sunder Raj argues that untouchable and tribal peoples of northeast India have never belonged to Sanskritic culture. Similarly, south Indians of Dravidian origin were not originally practitioners of Sanskrit-based religion. They worshiped different gods, adhered to different rites, and observed their own festivals. Indo-Aryan migrants from north India eventually drew south Indians into the orbit of Brahminical religion and its priestly order by forging powerful bonds between Brahmin missionaries (as Sunder Raj calls them), south Indian kings, and temples. Kings legitimated their rule by patronizing temples, while Brahmins provided ritual services as priests. The differentiation of labor that arose within this "sacred complex" became the caste system.[47]

Another iteration of this strategy of differentiation is presented in Kancha Ilaiah's depiction of the plight of "Dalit-Bahujans." This term, coined by the politician Kanshi Ram, envisioned a united political movement consisting of all Dalit communities along with other scheduled castes from the Sudra caste. In *Why I Am Not a Hindu*, Ilaiah narrates his experiences as a Dalit-Bahujan.[48] His book is not an example of Dalit Christian theology, but it illustrates the repositioning of Dalit identity that was central to this theology. Ilaiah stresses the difference between his familial customs and those of Hindu society. In addition to recounting the long history of oppression and discrimination that he and his fellow caste members (Kurumaas) suffered under caste Hindus, Ilaiah describes how every dimension of his caste culture can be differentiated from Hindu culture. These domains of difference include family relationships, the roles of women, deities, dietary habits, sexual mores, occupations, and education. Based on such differences, there are no grounds, Ilaiah argues, for regarding Dalit-Bahujans as part of the Hindu fold. Attacking the *Hindutva*-inspired cooption of his caste into the Brahminical social structure, Ilaiah writes:

> The question is what do we the lower Sudras and Ati-Sudras (whom I also call Dalitbahujans) have to do with Hinduism or with Hindutva itself? I, indeed not only I, but all of us, the Dalitbahujans of India, have never heard the word "Hindu"—not as a word, nor as the name of a culture, nor as the name of a religion in our early childhood days . . . But today we are suddenly being told that we have a common religious and cultural relationship with the Baapanoollu [Brahmins] and the Koomatoollu [Baniyas]. This is not merely surprising; it is shocking.[49]

The tools that Ilaiah employs to explain why he is not a Hindu are not centered on academic-sounding distinctions between different classes of people, but on the power of storytelling. This approach is similar to the one taken by the Roman Catholic Dalit author Bama. In *Karukku*, she narrates her life, skillfully weaving together her individual experiences and those of her community. Like Ilaiah, she eschews an academic presentation of Dalit experience, preferring instead to narrate pain, trauma, and humiliation in different episodes of her life.[50]

Ilaiah's reasoning taps into a tradition of non-Hindu confessionalism reflected in the work of anti-caste reformers such as Jyotirao Phule, B. R. Ambedkar, and E. V. Ramaswamy Naicker. The goal of this strategy is to differentiate Dalits from Hindu society while at the same time establishing them as people of the soil—indeed, as the original inhabitants of India who were colonized by the Aryan other.

The strategy of differentiating Dalit or Dalit-Bahujan identity from Hinduism does not come without risks. By forging a broad network of solidarity that stresses difference from Sanskritic society, they increase their capacity to counter Hindu majoritarianism with an alternative politics tailored to their interests. At the same time, India's system of affirmative action extends benefits only to Dalits who remain Hindu (discussed below). Dalits feel pressured to accept a Hindu identity in order to gain access to affirmative action benefits (called "reservations") in employment and education. This structural incentive undermines their politics of difference. For all practical purposes, the system of reservations has functioned as a form of inducement and a means of retaining Dalits within the Hindu fold. Brahmins and other upper castes have long employed strategies of cooption and assimilation in order to thwart rebellious assertions of difference among lower castes. By denying reservations to those who leave Hinduism for Islam or Christianity, a Hindu majoritarian state has found yet another way of coopting Dalits.[51]

Multiple Identities

In their classic study of a Telugu Christian community from south India's Medak Diocese, P. Y. Luke and John Carman describe a tension between the ties of converts to their village communities and their new Christian identity. Village Christians, they argued, often retained the customs of their caste traditions, and yet the Protestant theologies that underlay their conversions often demanded a clean break from the past. As a result, converts often assumed dual identities—one that was "separate and distinctive," the other that was "at one with the rest of the village."[52] Converts moved constantly between the domains of village life and those of the Church. As they did so, they negotiated their original identities with their new Protestant selves. Missionaries may have aspired to see converts make a clean break from their past, but this would have required them to provide those converts with an entirely new source of livelihood and an alternative social existence, removed from village life. As noted above, they neither aspired to nor were able to achieve such ends among their mass converts, who were compelled to maintain dual participation and dual identities.

The dilemma faced by Dalit Christians was not easily reduced either to living fully as Christians or to reverting to village practices. Instead, it was a dialectical task of living between Sanskritic and Christian social spaces. During the early twentieth century, this anxiety of being in between was captured in the poetry of a Dalit Christian named Gurram Joshua. The child of a Madiga mother and a Golla father, Joshua was born in the Vinukonda *taluk* (a subdistrict or village) of Guntur district. Experiences of caste-based mistreatment since his days as a youth profoundly shaped his poetic imagination and activism.[53] Joshua flourished as a poet during the most vibrant years of the Indian independence movement. His poems reflect his attentiveness to the politics of his day as much as they lament the stark realities of untouchability. They are conversant with Sanskritic and with biblical narratives; with the Hindu deity Shiva and with Jesus; with Indian nationality and with the painful exclusions faced by Dalits. His poem "My Story" describes how religion had failed him:

> Many a time did I read the Bible in the Church
> Sincerely did I pray for the removal of untouchability
> Took baptism like all others
> Loved even my enemy as my own brother
> Always kept my word of honor
> But the all-pervading false faith breaks my heart.[54]

Joshua represents that section of the Dalit Christian population that found themselves unable to fully identify with any one particular religion. As offspring of the mass movements, their lives rarely reflected the missionary ideal of an unadulterated Christian identity. Their post-baptismal experience may have been accompanied by a zeal to separate from their past; but, for many, the initial experience of radical change eventually receded. What remained were not devotees of a different religion, but persons shaped by many systems, none of which delivered on their promises to alleviate their oppressed conditions. Living in the margins of multiple societies, these Christians suffered from both social and religious discrimination. As a tool of survival, they found ways of asserting those aspects of their identity most likely to secure their wellbeing in a given environment.

Cultural Resources of Dalits

With an eye to recovering suppressed Dalit particularities and asserting their difference from dominant castes, some theologians draw upon the symbolic resources of Dalits to formulate their theologies. This sets them apart from Indian Christian theologians who made Sanskritic concepts and categories their primary reference point. The theologian Sathianathan Clarke draws upon the centrality of goddess worship and drum beating in the lives of south Indian Paraiyars. In an earlier era, missionaries would have dismissed goddess worship as demonic; from the standpoint of Dalit theology, however, the veneration of their deity Ellaiyamman represents an "alternative mode of religion making."[55] Paraiyars believed that Ellaiyamman protected the boundary that separated their village domains from those of caste Hindus. This deity, notes Clarke, "shields and polices the geographic, social, and cultural space of the Paraiyar from the continuous colonizing proclivity of the caste peoples."[56] Whereas some local myths linked Dalit goddesses to the Hindu divinities Shiva and Vishnu, Ellaiyamman remained independent. This shows the desire of Paraiyars to be "distinct, different, even separate" from Hindu society.[57] The veneration of Ellaiyamman is embedded deeply into the oral traditions of the Paraiyars, including in songs and stories that make derogatory references to caste Hindus.[58] Christian theology for Paraiyars would present Christ as one who incarnates himself into their social reality, thereby performing the role of protector, liberator, and resister once occupied by Ellaiyamman.

Paraiyars also differentiated themselves from Hindu society through their use of the drum. Drum beating is essential during marriage processions, ceremonies that invoke divine grace in everyday life, exorcisms, dances, and public declarations. The sound of the drum is related to the Paraiyar culture of oral transmission. Because it conveys meaning through sound as distinct from a written text, the drum differentiates Paraiyars from upper caste, literate elites. For Christian theology to speak to Dalits, it needed to penetrate this subaltern (non-elite) interior of Paraiyar experience. Upper castes withheld from Paraiyars the sacred word by denying them access to Sanskrit texts. Excluded from temples and sacred knowledge in Sanskrit, Paraiyars found in the drum the mediating presence of the divine. Within the context of Dalit theology, Clarke makes the case that the drum signifies the "immanental presence of God" in Christ, and that it is a powerful symbol of liberation for Paraiyars (see Figure 9.1).

Clarke's emphasis on sound and materiality resonates with the role of music in advancing the cause of Dalit liberation. The ethnomusicologist Zoe Sherinian describes how Tamil Christian folk music expresses the social experiences of Dalits and their aspirations for a more dignified life. Sherinian reflects on the

Figure 9.1 *Jesus and the Cosmic Drum* by Jyoti Sahi.

work of Reverend J. Theophilus Appavoo in "re-indigenizing" music and liturgy in ways that are "contextualized to be emblematic of the identity and culture of the oppressed."[59] When conveyed through the medium of Tamil folk music, this theology seeks to transform the outcaste's self-perception as "polluted" into a beloved and empowered person capable of waging a battle for social justice. In addition to composing over one hundred songs, Appavoo produced a sung liturgy, plays, and stories anchored in Tamil folklore. These capture the heart of the Dalit plight and instill hope for their final emancipation. His work is produced in dialogue with the Tamil Christians for whom it is intended; through incarnational living and conversation, he invites villagers to play an active role in producing the theology embedded in their music.

Appavoo's development of the notion of *oru olai* ("one pot") powerfully illustrates both the method and the content of this theologizing. It builds on New Testament passages that speak of different members of the Church as "one body" partaking of "one loaf." Following a conversation with a Dalit girl, it occurred to him that the basic experience of eating was far different for Dalits, who may eat nothing for long periods, or eat simple foods such as *kanji* (rice gruel), in contrast to the more substantial breakfast menu of well-to-do families. This awareness formed the basis of a focus on *oru olai*, which emphasizes "communal eating and shared labor as a daily Eucharistic lifestyle to address hunger in Dalit communities and to unify the oppressed."[60] The emphasis on communal eating connects motifs central to the New Testament with the experience of caste distinctions in south India. Within the New Testament (for example, 1 Corinthians 8, Galatians 2:12, Acts 10:9–16) and within caste society, eating defines one's social location. Inter-dining between Dalits and people of higher castes can "pollute" the latter. By theologizing about the very act of eating, *oru olai* recognizes it as a venue that either reinforces upper caste hegemony (by excluding some from the table) or promotes the alternative belief in a "universal family."[61] It challenges a long history within both Catholic and Protestant churches, whereby Dalits took communion separately from upper caste Christians.

Much of south Indian culture exalts the musical styles and classical forms that became the province of upper castes: for instance, Carnatic music and Bharatnatyam dance.[62] By contrast, Appavoo's theological work highlights the importance of subaltern folkloric traditions. The use of these traditions in theology works against the histories of Jesuits and other foreign missionaries, who privileged high caste, Sanskritic traditions in their attempts to contextualize the gospel. The use of music to cultivate alternative self-understandings, hopes, and transformations among Dalits resonates with liberationist frameworks arising in other contexts. The Brazilian educator Paulo Freire argued that oppressed people often internalize the assumptions and ideas of their oppressors in ways that reinforce their sense of inferiority. An alternative pedagogy is required to undo the damage and inspire them to be agents of their own liberation.[63] Tamil folk music presents itself not only as an affirmation of those who own its heritage, but also as a tool for their reeducation.

Other Theologies of Liberation

In addition to drawing upon the unique experience and symbols of Dalits, Dalit theology is committed to their liberation. The project is not merely incarnational (that is, rooted in Dalit localities and experiences); it is also emancipatory. It is a theology inspired by Latin America's liberation theology, which originated in the work of the theologian Gustavo Gutiérrez and called for a radical reading of the Bible through the lens of Marxist notions of class struggle and revolution. Such a reading draws liberationist themes from the story of the Exodus and portrays Christ as the liberator of the oppressed. Liberation theology applies this reading of the Bible to the sociopolitical struggles of poor and oppressed Latin American peoples. Eschewing notions of salvation that are centered on the afterlife, liberation theology fuses its doctrine of salvation with a praxis focused on challenging structures of inequality. Dalit theology does similar things, but tailors its liberationist vision to the context of Hindu caste oppression, as distinct from postcolonial Latin American struggle. The theologian Arvind Nirmal describes the profound *pathos* that defines Dalit consciousness:

> My dalit ancestor did not enjoy the nomadic freedom of the wandering Aramean. As an outcaste, he was also cast out of his/her village . . . When my dalit ancestor walked the dusty roads of his village, the *Sa Varnas* also tied an earthen pot around my dalit ancestor's neck to serve as a spittle. If ever my dalit ancestor tried to learn Sanskrit or some other sophisticated language the oppressors gagged him permanently by pouring molten lead down his throat.[64]

The memory of such experiences and their present-day reality are powerful shapers of Dalit Christian consciousness and inform the quest for liberation that runs through Dalit readings of the Gospels. Jesus is not a detached guru of contextual Indian Christian theology, but someone who was subjected to humiliation and crucifixion at the hands of the religious establishment of his day. Dalits—who are similarly crushed, broken, and humiliated—see both their experiences and their emancipation in the crucified Jesus.

The connections Dalits draw between their brokenness and the wounding of Christ's body resonate with powerful motifs of African American theology. This resonance is particularly strong in connection to the violence that both Dalits and African Americans face from whites or upper castes. Throughout their history in the segregated American South, Black Americans were victims of lynching, instances where a group of whites would hang a Black person publicly for alleged crimes without a trial. The theologian James Cone drew a parallel between the lynched African American body and the suffering of Christ. The poetics of Black preaching and the Black literary imagination saw the immediate resemblance, Cone observed, between the cross and the lynching tree. The same poetics portrayed Christ as the "first leaf in a line of trees on which a man should swing."[65] Christ, then, became the first lynchee and the lynching of Blacks became occasions on which Christ was lynched again.[66]

This identification with the suffering Christ is a salient feature of Dalit theology as well. Dalit theology recognizes Jesus as a Dalit, since the lowly birth, humiliation, and crucifixion of Jesus resonate with Dalit experience. Like African Americans, Dalits routinely are victims of atrocities and instances of humiliation, primarily by members of upper castes. India's National Crime Records Bureau indicates that a crime is committed against a Dalit by a non-Dalit every sixteen minutes. This includes rape, beatings, stripping and parading naked, seizing of land, and restricted access to water.[67] Dalit theology looks to Jesus as someone who embodies their pain and subjugation and opens the path for their liberation. The Son of Man's "rejection, mockery, contempt, suffering, and finally death" (Mark 8:31) occurred at the hands of "the dominant religious tradition

Figure 9.2 *Jesus the Dalit Man of Sorrows* by Jyoti Sahi.

and the established religion." In this manner, Jesus underwent Dalit experiences as the "prototype of all Dalits" (see Figure 9.2).[68] In contrast to theologies of substitutionary atonement, which stress how Christ suffered and died *for* or *in place of* others, the Dalit Jesus suffered and died *like* them.

In terms of their politics, Dalit Christians are inspired by Ambedkar's advocacy of legal and political solutions for Dalit problems. So inspired have they been by Ambedkar that they are inclined to view his methods as the praxis that flows from their liberation theology. In Ambedkar and Jesus, they find a special affinity, so much so that some theologians, such as Jayachitra Lalitha, read them in a complementary manner. Just as Jesus confronted the hypocrisy, purity laws, and exclusionary practices of the religious establishment of his day, Ambedkar attacked Brahminical laws of purity as practices that oppress and exclude Dalits. Jesus called for an "inclusive temple" and displayed a special concern for the poor. Similarly, Ambedkar decried the religious basis of caste discrimination, prohibitions of intermarriage and inter-dining, and discriminatory practices that reinforced economic disadvantage among Dalits.[69] Fired by this dynamic and contrapuntal reading of Jesus and Ambedkar, Dalit Christians are inspired to confront caste-ism within the life of the Church and in society at large. The radical social critique expressed by Dalit Christians through novels, poems, plays, and artwork is fired by a similar imagination.

Affirmative Action for Dalit Christians?

During the 1990s, the Government of India implemented a vast scheme of affirmative action in order to improve the lives of victims of caste discrimination. In 1979, the government established the Mandal Commission with the aim of identifying the most socially and educationally backward classes of India and recommending remedial action. When the recommendations were finally implemented in 1990, the government designated those caste communities that had suffered material and social disadvantages as "scheduled castes" (SCs). Members of SCs were entitled to quotas (or reservations) in state employment and education and other benefits aimed at rectifying their history of oppression. Another category—"other backward castes" (OBCs)—was also listed among those entitled to state assistance. Implementation of the Mandal Commission's recommendations led to widespread protests by Brahmin and other upper caste students. In some instances this took the form of public self-immolations. Protesters regarded SC quotas for educational admissions as a form of reverse discrimination.[70]

Roughly 76 percent of India's Christians belong to communities considered to be SCs, OBCs, or Scheduled Tribes (STs). This may seem like a disproportionately large number of people from disadvantaged backgrounds relative to other religious communities, but it is not. According to a 2021 study by the Pew Research Center, the SC, OBC, and ST population equates to about 75 percent of India's major religions collectively and comprises 77 percent of the Hindu population.[71]

These numbers become particularly important in relation to affirmative action. To this day, the government still refuses to recognize Dalit *Christians* as members of India's SCs who qualify for government assistance.[72] This policy can be traced back to the Constitutional (SC) Order of 1950, which established state-specific lists of communities that could be classified as SCs. It stipulated that "no person professing a religion different from Hinduism shall be deemed to be a member of a Scheduled Caste." The order was amended in 1956 to include

Sikhs and again in 1990 to include neo-Buddhists. Despite persistent appeals to make reservations completely "religion blind," Dalit Christians (and Muslims) find themselves excluded from SC status on the basis of their religious identity. Throughout the 1990s, Muslims disputed their exclusion from SC lists, arguing that much of their community in India was economically backward.[73] Christians have staged repeated protests across India, stressing the high degree of ritual discrimination that persists in their lives. Protesters feel that they are unduly penalized for being Christian. However, such advocacy appears to have landed on deaf ears, even during the long reign of the Congress Party, which purports to uphold religious freedom and secularism.

What seems to have informed the Constitutional (SC) Order of 1950 are three important assumptions: the casteless-ness of Christianity; its transformative impact on the lives of converts; and its capacity to bring foreign resources to bear upon the plight of India's untouchables. What has not been factored in to state policymaking is the persistence of caste consciousness and discrimination within churches and the economic deprivation faced by Dalit Christians. To change the 1950 Order, Dalit Christians must grapple not only with current Hindu nationalist winds but also with aspects of the missionary legacy. By claiming, on the one hand, that they remain socially and economically disadvantaged, they are working against a long history that emphasized the socially transformative impact of becoming Christian. By asserting, on the other hand, the primacy of their Christian identity, they mask insidious forms of discrimination that persist within and beyond the life of the Church and the adverse effects of such discrimination on their development.

Attempts to change the 1950 Order seem repeatedly to encounter the same road blocks. According to political scientist Zoya Hasan, the policy framework of independent India separated the needs of religious minorities from those of disadvantaged caste communities. Whereas the government had an interest in promoting the "cultural preservation" of religious minorities, it framed its policy toward Dalits and tribals in terms of their economic development and empowerment.[74] Within the nationalist imagination that underwrites this policy, religious minorities and untouchables occupy different spaces. The political scientist Gopal Guru describes how nationalism converts "minorities" into the "significant other" who needs to be managed and subordinated. Untouchables are the "insignificant other," consigned to a life of servility to upper castes.[75] These were two different constructions with two solutions. Constitutional protection for religious minorities placed such a strong emphasis upon religious identity that they ignored the inequality and deprivation often faced by Muslim or Christian converts.[76] This sharp bifurcation of religion and caste also seemed to be geared toward barring anyone from "double dipping" into minority rights and aid for the disadvantaged. The state's denial of intersectionality between religion and untouchability lies at the heart of the omission of Christian (and Muslim) Dalits from SC lists.

In 1985, Soosai, a Tamil Christian convert, challenged the SC Order in court, only to be met with the enduring logic of the state in excluding Christians from state benefits. He was a cobbler who worked on a roadside near an intersection in Madras. In May 1982, local officers surveyed the sites where the cobblers were working and subsequently granted many of them free bunks through the Khadi and Village Industries Board. Soosai did not receive one because he was a Christian. In his petition, he argued that he was a member of the Adi Dravida community, which was listed in the original SC list of 1950, and he had remained a member of that community after conversion. He argued that the Order of 1950 was invalid because it penalizes his change of religion, contrary to Articles 14 and 15 of the Indian constitution, which ensure equal protection under the law and freedom of religion respectively. Conversion, he argued, in no way eliminated the deprivations faced by members of his community.[77]

In its decision, the court did not deny the continuity of one's caste identity after conversion, but contended that this by itself was insufficient to classify someone as SC:

> To establish that paragraph 3 of the Constitution (Scheduled Castes) Order, 1950 discriminates against Christian members of the enumerated castes it must be shown that they suffer from a comparable depth of social and economic disabilities and cultural and educational backwardness and similar levels of degradation within the Christian community necessitating intervention by the State under provisions of the Constitution. It is not sufficient to show that the same caste continues after conversion. It is necessary to establish further that the disabilities and handicaps suffered from such caste membership in the social order of its origin—Hinduism—continue in their oppressive severity in the new environment of a different religious community. No authoritative or detailed study dealing with the present conditions of Christian society have been placed on the record in this case.[78]

The court's acknowledgment of the persistence of a caste identity after conversion is a marked change from earlier decisions, traceable to the colonial period, which simply regarded Christianity as a religion that did not teach caste distinctions and concluded from this that Christians possessed no caste identity.[79] What the court was willing to concede in 1985, however, would not be sufficient to overturn a long history of disassociating Christians from untouchable communities.

In 2005, the ruling United Progressive Alliance (UPA) government established a commission headed by Ranganath Mishra, the former Chief Justice of India. One of the main aims of this commission was to identify the criteria that define backwardness among linguistic and religious minorities and to recommend remedial measures on the basis of those criteria. Unlike the 1985 decision regarding Soosai, the Mishra Commission not only recognized caste as a pervasive institution in Indian society, irrespective of religion, but clearly acknowledged the persistence of ritual discrimination faced by Christian converts:

> The position of persons of Scheduled Caste origin converted to Christianity remains the same as before. They continue to be forced into the most demeaning occupations. Their position both in the Church as well as amongst fellow Christians is no better than that suffered by their counterparts in other religious denominations. They continue to be both poor and socially and educationally backward. Inter-marriages between them and upper caste Christians are rare. In the Churches they are segregated from the upper caste Christians. Even after death they are buried in different burial grounds.[80]

Dalit Christians could not have asked for a better statement to legitimize their claims for SC status than the one offered in the Mishra Report. When it was submitted to the government in 2007, it had the backing of several parties within the UPA. The Congress Party (the party of Gandhi and Nehru), however, was reluctant to act. Its members appear to have been pressured by certain members of parliament and ministers in the UPA who opposed the measure. Some of these members had expressed fears that extending SC status to Christian and Muslim Dalits would encourage Hindu Dalits to convert to those religions.[81]

These challenges to the 1950 Order reveal three recurring themes in the debate about religion and caste in India. First, they illustrate how both sides of the debate have deployed the notion of "inducement," which dates back to the era of mass movements. Opponents of the 1950 Order regard it as inducing Muslim or Christian converts to revert to Hinduism to qualify for state assistance. Some of the most strident defenders of the Order are Hindu nationalists, who believe that, by extending SC status to Muslims and Christians, the state would be encouraging conversion to those religions. They also maintain that the award would put Dalit Christians in a position to reap undue advantages arising from their conversion (for instance, access to education) as well as from state aid. This would be unfair to other SCs and neo-Buddhists, who do not benefit from Christian institutions.[82]

Second, these challenges show how the policy remains unchanged despite strong arguments on the ground for the persistence of caste-related disadvantage among Christian converts. The evidence set out in the Mishra Report has been joined by scholarly works by anthropologists and social scientists, and an official report by the National Commission for Minorities, that all enumerate the social disadvantages faced by Christian and Muslim communities.[83] Finally, responses to these challenges fail to adequately explain why Sikhs and Buddhists have been included in the SC lists while Muslims and Christians have not. Like Islam and Christianity, after all, Sikhism and Buddhism are egalitarian religions that disavow caste distinctions. The policy seems to invoke a longstanding distinction between religions of Indian origin and those of foreign origin. To this day, Hindu nationalists portray Muslims and Christians as members of foreign religions.[84]

Conclusion

This chapter has examined the role of the Christian gospel in promoting the liberation of Dalits. It began by comparing missionary approaches to caste in India with evolving Christian approaches to slavery in the Atlantic. Transitions from "Protestant supremacy" to "Christian slavery" and ultimately to the abolition of African slavery resonate with aspects of the missionary–Dalit–landlord relationship in India. In the face of mass conversions among Dalits, missionaries in India never embraced a "Protestant supremacy" paradigm, which opposed conversion to ensure white domination. Instead, they prioritized spiritual formation, doctrinal understanding, and abandonment of pre-Christian beliefs and practices among Dalits. This emphasis carried socially emancipatory possibilities but stopped well short of a radical critique of caste and a commitment to overturning exploitive bonded labor.

Dalit Christians occupied a space within Indian society that even Ambedkar, who became a Buddhist, could not foresee. Their double marginality as Dalits and Christians is compounded by a third dilemma: their complicated relationship with Ambedkar's legacy. As much as they want to appropriate Ambedkar to their cause and read the Gospels in light of Ambedkar's activism, they contend with unique prejudices associated with the Christian side of their identity. Should they reap the advantages that flow from Ambedkaresque advocacy and empowerment? Or did becoming Christian give them access to advantages not enjoyed by other Dalits? During the early twentieth century, the Congress Party official C. Rajagopalachari commended Christians from the depressed classes for their social transformation:

> As soon as people become Indian Christians, they go to school. In many places in India whole villages are converted, and they cease at once to be called "depressed classes" . . . Have you not seen with your own eyes in the villages, that the untouchables are not allowed to take water from the village well, but that the moment they are converted to Christ they can use the well of the village? . . . Therefore even the lowest in the social scheme in India's dark corners can by becoming a Christian enjoy these privileges.[85]

It is precisely these assumptions about "enjoying privileges" that alienate Dalit Christians from other Dalits. When joined to the notion that Christianity does not teach caste distinctions, such assumptions threaten to efface the Dalit side of their identity. Dalit Christians have made every effort to challenge stereotypes about their relatively elevated social location. They draw attention to the persistence of caste-based discrimination directed against them in village or urban settings. Dalit Christian theology provides a powerful medium for articulating their pain and their identification with Christ's suffering. It also provides tools not to be found in conventional Christian theology for addressing caste discrimination within the life of the Church.

10
Pentecostalism, Conversion, and Violence in India

At City of Harvest Assemblies of God Church in Bangalore, Pastor Shine Thomas delivered a stirring online message during the Covid-19 pandemic. He preached about Jesus healing ten lepers, based on the account given in Luke 17:11–14. Lepers in Jesus's day, he explained, were despised outcasts of society. The religious establishment shunned them because of their physical deformity, odor, and potential to pollute others with their skin disease. Unlike other instances when Jesus physically touched lepers to heal them, he did not touch the lepers in this passage. In accordance with Jewish ceremonial law, he instructed them to "go and show [themselves] to the priests." As the ten were on their way, Jesus healed them. Thomas used this as a launching point for his declaration of God's power to heal, even remotely:

> You may be thinking you are very far during these lockdown days from pastors or people who can pray for you for healing, but you don't have to go anywhere. He sends his word and He heals you. He can heal you at a distance, wherever you are watching in the name of Jesus! Receive your healing in the name of Jesus! Amen.[1]

Pastor Thomas and his message reveal important aspects of the Pentecostal legacy in India, both in what is stated explicitly and in things that are left unsaid. First, the sermon could very well have been about Dalits and their stigma of untouchability. Dalits, after all, are shunned on account of their pollution and are consigned to the outskirts of villages. In fact, the rapid expansion of Pentecostalism in India—and worldwide—is very much related to the movement's message of healing and spiritual deliverance, a message that resonates powerfully among society's poor and marginal, including members of Dalit castes.

Second, the Church's capacity to deliver its high-tech services during the pandemic in five different languages is extraordinary. It taps in to a deeper history of Pentecostalism's use of religious broadcasting to propagate its message and its ties to America-based religious networks. This aspect of the Pentecostal legacy is significant because it highlights their paradoxical shunning and embrace of modernity. Since the late nineteenth century, they have maintained a belief in supernatural activity in everyday life, while employing transnational media networks and new technologies (radio, television, and the internet) to reach audiences with the gospel. In post-Second World War America, religious fundamentalists and Pentecostals have broadcast over 1,600 different radio programs. Such undertakings laid the foundations for the proliferation of Christian television broadcasting in the USA and worldwide.[2] This history makes the online transition of Pentecostal services during the Covid-19 pandemic seem rather routine. It also raises important questions about Pentecostalism's origins. Is it indigenous or is it tied in some way to a distinctively American gospel?

Pastor Thomas's own life story reveals yet another aspect of the history of Pentecostalism. He came from a well-to-do "orthodox Christian family in Kerala." His parents placed their faith in Christ after his mother's terminal illness was healed. Eventually, Thomas himself committed his life to Christ in Calcutta when he responded to an altar call by the Canadian Pentecostal pastor Mark Buntain (1923–89).[3] Thomas's journey from an orthodox Christian tradition in Kerala to the Assemblies of God reflects a wider trajectory of parishioners from established or mainline churches to Pentecostal and Charismatic ones. Paradoxically, both Thomas Christians (who historically have claimed Brahmin status) and members of lower social classes are central to the story of Pentecostal growth in India. Understanding these patterns provides insights into trends in both South Asian and World Christianity.

This chapter examines factors that have contributed to the growth of Pentecostal churches in south India. It focuses on local and transnational factors that have energized the movement from its beginnings to the present day. Pentecostal preaching affirms the role of the supernatural in the lives of ordinary people. Possession by and deliverance from evil spirits, healing of physical illness, and spiritual gifts such as speaking in tongues are among the manifestations of the divine in the lives of believers. The mandate to advance God's kingdom by displays of supernatural acts is central to Pentecostal theology and praxis. The appeal of Pentecostalism among lower classes is a huge factor that explains why they stand at the forefront of missionary movements and rising Christian numbers in today's Global South.

In their commitment to evangelism, often through aggressive preaching, Pentecostals often face criticism or hostility. Their rising prominence in South Asian Christianity coincides with rising antipathy toward conversion, especially among those who champion the idea of India as a Hindu nation. The Hindu nationalist movement (*Hindutva*) in India vilifies Christians and Muslims as members of "foreign" religions. Drawing upon longstanding critiques of conversion from personalities such as Gandhi, members of the Sangh Parivar (literally "Saffron Brotherhood"—a coalition of Hindu nationalist organizations) often allege that Christian conversion arises from force or inducement. The rise to power in India of the Hindu nationalist Bharatiya Janata Party (BJP) has coincided with a spike in both anti-Christian and anti-Muslim violence.

Some view the methods and beliefs of Pentecostals, in addition to the rise of *Hindutva*, as contributing to anti-Christian violence. A recent study by the religion scholar Chad Bauman contends that the language of spiritual warfare employed by Pentecostals and their denunciation of other religions have singled them out as targets of attacks.[4] To what extent are Pentecostal methods aligned with or different from what can be seen in earlier phases of missionary encounters with local religions? How do we weigh their emergence as a force in World Christianity against the emergence of Hindu nationalism in today's globalized South Asia?

It is one thing to say that Pentecostals are attacked in India because they attack other faiths. It is perhaps more accurate to say that Pentecostals are attacked because they *attract*. Their steady numerical growth in south India indicates that their promise of tangible experiences of the Holy Spirit is appealing to a variety of social classes. The same holds for the northwestern state of Punjab, which has seen rapid growth of Pentecostal ministries, not simply among its sizeable Dalit and tribal population, but also among its middle classes. The "pastors of the Punjab" include doctors, engineers, attorneys, policemen, and businessmen who either double as clergy or have given up their jobs for the ministry. In recent years, the numbers of Pentecostal clergy have grown dramatically across the twenty-three districts of the state. The growth of their ministries has elicited opposition from Sikh and Hindu organizations.[5] In an effort to establish India as an officially Hindu nation, vigilante activists attack Pentecostals precisely because of their rising appeal among Dalits, tribals, and even middle classes in various parts of India. Pejorative terms such as "inducement" or "allurement" do little to help us understand this appeal, but they factor prominently in anti-conversion rhetoric and legislation. The intangible and affective goods provided in Pentecostal settings—interpersonal warmth, physical healing, a sense of belonging, exorcism, emotional uplift, and relief from caste stigmas—draw people to their tradition but cannot be grouped together with so-called "material inducements." The "prosperity gospel," for which Pentecostals are also known, declares that physical healing and material prosperity come to those who possess true faith. Prosperity preaching may be found in megachurches of the West and the Global South and explained in terms of its appeal to middle class and aspiring middle class communities.[6] Such preaching may be construed as a form of allurement, but it does not place a preacher or a church under any obligation to deliver prosperity to converts or other believers; rather, it is God who is believed to be the agent of such blessings.

Pentecostalism and *Hindutva* are clearly at odds with each other; and yet they appear to draw from a common set of tools arising from globalization. To explore these issues, this chapter first examines aspects of Pentecostal history and beliefs. It then turns to the rise of Hindu nationalism in India, increasing instances of interreligious riots, and violence against minorities. The chapter concludes with reflections on the Pentecostal legacy in South Asian and World Christianity.

Mapping Pentecostals

In his study of the Pentecostal movement in south India, Michael Bergunder argues that only a broad definition does justice to the term "Pentecostalism." This is because the movement does not easily conform to a fixed set of doctrines or a coherent institutional framework.[7] What is needed is a definition that highlights shared family traits across time and different world contexts. These family traits would eventually shape the identity of specific church bodies such as the Assemblies of God, the Church of God, or those influenced by the Latter Rain movement.

Defining Pentecostalism

Strictly speaking, Pentecostalism refers to a form of Christianity that places a strong emphasis on the direct experience of God through the work of the Holy Spirit. Pentecostals often speak of the "baptism of the Holy Spirit"; this event, which is distinct from water baptism, refers to a moment when one is filled with the Holy Spirit and equipped in a unique way to perform the work of missions. Within many Pentecostal contexts, the chief (and often defining) manifestation of Holy Spirit baptism is speaking in tongues. Charles Parham, who oversaw an early twentieth-century revival in Topeka, Kansas, believed that speaking in tongues is central to Holy Spirit baptism and the believer's bond with Christ. It also serves as a tool for revival during the last days before Christ's return.[8] Subsequent revivals reinforced the idea that Holy Spirit baptism would uniquely equip believers through tongues—believed literally to be foreign languages—to go to foreign lands to preach the gospel. In this respect, Pentecostalism bore a unique relationship to the great transatlantic revivals of the nineteenth century and to the Protestant missionary movement in Asia and Africa.[9] Later, the definition of tongues would include the utterance of spiritual languages intelligible only to God. Other manifestations of the Holy Spirit within these contexts include ecstatic visions, physical shaking or falling unconscious, and dreams or prophetic utterances that reveal divine guidance.

Early Revivals and Publicity

In 1860, an Indian evangelist named John Arulappan (1810–67) led a revival in the south Indian Tirunelveli district. Arulappan had studied under the German missionary C. T. E. Rhenius. He eventually became acquainted with the British Brethren missionary Anthony Norris Groves, with whom he undertook a preaching ministry in the Nilgiri Hills. During the course of his association with foreign missionaries, Arulappan became convinced that he needed to support himself financially. He raised funds from the people of Tirunelveli to support his ministry, receiving no payment from Groves.[10] As an educated man who was integrated into missionary networks, he read missionary periodicals. One in particular, *Missionary Reporter*, described a revival occurring in America and Britain over the past three years.

Moved by these events, Arulappan aspired to see similar developments in his own ministry. After months of prayer, a revival occurred in Tirunelveli district. It was marked initially by many of the same characteristics of later revivals: confession, groaning and weeping in remorse for sins, and an emphasis on holiness, trembling, and praising God. In the following months, Arulappan coordinated missionary outreach in local villages, combining preaching with the distribution of tracts and the construction of a large prayer hall. Over time, his movement began to assume characteristics of Pentecostalism: speaking in tongues, "great shaking," visions, prophetic utterances, falling down, swaying back and forth, and "rolling the eyes." Physical healing, however, does not seem to have factored prominently in Arulappan's movement.[11]

Despite late nineteenth-century manifestations such as those described in Arulappan's revival, people tend to associate the origins of Pentecostalism with later revivals occurring in different parts of the globe. One such revival occurred within the Khasi tribe of northeast India at a number of Welsh Presbyterian missionary stations. The Welsh revivals of 1904 also influenced the 1905 revival at Pandita Ramabai's Mukti mission. The Mukti revival (see Chapter 6) was accompanied by "tongues of fire" emanating from the heads of women as they prayed at the mission. Participants were inclined to confess their sins and also expressed feelings of intense joy.[12] In 1906, the African American preacher William J. Seymour led the Azusa Street Revival in Los Angeles. Seymour brought people of many races together for worship in a building that had once been an African Methodist Episcopal church. The congregants are said to have experienced a wide range of manifestations of the Holy Spirit, including physical healings, speaking in tongues, and other miraculous signs.

News of these revivals spread to other parts of the world through missionary publications. Account after account drew references to a common set of manifestations of the Spirit (as mentioned above). The simultaneous and global dimension of these revivals led leading evangelists of the day to believe that they were fulfilling biblical prophecy concerning a unique outpouring of the Spirit, a "latter rain," during the last days (Joel 2:28–9).

A closer examination of these events, however, diminishes the sense of autonomy and spontaneity suggested in missionary reports. What we find instead are networks of people and media that knitted different regions together by spreading the word about Pentecostal ideas and experiences. This is not to suggest that revivals were inauthentic or imitative, or that they moved from the West (i.e., Azusa Street or Wales) to the rest of the world. It only means that leaders of the revivals were in conversation with each other and that they benefited from local groundwork that was already in place. During her visit to America, Ramabai became acquainted with women missionaries and charismatic male evangelists who viewed the world through revivalist missionary lenses. Her close association with the American Methodist Minnie Abrams resulted in years of collaboration at the Mukti mission. Abrams, who championed Methodist holiness theology, promoted revival in various parts of India and conveyed her ideas about the Holy Spirit in a number of articles published in the *Guardian* and *Indian Witness* newspapers. Later, she compiled these articles into a book entitled *The Baptism of the Holy Ghost and Fire* (1906).[13]

Mission publications of the day describe spiritual awakenings occurring across many denominations that were at work in India, including the Anglican CMS, Lutherans, Baptists, Presbyterians, Church of Scotland, Brethren, Wesleyan Methodists, and the YMCA. Sensational accounts of visions, dreams, the "burning" work of the Spirit, and tongues were reported in their respective missionary publications. Some accounts found their way into newspapers such as the *Christian Patriot*, known for its commitment to Indianizing Christianity. As a common set of books and periodicals circulated across American and Indian church contexts, they disseminated a "holiness seed" among their readership.[14] How that seed would take root in South Asia and the forms of Christian expression it sprouted depended on earlier experiences and cultural frameworks. This convergence of global and local forces is a common theme in the history of South Asia's Christians. It was noted in connection to conversion movements among Dalit and tribal peoples (Chapter 7) and in the story of the Thomas Christians of Kerala (Chapter 1). Missionaries may have laid the infrastructure, but a range of indigenous factors drove these movements.

From the Old to the New

Local revivals and spiritual movements in South Asia set the stage for the reception of Pentecostalism and its global networks. The prevalence of *bhakti* devotional cult traditions and Sufi mysticism provided fertile soil for Pentecostal theology and practices in India. As movements that stressed the devotee's ability to experience God directly and intimately, Hindu *bhakti* and Sufi devotionalism could be accompanied by weeping or shaking, or, in the case of Sufism, entering trance-like states. The arrival of Pentecostalism in India did not constitute a departure from such practices; in fact, Pentecostalism built on them in much the same way that Catholic shrines in south India blended with local Sufi or Hindu warrior cult traditions. Such continuity aligns with the observations of the historian Andrew Walls, who emphasized how conversion constitutes a refashioning of already existing cultural material, not the imposition of an entirely new structure.[15]

In his discussion of events at Ramabai's Mukti mission, the scholar Arun Jones offers a provocative illustration of this dynamic of refashioning, drawing a connection between the Pentecostal "fire" at Mukti and the fire associated with the practice of *sati*.[16] Through the act of *sati*, a woman is believed to embody virtue and truth and acquire the status of a goddess. Without undertaking the cruel act of self-immolation, the girls and women at Mukti received the fire of the Holy Spirit. This, too, brought closeness to God (as distinct from becoming a *devi* or goddess) through being filled by the Spirit and empowered them to live lives of virtue and obedience.[17] At the time of the Mukti revival, *sati* was illegal, but it had been practiced in western India and was much talked about within missionary and reformist circles. With Ramabai's life work having been focused on the plight of Hindu widows, the strictures of *dharma* (moral duty) associated with *sati* would not have been far removed from the local cultural imagination.

The Appeal of Pentecostalism

By examining both Christian and non-Christian precursors to South Asian Pentecostalism, we avoid the mistake of assuming that Pentecostalism was purely derived from the West or that it arose in isolation from other developments. Doing so also helps us to appreciate the growing appeal of Pentecostal denominations in South Asia during the twentieth and twenty-first centuries. It was only a matter of time before experience-driven spirituality would consolidate itself in official denominations that distinguished themselves from older, mainline churches. Four in particular took hold in South Asia: the Indian Pentecostal Church (IPC), Ceylon Pentecostal Mission (CPM), the Assemblies of God, and the Church of God. With painstaking research, the historian Michael Bergunder has detailed their emergence and impact in South Asia. The birth of these denominations sheds light on the role of charismatic individuals who acquired followings within a particular region. Collaboration and conflict between Indians and Westerners are also part of their stories.[18] For the present purposes, it is important to observe in their histories several overarching patterns, as features associated with their beginnings become keys for understanding expressions of Pentecostalism in other places and times, including the present.

First, emerging Pentecostal congregations attracted people who were already Christian, often those who had attended mainline or orthodox churches. Many of the migrants to Pentecostalism in south India had once belonged to any number of Church of South India (CSI) churches. The CSI was inaugurated in 1947, the same year as India's independence, to unite many mainline denominations into one ecumenical, Indian body. These included the Anglican diocese of India, Myanmar (Burma), and Ceylon (Sri Lanka), the Methodist Church of South India, and the South Indian United Church (SIUC). The SIUC itself had been established in 1908 and included Presbyterian, Reformed, and Congregational churches. The goal of creating the CSI and its counterpart, the Church of North India (CNI), was to promote church unity in the Indian context. Awareness of the need to Indianize the Church was tied to the rejection of false divisions created by Western denominations. Despite the very real moments of revival that had shaped even mainline experiences, some CSI church programming receded into institutional practices and moralistic messages that suited a narrow clientele and did not address felt needs.

Pentecostalism presented a vision that was more energetic and democratic than the routinized mainline church culture; and it offered goods that were more tangible. Ordinary folk, including women and those lacking seminary degrees, could experience the power of the Spirit and lead small groups to do the same. A recent study documents the decline of CSI congregations in the south Indian state of Telangana and the rise of independent churches that embrace Pentecostal beliefs and practices (although they do not belong to any official Pentecostal denominations). The authors of this study, John Carman and Chilkuri Vasantha Rao, contend that the transition to independent, Pentecostal-like churches is chiefly related to the matter of healing. The authors documented seventy instances of healing after prayer to Christ. Many such healings were associated with deliverance from evil spirits, the effects of black magic, and physical ailments of various kinds. Those who were healed attributed their relief to prayer and Jesus's healing powers.[19] The newer congregations consisted of those who came to church with expectations relating to healing. Interestingly, the caste composition of these new churches was far more mixed than in the older CSI congregations they replaced. They consisted of people from different castes who shared worship experiences and meals in common, whereas older congregations consisted primarily of Dalits from Mala and Madiga communities.[20]

Pentecostalism Among Thomas Christians

A second feature of the emerging Pentecostalism in South Asia is the prominent role played by Thomas Christians. As noted in Chapter 1, the Thomas Christians underwent many divisions resulting from Portuguese and British efforts to reform them. By the early twentieth century, American Pentecostals such as George Berg, Mary Chapman, and Robert Cook were active in building congregations in Kerala. Malayali-speaking leaders such as K. E. Abraham also joined the Pentecostal movement and attracted followings. Eventually, Abraham and other Indians developed a strong opposition to foreign control and established congregations of their own. Some regard the quest for self-government as a defining feature of Indian Pentecostalism.[21] Opposing foreign control over local congregations, however, did not lead Indian Pentecostals to sever all ties to the West. Abraham and other Thomas Christians, such as K. C. Cherian and T. M. Verghese, maintained contact with Pentecostal leaders in Sweden and the USA. By means of foreign sponsors, they were able to establish and oversee churches of the IPC and Church of God. The emergence of Pentecostalism in Kerala and in South Asia as a whole involves many variables, sometimes in tension with each other. These include the role of overseas patrons, the quest for local autonomy, enterprising and visionary leadership by Indians, and interpersonal conflicts and church splits that created new churches. Out of this complex array of factors, Pentecostal and independent churches multiplied throughout South Asia and became the force in World Christianity that they are today.[22]

Currently, Pentecostal churches abound in Kerala among people who, like Pastor Shine Thomas, once belonged to the orthodox Syrian Christian tradition. They are accompanied by "Charismatic" Christians, those who embrace Pentecostal practices but remain within their mainline or orthodox churches, or those who join independent churches that employ elements such as contemporary music or spiritual gifts.[23] To date, no study has adequately explained the appeal of Pentecostalism among Thomas Christians. As a community that possessed its own ancient Christian tradition, why were so many drawn to an entirely different world of Christian practice and theology? Here, we can only speculate. At one level, we might explain the transition in terms similar to the path taken by many CSI congregants: They were drawn to the emotional modes of Pentecostal worship and the emphasis on miracles such as physical healing. Women found in Pentecostalism a more prominent role in ministry than was offered in orthodox churches. Lower castes found in its emphasis on experience an inroad into the life of the Church not found in a priestly liturgical tradition. In sum, the Pentecostal social and theological landscape stood in stark contrast to a more formal, high tradition that primarily served educated elites and upper caste men.

Another factor may relate to developments within Catholicism. After the Second Vatican Council (1962–5), the Catholic hierarchy placed a stronger emphasis on the role of lay people in the mission of the Church. This emboldened lay leaders to initiate gatherings that emphasized the capacity of each believer to experience God directly without intermediaries. During the 1980s, the Vincentian Fathers of Potta in Kerala hosted Charismatic retreats; these promoted grassroots forms of spirituality akin to Pentecostalism and were highly appealing to Syrian Catholics (*Pazhayakur*). Lay leaders played an active role in promoting and leading these retreats and in forming independent prayer units. They delivered sermons that stressed repentance and moral reform, outreach to the poor, and the outpouring of the Holy Spirit.[24] In some instances, the role of lay leaders even surpassed that of the hierarchy. Eventually, these types of spiritual services attracted Jacobite Thomas Christians as well and led to the establishment of independent churches (see Table 10.1).[25]

An Inclusive Vision

Pentecostalism is widely credited for its capacity to transcend barriers of race, class, and caste. The emphasis on the Holy Spirit who empowers the faithful draws people from mixed social backgrounds into shared ecclesiastical spaces. The Azusa Street Revival embodied the New Testament vision of Pentecost (Acts 2:1–4), where people of different races worship together and listen to the words of God in their own languages. It should be noted, however, that early Pentecostal revivals in the USA were not without elements of racism. When he was a student of Charles Parham in Houston, the African American James Seymour was required to sit separately from white students. When Parham visited the Azusa congregation in Los Angeles in 1906, the emotional worship and mingling of races deeply offended him and he blamed Seymour for promoting both.[26] Writers in local newspapers criticized the emotionalism of the movement, sometimes with language laced with racist innuendo. One referred to Seymour as a "one eyed, illiterate Negro" (Seymour had lost one eye to smallpox).[27] However, the capacity of the Azusa Street Revival to integrate African Americans, Latinx peoples, whites, and other ethnic groups into common worship is indisputable.

Scholars draw similar observations about Pentecostalism in India with respect to caste. Here, again, the literature is limited. A study by theologian V. V. Thomas points to several factors that explain the appeal of Pentecostalism to Dalits. First, Pentecostals tapped into an awakening of Dalit consciousness in Kerala, which expressed itself through organized protests and caste reform movements. Beginning in the late nineteenth century, reformers such as Sri Narayana Guru Swami (1856–1928) and Ayyankāli (1863–1941) launched movements that

Table 10.1 Pentecostals/Charismatics in India 1970–2020

Religion	Pop. 1970	% of country 1970	Pop. 2000	% of country 2020	Pop. 2020	% of country 2020	Growth rate % p.a. 2000–2020
Total population	553,579,000	100.0%	1,053,051,000	100.0%	1,383,198,000	100.0%	1.37%
Christians	20,598,000	3.7%	45,030,000	4.3%	67,356,000	4.9%	2.03%
Evangelicals	2,591,000	0.5%	8,455,000	0.8%	12,200,000	0.9%	1.85%
Pentecostals/Charismatics	2,714,000	0.5%	13,077,000	1.2%	21,000,000	1.5%	2.40%
Pentecostal	295,000	0.1%	1,283,000	0.1%	2,017,000	0.1%	2.29%
Charismatic	79,300	0.0%	3,318,000	0.3%	5,183,000	0.4%	2.25%
Catholic Charismatic	1,700	0.0%	1,337,000	0.1%	2,172,000	0.2%	2.45%
Orthodox Charismatic	75,800	0.0%	160,000	0.0%	225,000	0.0%	1.72%
Protestant Charismatic	1,800	0.0%	1,821,000	0.2%	2,786,000	0.2%	2.15%
Independent Charismatic	2,339,000	0.4%	8,476,000	0.8%	13,800,000	1.0%	2.47%

Data source: Todd M. Johnson and Gina A. Zurlo, eds, *World Christian Database* (Leiden/Boston: Brill, accessed March 2021).

championed the rights of Dalit groups such as the Ezhavas and Pulayas. They fought for Dalits to have access to common roads, temples, schools, wells, and markets. Discriminatory practices of the Syrian Christians also sparked uprisings within Thomas Christian circles. These events set the stage for their reception of the more inclusive vision of Pentecostals.[28]

Second, Pentecostals uniquely appealed to Dalits on account of their ability to address a wide range of their needs. According to V. V. Thomas, they advanced a "duel-faceted concept of salvation," one that affirmed one's place in heaven (as mainline churches had done) while at the same time addressing concrete struggles of Dalits in the here and now—financial, familial, physical, and social.[29] Dalits respond favorably to Pentecostal emphasis on the immediately accessible power of the Holy Spirit. On account of this belief in shared access to spiritual gifts, they sensed a more socially inclusive climate within Pentecostal church contexts.

Finally, the interests of Pentecostals in Kerala intersected with those of the ruling Communist Party. Communists were responsible for land reform schemes that addressed the plight of laboring classes, while their educational policies also benefited Dalit castes, including Dalit Christians. Due to such measures, a strong affinity developed between Pulaya Christians and communism. Many Christians participated in communist-led protests and worked alongside communists toward common goals in Kerala. Pentecostalism, according to Thomas, drew from this affinity.

Because of its democratic and inclusive message, Pentecostalism has drawn Dalits and other marginal classes into its orbit. Its theology and practices have presented the hope for liberation and dignity among those stigmatized by low caste status. Everyone, even "untouchables," can receive the gifts of the Holy Spirit and can be prayed for with the laying on of hands. Some contend that Pentecostalism has had a greater impact on the poor than liberation theology, despite the strong emphasis of the latter in Catholic and Protestant seminaries in South Asia. Although its message is not oriented to matters of social justice, Pentecostalism has had an impact on self-worth, empowerment, and dignity for the poor. In this respect, the aims of Pentecostalism intersect with those of liberation theology.

As a worldwide movement, Pentecostalism may have originated among society's outcasts, but it eventually made inroads into more educated and affluent social classes as well.[30] This is true of countries such as Korea, Nigeria, and South Africa as much as India, and it applies especially to major cities such as Mumbai, Hyderabad, and Bengaluru. Moreover, Pentecostalism may no longer be viewed as being fixated on spiritual or otherworldly interests, thus succumbing to the Marxist critique of being the "opiate of the people." Pentecostals have long been committed to medical aid, orphanages, and various forms of relief during times of crisis. Increasingly, its more educated constituency is demonstrating a greater interest in issues of justice and meeting the physical needs of people through so-called holistic ministry.

Both Pentecostalism and liberation theology address the needs of the poor and oppressed. They both rely upon the roles of women and have a transformational vision for human beings. As the theologian Felix Wilfred notes, justice and liberation often come in small increments, not in grand revolutionary events. The idea of emancipating women may be an ultimate dream of both the liberationist and the Pentecostal; but, in real life, the longing for liberation begins for women in practical, everyday changes—for instance, when husbands break their addiction to alcohol or drugs, desist from domestic violence, or stop having affairs; or, more positively, when husbands are able to contribute to the family's financial wellbeing. For Dalits, liberation begins when they cease to be stigmatized, excluded, or mistreated on the basis of their caste, and when they experience the genuine embrace of a community.[31] The oft-cited phrase "liberation theology opted for the poor, and the poor opted for Pentecostalism" points to how Dalits have realized many of their aspirations in Pentecostal churches.[32] Because of this substantial convergence of interests among the poor and the marginal, many believe that a more substantial dialogue between Pentecostals and liberation theologians is needed.

Commonality and Rupture

Pentecostalism maintains a paradoxical relationship with popular Hindu beliefs and practices. On the one hand, they share common convictions about the prevalence of spiritual forces that influence everyday life. Popular Hinduism traces the cause of illness, infertility, family conflict, personal tragedy, or financial misfortune and insecurity to supernatural causes. Hindus venerate various deities for healing diseases such as smallpox (Mariamman), or for providing wisdom in business (Ganesh) or financial prosperity (Lakshmi). Evil spirits are agents of misfortune and possession, and hence must be manipulated or expelled.

South Asian Pentecostals share many such beliefs. Their approach to the spiritual realm resembles what many have observed elsewhere in the Global South. African Christians (Pentecostals, Charismatics, and members of African Initiated Churches) believe in the reality and power of evil spirits in much the same way as practitioners of popular African religion. The main difference is that they profess Christ's conquest and authority over the demonic realm. South Asian Pentecostals, according to Bergunder, have "taken over the demonology of popular Hinduism, with some differences."[33] Conversion to Christ can liberate people from demonic oppression, but even baptized Christians can be in need of spiritual deliverance, especially if they have reverted to Hindu practices. Indian Pentecostals often speak in tongues while they are casting out spirits or healing an illness.

On the other hand, Pentecostals oppose many aspects of Hinduism, especially the veneration of idols. Bauman refers to their repudiation of their former Hindu beliefs as their "rhetoric of rupture."[34] In this sense, they share with Protestant missionaries of the nineteenth century a disdain for popular Hinduism. How Pentecostals relate to the Hindu other, however, vastly departs from their Evangelical predecessors of the nineteenth century. Evangelicals engaged in rational debate and invoked the superiority of the Bible over Hindu texts (see Chapter 5). This approach was heavily logocentric, or focused on the written or preached word. Pentecostals, by contrast, engage in what they call "spiritual warfare." This involves a combination of prayer (often in tongues), rebuking of evil spirits, faith healing, and even prayer against territorial spirits believed to preside over a village or neighborhood. The rhetoric of preachers can target Hindu practices such as the veneration of deities at *pujas* or popular festivals, but it can also attack what they regard as the lifeless and ineffectual practices of mainline Christianity. When coupled with its internal culture of warmth and inclusiveness, Pentecostalism has the capacity to appeal to various segments of Indian society. At the same time, its confrontational style can draw criticism or contempt from many quarters.

In recent decades, Pentecostals and Charismatics have also become a prevalent force on the airwaves. In 2010, there were four different twenty-four-hour Christian networks in India: Miraclenet, God TV, DayStar (which are all owned by Charismatics), and the Catholic Eternal Word Television Network. The majority of the programming on these networks originates from the USA, UK, and Australia.[35] Some programs, however, belong to well-known Indian Charismatic televangelists. D. G. S. Dhinakaran (1935–2008), the Tamil evangelist who founded Jesus Calls Ministries, developed twenty bases in India and elsewhere and made extensive use of radio and television broadcasts. K. P. Yohannan (1950–) founded Gospel for Asia, an organization that raised money from the West but promoted the use of native pastors to do the actual work of missions. Sam Chelladurai (1952–), the pastor of a megachurch in Chennai, is featured in a number of Christian television programs, including the Tamil *Vettriyum Vaazhvum* (*Victory and Life*) and *God Is Good*, aired on God TV.

The rising prevalence of the "prosperity gospel" in urban Pentecostal churches is displayed across Christian television networks. Prosperity preaching presents health and wealth as visible signs of true faith in Christ. According to Jonathan James, a scholar of global media, most Christian television draws from the Charismatic tradition and focuses almost exclusively on themes of wealth, success, and healing.[36] Some are inclined to view the rapid expansion of Christianity as a reproduction of the "American gospel" abroad. This is most evident in the use of mega-crusades and the growth of megachurches in places such as India, Nigeria, South Korea, and Brazil. The conflation of Protestantism, especially of the Charismatic/Pentecostal variety, with telecommunications, corporate dollars, and prosperity preaching through American broadcasting inclines scholars such as Paul Gifford to identify this "Global Christianity" as essentially American, despite the outward differences of language and culture.[37]

It is not difficult to see how the grandiose and flamboyant veneer of megachurches and the promises of prosperity preaching can impact different people in different ways. They may draw the attention of lower- or middle-class people who seek these material benefits, but they can also evoke the evil eye of resentment or envy within the competitive marketplace of religion. Whose gods and whose religion contribute to the greatest degree of health, wealth, and success?

A different picture is presented in Nathaniel Roberts' study of Pentecostalism in Anbu Nagar, a slum in the northern section of the city of Chennai. In contrast to an emphasis on prosperity seen within some Pentecostal circles, Roberts discovered a strong focus on mutual care within the slums. Slum dwellers faced rejection by other Indians, but they did not practice caste distinctions among themselves.[38] Because of this, amidst their everyday needs for drinking water, food, and money, protection from caste-based violence and humiliation, and other challenges arising from their poverty, residents of Anbu Nagar were able to care for each other in ways that crossed religious boundaries and participated in a shared "care-based moral ethos."[39] Pentecostalism made deep inroads into this environment, not through the infusion of big money or Western capital, but by preaching about Christ's love for the poor. Pentecostal and Hindu slum dwellers shared a belief that people should choose a religion that meets their concrete needs and evaluated gods based on what they could *do* for their devotees. Whereas Hindus stress the need to worship a powerful or potent deity, Christians stress Christ's love for the poor. Because of this love, he alone can intervene in their lives and deliver real benefits. Their discourse about Hindus is not the rhetoric of rupture seen in other contexts, and Hindu attitudes toward Christians are similarly non-othering.

The prominent role of women in Pentecostal circles is observable in many global contexts. They make up the majority of the movement's worldwide constituency and have become the chief agents of Pentecostal growth in the Global South. Direct access to the miraculous prophetic and healing power of the Spirit has a democratizing impact. This is partly why women embraced Pentecostalism in Anbu Nagar, but they also did so because of the moral pressure their faith exerted upon their men to avoid habits that jeopardized their family's wellbeing (drinking, frivolous spending, affairs, etc.). In the state of Rajasthan, Pentecostalism appealed to tribal women because of their desire for long-term change. It was not the allure of material inducements that drew them to the faith, argues the sociologist Sarbeswar Sahoo—such incentives would not overcome the ostracism or excommunication often suffered by converts. Instead, it was "faith and spiritual transformation, caused largely by miracle/faith healings" that led tribal women to convert.[40]

Hindutva and Anti-Christian Violence

Bauman believes that Pentecostals in India are disproportionately targeted in acts of anti-Christian violence, and he asks why that is the case. The context for many of these attacks is the rise of Hindu nationalism and its vilification of Islam and Christianity as expansionist "foreign" religions. Among the many forms of Christianity found in India, Pentecostals and "Pentecostalized Evangelicals" (more mainstream Christians who embrace Pentecostal worship styles and attitudes) tend to receive the brunt of anti-Christian violence for various reasons, according to Bauman. Their "more assertive, more critical, and more visible" forms of evangelism, including their loud and ecstatic form of worship, draw attention, which is sometimes hostile.

Pentecostals are at the forefront of those working among marginal populations. Their work among rural, low caste, and tribal communities can trigger opposition from those who oppose all conversions, or from those who claim that Pentecostals are forcing or inducing the poor to convert. Faced with threats or instances of violence, independent churches in villages or rural areas may lack denominational support, thereby increasing their vulnerability. Adding to this vulnerability, as noted above, is the rhetoric of combat employed in Pentecostal preaching. Preachers may portray their relationship to non-Christian India in terms of a battle against the spiritual forces venerated by non-believers.[41] For Bauman, factors such as these explain why Pentecostals are targets of violence, but they do not justify the violence. His analysis appears to walk a fine line between portraying Pentecostals as victims of unlawful violence while also identifying them as bringing the violence upon themselves through triumphalist rhetoric and practices. Another layer of the hostility they face concerns their relationship to Western modernity. Bauman argues that a residual anticolonialism fuels opposition toward Christianity among upper caste and traditional elites. They resent how humanitarian aid, education, and business have undermined older hierarchies and patronage systems. This resentment expresses itself in the targeting of Christian bodies with violence and Christian institutions with state scrutiny and delegitimization.[42]

The advancement of the agenda to make India a Hindu nation (*Hindutva*) has been accompanied by a surge in anti-Christian violence. From 1964 to

1996, the country registered only thirty-eight instances of such violence. This number increased dramatically after 1998, when the Hindu nationalist party, the BJP, headed a coalition government. The following year, Dara Singh, a Hindu activist of the Bajrang Dal organization, murdered the Australian missionary Graham Staines and his two sons while they were in Odisha's Manoharpur village attending an annual Christian gathering. Singh and his accomplices burned them alive while they were sleeping in a station wagon. This high-profile attack drew international attention. However, while some local leaders and commentators expressed lament and outrage, Hindu nationalists tended to frame the event as an angry reaction to conversion. Odisha is one of the states that has developed elaborate rules concerning conversion; these aim to ascertain motive and establish the "sincerity" of conversions. Conversion in Odisha is a police matter requiring detailed documentation, surveillance, and numerical tracking of potential mass conversions. Local inquiries into conversion have the effect of publicizing them and increasing the vulnerability of missionaries.[43]

By 1998, instances of anti-Christian violence had gone up to ninety; from 2001 to 2005, there were as many as 200 documented instances of anti-Christian attacks,[44] and the numbers have increased significantly over the past decade—to 365 in 2015 and roughly 500 in 2022.[45] Hindu activists claim that Christian conversion threatens the unity and integrity of a Hindu nation. Some attribute the surging violence in the years leading to the turn of the millennium to grand evangelistic Christian programs, such as the AD 2000 and Beyond Movement or the Joshua Project. These programs set targets for church planting endeavors worldwide and in north India specifically.[46] As word spread transnationally of these plans, the *Hindutva* agenda in India continued to gain traction among the nation's bourgeoning middle class. Quite often, it was the poorest and most vulnerable Christians in remote areas who suffered the worst of the violence.

During the late 1990s, Indian news media and human rights groups reported on churches being destroyed, nuns assaulted and raped, priests hacked to death, and social relief organizations solemnly warned not to engage in conversions.[47] Such events occurred in places such as Gujarat, Bihar, Odisha, and Madhya Pradesh amidst allegations of indifference or complicity on the part of state officials. In December 1998, a wave of attacks against tribal Christians in the Dang district of Gujarat drew the attention of political parties and national forums. Sonia Gandhi, then president of the Congress Party, described the "extreme fear and tension" felt by Christian minorities in the region. Spokespersons for the United Christian Forum for Human Rights declared the attacks to be part of a "systematic and orchestrated" agenda of Hindu nationalists.[48]

The theme of state complicity and premeditation is also evident in the Hindu–Muslim riots of 2002. These riots erupted at the Godhra train station in Gujarat when Hindus were returning from a pilgrimage to their holy city of Ayodhya, believed to be the birthplace of Rama, an incarnation of the Hindu deity Vishnu. When the pilgrims stepped off the train at Godhra, fighting erupted with Muslim residents of a nearby ghetto. In the course of the skirmish, one of the train's compartments—carrying more than 150 people—burst into flames. Fifty-two men, women, and children, nearly all Hindus, were burned to death. Hindus responded with a rampage that left more than 2,000 Muslims dead. The chief minister of Gujarat, Narendra Modi, who is the current prime minister of India, and the local police are widely believed to have been complicit in the violence. In a speech shortly following these incidents, the prime minister at the time, Atal Bihari Vajpayee, insisted that it was Muslims who had initiated the conflict by conspiring to burn alive the Hindu passengers. To this he added: "Wherever Muslims live, they don't like to live in co-existence with others, they don't like to mingle with others . . . they want to spread their faith by resorting to terror and threats."[49]

In 2008, riots erupted between Hindus and Christians in Kandhamal, a village in the state of Odisha. Tensions between members of these religions were not new to the region. The rising Christian presence among Odisha's tribal population had long elicited violent reactions from Hindus, including the destruction of nineteen churches in 1986–7 and of seventeen churches in 1990, and an attack on eleven Christian families in 1994. The latter involved "stripping and molesting seven Christian women and then removing them and others to a different village where they were forcibly tonsured and given cow dung to eat as part of their 'reconversion' ceremony."[50]

In 2007, riots broke out when Christians placed a Christmas arch and a tent on a site that Hindus claimed was the venue for their annual *puja* for the goddess Durga. The following year, tensions erupted into a much larger conflagration when Laxmanananda Saraswati, a leader of the Vishwa Hindu Parishad (VHP or World Hindu Federation), was murdered along with several of his associates. Hindus blamed Christians and, in a highly disputed verdict, seven Christians and a Maoist leader were convicted of Laxmanananda's murder.[51] In response to the murders, Hindu militants ransacked more than 600 villages, burned and looted 5,600 houses, and forced tens of thousands of Christians out of their homes. Many fled to the jungle and were bitten by snakes as they hid from their assailants. Roughly forty Christians were killed and more than 200 churches destroyed, according to human rights groups.[52] The violence resulted in dozens of instances of sexual assault and rape and the displacement of thousands of refugees.[53]

The events in Gujarat and Odisha involved large-scale acts of violence in which Muslims or Christians were the main victims. In its endeavors to establish India as a Hindu *Rashtra* (nation), the Sangh Parivar perpetrates or validates continued violence against anyone they view as getting in their way.

Their project also includes efforts to control state universities, since they perceive academicians as being "leftists" who criticize the government. India's premier university, Jawaharlal Nehru University (JNU), is among the chief targets of the Sangh's tactics of intimidation and violence. Toward the end of 2019, JNU students protested against various actions taken by the government. These included fee hikes as well as the introduction of the Citizenship Amendment Bill (now the Citizenship (Amendment) Act), which essentially made Indian citizenship available to migrants from border states, but only if they are not Muslim (the neighboring states are Muslim majority). In January 2020, a group of hooded people armed with metal rods and sticks entered the JNU campus at night and injured as many as thirty-nine students and teachers, some of them seriously. As in Gujarat and Odisha, the police did nothing to stop the violence.

In recent years, both Christians and Muslims have become victims of Hindu nationalist aggression. Hindus have attacked Muslims for their alleged beef consumption: From 2010 to 2017, "cow vigilantes" committed as many as sixty-three attacks on Muslims, resulting in twenty-four deaths and 124 injuries, according to a report by Reuters.[54] The Indian media often describe these attacks as acts of "lynching." Anti-Muslim rhetoric increased during the Covid-19 pandemic. A Muslim missionary organization, the Tablighi Jamaat, held a huge gathering in Delhi in March 2020 in breach of lockdown orders. After the government blamed them for contributing to the spread of the virus in the city, a surge of Islamophobic rhetoric followed along with attacks against Muslims in and around Delhi.[55]

Ghar Wapsi and Inducement

Current attempts to reconvert Dalits and tribals to Hinduism are based on the belief that these communities have been forced or induced to convert to "foreign religions" and must somehow be brought "home" to mother Hinduism.[56] This view assumes that tribal peoples were Hindu to begin with and that it is only the "foreign" proselytizing religions that engage in conversion. Recent studies, however, call into question this idea that tribal peoples were originally Hindu. They document instead a steady process whereby caste Hindus and nationalist leaders Sanskritized the tribals through the introduction of their gods, habits, and customs.[57] This alternative reading of the tribal past calls into question current attempts to "reconvert" tribals to Hinduism. The *Ghar Wapsi* (or "homecoming") campaign led by the VHP seeks to reconvert Christian converts to Hinduism; this presumes a stable "Hindu community" from which they were extracted and offers a mechanism for bringing them back.

In December 2014, the VHP reportedly reconverted thirty-seven families to Hinduism in Elappara, Kerala. As many as 100 of those reconverted belonged to the Pentecostal Church, which is quite prominent in Kerala, but had formerly been Hindus. The VHP claimed that, on the same day, it had also reconverted twenty-seven other Christians from five families in Kayamkulam. In both cases, priests at local temples performed the rites of reentry (*shuddhi kalashakriya*).[58] VHP spokesmen claim that these Christians had actively sought their assistance, citing "neglect from authorities in the name of caste and religion."[59]

Gaining the most press coverage was a reconversion drive in December 2014 on the outskirts of Agra, in which 200 Muslims were reconverted to Hinduism. There, fifty-seven Muslim families, mostly poor migrants from Bihar or Bengal, claimed that members of two militant Hindu organizations, the Dharma Jagran Manch and the Bajrang Dal, had employed both force and inducement to reconvert them.[60] A Muslim slum dweller named Farhan claimed that Hindu activists had forced him to participate in a *puja*, wash the feet of Hindu gods, and wear auspicious marks with vermilion on his forehead. "If forty people in saffron come and stand on your head," he charged, "you will do just as they want."[61] While Farhan insisted that his compliance was simply to get the saffron-clad activists "off his back," others who were reconverted claimed that they were offered ration cards and access to the local water supply in exchange for the decision to reconvert.[62]

The idea that India's poor were "induced" to leave Hinduism and hence must be reclaimed for Hinduism has a history that predates today's *Ghar Wapsi* campaign. During the nineteenth and twentieth centuries, the Arya Samaj, a reformist organization founded largely to stem the tide of Hindu conversion to other religions, employed the Vedic purification ceremony of *shuddhi* to readmit converts back into Hinduism. As Cassie Adcock has observed, however, Arya Samajist campaigns of the 1920s were not simply about "making Hindus"; they were also occasions for "adjusting" caste relations between Hindu communities. The "readmission" of Muslims or Christians into the Hindu fold required that high caste elites recognize the new status of reconverts and extend them the privileges due to them.[63] Mohandas Gandhi himself became an outspoken critic of conversion among the untouchables and was convinced that most of them converted because of the material inducements offered by foreign missionaries. He was so convinced of the falseness of their motives that, upon being asked whether reconverts should undergo the ritual of *shuddhi*, Gandhi replied that there was no need for the rite since the conversions were not "real" ones.[64]

The Hindu nationalist *Ghar Wapsi* campaign shares with Gandhi a belief in the illegitimacy of Dalit and tribal conversion out of Hinduism. But instead of becoming an excuse to eliminate the rite of *shuddhi*, today's Hindu nationalists assert that *Ghar Wapsi* is not conversion but "homecoming." Because of this distinction, they do not believe that their methods violate current anti-conversion laws, which prohibit conversion by force, fraud, or inducement.[65] In fact, financial contributions from Indians in the UK, USA, and various parts of Europe play an important role in funding *Ghar Wapsi* campaigns in India. A pamphlet circulated in Bihar and Uttar Pradesh by the Dharma Jagran Manch claimed that it costs one lakh rupees to convert a Muslim. It costs three times this amount to convert a Christian, however, because of the financial resources that circulate through churches and Christian organizations.[66]

Conclusion

South Asian Pentecostalism builds upon a long history of Protestant engagement with Hindu and Muslim societies in South Asia. The commitment to spreading the faith through aggressive preaching also belongs to a distinctively Protestant globalism. This is tied to the great revivals of the nineteenth-century missionary movement, the twentieth-century Azusa Street Revival, and the revivals at Mukti and other South Asian venues. The importance of the printed, preached, or broadcast word extends this long history into present times, with remote religious broadcasts prevalent during the Covid-19 pandemic.

Pentecostalism, however, departs from the "wordy-ness" (or logocentric tenor) of earlier missionary Protestantism. It eschews rational, scholarly, or apologetic modes of advancing the faith embraced by men such as Bartholomaeus Ziegenbalg, Alexander Duff, John Wilson, or Henry Martyn. It brings something new to the table—tangible experiences of the supernatural manifested in healing, tongues, and other gifts of the Spirit—and its message appeals to many classes of people in South Asia and across the Global South. In south India, Pentecostal understandings of the supernatural merged with Hindu demonology, but they declared Christ as sovereign over the demonic realm. Pentecostalism's message addressed the needs of poor and marginal classes, while its use of new technologies and networks of propaganda such as broadcast media also appealed to the middle classes. In the end, Pentecostalism and Pentecostalized spirituality (to use Bauman's phrase) provided churchgoers with a more tangible experience of the divine, something they were not finding in the established churches of the CSI and the CNI or in the Syrian Orthodox Church in Kerala.

The growth of Pentecostalism in South Asia coincided with the rise of India's Hindu nationalist movement. As a much larger movement that commands more levers of power, *Hindutva* has become the driving force behind violence against both Christian and Muslim minorities and the suppression of dissent in state universities. To say that Pentecostals are unique targets of violence and that their rhetoric contributes to their vulnerability has some validity. But this is mainly due to the fact that Pentecostals are more committed to propagating their message among non-believers than members of mainline church traditions. The very fact of their numerical growth—with or without the rhetoric of rupture or the idiom of spiritual warfare—makes them likely targets of opposition. *Hindutva*'s vilification of Christians and Muslims and the steady demise of liberal, constitutional protections has made anyone who openly dissents from the nationalist agenda a vulnerable target for violence or silencing. Just as Pentecostalism is a worldwide trend, the movement toward the right in politics is a global development resulting in violence against minorities.

Muslim and Christian minorities share a common plight in the face of militant Hindu nationalism. This creates unique opportunities for interreligious collaboration. Currently, the language of religious freedom and human rights frames the protests against violence toward minorities in India and elsewhere. If Christians and Muslims are fighting for their constitutional protections, this is a positive development. But what would it mean to move from a language of rights to one of mutual empathy and solidarity? Might it bridge the ecumenical impulses of mainline or liberal traditions with the struggles of Muslim and Christian victims of violence?

Conclusion

For centuries, South Asia's Christians have interacted with Hindu and Muslim peoples, institutions, and beliefs. What distinguishes them from other branches of World Christianity is not their strength in numbers, but their location within unique theaters of cross-cultural and interreligious encounters. Rarely have Christians remained ghettoed within their own enclaves or isolated from the cultural influences of the Indian Ocean world. Their encounters with adherents of other traditions resulted in mutual questioning and negotiations of identity for all parties involved. These interactions have assumed many forms, but this book has highlighted knowledge production, debate, and conversion.

The location of Christians *between Hindu and Muslim* did not begin in postcolonial South Asia but can be traced back to the experience of Thomas Christians. Well before the arrival of Islam in the Indian subcontinent, this ancient community navigated between a Persianate West Asia and Sanskritized segments of south India. After the arrival of Muslims in Malabar, Thomas Christians sustained largely peaceful relations with both Hindus and Muslims. This lasted until the arrival of the Portuguese, who infused south India with their new politics of difference, shaped by their contempt for Muslims and Jews in the Iberian Peninsula. They hoped that the discovery of a Christian army in India—that of the legendary Prester John—would allow them to outflank their Muslim rivals in the Mediterranean. What Portuguese Catholics found instead was an ancient community whom they eventually designated as heretics and proceeded to Latinize.

An Argumentative Heritage

Jesuit training in Europe involved language acquisition and preparation for theological debates. During the sixteenth century, Jesuits entered the courts of Akbar hoping to talk the emperor into being baptized; they encountered someone with a voracious appetite for learning and interreligious exchanges, but little interest in converting. Akbar appears to have enjoyed dialogue for dialogue's sake, a quality reflective of India's longstanding tradition of public reasoning and debate.

Jesuits such as Xavier, Nobili, and Bouchet brought to India a mapping of the world comprised of clearly defined categories. Identifying Christianity, Judaism, and Islam as the most recognizable religions on their map, they designated the rest of humanity—from Amerindian to Asian societies—as "Gentile" or "pagan" peoples. Bouchet likened Hindu polytheism to the landscape of the ancient Mediterranean, which eventually gave way to Christianity. Other missionaries either maintained that Christianity had in some way influenced India prior to the arrival of Europeans or likened Hindus to the Jews of the Old Testament awaiting Jesus the Messiah.

Portuguese colonists viewed Islam as a religion of heresy and violence and their Iberian-formed mindset inspired hostility toward Malabar's Muslims. Francis Xavier preferred to work among India's "pagans" because he viewed Jews or Muslims as too impenetrable or hostile to evangelize.[1] As Jesuits devoted more and more attention to understanding Hindu texts and institutions, they eventually recognized Brahmins as belonging to a bona fide "religion." Now located *between Hindu and Muslim*, they tended to prioritize their interaction with Hindus while either ignoring or downplaying the significance of Indian Islam.

Protestant missionaries who followed in the wake of Jesuits drew similar lines in the sand, but they added Catholics to their list of religious others. An important aspect of Protestant missionary endeavors involved the use of print media: By printing vernacular translations of the Bible, religious tracts, instructional materials, and hagiographies, missionaries introduced new modes for expressing religious ideas in public.[2] Their methods brought a new dimension to a longstanding tradition of debate and argumentation in South Asia, at times extending it in order to stage highly publicized debates, at times straining it through incendiary polemics against other religions. Missionaries eventually elicited sharp rebuttals from adherents of Hindu, Muslim, Parsi, and Buddhist traditions. Instead of succeeding at delegitimizing other faiths, missionaries activated a new self-awareness among members of other communities and a desire to defend their beliefs publicly.

World Christianity—Adjusting the Lens

A major issue addressed at the start of this book concerns the place of South Asian Christianity in the larger story of World Christianity. In important ways, scholars of Africa have taken the lead in explaining Christian growth outside Europe and North America. This is understandable, when one considers the striking rates of conversion in sub-Saharan Africa since the 1980s. In this connection, we must ask whether notions of translatability, local appropriation, and agency—so central to explaining rising Christian numbers in sub-Saharan Africa or South Korea—are as applicable to South Asian contexts.

South Asia's Christians share many features of the emerging World Christianity: for instance, the growth of Pentecostal, charismatic, and independent churches; the use of broadcast media; healing cults; and other populist or grassroots developments. However, their rates of numerical growth are lower than in other parts of the Global South. As Christian numbers surged in sub-Saharan Africa, Latin America, and other parts of Asia, they remained quite constant in South Asia. India's Christians account for hardly 3 percent of the country's population of 1.4 billion. It is no wonder that most discussions of World Christianity today tend to be centered in places with explosive church growth—where becoming Christian is perfectly consistent with being a proud Nigerian, Brazilian, or South Korean.

The numbers game changes significantly, however, if we adjust the lens to include a larger sweep of time. Going back to the mid-nineteenth century, the dramatic growth of Christianity among India's Dalit and tribal communities resembles trends in World Christianity occurring today. Indeed, from the standpoint of Dalit and tribal conversion histories, South Asia may be seen as a forerunner of Christian growth in the Global South, not as a region that lags behind. Dalit and tribal Christian voices, however, remain more subdued within the life of South Asian churches than their numerical strength clearly warrants.

Competing Religions and Dalits

The knowledge-producing aspect of Christian missions helped produce the public religions that competed for converts, including from among the poor. The same knowledge about "competing religions," however, does not appear to have inspired Dalits or tribals to place their faith in Christ. Dalit Christianity embraces Jesus as the one who heals, delivers, provides, and empathizes with their brokenness and pain. Far less does Dalit Christianity concern itself with the rational triumph of Christian ideas over and against those of other religions. Hence, to understand South Asia's Christians, more attention needs to be paid to the aspirations, experiences, and theologies of these communities than to large, dusty books produced by men such as Alexander Duff, John Wilson, or other offspring of the Scottish Enlightenment.

The infrastructure provided by missionaries—churches, schools, hospitals, orphanages, and relief sites—provided valuable services to those Dalits who were able to access them, but they hardly scratched the surface of the vast needs of this population. Today, Hindu nationalists are mapping Gandhi's notion of induced conversions (or conversions motivated by "material" rather than "spiritual" interests) onto alleged conversions among India's outcastes. They presume that, by becoming Christian, converts access an intact infrastructure once installed by missionaries and propped up by steady flows of global capital into India's churches.

The problems with this perspective become evident when we contrast Christian infrastructure with that of present-day "IT villages." In cities such as Pune, Hyderabad, Bengaluru, and Gurgaon, one can encounter oases of highly developed living quarters, medical facilities, roads, and shopping areas that service India's thriving information technology sector. These enclaves are in fact nodes of global capitalism. Becoming Christian in India today is not at all like becoming a software engineer and joining an IT village. Christian institutions are decentralized, unequally funded or staffed, and disparately connected to global resources; and they service a complex range of clientele who possess different levels of social and economic capital. The vast majority of Dalit Christians continue to face extraordinary degrees of social discrimination and material disadvantage, something amply demonstrated in the report of the Mishra Commission and other studies, discussed in Chapter 9. Their experience of exclusion, the demands and degradation tied to their hereditary occupations, and their dire socioeconomic conditions place them in a constant state of in-betweenness. When Dalits become Christian, it only compounds their sense of marginality and disadvantage. The denial of scheduled caste status for Dalit Christians compels many to conceal the Christian side of their identity in order to qualify for state assistance. Rather than validating Gandhi's belief that Dalits are fundamentally motivated by their "stomachs," such identity concealment indicates that their Christian identity does not eliminate caste disadvantages, but often accompanies them.

Manufacturing Foreigners

South Asia's Christians belong to a transnational religion, but they have nevertheless rooted themselves in the multireligious and multicultural ethos of the region. For Christians, as with members of other faith traditions, being global did not diminish their participation in local, regional, or national life. And yet, for much of their history, Christians, especially those from marginal classes, have shouldered a unique burden to prove their authenticity, gain access to public resources, and secure protections from their governments. Much of this burden arises from controversies associated with religious conversions and allegations of malevolent, external influences steering them.

Within the climate of rising nationalism, conversion is seen as a form of violence and a moment of rupture that separates converts from the institutions of family, caste, or nation. The birth of the modern nation-states of India, Sri Lanka, Bangladesh, Nepal, and Pakistan yielded clear-cut notions of majority and minority and strong impulses toward cultural homogeneity. The radicalizing tendencies of South Asian nations arise from their own notions of *swadeshi* religion. They "manufacture foreigners" through majoritarian politics and policies and institutionalized prejudice.[3] One might imagine that decolonization in South Asia would have softened the approach to ethnic or religious differences, especially considering the Indian subcontinent's precolonial history of global interactions. In India, the largest country of South Asia, a new rigidity threatens the very foundations of its democracy and its longstanding heritage of accommodating differences. For Christian minorities in a Hinduizing India, an Islamizing Pakistan, or a Buddhist Sri Lanka, experiences of marginalization, vilification, and violence have sadly become more frequent.

Much of this book was written during the Covid-19 pandemic. As devastating as this pandemic has been, it continues to provide challenging lessons about the connected nature of our world. As never before, we paid attention to various aspects of this global event: pathways and means of transmission; issues of blame and stereotyping; the possibility of international cooperation; networks of information and misinformation; the shared vulnerability of the human condition; and the quest for an effectively produced, distributed, and administered vaccine. Perhaps no single aspect of the pandemic, however, has become more painfully evident than the fact that certain classes contracted the disease and died from it more than others. In America, Black and Brown people who provide essential services and who simply could not afford to stay at home died at rates that were nearly double those of other social classes. In India, tens of thousands of laborers walked hundreds of kilometers to their villages as the government imposed lockdowns in cities. While citizens of developed countries gained access to vaccines and booster shots, those of underdeveloped countries remained largely unvaccinated.

Writing about South Asia's Christians during the pandemic led me to reflect in fresh ways on the global dimension of the faith and its unique inroads into poor, oppressed, and marginal communities. Today, the realities of the global poor are factoring more prominently in the globalization conversation. Climate catastrophes and refugees, the displacement of tribal peoples through "development," and widening wealth disparities in countries such as India (which have liberalized their economies) are casting new light on the struggles of the ever-expanding global poor. The history of South Asia's Christians makes contact with the many faces of globalization. It encompasses the stories of international church bodies and missionary societies, transnational religious broadcasting, and the aspirations of Dalit and tribal peoples. Many Dalits became Christian during periods of famine because of resources provided by missionaries and their message of hope. This raises questions about the role of churches in the midst of current and future global crises and the trajectories of Christian growth in the years to come.

Notes

Introduction

1. See Dana Robert, "Shifting Southward: Global Christianity Since 1945," *International Bulletin of Missionary Research*, Vol. 24, No. 2 (2000), pp. 50–8; Philip Jenkins, *The Next Christendom: The Coming of Global Christianity* (New York: Oxford University Press, 2007).
2. See Goldie Osuri, *Religious Freedom in India: Sovereignty and (Anti)Conversion* (London: Routledge, 2013); Goldie Osuri, "Foreign Swadeshi," *Frontline*, December 24, 2014, https://frontline.thehindu.com/the-nation/foreign-swadeshi/article6715524.ece.
3. See Rupam Jain and Tom Lasseter, "By Rewriting History, Hindu Nationalists Aim to Assert their Dominance Over India," Reuters, March 6, 2018, https://www.reuters.com/investigates/special-report/india-modi-culture/. For an example of a *Hindutva* portrayal of India's Christians as a force that is "breaking India," see Rajiv Malhotra and Aravindan Neelakandan, *Breaking India: Western Interventions in Dravidian and Dalit Faultlines* (Princeton: Infinity Foundation, 2011). For a series of articles on the history textbooks controversy in India, see Delhi Historians' Group, *Communalisation of Education: The History Textbooks Controversy* (New Delhi: Delhi Historians' Group, 2001).
4. The diffusion of Sanskritic influence in South Asia involved the interplay between poetic and literary texts (*kavya*) and notions of kingship (*rajya*). Sheldon Pollock, *Language of Gods in the World of Men: Sanskrit, Culture and Power in Premodern India* (Berkeley: University of California Press, 2006), pp. 6–7.
5. From the sixteenth to the twentieth century, the Muslims of South India and Southeast Asia were linked through the dissemination of Arabic texts. The translation of Ibn Salam's *Book of One Thousand Questions* into Javanese, Malay, and Tamil (a prominent South Indian language) belongs to a much larger corpus of "stories, poems, genealogies, histories and treatises" that circulated across many lands. These written texts integrated diverse Muslim societies into a common sphere, or "cosmopolis," of shared experiences and beliefs. Ronit Ricci, *Islam Translated: Literature, Conversion and the Arabic Cosmopolis in South and Southeast Asia* (Chicago: University of Chicago Press, 2011).
6. Throughout this book, I have preferred to use the name "Dalit" to designate those *jatis* (birth groups) who were referred to as "untouchable" during the colonial period. I do so against potential objections by historical purists that the term must not be deployed anachronistically to time periods predating this particular designation. In some instances, I do employ the term "untouchability" or "untouchable" or the

specific *jati* label when context demands it. However, because many of these traditional designations are in themselves derogatory, and in order to avoid causing offense to any particular community, I mostly employ "Dalit" throughout the text.

7. Ebenezer Sunder Raj employed a similar metaphor in his book. Ebenezer Sunder Raj, *The Confusion Called Conversion* (New Delhi: TRACI, 1988). Vegetable cups on an Indian *thali* meal tray represent various "religions," but the tray itself, he observes, is Hinduism. By this, Sunder Raj critiques the common sense that has prevailed in postcolonial India, which counts everyone who is not Christian, Muslim, Parsi, or Sikh as a "Hindu"—a logic that factors prominently in census tabulations. For a more recent critique of the category "Hindu," see Joel Lee, *Deceptive Majority: Dalits, Hinduism, and Underground Religion* (Cambridge: Cambridge University Press, 2021).

8. For a recent discussion of Dalit identity as a fluid identity, see Philip Vinod Peacock, "Now We Will Have the Dalit Perspective," *Ecumenical Review*, Vol. 72, No. 1 (2020), pp. 116–27.

9. Many Dalits and tribals lived under the weight of sacred texts that sanctioned their subordination or enslavement by upper castes. See Jose Maleikal, *Standstill Utopias: Dalits Encountering Christianity* (New Delhi: ISPCK, 2017). Maleikal examines the Madigas of Konaseema (South India) by making use of theoretical tools from development studies and the subaltern studies collaborative in South Asian history.

10. They sought to liberate Indian Christianity from its Western mold. See R. S. Sugirtharajah and Cecil Hargreaves (eds.), *Readings in Indian Christian Theology* (New Delhi: ISPCK, 1995); Robin Boyd, *India and the Latin Captivity of the Church: The Cultural Context of the Gospel* (Cambridge: Cambridge University Press, 1974). Dalits, however, criticized this project for replacing the Western mold with a Sanskritic one, as discussed in Chapter 8.

11. Jackie Assayag's study of Hindus and Muslims in South India contests the idea that they constitute two monolithic communities with sharply defined boundaries. Instead, he points to numerous instances of shared traditions, cults and shrines. See Jackie Assayag, *At the Confluence of Two Rivers: Muslims and Hindus in South India* (New Delhi: Manohar, 2004). For instances of Hindu–Christian reciprocity and hybridity, see Alexander Henn, *Hindu-Catholic Encounters in Goa: Religion, Colonialism, and Modernity* (Bloomington: Indiana University Press, 2014); Susan Bayly, *Saints, Goddesses and Kings: Muslims and Christians in South Indian Society, 1700–1900* (Cambridge: Cambridge University Press, 1989).

12. A deceptive majority, as the anthropologist Joel Lee has noted. See Lee, *Deceptive Majority*.

13. Sonja Thomas, *Privileged Minorities: Syrian Christians, Gender, and Minority Rights in Postcolonial India* (Seattle: University of Washington Press, 2018).

14. See Chandra Mallampalli, *Christians and Public Life in Colonial South India, 1863–1937: Contending with Marginality* (London: Routledge Curzon, 2004); Nandini Chatterjee, *The Making of Indian Secularism: Empire, Law and Christianity, 1830–1960* (London and New York: Palgrave Macmillan, 2011).

15. See Ian Copland's discussion of missionaries and cultural hegemony in India. Ian Copland, "The Limits of Hegemony: Elite Responses to Nineteenth-Century Imperial and Missionary Acculturation Strategies in India," *Comparative Studies in Society and History*, Vol. 49, No. 3 (2007), pp. 637–65. For a discussion of "conversion as assimilation," see Gauri Vishwanathan, *Outside the Fold: Conversion, Modernity and Belief* (Princeton: Princeton University Press, 1998). For discussions of colonial Christianity, see Stephen Neill, *Colonialism and Christian Missions* (New York: McGraw Hill, 1966); Gauri Vishwanathan, *Masks of Conquest: Literary Study and British Rule in India* (New York: Columbia University Press, 2015); Jeffrey Cox, *Imperial Fault Lines: Christianity and Colonial Power in India, 1818–1940* (Stanford: Stanford University Press, 2002).
16. The failure to recognize Christianity as a South Asian religion in world religions textbooks is noted by Selva Raj, "The Quest for a Balanced Representation of South Asian Religions in World Religions Textbooks," *Religious Studies Review*, Vol. 31, Nos. 1–2 (2005), pp. 14–16. Note the recognition of Christianity as a South Asian religion in Karen Pechilis and Selva Raj (eds.), *South Asian Religions: Tradition and Today* (London: Routledge, 2013).
17. This plurality of Christian experiences and the degree to which India's regional cultures have shaped them is highlighted in Rowena Robinson, *Christians of India* (New Delhi: Sage, 2003).
18. Lamin Sanneh, *Whose Religion is Christianity? The Gospel Beyond the West* (Grand Rapids, MI: Eerdmans, 2003), p. 10.
19. For a discussion of these developments, see Andrew Walls, *The Missionary Movement in Christian History: Studies in the Transmission of Faith* (Maryknoll, NY: Orbis, 1996); Dana Robert, *Christian Mission: How Christianity Became a World Religion* (Malden, MA: Wiley-Blackwell, 2009); Jenkins, *The Next Christendom*.
20. Lamin Sanneh, *Translating the Message: The Missionary Impact on Culture*, 2nd edition revised and expanded (Maryknoll, NY: Orbis, 2009), pp. 193–5.
21. Andrew Walls, *The Cross-Cultural Process in Christian History* (Maryknoll, NY: Orbis, 2002), p. 74.
22. Ibid., pp. 31, 33, 65.
23. See John L. Comaroff and Jean Comaroff, *Of Revelation and Revolution: The Dialectics of Modernity on a South African Frontier* (Chicago: University of Chicago Press, 1997); Robert Wuthnow, *Boundless Faith: The Global Outreach of American Churches* (Berkeley: University of California Press, 2009); David Maxwell, *African Gifts of the Spirit: Pentecostalism and the Rise of a Zimbabwean Transnational Religious Movement* (Athens: Ohio University Press, 2006).
24. See, for instance, Mark Noll, *The New Shape of World Christianity: How American Experience Reflects Global Faith* (Downers Grove, IL: Intervarsity Press, 2009).
25. Lamin Sanneh, "Christian Missionaries and the Western Guilt Complex," *The Christian Century*, p. 331.
26. For an excellent summary of missionary contributions to print culture in South India, see A. R. Venkatachalapathy, *The Province of the Book: Scholars, Scribes, and Scribblers in Colonial Tamilnadu* (Ranikhet: Permanent Black, 2012), pp. 5–15.

27. Sumathy Ramaswamy, *Passions of the Tongue: Language Devotion in Tamil India, 1891–1970* (Berkeley: University of California Press, 1997). The worship or divinization of language formed an essential component of devotion to "Mother India," conceived of as a goddess possessing great power. See also the discussion of Saraswat Brahmins and the Konkani language in Goa in Jason Keith Fernandez, *Citizenship in a Caste Polity: Religion, Language and Belonging in Goa* (Hyderabad: Orient Black Swan, 2020).
28. Joel Cabrita, David Maxwell, and Emma Wild-Wood (eds.), *Relocating World Christianity: Interdisciplinary Studies in Universal and Local Expressions of the Christian Faith* (Leiden: Brill, 2017), p. 21.
29. J. Kwabena Asamoah-Gyadu, "Symbolising Charismatic Influence: Contemporary African Pentecostalism and Its Global Aspirations" in ibid., pp. 302–23; Chad Bauman, "Pentecostals and Interreligious Conflict in India: Proselytization, Marginalization, and Anti-Christian Violence," *PentecoStudies*, Vol. 16, No. 1 (2017), pp. 8–34.
30. Cabrita, Maxwell, and Wild-Wood (eds.), *Relocating World Christianity*, p. 324.
31. Klaus Koschorke, "Polycentric Structures in the History of World Christianity" in Klaus Koschorke and Adrian Hermann (eds.), *Polycentric Structures in the History of World Christianity* (Wiesbaden: Harrassowitz, 2014), p. 23.
32. During the 1970s, the Church History Association of India (CHAI) adopted a "New Perspective" that diverted attention away from an exclusive focus on missions to one that is grounded in the social and cultural history of Christian people, as their lives are integrated into Indian society. This study's emphasis on interactions resonates with the redirection envisioned by CHAI. See "A Scheme for a Comprehensive History of Christianity in India" (mimeographed), pp. 1–2, *Indian Church History Review*, Vol. 8 (1974), pp. 89–90. Discussed in John C. B. Webster, "Writing a Social History of Christianity in India," *International Bulletin of Missionary Research*, Vol. 32, No. 1 (2008), pp. 10–12.
33. P. Y. Luke and John B. Carman, *Village Christians and Hindu Culture: Study of a Rural Church in Andhra Pradesh, South India* (Cambridge: Lutterworth Press, 1969).

Chapter 1

1. During these early centuries, Syria belonged to the western region of Persia. I am grateful to the historian Pius Malekandathil for stimulating and highly informative exchanges about the Persian heritage of the Thomas Christians. I draw significantly upon his work in this chapter.
2. The Malayalam-speaking state of Kerala was founded in 1956 by merging together the princely states of Travancore and Cochin. Parts of Malabar, which belonged to British India, also joined Kerala.
3. For a summary of the scholarly debate concerning the designation of Thomas as Jesus's twin brother and of the theology of "twinning" in New Testament times, see

Charles Stang, *Our Divine Double* (Cambridge, MA: Harvard University Press, 2016), pp. 64–106.
4. Ibid., p. 67. Here, Stang draws from the scholar Bentley Layton.
5. Albertus F. J. Klijn, *The Acts of Thomas: Introduction, Text and Commentary* (Leiden: Brill, 2003), p. 17.
6. These possibilities are discussed in Johnson Thomaskutty, *Saint Thomas the Apostle: New Testament, Apocrypha and Historical Traditions* (London: Bloomsbury, 2018), pp. 129–31.
7. Klijn, *The Acts of Thomas*, p. 26.
8. Ibid., p. 40.
9. Ibid., pp. 52–3.
10. Ibid., p. 65.
11. Samuel Hugh Moffett, *A History of Christianity in Asia. Volume I: Beginnings to 1500* (Maryknoll, NY: Orbis, 2004), p. 28.
12. Klijn, *The Acts of Thomas*, p. 247.
13. Ibid., pp. 248–9.
14. Stang, *Our Divine Double*, p. 72.
15. Ibid., p. 67.
16. Klijn, *The Acts of Thomas*, p. 115.
17. For a detailed discussion of the historicity of the apostle Thomas's visit to India, see Moffett, *A History of Christianity in Asia. Volume I*, pp. 29–36; Pius Malekandathil, "St. Thomas Christians: A Historical Analysis of their Origins and Development up to the 9th Century AD" in Bosco Puthur (ed.), *St. Thomas Christians and Nambudiris, Jews and Sangam Literature: A Historical Appraisal* (Kochi: LRC Publications, 2003), pp. 1–48.
18. Moffett, *A History of Christianity in Asia. Volume I*, pp. 34–5.
19. Malekandathil, "St. Thomas Christians," p. 2.
20. For an excellent summary of the different perspectives on Thomas's visit to India and the different source data, see Pius Malekandathil, "Debate on the Apostolate of St. Thomas in Kerala: A Response," *Journal of St. Thomas Christians*, Vol. 29, No. 2 (2018), pp. 32–58.
21. For a concise summary of the ties the Thomas Christians formed with both Eastern and Western Syriac liturgy, see Placid J. Podipara, *The Thomas Christians and Their Syriac Treasures* (Alleppey, India: Prakasam Publications, 1974).
22. Malekandathil, "Debate on the Apostolate of St. Thomas in Kerala: A Response," p. 42.
23. Malekandathil, "St. Thomas Christians," p. 15.
24. Robert E. Frykenberg, *Christianity in India from Beginnings to the Present* (Oxford: Oxford University Press, 2008), p. 104.
25. Moffett, *A History of Christianity in Asia. Volume I*, p. 176.
26. Clara Joseph, *Christianity in India: An Anti-Colonial Turn* (London: Routledge, 2019), pp. 101–6.
27. Moffett, *A History of Christianity in Asia*, p. 266.
28. Sonja Thomas, *Privileged Minorities: Syrian Christianity, Gender and Minority Rights in Postcolonial India* (Seattle: University of Washington Press, 2018), pp. 25–6.

29. Moffett, *A History of Christianity in Asia. Volume I*, p. 268; Roderick Mullen, *The Expansion of Christianity: A Gazetteer of Its First Three Centuries* (Leiden: Brill, 2003), p. 70.
30. Malekandathil, "St. Thomas Christians," p. 30.
31. Ibid., p. 37.
32. Moffett, *A History of Christianity in Asia. Volume I*, p. 267.
33. Leslie Brown, *The Indian Christians of St. Thomas* (Cambridge: Cambridge University Press, 1956), p. 17.
34. Stephen Dale, *Islamic Society on the South Asian Frontier: The Māppiḷas of Malabar, 1498–1922* (Oxford: Clarendon Press, 1980), p. 34.
35. Susan Bayly, "Hindu Kingship and the Origin of Community: Religion, State and Society in Kerala, 1750–1850," *Modern Asian Studies*, Vol. 18, No. 2 (1984), pp. 177–213. See also Dale, *Islamic Society on the South Asian Frontier*.
36. Roland Miller, "The Dynamics of Religious Coexistence in Kerala: Muslims, Christians, and Hindus" in Yvonne Haddad and Wadi Haddad (eds.), *Christian-Muslim Encounters* (Gainesville: University Press of Florida, 1995), p. 268.
37. C. J. Fuller, "Kerala Christians and the Caste System," *Man*, Vol. 11, No. 1 (1976), pp. 61–2.
38. Malekandathil, "Debate on the Apostolate of St. Thomas," p. 43.
39. Thomas, *Privileged Minorities*, p. 38.
40. Ibid., pp. 67–75.
41. Frykenberg, *Christianity in India*, p. 245. This is a variant on Placid Podipara's essay, "Hindu in Culture, Christian in Religion, Oriental in Worship" in George Menachery (ed.), *The St. Thomas Christian Encyclopedia of India. Volume 2* (Madras: P. N. K. Press, 1973), p. 107.
42. Sanjay Subrahmanyam, *The Career and Legend of Vasco da Gama* (Cambridge: Cambridge University Press, 1997), p. 129.
43. Ananya Chakravarty, *Empire of the Apostles: Religion, Accommodatio, and the Imagination of Empire in Early Modern Brazil and India* (New Delhi: Oxford University Press, 2018), p. 32.
44. This perception of the Thomas Christians as allies coincides with their hopes of discovering the lost kingdom of Prester John, a topic explored in Chapter 4.
45. Brown, *The Indian Christians of St. Thomas*, p. 6, 15.
46. Ibid., p. 19.
47. As noted by one observer: "The sacrifice of mass was established according to the manner of the Nestorians. The wine which they consecrated was palm wine (arrack): the host consisted of some wheaten flour, mixed with salt and oil." In Mar Aprem, *Nestorian Missions* (Trichur: Mar Narsai Press, 1976), pp. 60–1.
48. Pius Malekandathil, "Religious Rhetoric, Mercantile Strategies and a Revolting Community: A Study on the Conflicts Between the St. Thomas Christians and the Portuguese *Padroado*" in Rameshwar Prasad Bahuguna, *Negotiating Religion: Perspectives from Indian History* (New Delhi: Manohar, 2012), p. 362.
49. Ibid., p. 360.
50. Brown, *The Indian Christians of St. Thomas*, p. 38.

51. Ibid., p. 32.
52. Frykenberg, *Christianity in India*, p. 136.
53. Malekandathil, "Debate on the Apostolate of St. Thomas," pp. 35–6.
54. Samuel Hugh Moffett, *A History of Christianity in Asia. Volume II: 1500–1900* (Maryknoll, NY: Orbis, 2005), p. 18.
55. Ibid.
56. Dyron Daughrity and Jesudas Athyal, *Understanding World Christianity: India* (Minneapolis: Fortress Press, 2016), p. 31.
57. Susan Bayly, *Saints, Goddesses and Kings: Muslims and Christians in South Indian Society, 1700–1900* (Cambridge: Cambridge University Press, 1989), pp. 275–6.
58. Ibid., p. 282.
59. Buchanan expresses this vision in Claudius Buchanan, *Memoir of the Expediency of an Ecclesiastical Establishment for British India* (Oxford: Oxford University Press, 1813).
60. Quote taken from Susan Visvanathan, *The Christians of Kerala: History, Belief and Ritual Among the Yakoba* (New Delhi: Oxford University Press, 1999), p. 20.
61. Ibid., p. 173.
62. Thomas, *Privileged Minorities*, p. 45.
63. Robert Hardgrave, "The Breast-Cloth Controversy: Caste Consciousness and Social Change in Southern Travancore," *Indian Social and Economic History Review*, Vol. 5, No. 2 (1968), p. 176.
64. Thomas, *Privileged Minorities*, p. 50.
65. Visvanathan, *The Christians of Kerala*, pp. 21–2.
66. See Bayly, *Saints, Goddesses and Kings*.
67. Ramachandra Guha, *India After Gandhi: History of the World's Largest Democracy* (London: Picador, 2007), pp. 289–90.
68. For a more detailed discussion of the paradoxes associated with Kerala's model of development, see Thomas, *Privileged Minorities*, pp. 31–4.
69. Ajoy Ashirwad Mahaprashasta, "Wahhabi Impact," *Frontline*, November 29, 2013, https://frontline.thehindu.com/cover-story/wahhabi-impact/article5338336.ece (accessed January 9, 2022).
70. Stanley John, *Transnational Religious Organization and Practice: A Contextual Analysis of Kerala Pentecostal Churches in Kuwait* (Leiden: Brill, 2018), p. 45.
71. Ibid., pp. 84–107.
72. Ibid.

Chapter 2

1. The portrait is originally found in Abu'l-fazl's *Akbarnama*. The commentary is from Edward Maclagan, *The Jesuits and the Great Mogul* (London: Burns, Oates and Washbourne, 1932), pp. 30, 258. Maclagan was an early twentieth-century British civil servant in India.

2. Instead of viewing the Mughals as a theocratic regime informed by Muslim doctrines, some scholars today prefer to use the term "Islamicate," which designates regimes whose institutions were generally shaped by Muslim culture but that governed populations consisting of adherents of many religions. See David Gilmartin and Bruce Lawrence (eds.), *Beyond Turk and Hindu: Rethinking Religious Identities in Islamicate South Asia* (Gainsville: University Press of Florida, 2000); Catherine B. Asher and Cynthia Talbot, *India Before Europe* (Cambridge: Cambridge University Press, 2006), p. 72; Agnieszka Kuczkiewicz-Fraś (ed.), *Islamicate Traditions in South Asia: Themes from Culture and History* (New Delhi: Manohar, 2013).
3. See Hassan Bashir, *Europe and the Eastern Other: Comparative Perspectives on Politics, Religion and Culture Before the Enlightenment* (Lanham: Lexington Books, 2013).
4. Bamber Gascoigne, *The Great Moghuls* (London: Jonathan Cape, 1987), pp. 110–11.
5. C. A. Bayly, *Empire and Information: Intelligence Gathering and Social Communication in India, 1780–1870* (Cambridge: Cambridge University Press, 1996), pp. 182–5; Amartya Sen, *The Argumentative Indian: Writings on Indian History, Culture and Identity* (London: Penguin, 2006).
6. Ines G. Županov, "The Historiography of the Jesuit Missions in India (1500–1800)," *Jesuit Historiography Online* (first published 2016), http://dx.doi.org/10.1163/2468-7723_jho_COM_192579 (accessed January 19, 2021).
7. Sanjay Subrahmanyam, *Europe's India: Words, People, Empires, 1500–1800* (Cambridge, MA: Harvard University Press, 2017); Thomas Banchoff and José Casanova, *The Jesuits and Globalization: Historical Legacies and Contemporary Challenges* (Washington, DC: Georgetown University Press, 2016), pp. 3–4.
8. Subrahmanyam, *Europe's India*, pp. 45–55.
9. Ibid.
10. Sanjay Subrahmanyam, *The Career and Legend of Vasco da Gama* (Cambridge: Cambridge University Press, 1997), pp. 79, 90–1.
11. See Jorge Flores, *Unwanted Neighbors: The Mughals, the Portuguese, and Their Frontier Zones* (New Delhi: Oxford University Press, 2018). According to Hugh Cagle, "Portugal's empire in Asia depended on a vision that situated the *Estado da India* within an emerging metropolitan vision of nature globally—a cartographic vision recognizable to private traders, royal factors, and Crown advisers alike." See Hugh Cagle, *Assembling the Tropics: Science and Medicine in Portugal's Empire, 1450–1700* (Cambridge: Cambridge University Press, 2018), p. 148.
12. John Correia-Afonso (ed.), *Letters from the Mughal Court: The First Jesuit Mission to Akbar, 1580–83* (St. Louis: Institute of Jesuit Sources, 1981), p. 56.
13. Badauni, *Muntakhab-ut-Tawarikh. Volume II*, translated by W. H. Lowe (Calcutta: J. W. Thomas Baptist Mission Press, 1884), p. 206. See also Correia-Afonso, *Letters from the Mughal Court*, p. 96 (note 4); Agnieszka Kuczkiewicz-Fraś, "Akbar the Great (1542–1605) and Christianity: Between Religion and Politics," *Orientalia Christiana Cracoviensia*, Vol. 3 (2011), p. 75 (note 1).
14. Iris Macfarlane, "Akbar and the Jesuits," *History Today*, Vol. 20, No. 7 (1970), p. 466.
15. Maclagan, *The Jesuits and the Great Mogul*, pp. 23–4.
16. Correia-Afonso, *Letters from the Mughal Court*, p. 7.

17. Maclagan, *The Jesuits and the Great Mogul*, p. 25.
18. Arnulf Camps, *An Unpublished Letter of Father Christoval de Vega, SJ: Its Importance for the History of the Second Mission to the Mughal Court and for the Knowledge of the Religion of Akbar* (Cairo: Franciscan Centre for Christian Oriental Studies, 1956), p. 11.
19. Michael Wood, "Episode 5: The Meeting of Two Oceans" in the documentary The Story of India, 41:30–42:13.
20. According to Richard Eaton, "many of the ideological and institutional foundations of Mughal rule commonly associated with the reign of Akbar (r. 1556–1605) were already in place during Humayun's turbulent reign, or during the interregnum of Sher Shah and his successors." Richard Eaton, *India in the Persianate Age, 1000–1765* (Berkeley: University of California Press, 2019), pp. 214–15.
21. The quote is from Badauni, *Muntakhab-ut-Tawarikh*, pp. 255–6. Taken from Kuczkiewicz-Fraś, "Akbar the Great," p. 82 (note 27).
22. J. S. Hoyland (translator), *The Commentary of Father Monserrate on His Journey to the Court of Akbar* (London: Oxford University Press, 1922), pp. 64–5.
23. André Wink, *Akbar* (Oxford: One World, 2009), p. 33.
24. Hoyland, *The Commentary of Father Monserrate*, p. 70.
25. Wink, *Akbar*, p. 103.
26. Azfar Moin, *The Millennial Sovereign: Sacred Kingship and Sainthood in Islam* (New York: Columbia University Press, 2014), pp. 9–11.
27. Ibid., p. 135.
28. Wink, *Akbar*, p. 103.
29. Ibid., p. 81.
30. See H. Beveridge (translator), *The Akbar Nama of Abu-l-Fazl* (New Delhi: Asiatic Society of Bengal, 1972), pp. 85–95.
31. Wink, *Akbar*, pp. 48, 105.
32. Beveridge, *The Akbar Nama of Abu-l-Fazl*, p. 1 (note 1).
33. Wink, *Akbar*, p. 103.
34. Moin, *The Millennial Sovereign*, p. 167.
35. Hoyland, *The Commentary of Father Monserrate*, p. 115.
36. Ibid., p. 28.
37. Ibid., p. 64.
38. For an excellent description of the political significance of gift exchange in princely India, see Stewart Gordon, *Robes of Honor: Khilat in Pre-Colonial and Colonial India* (Delhi: Oxford University Press, 2003).
39. Hoyland, *The Commentary of Father Monserrate*, p. 64.
40. Ibid., p. 61.
41. Ibid., p. 62.
42. Ibid.
43. Ibid., p. 63.
44. Pierre Jarric, *Akbar and the Jesuits: An Account of the Jesuit Missions to Akbar's Court* (New Delhi and New York: Asian Educational Services and Harper and Brothers, 1996 [1926]), p. 30 (hereafter, "Jarric").

45. Monserrate to Fr. Rui Vincente, Provincial, September 9, 1580 in Correia-Afonso, *Letters from the Mughal Court*, p. 78.
46. Ibid., p. 74.
47. Jarric, p. 31.
48. Monserrate to Fr. Rui Vincente, Provincial, September 9, 1580 in Correia-Afonso, *Letters from the Mughal Court*, p. 74.
49. Acquaviva to Vicente, Fatehpur Sikri, July 20, 1580 in ibid., p. 67.
50. Moin, *The Millennial Sovereign*, p. 156.
51. Ines Županov, *Disputed Mission: Jesuit Experiments and Brahminical Knowledge in Seventeenth Century India* (New Delhi: Oxford University Press, 1999), p. 45.
52. Jesuits were actively engaged in debates with Lutheran theologians and were similarly influenced by notions of argumentation arising from the Enlightenment. See Susan Rosa, "Seventeenth-Century Catholic Polemic and the Rise of Cultural Rationalism: An Example from the Empire," *Journal of the History of Ideas*, Vol. 57, No. 1 (1996), pp. 93–4.
53. Jarric, p. 21.
54. Joint missive to Vicente, Agra, July 13, 1580 in Correia-Afonso, *Letters from the Mughal Court*, p. 43.
55. Hoyland, *The Commentary of Father Monserrate*, pp. 132–3; Jarric, p. 27.
56. Monserrate to Fr. Rui Vincente, Provincial, September 9, 1580 in Correia-Afonso, *Letters from the Mughal Court*, p. 74.
57. Hoyland, *The Commentary of Father Monserrate*, p. 49.
58. Ibid.
59. Ibid., p. 75.
60. Jarric, p. 25.
61. Ibid., p. 26.
62. Ibid., p. 25.
63. Ibid., p. 29.
64. Various extracts in Correia-Afonso, *Letters from the Mughal Court*, p. 29.
65. Joint missive to Vicente, Agra, July 13, 1580 in ibid., pp. 43–4.
66. Jarric, p. 26.
67. Wink, *Akbar*, p. 98.
68. Jarric, p. 16.
69. Ibid.
70. From Badauni, *Muntakhab-ut-Tawarikh*, p. 163. Taken from Wink, *Akbar*, p. 99.
71. Hoyland, *The Commentary of Father Monserrate*, p. 40.
72. Ibid.
73. Moin, *The Millennial Sovereign*, p. 149.
74. Macfarlane, "Akbar and the Jesuits," p. 466.
75. Moin, *The Millennial Sovereign*, p. 149.
76. Ibid., pp. 42–3.
77. Monserrate to Vincente, September 9, 1580 in Correia-Afonso, *Letters from the Mughal Court*, p. 73.
78. Acquaviva to Rodrigues, September 10, 1580 in ibid., p. 89.

79. Ibid.
80. Monserrate to Vicente, Fatehpur Sikri, September 9, 1580 in ibid., p. 74.
81. Ibid., p. 76.
82. Maclagan, *The Jesuits and the Great Mogul*, p. 29.
83. This quote from Badauni is taken from ibid., p. 30.
84. Kuczkiewicz-Fraś, "Akbar the Great," p. 87.
85. Maclagan, *The Jesuits and the Great Mogul*, p. 36.
86. From Akbar's *farman*, permitting Acquaviva's departure, in ibid., p. 39.
87. Ibid., p. 38.
88. In ibid., p. 47.
89. Ibid.
90. Ibid.
91. Excerpt of Leitão's letter taken from Camps, *An Unpublished Letter*, p. 10.
92. Jerome Xavier stayed in India after Akbar's death in 1605 and sustained his dialogues with Akbar's son and successor, Salim, better known as Jahangir.
93. Maclagan, *The Jesuits and the Great Mogul*, p. 55.
94. See Gauvin Alexander Bailey, *The Jesuits and the Grand Mogul: Renaissance Art and the Imperial Court of India, 1580–1630* (Washington, DC: Smithsonian Institute, 1998).
95. Adrija Roychaudhury, "When Mughal Rulers Borrowed from Christianity to Produce Exquisite Art Works," *Indian Express*, December 23, 2016, https://indianexpress.com/article/research/when-mughal-rulers-borrowed-from-christianity-to-produce-exquisite-art-works-4440469/ (accessed July 31, 2022).
96. Michael Fisher, *The Inordinately Strange Life of Dyce Sombre, Victorian Anglo-Indian MP and Chancery "Lunatic"* (London: Hurst and Co., 2010), pp. 18–19.
97. Jyoti Pandey Sharma, "Architectural Adventurism in Nineteenth-Century Colonial India: Begum Samru and Her Sardhana Church," *International Journal of Islamic Architecture*, Vol. 9, No. 1 (2020), pp. 61–89.
98. Cagle, *Assembling the Tropics*, p. 148.
99. Jarric, p. 203.
100. Ainslee Embree, *Utopias in Conflict: Religion and Nationalism in Modern India* (Berkeley: University of California Press, 1990), p. 44.

Chapter 3

1. Samuel Hugh Moffett, *A History of Christianity in Asia. Volume II: 1500–1900* (Maryknoll: Orbis, 2005), pp. 88–9.
2. Ibid., p. 147.
3. Ibid.
4. A version of this chapter has appeared as "Re-examining Cultural Accommodation and Difference in the Historiography of South Indian Catholicism," Madras Institute of Development Studies (MIDS), Working Paper No. 237 (December 2019).

5. Ronald Inden, "Orientalist Constructions of India," *Modern Asian Studies*, Vol. 20, No. 3 (1986), pp. 401–46; more recently, Jyoti Mohan, *Claiming India: French Scholars and the Preoccupation with India During the Nineteenth Century* (New Delhi: Sage, 2018).
6. Susan Bayly, *Saints, Goddesses and Kings: Muslims and Christians in South Indian Society, 1700–1900* (Cambridge: Cambridge University Press, 1989), p. 107.
7. The work of Ines Županov, Susan Bayly, and David Mosse provides rich insights into the dynamics of Catholic acculturation and are discussed in this chapter.
8. J. A. Dubois, *Letters on the State of Christianity; in which the Conversion of the Hindus Is Considered as Impracticable* (London: A. R. Spottiswoode, 1823).
9. In fact, it is more accurate to say that Roman Catholics employed different approaches to address different conditions. Their models of cultural engagement varied depending on the traditions, social classes, regimes, and languages that prevailed in a given region. See Joan-Pau Rubiés, "Ethnography and Cultural Translation in the Early Modern Missions," *Studies in Church History*, Vol. 53 (2017), pp. 272–310.
10. Bayly, *Saints, Goddesses and Kings*.
11. Alexander Henn, *Hindu-Catholic Encounters in Goa: Religion, Colonialism, and Modernity* (Bloomington: Indiana University Press, 2014), pp. 13–18; Charles Stewart and Rosalind Shaw (eds.), *Syncretism/Anti-Syncretism: The Politics of Religious Synthesis* (London: Routledge, 1994).
12. See Joel Robbins, "Continuity Thinking and the Problem of Christian Culture," *Current Anthropology*, Vol. 48, No. 1 (2007), pp. 5–17.
13. Filipo and Caroline Osella make this observation relative to the history of Indian Islam and its privileging of Sufism as authentically South Asian. The observations are applicable to the history of Christianity as well, particularly when syncretistic expressions of Christianity are viewed as more indigenous and more bounded expressions are viewed as more foreign. See Filipo Osella and Caroline Osella, "Islamism and Social Reform in Kerala, South India," *Modern Asian Studies*, Vol. 42, Nos. 2–3 (2008), pp. 317–19.
14. Bayly, *Saints, Goddesses and Kings*; Gyanendra Pandey, *The Construction of Communalism in Colonial North India* (New Delhi: Oxford University Press, 1990); Ashish Nandy, "The Politics of Secularism and the Recovery of Tolerance," *Alternatives*, Vol. 13, No. 2 (1988), pp. 177–94.
15. Today, Bombay is called Mumbai. In this chapter, I employ the names of places as they were used at the time.
16. Henriette Bugge, *Mission and Tamil Society: Social and Religious Change in South India, 1840–1900* (Richmond: Curzon Press, 1994), p. 42.
17. Robert E. Frykenberg, *Christianity in India: From Beginnings to the Present* (Oxford: Oxford University Press, 2008), p. 127.
18. Henn, *Hindu-Catholic Encounters in Goa*, p. 43.
19. M.N. Pearson, *The Portuguese in India* (Cambridge: Cambridge University Press, 1987), pp. 118–19.
20. Frykenberg, *Christianity in India*, pp. 121–8.
21. Bayly, *Saints, Goddesses and Kings*, p. 325.
22. Ibid., p. 328.
23. Henry James Coleridge, *The Life and Letters of Francis Xavier. Volume I* (London: Burns and Oates, 1872), pp. 182–3, 187.

24. Frykenberg, *Christianity in India*, p. 138.
25. Letter from Xavier to the Society at Rome. December 31, 1543; Coleridge, *The Life and Letters of Francis Xavier*, p. 151.
26. Bayly, *Saints, Goddesses and Kings*, p. 328.
27. Ibid.
28. Ibid., p. 332.
29. Letter from Xavier to the Society at Rome. December 31, 1543; Coleridge, *The Life and Letters of Francis Xavier*; p. 161.
30. Ibid., p. 160.
31. Ibid.
32. Ines Županov, "Twisting a Pagan Tongue: Portuguese and Tamil in Sixteenth Century Jesuit Translations" in Kenneth Mills and Anthony Grafton (eds.), *Conversion: Old Worlds and New* (Rochester: University of Rochester Press, 2003), p. 109.
33. Ananya Chakravarti, *Empire of the Apostles: Religion, Accommodatio, and the Imagination of Empire in Early Modern Brazil and India* (New Delhi: Oxford University Press, 2018), pp. 63–4.
34. Bayly, *Saints, Goddesses and Kings*, p. 334.
35. See Chandra Mallampalli, *Race, Religion and Law in Colonial India: Trials of an Interracial Family* (Cambridge: Cambridge University Press, 2011), pp. 8, 36.
36. Coleridge, *The Life and Letters of Francis Xavier*, p. 189.
37. Ibid., p. 197.
38. Bayly, *Saints, Goddesses and Kings*, p. 332.
39. Ibid., pp. 56–7.
40. Hermann Kulke and Deitmar Rothermund, *A History of India*, 4th edition (London: Routledge, 2004), pp. 127–41.
41. Bayly, *Saints, Goddesses and Kings*, pp. 328–9.
42. David Mosse, *The Saint in the Banyan Tree: Christianity and Caste Society in India* (Berkeley: University of California Press, 2012), pp. 76–7.
43. Bayly, *Saints, Goddesses and Kings*, p. 329.
44. Richard Eaton, *The Rise of Islam and the Bengal Frontier, 1204–1760* (Berkeley: University of California Press, 1993), pp. 113–34.
45. Stephen Neill, *A History of Christianity in India: Beginnings to AD 1707* (Cambridge: Cambridge University Press, 1984), p. 280.
46. Bayly, *Saints, Goddesses and Kings*, p. 389.
47. Francis Clooney, *Western Jesuit Scholars in India: Tracing Their Paths, Reassessing Their Goals* (Leiden: Brill, 2020), p. 27.
48. Ibid., p. 390.
49. Bayly, *Saints, Goddesses and Kings*, p. 392.
50. Ibid.
51. The assertion is first made in Joan-Pau Rubiés, *Travel and Ethnology in the Renaissance: South India through European Eyes, 1250–1625* (Cambridge: Cambridge University Press, 2000), p. 321. More recently, Chakravarti makes the same point, without citing Rubiés, in Empire of the Apostles, p. 10.
52. Ananya Chakravarti, "The Many Faces of Baltasar da Costa: *Imitatio* and *Accommodatio* in the Seventeenth Century Madurai Mission," *Etnografica*, Vol. 18, No. 1 (2014), pp. 135–58.

53. Ibid.
54. Ines Županov, *Disputed Mission: Jesuit Experiments and Brahminical Knowledge in Seventeenth-Century India* (New Delhi: Oxford University Press, 1999), p. 44.
55. It is possible to overinterpret the class differences of these two men and how they shaped their approaches to Hindu society. Rubiés notes that Alessandro Valignano, the head of the Jesuit mission to the East, shared many of the sensibilities of Fernandes despite his humanist education. See Rubiés, Travel and Ethnology in the Renaissance, pp. 339–40.
56. Quote taken from Županov, *Disputed Mission*, p. 49.
57. Ibid.
58. Ibid., p. 58.
59. Ibid., p. 66.
60. Ibid., p. 68. Ultimately, Nobili would find a degree of vindication within the ranks of the Catholic Church and his critics would not succeed in branding him a heretic. In 1623, Pope Gregory XV cleared Nobili of practically every charge that was brought against him, but he was advised to "avoid even the appearance of idolatry and superstition." Quote from Moffett, *A History of Christianity in Asia. Volume II*, p. 22.
61. Frykenberg, *Christianity in India*, p. 138.
62. Bayly, *Saints, Goddesses and Kings*, p. 398.
63. Mosse, *The Saint in the Banyan Tree*, pp. 36–7.
64. See Sascha Ebeling and Margherita Trento, "From Jesuit Missionary to Tamil *Pulavar*: Constanzo Gioseffo Beschi SJ (1680–1747), 'The Great Heroic Sage'" in Tiziana Leucci, Claude Markovits, and Marie Fourcade (eds.), *L'Inde et L'Italie: Recontres Intellectuelles, Politiques et Artistiques* (Paris: Éditions de l'École des Hautes Études en Sciences Sociales, 2018), pp. 1–37.
65. Frykenberg, *Christianity in India*, p. 140.
66. One biographer claims that Chanda Saheb bestowed upon him a royal title, appointed him *diwan* (minister), and awarded him a tax-exempt land grant of four villages. This, however, has been dismissed as unsubstantiated exaggeration. See Margherita Trento, *Writing Tamil Catholicism: Literature, Persuasion, and Devotion in the Eighteenth Century* (Leiden: Brill, 2022), pp. 144–5.
67. Ibid., pp. 159–61.
68. Mosse, *The Saint in the Banyan Tree*, pp. 39–40.
69. Ibid., p. 78.
70. Ibid., p. 87.
71. Ibid., p. 14.
72. The Jesuit order made the universal salvation of "souls" central to its mission. This went hand in hand with the belief in an "overarching world culture" and the role of Jesuits as "pioneer cultural brokers and translators between North and South and East and West." José Casanova, "The Jesuits Through the Prism of Globalization: Globalization Through a Jesuit Prism" in Thomas Banchoff and José Casanova (eds.), *The Jesuits and Globalization: Historical Legacies and Contemporary Challenges* (Washington, DC: Georgetown University Press, 2016), p. 266.
73. In the absence of conversion, Catholics also became more astute observers of local polities, such as the Wodeyar dynasty, which controlled the princely state of Mysore. Sanjay Subrahmanyam, *Penumbral Visions: Making Polities in Early Modern South Asia* (New Delhi: Oxford University Press, 2001), p. 65.

74. Dubois has long been associated with the book *Hindu Manners, Customs and Ceremonies* (Oxford: Clarendon Press, 1906). Sylvia Murr has shown how Dubois had substantially plagiarized a manuscript from the 1760s written by Pere Coeurdoux. Later, he added his own material to it. The colonial government prized the ethnographic information contained in this work as vital to the administration of Indian society. See Nicolas Dirks, *Castes of Mind: Colonialism and the Making of Modern India* (Princeton: Princeton University Press, 2002), p. 21.
75. Dubois's ethnographic work stressed the orientation of Brahmins toward the body and its cleanliness. This consciousness pervades restrictions concerning contact with corpses or other articles such as dishes, clothing, or cooking vessels, which could be polluted through the mere touch of lower caste members or non-Hindus. Hindu homes undergo daily purification rituals due to defilement from occasional visits from outsiders. Contact with a pariah is among the worst sources of pollution and accounts for Brahmins' constant efforts to retain physical distance from them. J. A. Dubois, *Description of the Character, Manners and Customs of the People of India and of Their Institutions, Religious and Civil* [translation from the French] (London: Longman, Hurst, Rees, Orme, and Brown, 1817), pp. 108–9, 117. As much as this is a plagiarized manuscript, the views resemble those in Dubois, *Letters on the State of Christianity*.
76. "An Hindoo, and above all, a Brahmin, by his institutions, his usages, his education and customs, must be considered as a kind of moral monster, as an individual placed in a state of continual variance and opposition with the rest of the human race ... The crafty Brahmins (in order that the system of imposture that establishes their unmolested superiority over the other tribes, and brings the latter under their uncontrolled bondage, might in no way be discovered or questioned) had the foresight to draw up between the Hindoos and the other nations on earth an impassable, and impregnable line, that defies all attacks from foreigners." Ibid., p. 100.
77. Dubois doubted whether they were in fact true converts. Ibid., p. 69.
78. Ibid., p. 18.
79. Ibid.
80. Houpert's figures are cited in Danna Agmon, "Conflicts in the Context of Conversion: French Jesuits and Tamil Religious Intermediaries in Madurai, India" in Anand Amaldass and Ines Županov (eds.), *Intercultural Encounter and the Jesuit Mission in South Asia (16th–18th Centuries)* (Bangalore: Asian Trading Corporation, 2014), p. 184.
81. Agmon, "Conflicts in the Context of Conversion," p. 182.
82. Sanjay Subrahmanyam, *Europe's India: Words, People, Empires, 1500–1800* (Cambridge, MA: Harvard University Press, 2017), p. 127.
83. Agmon, "Conflicts in the Context of Conversion," p. 189.
84. Hugald Grafe, *History of Christianity in India. Volume IV, Part 2: Tamilnadu in the Nineteenth and Twentieth Centuries* (Bangalore: Church History Association of India, 1990), p. 49.
85. Danna Agmon, "Striking Pondicherry: Religious Disputes and French Authority in an Indian Colony of the Ancien Regime," *French Historical Studies*, Vol. 37, No. 3 (2014), p. 443.
86. Bugge, *Mission and Tamil Society*, p. 51.
87. Grafe, *History of Christianity in India*, pp. 35–9.

88. Agmon, "Striking Pondicherry," p. 445.
89. Ibid., p. 454.
90. Ibid., p. 437.
91. After capturing these islands in 1534, the Portuguese established a factory along the coast in order to advance the trade in spices and cotton and silk textiles, among other things. In due course, the Portuguese were compelled to develop closer ties to the British, largely in the hope of countering Dutch aggression and expanding influence in the Indian Ocean trade. William Foster, "The East India Company, 1600–1740" in H. H. Dodwell (ed.), *The Cambridge History of India. Volume V: British India* (Cambridge: Cambridge University Press, 1929), pp. 85–8.
92. Sidh Daniel Losa Mendiratta, "Framing Identity: Bombay's East Indian Community and Its Indo-Portuguese Historical Background, 1737–1928," *Anais de Historia de Alem-Mar*, Vol. 18 (2017), pp. 207–48.
93. See Kenneth Ballhatchet, *Caste, Class and Catholicism in India, 1789–1914* (Richmond: Curzon Press, 1998).
94. Mendiratta, "Framing Identity," pp. 212–13.
95. Ibid., p. 225.
96. Sylvester McGoldrick, *Bellary Mission* (Buckingham: Franciscan Missionary Union, 1960), pp. 207–8. Perozy remained in Bellary for some years after Doyle replaced him.
97. Hastings Fraser, *Memoir and Correspondence of General James Stuart Fraser of the Madras Army* (London: Whiting and Co., 1885), pp. 274–6.
98. Jason Keith Fernandez, *Citizenship in a Caste Polity: Religion, Language, and Belonging in Goa* (Hyderabad: Orient Black Swan, 2020), pp. 87–97.
99. Kristin Bloomer, *Possessed by the Virgin: Hinduism, Roman Catholicism, and Marian Possession in South India* (New York: Oxford University Press, 2018), p. 6.
100. Bayly, *Saints, Goddesses and Kings*, p. 73.
101. See Stewart and Shaw, *Syncretism/Anti-Syncretism*.

Chapter 4

1. Jean-Baptiste Tavernier, *Travels in India. Volume II*, translated by V. Ball (London: Macmillan and Co., 1889), p. 182.
2. Joan-Pau Rubiés argues that the lay traveler had become an increasingly influential voice in European society, bridging a humanist education with the "empirical reality of human diversity" gleaned from exposure to other lands. See Joan-Pau Rubiés, *Travel and Ethnology in the Renaissance: South India Through European Eyes, 1250–1625* (Cambridge: Cambridge University Press, 2000), p. 348.
3. The notion of a conceptual map in which Europeans placed adherents of other religions is developed in Joan-Pau Rubiés, "Ethnography and Cultural Translation in the Early Modern Missions," *Studies in Church History*, Vol. 53 (2017), pp. 272–310; Tomoko Masuzawa, *The Invention of World Religions: Or, How European*

Universalism Was Preserved in the Language of Pluralism (Chicago: University of Chicago Press, 2005); Brian Pennington, *Was Hinduism Invented? Britons, Indians and the Colonial Construction of Religion* (New York: Oxford University Press, 2005).
4. Edward Said, *Orientalism* (New York: Random House, 1978).
5. Sven Beckert, *Empire of Cotton: A Global History* (New York: Alfred Knopf, 2014), pp. 29–57.
6. For an account of the British East India Company's evolution into a ruling political power in India and its sponsorship of violent campaigns of expansion, see William Dalrymple, *The Anarchy: The East India Company, Corporate Violence, and the Pillage of an Empire* (New York: Bloomsbury, 2019).
7. Rubiés, "Ethnography and Cultural Translation," pp. 274–5.
8. Alexander Henn, *Hindu–Catholic Encounters in Goa: Religion, Colonialism, and Modernity* (Bloomington: Indiana University Press, 2014), p. 26.
9. See Clara Joseph, *Christianity in India: An Anti-Colonial Turn* (London: Routledge, 2019), p. 35.
10. This section's discussion of the "similarity motif" draws from Chapter 1 in Henn, *Hindu–Catholic Encounters in Goa*.
11. Ernest George Ravenstein (translator), Alvaro Velho, and João de Sá, *A Journal of the First Voyage of Vasco da Gama, 1497–1499* (London: Hakluyt Society, 1898), pp. 52–3.
12. He bases this on the appearance of a bird's figure on the *stambha* (a sacred or auspicious column) outside the temple. See Sanjay Subrahmanyam, *The Career and Legend of Vasco da Gama* (Cambridge: Cambridge University Press, 1997), p. 132.
13. Henn, *Hindu–Catholic Encounters in Goa*, p. 21.
14. See, for instance, M. N. Pearson, *The Portuguese in India* (Cambridge: Cambridge University Press, 1987), pp. 116–17.
15. Ibid.; Stephen Dale, "Communal Relations in Pre-Modern India: 16th-Century Kerala," *Journal of the Social and Economic History of the Orient*, Vol. 16, Nos. 2–3 (1973), pp. 319–27.
16. Subrahmanyam, *The Career and Legend of Vasco da Gama*, p. 133.
17. Sanjay Subrahmanyam, "The Birth-Pangs of Portuguese Asia: Revisiting the Fateful 'Long Decade', 1498–1509," *Journal of Global History*, Vol. 2, No. 3 (2007), p. 262.
18. Paul Shore, "Contact, Confrontation, Accommodation: Jesuits and Islam, 1540–1770," *Al-Qantara*, Vol. 36, No. 2 (2015), p. 434.
19. Jerome Xavier's letter dated 14 September 1609, "Eulogy of Father Jerome Xavier," pp. 120–1. The quote is taken from Faraz Anjam, "Islam and Hinduism in the Eyes of Early European Travellers to India," *Journal of the Research Society of Pakistan*, Vol. 44, No. 2 (2007), p. 62.
20. M. N. Pearson, *The Indian Ocean* (London: Routledge, 2003), p. 127.
21. Richard Eaton, *India in the Persianate Age, 1000–1765* (Berkeley: University of California Press, 2019), p. 189.
22. Pearson, *The Indian Ocean*, p. 122.
23. Taken from ibid., p. 124.

24. Dale, "Communal Relations in Pre-Modern India," p. 323.
25. Exceptions would be the Mughals and the southern kingdom of Vijayanagara. These too were regional kingdoms and therefore contributed to a sense of India's cultural and religious complexity, not unity. See Rubiés, *Travel and Ethnology in the Renaissance*, pp. 7–10.
26. For a perceptive analysis of the relationship between Jesuit Orientalism and missionary work, see Francis Clooney, "Understanding in Order to be Understood, Refusing to Understand in Order to Convert" in Francis Clooney, *Western Jesuit Scholars in India: Tracing Their Paths: Reassessing Their Goals* (Leiden: Brill, 2020), pp. 112–26.
27. Ines Županov, "*Antiquissime Christianita*: Indian Religion or Idolatry?," *Journal of Early Modern History*, Vol. 24 (2020), p. 472.
28. Francis Clooney, "Excerpts from Fr. Bouchet's India: An Eighteenth-Century Jesuit's Encounter with Hinduism" in Clooney, *Western Jesuit Scholars in India*, p. 148.
29. Quote taken from ibid., p. 149.
30. The French philosopher Voltaire was among those who drew from the beliefs of other societies to challenge European ethnocentrism. See Joan-Pau Rubiés, "From Antiquarianism to Philosophical History: India, China, and the World History of Religion in European Thought" in Peter Miller and Francois Louis (eds.), *Antiquarianism and Intellectual Life in Europe and China, 1500–1800* (Ann Arbor: University of Michigan Press, 2012), pp. 313–67.
31. Jan Peter Schouten, *The European Encounter with Hinduism in India*, translated by Henry Jansen (Leiden: Brill, 2020), p. 26.
32. Schouten, *The European Encounter*, p. 37.
33. Pearson, *The Indian Ocean*, p. 146.
34. Kerry Ward, *Networks of Empire: Forced Migration in the Dutch East India Company* (Cambridge: Cambridge University Press, 2009), pp. 5, 56.
35. S. Arasaratnam, *Ceylon and the Dutch, 1600–1800: External Influences and Internal Change in Early Modern Sri Lanka* (Aldershot: Variorum, 1996), p. 18.
36. James Emerson Tennent, *Christianity in Ceylon: Its Introduction and Progress Under the Portuguese, the Dutch, the British and American Missions with an Historical Sketch of the Brahmanical and Buddhist Superstitions* (Cambridge: Cambridge University Press, 2018 [1850]), p. 41.
37. Arasaratnam, *Ceylon and the Dutch*, p. 19.
38. Ibid.
39. Sanjay Subrahmanyam, *Europe's India: Words, People, Empires, 1500–1800* (Cambridge, MA: Harvard University Press, 2017), p. 108.
40. They did so in the footnotes of La Créquinière's text. Ibid., p. 116.
41. Will Sweetman (ed.), *A Discovery of the Banian Religion and the Religion of the Persees: A Critical Edition of Two Early English Works on Indian Religions* (Lewiston: Edwin Mellen Press, 1999), p. xxiii.
42. Ibid., pp. 43–4.
43. Subrahmanyam, *Europe's India*, p. 118.

44. Philip J. Stern, *The Company State: Corporate Sovereignty and the Early Modern Foundations of the British Empire in India* (Oxford: Oxford University Press, 2011), p. 101.
45. Ibid., p. 111.
46. See Markus Balkenhol, "Silence and the Politics of Compassion: Commemorating Slavery in the Netherlands," *Social Anthropology*, Vol. 24, No. 3 (2016), pp. 278–93; Liam Stack, "Amsterdam Considers Apology for Slavery in Former Colony," *New York Times*, February 10, 2020, https://www.nytimes.com/2020/02/10/world/europe/amsterdam-considers-apology-for-slavery-in-former-colony.html.
47. See Amitav Ghosh, *The Nutmeg's Curse: Parables for a Planet in Crisis* (Chicago: University of Chicago Press, 2021).
48. Stern, *The Company State*, p. 102.
49. Jill Lepore, *These Truths: A History of the United States* (New York: W. W. Norton and Co., 2019), pp. 54–5.
50. The German Pietist tradition to which Ziegenbalg belonged placed a strong emphasis on heartfelt devotion to Christ and the renewal of Christian faith and practice. The tradition can be traced back to the initiatives of several theologians from the University of Halle, most notably Philipp Jakob Spener (1635–1705) and August Hermann Francke (1663–1727). These men and their successors viewed the state-sponsored Lutheranism of their day as having fallen asleep amidst an overemphasis on theology and scholasticism. Christian leaders could be well versed in theology while leading decadent lifestyles. This disjunction between the life of the mind and Christian praxis made them ineffective in transforming the culture around them.
51. "300 Years On: Ziegenbalg Set to Get his Due," *The Hindu*, June 29, 2006.
52. Susan Viswanathan, "Memorable Mission," *Frontline*, July 28, 2006, https://frontline.thehindu.com/arts-and-culture/article30210267.ece.
53. Daniel Jeyaraj, *A German Exploration of Indian Society: Ziegenbalg's "Malabarian Heathenism." An Annotated English Translation with an Introduction and a Glossary* (Chennai: Mylapore Institute for Indigenous Studies and ISPCK, 2006), p. 250.
54. Brijraj Singh argues that, because of his commitment to learning Tamil and his deep interest in the local religions, and because of the high regard he had for Tamils, Ziegenbalg was not a colonialist. Brijraj Singh, *The First Protestant Missionary to India: Bartholomaeus Ziegenbalg, 1683–1719* (New Delhi: Oxford University Press, 1999), p. 163.
55. Robert E. Frykenberg, *Christianity in India: From Beginnings to the Present* (New York: Oxford University Press, 2008), p. 144.
56. Jeyaraj, *A German Exploration of Indian Society*, pp. 93–5, 126–41.
57. Frykenberg, *Christianity in India*, p. 149.
58. Jeyaraj, *A German Exploration of Indian Society*, p. 35.
59. This point is made in the documentary, "Beyond Empires: Why India Celebrates Bartholomaeus Ziegenbalg," produced by Christopher Gilbert and Lamp Post Media (2013).
60. From Daniel Jeyaraj, *Inkulturation in Tranquebar: der Beitrag der frühen dänisch-halleschen Mission zum Werden einer indisch-einheimischen Kirche (1706–1730)*

(Erlangen: Verlag der Ev.-Luth. Mission Erlangen, 1996), p. 84. Taken from Singh, *The First Protestant Missionary to India*, p. 16.
61. Singh, *The First Protestant Missionary to India*, p. 26.
62. Ibid., pp. 22–3.
63. For a comparative examination of Jesuits and Pietists, see Ines Županov and Will Sweetman, "Rival Mission, Rival Science? Jesuits and Pietists in Seventeenth- and Eighteenth-Century South India," *Comparative Studies in Society and History*, Vol. 61, No. 3 (2019), pp. 624–53.
64. Dennis Hudson, *Protestant Origins in India: Tamil Evangelical Christians, 1706–1835* (Grand Rapids and Richmond: Eerdmans and Curzon Press, 2000), p. 52. See also Amartya Sen, *The Argumentative Indian: Writings on Indian History, Culture and Identity* (London: Penguin, 2006); C. A. Bayly, *Empire and Information: Intelligence Gathering and Social Communication in India, 1780–1870* (Cambridge: Cambridge University Press, 1996), p. 200.
65. Singh, *The First Protestant Missionary to India*, p. 142, citing Bartholomaeus Ziegenbalg, *An Account of the Religion, and Government, Learning, and Oeconomy, &c. of the Malabarians* (London: Joseph Downing, 1717), p. 37.
66. Daniel Jeyaraj, *Bartholomaeus Ziegenbalg, The Father of Modern Protestant Missions: An Indian Assessment* (New Delhi and Chennai: ISPCK and Gurukal Theological College and Research Institute, 2006), p. 145.
67. Bartholomaeus Ziegenbalg, *Thirty-Four Conferences Between the Danish Missionaries and the Malabarian Brahmins (or Heathen Priests) in the East Indies* (London: H. Clemens, 1719), p. 22.
68. Hudson, *Protestant Origins in India*, pp. 51–9.
69. Ibid., p. 54.
70. Ziegenbalg, *Thirty-Four Conferences*, pp. 30–1.
71. Ibid., pp. 33–4.
72. Ibid., pp. 124–8.
73. Ibid., p. 128.
74. See A. Madhaviah, *Clarinda: A Historical Novel*, 2nd edition (Tirunelveli: Nambar Vattam, 1992 [1915]). See also Kristen Bergmen Waha, "Synthesizing Hindu and Christian Ethics in Madhaviah's English Novel, *Clarinda*," *Victorian Literature and Culture*, Vol. 46 (2018), pp. 237–55.
75. Lamin Sanneh, *Whose Religion Is Christianity? The Gospel Beyond the West* (Grand Rapids: Eerdmans, 2003), pp. 15–22, 73–4. See also Lamin Sanneh, *Translating the Message: The Missionary Impact on Culture*, 2nd edition, revised and expanded (Maryknoll, NY: Orbis, 2009).
76. Frykenberg, *Christianity in India*, pp. 144–5.
77. See, for instance, Henriette Bugge, *Mission and Tamil Society: Social and Religious Change in South India, 1840–1900* (Richmond: Curzon Press, 1994); Susan Billington Harper, *In the Shadow of the Mahatma: Bishop V. S. Azariah and the Travails of Indian Christianity* (Grand Rapids and Richmond: Eerdmans and Curzon Press, 2001); Hephzibah Israel, *Religious Transactions in Colonial South*

India: Language, Translation, and the Making of Protestant Identity (New York: Palgrave Macmillan, 2011).
78. Indira Peterson, "*Bethlehem Kuṟavañci* of Vedanayaka Sastri of Tanjore: The Cultural Discourses of an Early Nineteenth-Century Tamil Christian Poem" in Judith Brown and Robert Frykenberg (eds.), *Christians, Cultural Interactions, and India's Religious Traditions* (London and Grand Rapids: Routledge and Curzon Press, 2002), p. 12.
79. Hudson, *Protestant Origins in India*, p. 141.
80. Ibid., pp. 140–67.
81. Ibid., pp. 161–3.
82. Israel, *Religious Transactions in Colonial South India*, p. 38.
83. Ibid., p. 42.
84. Ibid., p. 116.
85. Ibid., p. 133.
86. Singh, *The First Protestant Missionary to India*, p. 163.
87. Sunil Amrith, *Crossing the Bay of Bengal: The Furies of Nature and the Fortunes of Migrants* (Cambridge, MA: Harvard University Press, 2013), pp. 80–3.
88. N. S. Sargant, *The Dispersion of the Tamil Church* (New Delhi: ISPCK, 1940), p. 70.
89. Ibid., p. 81.
90. Ibid., p. 83.
91. Ibid., p. 92.
92. Robbie Goh, *Protestant Christianity in the Indian Diaspora: Abjected Identities, Evangelical Relations, and Pentecostal Visions* (Albany, NY: SUNY Press, 2018), pp. 57–61.

Chapter 5

1. Brad Gregory, *The Unintended Reformation* (Cambridge, MA: Harvard University Press, 2012).
2. See Alec Ryrie, *Protestants: The Faith that Made the Modern World* (New York: Viking Press, 2017); Alec Ryrie, "Protestantism as a Historical Category," *Transactions of the Royal Historical Society*, Vol. 26 (2016), pp. 59–77.
3. Amartya Sen, *The Argumentative Indian: Writings on Indian History, Culture and Identity* (London: Penguin, 2006); C. A. Bayly, *Empire and Information: Intelligence Gathering and Social Communication in India, 1780–1870* (Cambridge: Cambridge University Press, 1996), p. 200.
4. Bayly, *Empire and Information*, p. 210.
5. Frank Conlon, "The Polemic Process in Nineteenth-Century Maharashtra: Visnubawa Brahmachari and Hindu Revival" in Kenneth Jones (ed.), *Religious Controversy in British India: Dialogues in South Asian Languages* (Albany: State University of New York Press, 1992), p. 8.
6. B. S. Kesavan describes presses established in South India in *History of Printing and Publishing in India* (New Delhi: National Book Trust, 1988).

7. This was a process that resembles what Benedict Anderson has associated with the origins of nationalism. Benedict Anderson, *Imagined Communities: Reflections on the Origins and Spread of Nationalism* (London: Verso, 1983); Derek Peterson, *The Invention of Religion: Rethinking Belief in Politics and History* (New Brunswick: Rutgers University Press, 2002).
8. Nile Green describes this competitive economy of religion in terms of "religious entrepreneurs" and "firms" arising within the context of colonial and industrial expansion of the nineteenth century. He describes how Muslims in West and South Asia employed the organizational methods of Christian missionaries to propagate Islam globally. See Nile Green, *Terrains of Exchange: Religious Economies of Global Islam* (New York: Oxford University Press, 2015). My interests in this chapter overlap with Green's, but are less tied to the language of business and capitalism and more to traditions of debate and argumentation, developed in the work of C. A. Bayly and Amartya Sen.
9. William Dalrymple, *White Mughals: Love and Betrayal in Eighteenth-Century India* (New York: Penguin, 2003), pp. 20–1.
10. Dalrymple, *White Mughals*, pp. 9–12.
11. Under the auspices of this state-sponsored Orientalism, the Sanskritist William Jones developed the theory of an Indo-European family of languages, in which Indians and Europeans shared a common classical heritage. In South India, the civil servant Francis Whyte Ellis and missionary Robert Caldwell advanced a parallel theory of another family of languages known as "Dravidian." This view of this "Madras School" of Orientalism in turn informed an anti-Brahminical, anti-Sanskrit politics of identity. See Thomas Trautmann, *The Madras School of Orientalism: Producing Knowledge in Colonial South India* (Delhi: Oxford University Press, 2009).
12. See Eric Stokes, *The English Utilitarians and India* (Oxford: Oxford University Press, 1989); Jennifer Pitts, *A Turn to Empire: The Rise of Imperial Liberalism in Britain and France* (Princeton: Princeton University Press, 2006).
13. According to Bebbington, Evangelicalism was marked by four defining characteristics: conversionism, crucicentrism, biblicism, and activism. See David Bebbington, *Evangelicalism in Modern Britain: A History from the 1730s to the 1980s* (London: Routledge, 1989).
14. David Kopf, *British Orientalism and the Bengal Renaissance: Dynamics of Indian Modernization, 1773–1835* (Calcutta: Firma K. L. Mukhopadyay, 1969), p. 134.
15. Penelope Carson, *The East India Company and Religion, 1698–1858* (Woodbridge: Boydell Press, 2012), pp. 90–4.
16. William Carey, *An Inquiry into the Obligations of Christians to Use Means for the Conversion of the Heathen* (London: Hodder and Stoughton, 1891).
17. Claudius Buchanan, *Memoir of the Expediency of an Ecclesiastical Establishment for British India; Both as the Means of Perpetuating the Christian Religion Among our Own Countrymen; and as a Foundation for the Ultimate Civilization of the Natives* (London: T. Cadell and W. Davies, 1805). See also Claudius Buchanan, *An Apology for Promoting Christianity in India* (London: Nathaniel Willis, 1812).
18. Carson, *The East India Company and Religion*, pp. 15–16.

19. This is the impression that one derives from William Dalrymple's book about the Great Rebellion of 1857. He attributes the rebellion in no small part to the "aggressively self-confident" activities of missionaries in Delhi. See William Dalrymple, *The Last Mughal: The Fall of a Dynasty, Delhi, 1857* (New York: Alfred A. Knopf, 2007), p. 61. Dalrymple overemphasizes the role of missionary polemics in fomenting the Great Rebellion, as many other factors came into play: among them, policies toward India's princely states, the erosion of what C. A. Bayly calls the "information order" of imperialism, changing policies of military recruitment, changing policies on land tenure and revenue collection, and a declining sense of dialogue between rulers and the ruled (maintained by the Mughals, but lost under the East India Company). Many such factors led to a collapse in the relationship between the Company and various sections of Indian society. See Bayly, *Empire and Information*; Jon Wilson, *India Conquered: Britain's Raj and the Chaos of Empire* (New York: Perseus Books, 2016).
20. For an examination of the ebb and flow of the Company's educational policies, see Kopf, *British Orientalism and the Bengal Renaissance*; Nandini Chatterjee, *The Making of Indian Secularism: Empire, Law and Christianity, 1830–1960* (London and New York: Palgrave Macmillan, 2011).
21. Lata Mani, *Contentious Traditions: The Debate on Sati in Colonial India* (New Delhi: Oxford University Press, 1998).
22. As the *sati* debate illustrates, missionary views about Indian society did not arise in a vacuum, but intersected with the Orientalist projects of the Asiatic Society, the efforts to translate and codify Hindu and Muslim law, and the employment of court pandits. The affinity and overlapping personnel between missionaries and scholar administrators of the Raj have led some to regard British rule in India as advancing an essentially Protestant agenda. See Robert Yelle, *The Language of Disenchantment: Protestant Literalism and Colonial Discourse in British India* (New York: Oxford University Press, 2013).
23. Mani, *Contentious Traditions*, p. 109.
24. Carey, Journal, January 19, 1794, BMS Archive. Taken from Mani, *Contentious Traditions*, p. 93.
25. Ibid., p. 96.
26. Samuel Hugh Moffett, *History of Christianity in Asia. Volume II: 1500–1900* (Maryknoll, NY: Orbis, 2005), p. 265.
27. See Parna Sengupta, *Pedagogy for Religion: Missionary Education and the Fashioning of Hindus and Muslims in Bengal* (Berkeley: University of California Press, 2011).
28. For a more detailed examination of identity, conflict, and controversy associated with prominent Bengali converts, see Mou Banerjee, "Questions of Faith: Christianity, Conversion and the Ideological Origins of Political Theology in Colonial India, 1813–1907," PhD thesis, Harvard University, 2018, p. 92. Banerjee draws from *Converts from the Government and Missionary Colleges and Schools* (Calcutta: Baptist Mission Press, 1852), pp. 10–26 [no author]. Chapter 6 of this book discusses Brahmin conversion in more detail. See also Sudhir Chandra, "Hindu Conservatism in the Nineteenth Century," *Economic and Political Weekly*, Vol. 5, No. 50 (1970), pp. 2003–7.

29. Geoffrey Oddie, "Constructing 'Hinduism': The Impact of the Protestant Missionary Movement on Hindu Self-Understanding" in Robert Eric Frykenberg (ed.), *Christians and Missionaries in India: Cross-Cultural Communication Since 1500* (Grand Rapids and London: Eerdmans and Routledge, 2003), p. 162. See also Geoffrey Oddie, *Imagined Hinduism: British Protestant Missionary Constructions of Hinduism, 1793–1900* (New Delhi: Sage, 2006).
30. Oddie, "Constructing 'Hinduism,'" p. 163. See also Jones, *Religious Controversy in British India*; Kenneth Jones, *Socio-Religious Reform Movements in British India* (Cambridge: Cambridge University Press, 1994); David Kopf, *The Brahmo Samaj and the Shaping of Modern India* (Princeton: Princeton University Press, 1979); Brian Pennington, *Was Hinduism Invented? Britons, Indians, and the Colonial Construction of Religion* (New York: Oxford University Press, 2005).
31. Richard Fox Young, *Resistant Hinduism: Sanskrit Sources of Anti-Christian Apologetics* (Leiden: Brill, 1981), pp. 144–5.
32. Ibid., p. 101. See also Jon Keune, "The Intra- and Inter-Religious Conversions of Nilakantha Goreh," *Journal of Hindu–Christian Studies*, Vol. 17 (2004), pp. 45–54.
33. Dennis Hudson, "Tamil Hindu Responses to Protestants" in Steven Kaplan (ed.), *Indigenous Responses to Western Christianity* (New York: New York University Press, 1995), p. 97.
34. Ibid., p. 107.
35. Mitch Numark, "Hebrew School in 19th Century Bombay: Protestant Missionaries, Cochin Jews, and the Hebraization of India's Bene Israel Community," *Modern Asian Studies*, Vol. 46, No. 6 (2012), pp. 1765–8.
36. Ibid., p. 1768.
37. John Wilson, *The Parsi Religion as Contained in the Zand Avasta* (Bombay: American Mission Press, 1843), p. 26.
38. Reuben Louis Gabriel, "Migration, Human Dislocation and the Good News: The Case of the Parsees in Nineteenth-Century Western India," *Mission Studies*, Vol. 31 (2014), p. 210.
39. The Parsi who debated with Wilson wrote under the pen name Nauroz Goosequill, which was later modified to Swanquill, but his actual identity is disputed among scholars. See Gabriel, "Migration, Human Dislocation and the Good News," p. 212, note 5.
40. For a detailed account of Parsi legal reforms and the shaping of the legal profession in Bombay, see Mitra Sharafi, *Law and Identity in Colonial South Asia: Parsi Legal Culture, 1772–1947* (Cambridge: Cambridge University Press, 2014).
41. The account is detailed in Wilson, *The Parsi Religion as Contained in the Zand Avasta*, pp. 87–94.
42. Gabriel, "Migration, Human Dislocation and the Good News," pp. 218–20.
43. Harlan Pearson, *Islamic Reform and Revival in Nineteenth-Century India: The Tariqah-i-Muhammadiyah* (New Delhi: Yoda Press, 2008), p. 133.
44. Avril Powell, *Muslims and Missionaries in Pre-Mutiny India* (Richmond: Curzon Press, 1993), p. 98.
45. Ibid., p. 95.

46. Ibid., p. 96.
47. See Avril Powell, "Creating Christian Community in Early Nineteenth-Century Agra" in Richard Young (ed.), *India and the Indianness of Christianity: Essays on Understanding—Historical, Theological, and Bibliographical—in Honor of Robert Frykenberg* (Grand Rapids: Eerdmans, 2009), pp. 82–107.
48. T. P. Hughes, "The Wahhabis of Najd and India" in *Church Missionary Intelligencer and Record: A Monthly Journal of Missionary Record* (London: Seeley, Jackson, and Halliday, 1878), pp. 98ff., 160ff.
49. Nile Green, *Terrains of Exchange*, pp. 68–9.
50. Pearson, *Islamic Reform and Revival*, pp. 65–6.
51. Ibid., p. 141.
52. Avril Powell, "Maulana Rahmat Allah Kairanawi and Muslim–Christian Controversy in India in the Mid-19th Century," *Journal of the Royal Asiatic Society of Great Britain and Ireland*, Vol. 108, No. 1 (1976), pp. 45–6.
53. Ibid., p. 49.
54. Ibid., p. 51.
55. Ibid., p. 55.
56. Sayyid Ahmad Khan, *The Causes of the Indian Revolt* (Benares: Medical Hall Press, 1873), p. 18.
57. See Youcef Djadi, "Max Weber, Islam and Modernity," *Max Weber Studies*, Vol. 11, No. 1 (2011), pp. 35–47.
58. Nile Green, *Bombay Islam: The Religious Economy of the West Indian Ocean, 1840–1915* (Cambridge: Cambridge University Press, 2011), p. 26. For a detailed description of charms, amulets, rites, and objects utilized in local Muslim customary observances in India, see Ja'Far Sharif, *Islam in India or the Qanum-i-Islam: The Customs of the Musalmans of India*, translated by G. A. Herklots (London: Oxford University Press, 1921).
59. Mou Banerjee, "The Tale of the Tailor: Munshi Mohammed Meherullah and Muslim–Christian Apologetics in Bengal, 1885–1907," *South Asian Studies*, Vol. 33, No. 2 (2017), p. 123. See also Rafiuddin Ahmed, "Muslim–Christian Polemics and Religious Reform in Nineteenth-Century Bengal: Munshi Meheru'llah of Jessore" in Jones, *Religious Controversy in British India*, pp. 93–122.
60. Banerjee, "The Tale of the Tailor," p. 123.
61. See Ussama Makdisi, *Artillery of Heaven: American Missionaries and the Failed Conversion of the Middle East* (Ithaca: Cornell University Press, 2008); Daniel Bays, *A New History of Christianity in China* (Chichester: Wiley-Blackwell, 2012).
62. Hastie's letters and Bankim's responses are published in William Hastie, *Hindu Idolatry and English Enlightenment: Six Letters Addressed to Educated Hindus Containing a Practical Discussion of Hinduism* (Calcutta: Thacker, Spink and C., 1883).
63. Ibid., p. 128.
64. Tapan Raichaudhury, *Europe Reconsidered: Perceptions of the West in Nineteenth-Century Bengal* (Oxford: Oxford University Press, 1988), pp. 114–16.
65. Ibid., p. 138.

66. Hastie, *Hindu Idolatry and English Enlightenment*, pp. 141–3.
67. Ibid., p. 143.
68. Raichaudhury, *Europe Reconsidered*, p. 146.
69. Hinduism, Bankim asserted, consisted of doctrine or creed, worship and rites, and morality, and thus replicates the structure of Christian tradition. Ibid., p. 145.
70. Harald Fischer-Tiné, "Third Stream Orientalism? J. N. Farquhar, the Indian YMCA's Literature Department and the Representation of South Asian Cultures and Religions (ca. 1910–1940)," *Journal of Asian Studies*, Vol. 79, No. 3 (2020), pp. 659–83.
71. Ibid., p. 663. See also Eric J. Sharpe, *Not to Destroy but to Fulfill: The Contribution of J. N. Farquhar to Protestant Missionary Thought in India Before 1914* (Lund: C. W. K. Gleerup, 1965).
72. See Djadi, "Max Weber, Islam and Modernity," pp. 35–47.
73. Another discussion of Protestantization is provided in J. Barton Scott, "Luther in the Tropics: Karsandas Mulji and the Colonial 'Reformation' of Hinduism," *Journal of the American Academy of Religion*, Vol. 83, No. 1 (2015), pp. 181–209.
74. Mitch Numark, "Translating *Dharma*: Scottish Missionary Orientalists and the Politics of Religious Understanding in Nineteenth-Century Bombay," *Journal of Asian Studies*, Vol. 7, No. 2 (2011), p. 475. Numark draws the phrase "legislative intellectuals" from Zygmut Bauman, *Legislators and Interpreters: On Modernity, Post-Modernity, and Intellectuals* (Ithaca: Cornell University Press, 1987).
75. Nile Green discusses this in connection to the Muslims of Bombay. He is careful to point out that it was not the Islam based on "scripture, reason and salvation" that ultimately won the hearts of Bombay Muslims, but the "disenchanted" forms based on "miracles, rituals, and intercession of charismatic saviours." Green, *Bombay Islam*, pp. 26–8.
76. Peter Berger, "Pluralism, Protestantization, and the Voluntary Principle" in Thomas Banchoff (ed.), *Democracy and the New Religious Pluralism* (Oxford: Oxford University Press, 2007), pp. 21–2.
77. Talal Asad, *Genealogies of Religion: Discipline and Reasons of Power in Christianity and Islam* (Baltimore: Johns Hopkins University Press, 1993), pp. 28–9.
78. Bhudev Mukhopadyay, from Raichaudhury, *Europe Reconsidered*.
79. *Harvest Field*, June 1889, p. 423.
80. Numark, "Translating *Dharma*," p. 475.
81. See Brian Stanley, "Church, State and the Hierarchy of Civilization" in Andrew Neil Porter (ed.), *The Imperial Horizons of British Protestant Missions, 1880–1914* (Grand Rapids: Eerdmans, 2003), pp. 58–84.
82. Robert E. Frykenberg, *Christianity in India: From Beginnings to the Present* (Oxford: Oxford University Press, 2008), pp. 383–4.
83. Klaus Koschorke, *Polycentric Structures in the History of World Christianity* (Wiesbaden: Harrassowitz, 2014).
84. Andrew Walls, *The Cross-Cultural Process in Christian History* (Maryknoll, NY: Orbis, 2002), pp. 29, 67.

Chapter 6

1. Monier Monier-Williams, *The Study of Sanskrit in Relation to Missionary Work in India* (London: Williams and Norgate, 1861), p. 39.
2. Ibid., p. 41. Sections of this chapter can be found in my contribution to Joel Cabrita, David Maxwell, and Emma Wild-Wood (eds.), *Relocating World Christianity: Interdisciplinary Studies in Universal and Local Expressions of the Christian Faith* (Leiden: Brill, 2017) and in Chandra Mallampalli, "Dalit Christian Reservations: Colonial Moorings of a Live Debate," *International Journal of Asian Christianity*, Vol. 1 (2018), pp. 25–44.
3. By "Orientalist," I am referring specifically to the study of India by Europeans during the eighteenth and nineteenth centuries. For an excellent description of how Orientalist scholarship gave rise to enduring notions of race tied to the concept of the "Aryan," see Thomas Trautmann, *The Aryans of British India* (Berkeley: University of California Press, 1997); Thomas Trautmann, *Languages and Nations: The Dravidian Proof in Colonial Madras* (Berkeley: University of California Press, 2006).
4. Monier-Williams, *The Study of Sanskrit*, pp. 2–5.
5. Ibid., p. 39. He drew no references to so-called "Dravidian people," who, according to another thread of Orientalism, the Madras School, derived their identity from a different family of languages. See Trautmann, *Languages and Nations*, pp. 151–85.
6. A broader discussion of Protestant missionary knowledge about India is provided in Geoffrey Oddie, "Orientalism and British Protestant Missionary Constructions of India in the Nineteenth Century," *South Asia*, New Series, Vol. 18, No. 2 (1994), pp. 27–42.
7. Within South Indian contexts, such developments are discussed in Geoffrey Oddie, *Hindu and Christian in South-East India* (London: Curzon Press, 1991); Henriette Bugge, *Mission and Tamil Society: Social and Religious Change in South India, 1840–1900* (Richmond: Curzon Press, 1994); Hugald Grafe, *History of Christianity in India. Volume IV, Part 2: Tamilnadu in the Nineteenth and Twentieth Centuries* (Bangalore: Church History Association of India, 1990). For West Bengal, see Mou Banerjee, "Questions of Faith: Christianity, Conversion and the Ideological Origins of Political Theology in Colonial India, 1813–1907," PhD thesis, Harvard University, 2018.
8. Robert E. Frykenberg, *Christianity in India: From Beginnings to the Present* (Oxford and New York: Oxford University Press, 2008), p. 381.
9. Felix Wilfred, *Christians for a Better India* (New Delhi: ISPCK, 2014), p. 169.
10. See Swami Dayananda Saraswati in *Indian Express*, October 29, 1999. Cited in Nathaniel Roberts, "Is Conversion a 'Colonization of Consciousness'?," *Anthropological Theory*, Vol. 12, No. 3 (2012), p. 272.
11. Ibid., p. 276.
12. See Talal Asad, "Comments on Conversion" in Peter van der Veer (ed.), *Conversion to Modernities: The Globalization of Christianity* (New York: Routledge, 1996), pp. 263–73.

13. Deepra Dandekar, *The Subhedar's Son: A Narrative of Brahmin-Christian Conversion from Nineteenth-Century Maharashtra* (New York: Oxford University Press, 2019), pp. 16–17.
14. Ibid., p. xxx.
15. Frykenberg, *Christianity in India*, p. 414.
16. H. L. Richard, *Following Jesus in the Hindu Context: The Intriguing Implications of N. V. Tilak's Life and Thought* (Pasadena: William Carey Library, 1998), p. 5.
17. Frykenberg, *Christianity in India*, p. 415.
18. Deepra Dandekar, *Baba Padmanji: Pioneering Vernacular Christianity in Colonial India* (London: Routledge, 2020), p. 2.
19. Ibid., pp. 2–3.
20. Ibid., p. 4.
21. Nile Green, *Bombay Islam: The Religious Economy of the West Indian Ocean, 1840–1915* (Cambridge: Cambridge University Press, 2011).
22. Gauri Viswanathan, *Outside the Fold: Conversion, Modernity and Belief* (Princeton: Princeton University Press, 1998).
23. Quote taken from ibid., p. 84.
24. Quote taken from ibid., p. 85.
25. See Andrew Walls, "Converts or Proselytes? The Crisis Over Conversion in the Early Church," *International Bulletin of Missionary Research*, Vol. 28, No. 1 (2004), pp. 2–6.
26. Ibid., p. 5.
27. Pandita Ramabai, *A Testimony of Our Inexhaustible Treasure*, 12th edition (Kedgaon: Mukti Mission, 2001), p. 15.
28. Robert Frykenberg (ed.), *Pandita Ramabai's America: Conditions of Life in the United States*, translated by Kshitija Gomes (Grand Rapids: Eerdmans, 2003), pp. 6–8.
29. Uma Chakravarty, *Rewriting History: The Life and Times of Pandita Ramabai* (New Delhi: Zubaan, 2013), p. 308.
30. Ramabai, *A Testimony*, p. 21.
31. Meera Kosambi, *Pandita Ramabai Through Her Own Words* (New Delhi: Oxford University Press, 2000), p. 8.
32. See, in particular, her commentary on the laws of Manu, family, and women in her book *The High Caste Hindu Woman*. Its text is reproduced in Kosambi, *Pandita Ramabai*, pp. 130–80.
33. Ramabai, *A Testimony*, p. 23.
34. Hers was not "conversion as assimilation," a point made by Viswanathan in *Outside the Fold*.
35. Meera Kosambi, *Returning the American Gaze: Situating Pandita Ramabai's American Encounter* (Bloomington: Indiana University Press, 2003), pp. 31–2.
36. Antoinette Burton, "Colonial Encounters in Late Victorian England: Pandita Ramabai at Cheltenham and Wantage, 1883–6," *Feminist Review*, Vol. 49 (1995), p. 33.
37. Chakravarty, *Rewriting History*, pp. 317–18.
38. For our purposes, the phrase "Anglo-Catholic" refers to the High Church tradition within Anglicanism, which aligns itself doctrinally and through its worship forms with Catholicism.

39. Ramabai, *A Testimony*, p. 29.
40. Letter from Sister Geraldine at Bath to Ramabai; A. B. Shah (ed.), *Letters and Correspondence of Pandita Ramabai* (Bombay: Maharashtra State Board for Literature and Culture, 1977), p. 106.
41. Shah, *Letters and Correspondence*, p. 99.
42. Ibid.
43. Ibid., p. 108.
44. Viswanathan, *Outside the Fold*, p. 132.
45. Chakravarty, *Rewriting History*, p. 318.
46. Ibid., p. 319.
47. Quote taken from ibid., p. 319.
48. Ibid., p. 320.
49. Meera Kosambi (translator), *Pandita Ramabai's American Encounter: The Peoples of the United States* (Bloomington: Indiana University Press, 2003), p. 6.
50. For an excellent treatment of these impulses in American Christianity, see Nathan Hatch, *The Democratization of American Christianity* (New Haven: Yale University Press, 1989).
51. Frykenberg (ed.), *Pandita Ramabai's America*, p. 49.
52. Allan Anderson, "Pandita Ramabai, the Mukti Revival and Global Pentecostalism," *Transformation*, Vol. 23, No. 1 (2006), p. 37.
53. Ibid., p. 40.
54. Ibid., p. 41.
55. Dandekar, *Baba Padmanji*, p. 9.
56. Klaus Koschorke, *Owned and Conducted Entirely by the Native Christian Community: Der "christian Patriot" und die Indigen-Christliche Presse im Kolonialen Indien um 1900* (Wiesbaden: Harrassowitz, 2019).
57. Chandra Mallampalli, *Christians and Public Life in Colonial South India, 1863–1937: Contending with Marginality* (London: Routledge Curzon, 2004), pp. 114–16.

Chapter 7

1. See note 7 in the Introduction for my explanation for why I use the term "Dalit" throughout this chapter and book.
2. Sujatha Gidla, *Ants Among Elephants: An Untouchable Family and the Making of Modern India* (New York: Farrar, Straus and Giroux, 2017).
3. Y. B. Satyanarayana, *My Father Baliah* (Noida: HarperCollins, 2011).
4. Arundhati Roy, "The Doctor and the Saint" in B. R. Ambedkar, *Annihilation of Caste* (New Delhi: Navayana, 2014), pp. 35–6.
5. Satyanarayana, *My Father Baliah*, pp. 22–3.
6. The Sikh religion originated in the Punjab toward the end of the fifteenth century under the influence of Guru Nanak (1469–1539). It drew inspiration from both Hindu and Muslim faith traditions. Guru Gobind Singh (1666–1708) established

the Khalsa (the Sikh order or brotherhood) and set out the distinctive markers of male Sikh identity. Harjot Oberoi, *The Construction of Religious Boundaries: Culture, Identity and Diversity in the Sikh Tradition* (New Delhi: Oxford University Press, 1997), pp. 24–5.

7. Eliza Kent notes that material motivations for conversion were combined with psychological, spiritual, and social ones. The dualism between material and spiritual is something inherited from the Western Christian tradition. See Eliza Kent, *Converting Women: Gender and Protestant Christianity in Colonial South India* (New York: Oxford University Press, 2004), p. 18.

8. Those who converted in the interest of gaining access to foreign aid are often referred to as "rice Christians." M. Christu Doss, "Repainting Religious Landscape: Economics of Conversion and Making Rice Christians in Colonial South India (1781–1880)," *Studies in History*, Vol. 30, No. 2 (2014), p. 181.

9. The poor bear a greater burden to demonstrate the autonomy and authenticity of their religious choices, according to Rupa Viswanath. See Rupa Viswanath, "The Emergence of Authenticity Talk and the Giving of Accounts: Conversion as Movement of the Soul in South India, ca. 1900," *Comparative Studies in Society and History*, Vol. 55, No. 1 (2013), p. 122.

10. Joel Robbins, "Continuity Thinking and the Problem of Christian Culture," *Current Anthropology*, Vol. 48, No. 1 (2007), pp. 5–17; Joel Robbins, "On the Paradoxes of Global Pentecostalism and the Perils of Continuity Thinking," *Religion*, Vol. 33 (2003), pp. 221–31.

11. This is not to suggest that there are no real instances of continuity with past beliefs or instances of radical transformation. Debates over rupture versus continuity reveal how disciplinary or ideological currents can place the stories of converts in service to larger agendas. Proving that Christianity is Indian and not colonial, advancing or eschewing whiggish triumphalism, or demonstrating the authenticity of conversions are examples of how such agendas can steer one's interpretation in different directions. When examining any particular account of a mass conversion movement, it is important to consider not only the facts being presented, but also the kinds of questions the narrator feels obliged to address. The need to prove that conversions are "sincere" or "authentic" arose within both Roman Catholic and Protestant contexts well before Hindu nationalists made it a pillar of their own campaigns against conversion.

12. For a detailed account of the deliberations of Protestant ministers in India on the topic of caste, see Joseph Roberts (ed.), *Caste, in Its Religious and Civil Character, Opposed to Christianity* (London: Longman, Brown, Green, and Longmans, 1847).

13. See Duncan B. Forrester, *Caste and Christianity: Attitudes and Policies on Caste of Anglo-Saxon Protestant Missions in India* (London: Curzon Press, 1980).

14. Eliza Kent, "'Mass Movements' in South India, 1877–1936" in Dennis Washburn and Kevin Reinhart (eds.), *Converting Cultures: Religion, Ideology and Transformations of Modernity* (Leiden: Brill, 2007), p. 372.

15. John E. Clough, *Social Christianity in the Orient: The Story of a Man, a Mission and a Movement* (New York: Macmillan, 1914), pp. 244–7.

16. Ibid., p. 249.
17. Chakali Chandra Sekhar, "In Search of a Touchable Body: Christian Mission and Dalit Conversions," *Religions*, Vol. 10, No. 12 (2019), p. 644.
18. Ibid.
19. Ibid., p. 6.
20. Ibid., p. 263.
21. Kent, "'Mass Movements' in South India," p. 379.
22. Jesuits had addressed this matter centuries before them. Roberto de Nobili concluded that caste distinctions were civil observances similar to European class distinctions and should therefore be tolerated (see Chapter 3).
23. Susan Billington Harper, "Azariah, Vedanayagam Samuel (1874-1945)" in Gerald H. Anderson (ed.), *Biographical Dictionary of Christian Missions* (Grand Rapids: Eerdmans, 1999), pp. 35-6.
24. Azariah, "The Indian Church and the Depressed Classes," *Guardian*, May 21, 1936, p. 325. Cited in Chandra Mallampalli, *Christians and Public Life in Colonial South India, 1863-1937: Contending with Marginality* (London: Routledge Curzon, 2004), p. 186.
25. John Webster, *The Dalit Christians: A History*, 2nd edition (Delhi: ISPCK, 2009), pp. 16-17, 24.
26. Susan Billington Harper, *In the Shadow of the Mahatma: Bishop V. S. Azariah and the Travails of Christianity in British India* (Grand Rapids and Richmond: Eerdmans and Curzon Press, 2000), pp. 251-61.
27. Ibid., p. 252.
28. Kent, Converting Women, pp. 134-9.
29. Ibid., p. 160.
30. Chakali Chandra Sekhar, "Dalit Women and Colonial Christianity: First Telugu Bible Women as Teachers of Wisdom," *Economic and Political Weekly*, Vol. 56, No. 11 (2021), p. 59.
31. The nursing profession attracted many Indian women and equipped them with specialized knowledge of the body and modern medical practices. See Ashok Kumar Mocherla, "We Called Her Peddamma: Caste, Gender, and Missionary Medicine in Guntur, 1880-1930," *International Journal of Asian Christianity*, Vol. 3 (2020), pp. 69-84.
32. Paul William Harris, "The Social Dimensions of Foreign Missions: Emma Rauschenbusch Clough and Social Gospel Ideology" in Wendy J. Deichmann Edwards and Carolyn De Swarte Gifford (eds.), *Gender and the Social Gospel* (Urbana: University of Illinois Press, 2003), pp. 87-102.
33. Frederick Downs, "Christianity as a Tribal Response to Change in Northeast India," *Missiology*, Vol. 8, No. 4 (1980), pp. 407-16.
34. Robert E. Frykenberg, *Christianity in India: From Beginnings to the Present* (Oxford and New York: Oxford University Press, 2008), p. 420.
35. However, dominant groups have attempted to Sanskritize tribals by incorporating them into lower echelons of village life. As they assumed menial roles as laborers, this process of Sanskritization led some tribal peoples to absorb Hindu deities into their pantheon and observe laws of purity and pollution in keeping with Brahminical

notions of caste. Frederick Downs, *The History of Christianity in India. Volume V, Part 5: North East India in the Nineteenth and Twentieth Centuries* (Bangalore: Church History Association of India, 1992), pp. 2–4; see also Gail Omvedt, "Adivasis, Culture and Modes of Production in India," *Critical Asian Studies*, Vol. 12, No. 1 (1980), p. 17; Srinivas, "A Note on Sanskritization and Westernization," p. 200.

36. With regard to the societies to the east of Bhutan, such as those of Arunachal Pradesh, historian Berenice Guyot-Rechard writes: "In the absence of an easily enforceable border and of strong legal, cultural, emotional, or historical claims to the eastern Himalayas' inhabitants, China and India's proximity became inherently threatening." Berenice Guyot-Rechard, *Shadow States: India, China and the Himalayas, 1910–1962* (Cambridge: Cambridge University Press, 2017), p. 4.

37. Robin Horton, "African Conversion" in Brendon Carmody (ed.), *Religious Conversion: An African Perspective* (Lusaka: Gadsden, 2015), pp. 45–54.

38. Ibid., p. 47.

39. Richard Eaton, "Comparative History as World History: Religious Conversion in Modern India" in Richard Eaton, *Essays on Islam and Indian History* (New Delhi: Oxford University Press, 2000), p. 47.

40. Mary Mead Clark, *A Corner in India* (Philadelphia: American Baptist Publication Society, 1907), pp. 57–60; Eaton, "Comparative History as World History," pp. 52, 60.

41. By the early nineteenth century, the British had made inroads into northeast India. In 1826, the British government in Bengal and the leaders of Burma signed the Treaty of Yandabo. This treaty stopped the imperialistic advances of the Burmese, especially into parts of Assam where the British were developing their commercial interests. Joy Pachuau, *Being Mizos: Identity and Belonging in Northeast India* (New Delhi: Oxford University Press, 2014), p. 87.

42. The governor-general, William Bentinck, formed a ten-member Tea Committee whose task was to determine whether tea was already growing in Assam and if, by annexing Assam, the British could challenge China's hold on the global tea market. Erica Rappaport, *A Thirst for Empire: How Tea Shaped the Modern World* (Princeton: Princeton University Press, 2017), p. 87.

43. The appellation "Nagas" has unknown origins. Quite likely, it is a colonial construction, intended to group the nearly fifty tribes of this region under one identity heading. Colonial records dating as far back as the 1840s indicate a lack of any evidence that the Nagas themselves used the term for self-designation. Sangamitra Misra, "The Nature of Colonial Intervention in the Nagas Hills, 1840–80," *Economic and Political Weekly*, Vol. 33, No. 51 (1998), p. 3276.

44. Frykenberg, *Christianity in India*, p. 426.

45. Downs, *The History of Christianity in India*, p. 82.

46. Eaton, "Comparative History as World History," p. 63.

47. Misra, "The Nature of Colonial Intervention," p. 3273.

48. Frykenberg, *Christianity in India*, p. 437.

49. Lamin Sanneh, *Whose Religion is Christianity? The Gospel Beyond the West* (Grand Rapids: Eerdmans, 2003), p. 10.

50. Eaton, "Comparative History as World History," p. 66. See the classic work, John Henry Hutton, *The Sema Nagas* (London: Macmillan and Co., 1921).
51. Eaton, "Comparative History as World History," pp. 67–8.
52. John Thompson, *Evangelizing the Nation: Religion and the Formation of Naga Political Identity* (New York: Routledge, 2016), pp. 100–1.
53. See Benedict Anderson, *Imagined Communities: Reflections on the Origin and Spread of Nationalism* (London: Verso, 1983).
54. Arkotong Longkumer, "'Along Kingdom's Highway': The Proliferation of Christianity, Education, and Print Amongst the Nagass in Northeast India," *Contemporary South Asia*, Vol. 27, No. 2 (2019), pp. 160–78.
55. Frederick Downs, *Essays on Christianity in Northeast India* (New Delhi: Indus, 1994), p. 148.
56. Ibid., p. 155.
57. Frykenberg, *Christianity in India*, p. 167.
58. Downs, *The History of Christianity in India*, pp. 16–22. See also David Kling, *A History of Christian Conversion* (New York: Oxford University Press, 2020), pp. 550–70.
59. Lalsangkima Pachuau, "Mizos Sakhua in Transition: Change and Continuity from Primal Religion to Christianity," *Missiology: An International Review*, Vol. 34, No. 1 (2006), p. 49.
60. Ibid., p. 43.
61. Downs, *The History of Christianity in India*, p. 96.
62. Ibid., pp. 96–7.
63. Ibid., p. 99.
64. Ibid., p. 149.
65. Joy Pachuau, "Christianity in Mizoram: An Ethnography" in Pius Malekandathil, Joy Pachuau, and Tanika Sarkar (eds.), *Christianity in Indian History: Issues of Culture, Power and Knowledge* (New Delhi: Primus Books, 2016), p. 50.
66. Lalsangkima Pachuau, "'Assistants' or 'Leaders'? The Contributions of Early Native Christian Converts in North-East India" in Malekandathil, Pachuau, and Sarkar, *Christianity in Indian History*, p. 105.
67. Arun Jones, *Missionary Christianity and Local Religion: American Evangelicalism in North India, 1836–1870* (Waco, TX: Baylor University Press, 2017), p. 33.
68. Ibid., pp. 5–6. Jones draws from the work of Edward Soja and Henri Lefebvre to develop his own application of "Thirdspace" to understand religious dynamics in north India.
69. Ibid., pp. 37–9.
70. Ibid., p. 279.
71. Ibid., pp. 254–7.
72. John C. B. Webster, *A Social History of Christianity: Northwest India Since 1800* (New Delhi: Oxford University Press, 2007), pp. 61–2.
73. Rupa Viswanath, *The Pariah Problem: Caste, Religion and the Social in Modern India* (New York: Columbia University Press, 2014), pp. 80–1.

74. Navyug Gill, "Limits of Conversion: Caste, Labor and the Question of Emancipation," *Journal of Asian Studies*, Vol. 78, No. 1 (2019), pp. 5–6.
75. Ibid., p. 6.
76. Joel Lee, "Lal Beg Underground: The Passing of an 'Untouchable' God" in Knut Jacobsen et al. (eds.), *Objects of Worship in South Asian Religion: Forms, Practices and Meanings* (New York: Routledge, 2014), p. 144.
77. Joel Lee, *Deceptive Majority: Dalits, Hinduism, and Underground Religion* (Cambridge: Cambridge University Press, 2021), p. 10.
78. Lee, "Lal Beg Underground," p. 144.
79. Christopher Harding, *Religious Transformation in South Asia: The Meanings of Conversion in Colonial Punjab* (New York: Oxford University Press, 2008), p. 40.
80. Kling, *A History of Christian Conversion*, p. 17. Taken from Jeffrey Cox, *Imperial Fault Lines: Christianity and Colonial Power in India, 1818–1940* (Stanford: Stanford University Press, 2002), p. 124.
81. John O'Brien, *The Unconquered People: The Liberation Journey of an Oppressed Caste* (Oxford: Oxford University Press, 2012), pp. 169–78.
82. Webster, *A Social History of Christianity*, p. 168.
83. Ibid., p. 170.
84. Ibid., pp. 175–6.
85. Harding, *Religious Transformation in South Asia*, pp. 133–5.
86. Webster, *The Dalit Christians*, p. 48.
87. Harding, *Religious Transformation in South Asia*, p. 33.
88. Ibid., pp. 136–40.
89. Hervey De Witt Griswold, "Admission of Village Christians to the Lord's Supper" (n.d.), Burke Library, Union Theological Seminary, New York.
90. David Hardiman, "Purifying the Nation: The Arya Samaj in Gujarat, 1895–1930," *Indian Economic and Social History Review*, Vol. 44, No. 1 (2007), p. 42.
91. Ibid., p. 43.
92. Viswanath, "The Emergence of Authenticity Talk," p. 120.
93. Webster, *The Dalit Christians*, p. 44.
94. Clough, *Social Christianity in the Orient*, pp. 265–6.
95. Ibid., p. 267.
96. Sanneh, *Whose Religion is Christianity?*, p. 18.

Chapter 8

1. Dorothy Clark Wilson, "The Legacy of Ida S. Scudder," *International Bulletin of Missionary Research*, Vol. 11, No. 1 (1987), pp. 24–5.
2. Gandhi develops his understanding of *swadeshi* in his political manifesto *Hind Swaraj*. See Anthony Parel (ed.), *Gandhi: Hind Swaraj and Other Writings* (Cambridge: Cambridge University Press, 2009).
3. Jason Keith Fernandez, *Citizenship in a Caste Polity: Religion, Language, and Belonging in Goa* (Hyderabad: Orient Black Swan, 2020).

4. Sumit Sarkar, *The Swadeshi Movement in Bengal, 1903–1908* (New Delhi: People's Publishing, 1973), p. 303.
5. Ibid., p. 303. In *Hindutva* ideology, Shivaji's defiance and masculinity represented the pursuit of a Hindu Rashtra or kingdom.
6. *Harijan*, December 12, 1936. The quote is from Jon Bonk, *Missions and Money: Affluence as a Missionary Problem—Revisited* (Maryknoll, NY: Orbis, 2006), p. 81.
7. See M. K. Gandhi, *An Autobiography: The Story of My Experiments With Truth* (London: Jonathan Cape, 1966), p. 33.
8. Gail Minault, *The Khilafat Movement: Religious Symbolism and Political Mobilization in India* (New York: Columbia University Press, 1982), p. 11.
9. See Chandra Mallampalli, *Christians and Public Life in Colonial South India, 1863–1937: Contending with Marginality* (London: Routledge Curzon, 2004).
10. Vengal Chakkarai, *Jesus the Avatar* (Madras: Christian Literature Society, 1926). See Schouten's discussion of Chakkarai in Jan Peter Schouten, *Jesus as Guru: The Image of Christ Among Hindus and Christians of India* (New York: Rodopi, 2008), pp. 115–30.
11. M. S. S. Pandian, "Nation as Nostalgia: Ambiguous Spiritual Journeys of Vengal Chakkarai," *Economic and Political Weekly*, Vol. 38, Nos. 51–2 (2003–4), pp. 5357–65.
12. A. J. Appasamy, *Sundar Singh: A Biography* (Cambridge: Lutterworth Press, 1958), p. 189.
13. There were, of course, exceptions to this rule. The ardent Catholic nationalist and theologian Brahmabandhab Upadhyay (1861–1907) espoused a contextualized Catholicism, retaining the customs of the Kulin Brahmin caste from which he hailed. He wore saffron robes, walked barefoot, and called himself a "Hindu-Catholic." See Julius Lipner, *Brahmabandhab Upadhyay: The Life and Thought of a Revolutionary* (New York: Oxford University Press, 1999).
14. *The Catholic Laymen's Directory of India* (Mangalore: C. J. Varkey, 1933), pp. 48, 164.
15. *The Catholic Directory of India for the Year of Our Lord 1969* (New Delhi: St. Paul Publishers, 1969), p. 6.
16. Mallampalli, *Christians and Public Life*, p. 135.
17. Ibid.
18. *Address by Quaid-i-Azam Mohammad Ali Jinnah at Lahore Session of Muslim League, March, 1940* (Islamabad: Directorate of Films and Publishing, Ministry of Information and Broadcasting, Government of Pakistan, 1983), pp. 5–23.
19. See Joya Chatterji, *Bengal Divided: Hindu Communalism and Partition, 1932–1947* (Cambridge: Cambridge University Press, 1994); Joya Chatterji, *Partition's Legacies* (Ranikhet: Permanent Black, 2019); see also Ayesha Jalal, *The Sole Spokesman: Jinnah, the Muslim League, and the Demand for Pakistan* (Cambridge: Cambridge University Press, 1985); Neeti Nair, *Changing Homelands: Hindu Politics and the Partition of India* (Cambridge, MA: Harvard University Press, 2011).
20. *Address by Quaid-i-Azam Mohammad Ali Jinnah*.
21. The quote is taken from Frederick Puckle, "The Gandhi-Jinnah Conversations," Vol. 23, No. 2 (1945), p. 320.
22. He did not approach Christian converts in the same manner, but treated them as denationalized products of inducements.

23. P = Punjab, A = Afghan provinces, K = Kashmir, and S = Sindh. "Stan" simply means "place of."
24. See Urvashi Butalia, *The Other Side of Silence: Voices from the Partition of India* (Durham, NC: Duke University Press, 2000).
25. John O'Brien, *The Unconquered People: The Liberation Journey of an Oppressed Caste* (Oxford: Oxford University Press, 2012), pp. 274–5.
26. Linda Walbridge, *The Christians of Pakistan: The Passion of Bishop John Joseph* (London: Routledge Curzon, 2004), p. 177.
27. Theodore Gabriel, *Christian Citizens in an Islamic State: The Pakistan Experience* (Burlington, VT: Ashgate, 2007), p. 19.
28. Ibid., p. 276.
29. From *Tidings: Bengal, Orissa Baptist Mission*, Vol. 27, No. 3 (1947), p. 6, in Day Missions Library Digital Collection, Yale Divinity School.
30. "A Message of Goodwill to the Country," Proceedings of the Tenth Meeting of the National Christian Council of India, Burma, and Ceylon held at Nagpur, November 26–29, 1946, p. 43.
31. Ibid.
32. Salman Tarik Kureshi, "How Four Christian Votes Made Pakistan Possible," *The Friday Times*, June 1, 2018, updated September 21, 2021, https://www.thefridaytimes.com/how-four-christian-votes-made-pakistan-possible/.
33. Mehak Arshad and Youshib Matthew John, "Pakistan" in Kenneth Ross, Daniel Jeyaraj, and Todd Johnson (eds.), *Christianity in South and Central Asia* (Peabody, MA: Hendrickson, 2019), pp. 108–9.
34. Kureshi, "How Four Christian Votes Made Pakistan Possible."
35. Yaqoob Khan Bangash, "Eyewitness to Perils of Partition," *The News on Sunday*, October 28, 2018, https://www.thenews.com.pk/tns/detail/566571-eyewitness-perils-partition. All subsequent discussions of Forman are derived from this article.
36. Ibid.
37. Ibid.
38. "Partition Affects Catholic Union of India," *Indian Daily Mail*, November 21, 1947, https://eresources.nlb.gov.sg/newspapers/Digitised/Article/indiandailymail19471121-1.2.22.
39. "Death Sentence Passed on a Christian Accused of Blasphemy," *Anglican Communion News Service*, May 11, 1998, https://www.anglicannews.org/news/1998/05/death-sentence-passed-on-a-christian-accused-of-blasphemy.aspx.
40. Walbridge, *The Christians of Pakistan*, pp. 88–9.
41. Altaf Gauhar, "A Short Course on Blasphemy," *Index on Censorship*, Vol. 24, No. 3 (1995), p. 103; John Thor Dahlberg, "Two Pakistani Christians to Hang for Blasphemy," *Washington Post*, February 21, 1995, https://www.washingtonpost.com/archive/politics/1995/02/21/2-pakistani-christians-to-hang-for-blasphemy/9a88f707-b28f-4c12-9651-26a701347edf/.
42. Walbridge, *The Christians of Pakistan*, p. 90.
43. "Asia Bibi: Christian Leaves Pakistan After Blasphemy Acquittal," BBC News, May 8, 2019, https://www.bbc.com/news/world-asia-48198340.

44. "Eight-Year-Old Becomes Youngest Person Charged With Blasphemy in Pakistan," *Guardian*, August 9, 2021, https://www.theguardian.com/global-development/2021/aug/09/eight-year-old-becomes-youngest-person-charged-with-blasphemy-in-pakistan.
45. "Taslima Nasreen Sentenced for Blasphemy," *Times of India*, October 14, 2002, https://timesofindia.indiatimes.com/taslima-nasreen-sentenced-for-blasphemy/articleshow/25104332.cms.
46. See pp. 29–30 at https://www.constituteproject.org/constitution/India_2015.pdf?lang=en.
47. Sebastian Kim, *In Search of Identity: Debates on Religious Conversion in India* (New Delhi: Oxford University Press, 2003), pp. 60–9.
48. K. W. Christopher, "Between Two Worlds: The Predicament of Dalit Christians in Bama's Works," *Journal of Commonwealth Literature*, Vol. 47, No. 1 (2012) p. 10.
49. "State Anti-Conversion Laws in India," Law Library of Congress, LL File No. 2018-016806, updated October 2018, p. 26.
50. Bal Krishna Sharma, "Nepal" in Roger Hedlund et al. (eds.), *The Oxford Encyclopedia of South Asian Christianity* (New Delhi: Oxford University Press, 2011), online version at https://www-oxfordreference-com.ezp-prod1.hul.harvard.edu/view/10.1093/acref/9780198073857.001.0001/acref-9780198073857-e-0702?rskey=bfhxQ0&result=705.
51. Sharma, "Nepal" in Ross, Jeyaraj, and Johnson (eds.), *Christianity in South and Central Asia*, p. 171.
52. Todd Johnson (ed.), *Christianity in Its Global Context, 1970—2020: Society, Religion, and Mission* (South Hamilton, MA: Center for the Study of Global Christianity, Gordon Conwell Theological Seminary, 2013), p. 38.
53. Kate Shellnut, "Nepal Criminalizes Christian Conversion and Evangelism," *Christianity Today*, October 25, 2017, https://www.christianitytoday.com/news/2017/october/nepal-criminalizes-conversion-christianity-evangelism-hindu.html.
54. S. Arasaratnam, "Christians of Ceylon and Nationalist Politics" in G. A. Oddie (ed.), *Religion in South Asia* (New Delhi: Manohar, 1991), p. 238.
55. Ibid., pp. 246–7.
56. "2019 Report on International Religious Freedom: Sri Lanka," Office of International Religious Freedom, US State Department, https://www.state.gov/reports/2019-report-on-international-religious-freedom/sri-lanka/.
57. Thant Myint-U, *The Making of Modern Burma* (Cambridge: Cambridge University Press, 2004), pp. 243–4.
58. Pum Za Mang, "Counteracting Resurgent Buddhist Nationalism and Fostering Interreligious Collaboration in Contemporary Burma" in Richard Fox Young (ed.), *World Christianity and Interfaith Relations* (Minneapolis: Fortress Press, 2022), pp. 13–14.
59. See Sunil Amrith, *Crossing the Bay of Bengal: The Furies of Nature and the Fortunes of Migrants* (Cambridge: Harvard University Press, 2013).
60. Pum Za Mang, "Counteracting Resurgent Buddhist Nationalism," p. 19.

61. See Sonja Thomas, *Privileged Minorities: Syrian Christians, Gender, and Minority Rights in Postcolonial India* (Seattle: University of Washington Press, 2018).
62. Fernandez, *Citizenship in a Caste Polity*, pp. 104–5.

Chapter 9

1. A recent decision of the Madras High Court upheld the notion that caste identities persist in the lives of converts. See "Religious Conversion Won't Change a Person's Caste: Madras HC," *The Wire*, November 26, 2021, https://thewire.in/law/religious-conversion-wont-change-a-persons-caste-madras-hc.
2. Joseph Roberts (ed.), *Caste, in Its Religious and Civil Character, Opposed to Christianity* (London: Longman, Brown, Green, and Longmans, 1847), pp. vi–vii. Roberts, a member of the Royal Asiatic Society who wrote extensively about religious texts, writes: "[T]hose who set themselves in array against [caste], in all or any of its relations, are conferring a boon which looks to both worlds; they are contributing towards an emancipation, not inferior to that of the Negro, who so long in vain lifted up his chains to Britain, and inquired, 'Am I not a man and a brother?'" Ibid., p. 22.
3. Colonial India was divided between three main provinces or "presidencies" directly ruled by the British—Bombay, Bengal, and Madras—and nearly 600 princely states that maintained a degree of control over their own affairs. Many of these princely states, including Travancore and Cochin, would eventually be "indirectly ruled" by the British. The East India Company would station a "resident" in a princely state to "advise" the prince and offer British protection in exchange for loyalty. See Michael Fisher, *Indirect Rule in India: Residents and the Residency System, 1764–1858* (New Delhi: Oxford University Press, 1991).
4. Vinil Baby Paul, "In His Radiance I Would Be Cleared of My Black Color: Life and Songs of Dalit Christians in Colonial Kerala," *Nidan*, Vol. 4, No. 1 (2019), p. 146; see also Robin Jeffrey, *The Decline of Nair Dominance: Society and Politics in Travancore, 1847–1908* (New Delhi: Manohar, 1994), p. 40.
5. Katharine Gerbner, *Christian Slavery: Conversion and Race in the Protestant Atlantic World* (Philadelphia: University of Pennsylvania Press, 2018), p. 13.
6. Ibid., pp. 14–17.
7. Ibid., pp. 40–5.
8. The increasing emphasis on whiteness in law books and vernacular speech, according to Gerbner, coincided with the "growing population of free black Christians." Ibid., pp. 97–8, Chapter 4: "From Christian to White."
9. Rupa Viswanath, *The Pariah Problem: Caste, Religion, and the Social in Modern India* (New York: Columbia University Press, 2014), pp. 100–5, 177.
10. In Bengal, "networks of executive, legal and judicial influence . . . wielded by the planters and native landowners, was in direct competition with the moral, religious and righteous influence nominally wielded by the missionaries." Landlords in Bengal subjected Christian converts to severe violence in order to enforce their labor

demands. See Mou Banerjee, "Questions of Faith: Christianity, Conversion and the Ideological Origins of Political Theology in Colonial India, 1813–1907," PhD thesis, Harvard University, 2018, p. 135.

11. John C. B. Webster, *A Social History of Christianity: Northwest India Since 1800* (New Delhi: Oxford University Press, 2007), p. 177.
12. Rupa Viswanath, "The Emergence of Authenticity Talk and the Giving of Accounts: Conversion as Movement of the Soul in South India, ca.1900," *Comparative Studies in Society and History*, Vol. 55, No. 1 (2015), p. 138–9.
13. Viswanath, *The Pariah Problem*, pp. 56–7.
14. Ibid., pp. 96–7.
15. Ibid., p. 17.
16. Parts of this section of the chapter are adapted from my book *Christians and Public Life in Colonial South India, 1863–1937: Contending with Marginality* (London: Routledge Curzon, 2004).
17. For the background to this debate, see Ramachandra Guha, "The Rise and Fall of the Term 'Harijan,'" *The Telegraph*, June 10, 2017; Robert Frykenberg, "Religion, Nationalism and Hindu Fundamentalism: The Challenge to Indian Unity," *Ethnic Studies Report*, Vol. 11, No. 2 (1993), pp. 125–42.
18. Rudolph Heredia, "No Entry, No Exit: Savarna Aversion Towards Dalit Conversions," *Economic and Political Weekly*, October 9, 2004, pp. 4543–55.
19. Gandhi, "Conversions for Convenience," *Harijan*, June 12, 1937. In Bharatan Kumarappa (ed.), *Christian Missions: Their Place in India* (Ahmedabad: Navajivan Publishing House, 1957), p. 58. Kumarappa's book consists of Gandhi's writings on Christianity and conversion in India. When possible, in the notes I include the original title and date of Gandhi's article, followed by *CMPI* (*Christian Missions: Their Place in India*) and page number.
20. Gandhi, "With an American Clergyman," *Harijan*, March 6, 1937. *CMPI*, p. 113.
21. Ibid.
22. Laura Jenkins, *Religious Freedom and Mass Conversion in India* (Philadelphia: University of Pennsylvania Press, 2019), p. 41.
23. Jarrell Waskom Pickett, *Christian Mass Movements in India: A Study with Recommendations* (New York: Abingdon Press, 1933).
24. Jenkins, *Religious Freedom and Mass Conversion in India*, p. 44.
25. "Dr. Mott's Visit," *Harijan*, December 19, 1936. *CMPI*, p. 174.
26. Gandhi, "Missionary Methods," *Harijan*, December 5, 1937. *CMPI*, p. 147.
27. Gandhi, "The Cow and the Harijan," *Harijan*, March 13, 1937. *CMPI*, p. 58.
28. The philosopher Andrew J. Krzesinski had argued for the existence of a single truth to be found in Catholicism. See Government of India, *The Collected Works of Mahatma Gandhi. Volume 64* (New Delhi: Publications Division, 1969), p. 203.
29. In *Harijan*, March 21, 1996. Quoted in P. L. John Panicker, *Gandhi on Pluralism and Communalism* (New Delhi: ISPCK, 2006), p. 188.
30. "As I have said repeatedly, if untouchability lives Hinduism perishes, and even India perishes; but if untouchability is eradicated from the Hindu heart root and branch,

then Hinduism has a definite message for the world." "Dr. Mott's Visit," *Harijan*, December 19, 1936. *CMPI*, p. 169.

31. Quote taken from Sukumar Muralidharan, "Patriotism Without People: Milestones in the Evolution of the Hindu Nationalist Ideology," *Social Scientist*, Vol. 21, No. 7 (1993), p. 32.
32. For a more detailed critique of Gandhi's attitudes toward race, caste, and untouchability, see Arundhati Roy, "The Doctor and the Saint" in B. R. Ambedkar, *Annihilation of Caste* (New Delhi: Navayana, 2014).
33. Eleanor Zelliot, *From Untouchable to Dalit: Essays on the Ambedkar Movement* (New Delhi: Manohar, 1996), pp. 150–77.
34. Christophe Jaffrelot, *Dr. Ambedkar and Untouchability: Analyzing and Fighting Caste* (New Delhi: Permanent Black, 2005), pp. 36–7.
35. See B. R. Ambedkar, *Writings and Speeches. Volume 5* (Bombay: Education Department, Government of Maharashtra, 1989), pp. 445–8.
36. Cited in Jaffrelot, *Dr. Ambedkar and Untouchability*, p. 121. From Mallampalli, Christians and Public Life in Colonial South India, p. 164.
37. Ambedkar, *Writings and Speeches*, p. 450.
38. B. R. Ambedkar, *Why Go for Conversion?* (New Delhi: Dalit Sahitya Academy, 1981), p. 12.
39. Ibid., p. 17.
40. Cited in Jaffrelot, *Dr. Ambedkar and Untouchability*, p. 120.
41. Arthur McPhee, *The Road to Delhi: J. Waskom Pickett Remembered* (Bangalore: SAIACS Press, 2005), p. 241.
42. Jaffrelot, *Dr. Ambedkar and Untouchability*, p. 122.
43. Nidhin Shobhana, "Caste in the Name of Christ: An Angry Note on the Syrian Christian Caste," *Round Table India: For an Informed Ambedkar Age*, March 21, 2014, https://roundtableindia.co.in/index.php?option=com_content&view=article&id=7301:caste-in-the-name-of-christ-caste-in-the-name-of-christ-an-angry-note-on-the-syrian-christian-caste&catid=119&Itemid=132.
44. Peniel Rajkumar, *Dalit Theology and Dalit Liberation: Problems, Paradigms and Possibilities* (London: Ashgate, 2010), pp. 25–9.
45. Sathianathan Clarke, *Dalits and Christianity: Subaltern Religion and Liberation Theology in India* (New Delhi: Oxford University Press, 1998), pp. 41–3.
46. Clarke, *Dalits and Christianity*, p. 40.
47. Here, he cites the anthropologist L. P. Vidhyarti. Ebenezer Sunder Raj, *The Confusion Called Conversion* (New Delhi: TRACI, 1988), pp. 39, 68–71; see also James Massey, *Roots: A Concise History of Dalits* (New Delhi: ISPCK, 1994).
48. The term "Dalit-Bahujan" encompasses all groups classified as scheduled castes, scheduled tribes, or other backward castes. It combines the term "Dalit," which includes only the untouchables, with the term "Bahujan," a term popularized by Kanshi Ram and meaning literally "majority." Kancha Ilaiah, *Why I Am Not a Hindu* (Calcutta: Samya, 1996), p. viii.
49. Ibid., p. xi.

50. Bama, *Karukku*, translated by Lakshmi Holmstrom (New York: Oxford University Press, 2012).
51. Their strategy of cooption has also included their incorporation of Ambedkar into their "pantheon of great men." See Jaffrelot, Dr. Ambedkar and Untouchability, pp. 145–7.
52. See P. Y. Luke and John B. Carman, *Village Christians and Hindu Culture: A Study of a Rural Church in Andhra Pradesh, South India* (Cambridge: Lutterworth Press, 1969), p. 190.
53. Jangam Chinnaiah, "Desecrating the Sacred Taste: The Making of Gurram Joshua—the Father of Dalit Literature in Telugu," *Indian Economic and Social History Review*, Vol. 51, No. 2 (2014), pp. 177–98.
54. Gurram Joshua, *My Story*. Cited in Mallampalli, Christians and Public Life in Colonial South India, p. 189.
55. Clarke, *Dalits and Christianity*, p. 128.
56. Ibid., p. 102.
57. Ibid., p. 103.
58. Why exactly a belief in Jesus (as distinct from Ellaiyamman) is unable to provide this shield of protection from caste oppression for Clarke's Paraiyars, however, remains unclear.
59. Zoe Sherinian, *Tamil Folk Music as Dalit Liberation Theology* (Bloomington: Indiana University Press, 2014), p. 3.
60. Ibid., p. 55.
61. Ibid., p. 144.
62. Bharatnatyam dance became the province of upper castes, but it originated in the dance performances of *devadasis*, low caste courtesans who danced in temples, at private gatherings, and at court. For a vivid account of their rich tradition and its criminalization during the nineteenth and twentieth centuries, see Davesh Soneji, *Unfinished Gestures: Devadasis, Memory and Modernity in South India* (Chicago: Chicago University Press, 2012).
63. Paulo Freire, *Pedagogy of the Oppressed*, translated by Myrna Bergman Ramos (New York: Continuum, 2005).
64. Arvind P. Nirmal, "Towards a Christian Dalit Theology" in Arvind P. Nirmal (ed.), *A Reader in Dalit Theology* (Madras: Gurukul Lutheran Theological College and Research Institute, 1990), p. 61.
65. James Cone, *The Cross and the Lynching Tree* (Maryknoll, NY: Orbis, 2011), p. 96.
66. Ibid.
67. Roy, "The Doctor and the Saint," p. 21.
68. Nirmal, "Towards a Christian Dalit Theology," pp. 66–7.
69. Jayachitra Lalitha, "Jesus and Ambedkar: Exploring Common Loci for Dalit Theology and Dalit Movements" in Sathianathan Clarke, Deenabandhu Manchala, and Philip Vinod Peacock (eds.), *Dalit Theology in the Twenty-First Century: Discordant Voices, Discerning Pathways* (New Delhi: Oxford University Press, 2010), pp. 124–5.
70. Ramachandra Guha, *India After Gandhi: The History of the World's Largest Democracy* (London: Picador, 2007), pp. 608–9.

71. Stephanie Kramer, "Religious Composition of India," Pew Research Center, September 21, 2021, p. 15, https://www.pewresearch.org/religion/2021/09/21/population-growth-and-religious-composition/.
72. This discussion of SC status for Dalit Christians is taken from Chandra Mallampalli, "Dalit Christian Reservations: Colonial Moorings of a Live Debate," *International Journal of Asian Christianity*, Vol. 1 (2018), pp. 25–44.
73. Laura Jenkins, *Identity and Identification in India: Defining the Disadvantaged* (New York: Routledge, 2003), pp. 114–15.
74. Zoya Hasan, *Politics of Inclusion: Castes, Minorities, and Affirmative Action* (Delhi: Oxford University Press, 2009), pp. 42–3.
75. Gopal Guru, "Rejection of Rejection: Foregrounding Self-Respect" in Gopal Guru (ed.), *Humiliation: Claims and Context* (New Delhi: Oxford University Press, 2009), p. 14.
76. Hasan, *Politics of Inclusion*, p. 47.
77. *Soosai & Others v. Union of India and Others*, 1986, All India Reporter, 733 1985 SCR Supl. (3), pp. 242–3.
78. Ibid., p. 250.
79. See, for instance, *K. Michael Pillai v. J. M. Barthe and Others*, 1917, All India Reporter, Madras, pp. 432–6.
80. Justice Ranganath Mishra, *Report of the National Commission for Linguistic and Religious Minorities* (New Delhi: Government of India, 2007), p. 140.
81. Hasan, *Politics of Inclusion*, p. 215.
82. This view was voiced by Shri Kalka Das, a leader of the Hindu nationalist BJP party, in deliberations of the Rajya Sabha (the upper house of the Indian parliament) in May 1990. Taken from Jose Kananaikil, *Scheduled Caste Converts in Search of Justice: Constitution (Scheduled Castes) Orders (Amendment) Bill, 1990, Part III* (New Delhi: Indian Social Institute, 1993), p. 16.
83. Hasan, *Politics of Inclusion*, p. 218.
84. Jenkins, *Identity and Identification in India*, pp. 134–9.
85. Cited in Mallampalli, *Christians and Public Life in Colonial South India*, p. 160.

Chapter 10

1. Sunday English service at City of Harvest Assemblies of God Church, Bangalore, May 24, 2020 (56:05), https://www.youtube.com/watch?v=A4KsVEW8w3w.
2. Nathan Hatch, *The Democratization of American Christianity* (New Haven: Yale University Press, 1989), p. 217.
3. Buntain, an Assemblies of God pastor of Canadian origin, had founded a hospital and numerous ministries to serve Calcutta's poor. For Thomas's testimony, see https://www.cityharvestagchurch.in/about/shine-thomas/.
4. Chad Bauman, *Pentecostals, Proselytization, and Anti-Christian Violence in Contemporary India* (New York: Oxford University Press, 2015).

5. Sunil Menon, "The Pastors of the Punjab," *India Today*, November 14, 2022. https://www.indiatoday.in/magazine/14-11-2022.
6. Chad Bauman, "Global Megachurch Studies: The State, Evolution, and Maturation of a Field," *The Journal of World Christianity*, Vol. 12, No. 1 (2022), p. 122.
7. Michael Bergunder, *The South Indian Pentecostal Movement in the Twentieth Century* (Grand Rapids: Eerdmans, 2008), pp. 2–3.
8. Ibid., p. 5.
9. Ibid., p. 4; see also Arun Jones, "Faces of Pentecostalism in North India Today," *Society*, Vol. 46 (2009), p. 505.
10. Allen Anderson, *From the Ends of the Earth: Pentecostalism and the Transformation of World Christianity* (New York: Oxford University Press, 2013), p. 19.
11. Ibid., pp. 22–4.
12. Edith Blumhofer, "Consuming Fire: Pandita Ramabai and the Global Pentecostal Impulse" in Ogbu Kalu (ed.), *Interpreting Contemporary Christianity: Global Processes and Local Identities* (Grand Rapids: Eerdmans, 2008), pp. 224–5.
13. "Abrams, Minnie" in Gerald Anderson (ed.), *Biographical Dictionary of Christian Missions* (Grand Rapids: Eerdmans, 1997), p. 3.
14. Gary B. McKee, "Latter Rain Falling in the East: Early Twentieth Century Pentecostalism in India and the Debate Over Speaking in Tongues," *Church History*, Vol. 68, No. 3 (1999), pp. 652–4.
15. See Andrew Walls, *The Missionary Movement in Christian History: Studies in the Transmission of Faith* (Maryknoll, NY: Orbis, 1996), pp. 28–9.
16. We might add to Jones's parallel the story of Sita in the Hindu epic the *Ramayana*. Having been abducted by an evil king and later rescued by her husband Rama, Sita endured a trial by fire to prove her purity.
17. Jones, "Faces of Pentecostalism," p. 508.
18. See Bergunder, *The South Indian Pentecostal Movement*, pp. 23–57.
19. John Carman and Chilkuri Vasantha Rao, *Christians in South Indian Villages, 1959–2009: Decline and Revival in Telangana* (Grand Rapids: Eerdmans, 2014), p. 175.
20. Ibid., p. 177.
21. Thomas George and K. R. Rajani, "Origin and Development of Pentecostalism in India with Special Reference to the Indian Pentecostal Church (IPC): An Expression of Indigenous Spirituality," *International Journal of Humanities and Social Science Research*, Vol. 4, No. 6 (2018), pp. 115–21.
22. Bergunder, *The South Indian Pentecostal Movement*, p. 29.
23. Jones, "Faces of Pentecostalism," p. 504.
24. Joseph Pampackal, "Vincentian Congregation of the Syro-Malabar Church in Kerala (India)," *Vincentiana*, November–December 2011, pp. 417–27.
25. Pius Malekandathil, consultation, July 27, 2020.
26. "William J. Seymour and the Azusa Street Revival," *AG News*, April 4, 1999, https://news.ag.org/Features/William-J-Seymour-and-the-Azusa-Street-Revival.
27. "Azusa Street Revival, 1906–1908," Apostolic Archives International, M. E. Golder Library and Research Center, https://www.apostolicarchives.com/articles/article/8801925/173190.htm.

28. V. V. Thomas, *Dalit Pentecostalism: Spirituality of the Empowered Poor* (Bangalore: Asian Trading Corporation, 2008), pp. 115–27.
29. Ibid., p. 349.
30. Donald Miller, "2006 SSSR Presidential Address—Progressive Pentecostals: The New Face of Christian Social Engagement," *Journal for the Scientific Study of Religion*, Vol. 46, No. 4 (2007), p. 438.
31. Felix Wilfred, *Christians for a Better India* (New Delhi: ISPCK, 2014), p. 145.
32. David Lindenfeld, *World Christianity and Indigenous Experience: A Global History, 1500–2000* (Cambridge: Cambridge University Press, 2021), p. 48. Lindenfeld cites Brian Stanley, *Christianity in the Twentieth Century: A World History* (Princeton: Princeton University Press, 2018), p. 309.
33. Bergunder, *The South Indian Pentecostal Movement*, p. 125.
34. Chad Bauman, "Pentecostals and Interreligious Conflict in India: Proselytization, Marginalization, and Anti-Christian Violence," *PentecoStudies*, Vol. 16, No. 1 (2017), pp. 8–34.
35. Jonathan James, *McDonaldization, Masala McGospel and Om Economics* (New Delhi: Sage, 2010), pp. 104–5.
36. James, *McDonaldization*, p. 106.
37. Steve Brouwer, Paul Gifford, and Susan Rose, *Exporting the American Gospel: Global Christian Fundamentalism* (New York: Routledge, 1996).
38. Nathaniel Roberts, *To Be Cared For: The Power of Conversion and the Foreignness of Belonging in an Indian Slum* (Oakland: University of California Press, 2016), p. 79.
39. Ibid., p. 169.
40. Sarbeswar Sahoo, *Pentecostalism and the Politics of Conversion in India* (Cambridge: Cambridge University Press, 2018), pp. 88–9.
41. Bauman, *Pentecostals, Proselytization, and Anti-Christian Violence*, pp. 76, 114–15.
42. Chad Bauman, *Anti-Christian Violence in India* (Ithaca: Cornell University Press, 2020), p. 209.
43. Laura Jenkins, *Religious Freedom and Mass Conversion in India* (Philadelphia: University of Pennsylvania Press, 2019), pp. 146–7.
44. These figures are drawn from Sahoo, Pentecostalism and the Politics of Conversion in India, p. 5.
45. Each incident is carefully documented in "Hate and Targeted Violence Against Christians in India, Yearly Report 2021," Religious Liberty Commission of the Evangelical Fellowship of India.
46. Ibid., p. 3.
47. For a list of newspaper articles, see Chandra Mallampalli, *Christians and Public Life in Colonial South India, 1863–1937: Contending with Marginality* (London: Routledge Curzon, 2004), p. 4, note 10.
48. "Sonia Gandhi Warns Gujarat Government," *The Hindu*, January 9, 1999.
49. Quote taken from Martha Nussbaum, *The Clash Within: Democracy, Religious Violence, and India's Future* (Cambridge, MA: Harvard University Press, 2007), p. 29.
50. Bauman, *Anti-Christian Violence in India*, p. 147.

51. "Maoist Leader Convicted in Laxmanananda Murder Case," *The Hindu*, October 1, 2013, https://www.thehindu.com/news/national/maoist-leader-convicted-in-laxmananandamurder-case/article5189513.ece; see also Guarav Vivek Bhatnagar, "New Book Reignites Questions Over Alleged Cover-Up of Kandhamal Killings," *The Wire*, December 29, 2017, https://thewire.in/communalism/new-book-reignites-questions-alleged-cover-kandhamal-killings.
52. "They Don't Feel Sorry: Revisiting Kandhamal Ten Years After the Violence Against Christians," Scroll.in, August 9, 2020, https://scroll.in/article/891587/they-dont-feel-sorry-revisiting-kandhamal-10-years-after-the-violence-against-christians.
53. Bauman, *Pentecostals, Proselytization, and Anti-Christian Violence*, p. 53.
54. Zeba Siddiqui, Krishna N. Das, Tommy Wilkes, and Tom Lasseter, "Emboldened by Modi's Ascent, India's Cow Vigilantes Deny Muslims Their Livelihood," Reuters, November 6, 2017, https://www.reuters.com/investigates/special-report/india-politics-religion-cows/#:~:text=Separately%2C%20Reuters%20surveyed%20110%20cow,after%20Modi's%202014%20election%20win.&text = But%20of%20the%20110%20cattle,from%20the%20Hindu%20vigilante%20groups.
55. Jeffrey Gettleman, Kai Schultz, and Suhasini Raj, "In India, Coronavirus Fans Religious Hatred," *New York Times*, April 12, 2020, https://www.nytimes.com/2020/04/12/world/asia/india-coronavirus-muslims-bigotry.html.
56. Goldie Osuri traces current reconversion drives to developments of the late colonial period, in which Hindu activists drew their inspiration from European fascists to advance their agenda. Goldie Osuri, "Foreign Swadeshi," *Frontline*, December 24, 2014, http://www.frontline.in/thenation/foreignswadeshi/article6715524.ece.
57. See Biswamoy Pati, *Identity, Hegemony, Resistance: Towards a Social History of Conversions in Orissa, 1800–2000* (New Delhi: Three Essays, 2003), pp. 3–27.
58. "'Ghar Wapsi' in Idukki, Alappuzha," *The Hindu*, January 19, 2015.
59. Ibid.
60. "Agra Reconversion Row: Uproar in Parliament as Opposition Seeks Prime Minister's Reply; UP Cops on High Alert," *Hindustan Times*, December 11, 2014, http://www.hindustantimes.com/india-news/agra-conversion-that-muslims-say-wasn-t-rocks-parliament-bsp-cong-target-bjp/article1-1295082.aspx.
61. Ibid.
62. This was the claim of Haji Jamiluddin Qureshi, president of the Rashtriya Sarvdaliya Muslim Action Committee. Ibid.
63. See the discussion of *shuddhi* and religious rights of Hindus in Cassie Adcock, *The Limits of Tolerance: Indian Secularism and the Politics of Religious Freedom* (Oxford: Oxford University Press, 2014), pp. 124–6.
64. Gandhi, "Four Questions," *Harijan*, September 25, 1937 in Bharatan Kumarappa (ed.), *Christian Missions: Their Place in India* (Ahmedabad: Navajivan Publishing House, 1957), p. 84.
65. Such laws are in place in Odisha, Madhya Pradesh, Gujarat, Rajasthan, Chhattisgarh, and Himachal Pradesh.
66. "Project Hindutva," *Frontline*, December 22, 2014.

Conclusion

1. Ananya Chakravarti, *Empire of the Apostles: Religion,* Accommodatio, *and the Imagination of Empire in Early Modern Brazil and India* (New Delhi: Oxford University Press, 2018), p. 58.
2. For an excellent summary of missionary contributions to print culture in South India, see A. R. Venkatachalapathy, *The Province of the Book: Scholars, Scribes, and Scribblers in Colonial Tamilnadu* (Ranikhet: Permanent Black, 2012), pp. 5–15.
3. Siddhartha Deb, "They Are Manufacturing Foreigners: How India Disenfranchises Muslims," *New York Times*, September 15, 2021, https://www.nytimes.com/2021/09/15/magazine/india-assam-muslims.html.

Glossary

Accommodatio—Policy of cultural adaptation observed by the Jesuits.

Adivasi—"Original inhabitants," designating the tribal peoples of mainland India.

Agraharam—In villages, the areas where Brahmins reside.

Ammans—Blood-taking goddesses.

Ashraf—Honorable or noble; a class of high-born Muslims.

Avarna—Literally, "without caste."

Avatar—Literally, "descent" of the Hindu deity Vishnu (the "preserver") into the world.

Azaan—Evening calls to prayer in Islam.

Batleli—Pejorative word in Marathi for a convert (female) with overtones of anti-nationalism, and betrayal of community and society.

Bhadralok—Respectable or upper middle-class people in Bengali society.

Bhakti—Devotion to a Hindu deity.

Bidat—Religious innovations not taught in the Qur'an.

Brahmacharya—Usually a practice in which celibate male youths study the Veda under a teacher.

Cadjan—Palmyra leaves, often used for manuscripts.

Cartaz—Pass or license required at Portuguese ports.

Cutcherry—District administrative office; may also refer to a less refined or less pure version of Tamil.

Dalit—Broken or oppressed; the name given to those formerly called "untouchables."

Degredado—Exiled convict (Portuguese).

Descendentes—Indian-born persons of Portuguese descent (also *casados*).

Devi—Goddess.

Dharma—Duty as defined by caste, or a righteous order.

Dharmashastras—Hindu legal treatises.

Din-i-Ilahi—"Religion of God" instituted by the emperor Akbar.

Dvija—"Twice-born"; a term applied especially to Brahmins who have undergone initiation (*upanayana*).

Estado da India—Portuguese state in India.

Fakirs—Itinerant Muslim holy men

Farangi—"Franks," aliens, Westerners, or foreigners.

Farman—Royal invitation or decree.

Ghar Wapsi—"Homecoming" or reconversion to Hinduism from another religion.

Gnosis—Secret knowledge that liberates the soul.

Gurdwara—Sikh place of worship.

Hijra—Eunuch or member of a transgender or intersex community.

Hindutva—Literally, "Hindu-ness," or the pursuit of an officially Hindu nation.

Hypostasis—Union of divine and human qualities, attributed to Christ.

Ibadat-Khana—Akbar's House of Worship, in which he hosted interreligious dialogues.

Idjtihad—Independent judgment in Islam.

Izzat—Honor, reputation, or prestige (in Punjabi society).

Jacoba—Jacobite Christians.

Jagir—Land grant.

Jati—Birth group, or sub-caste.

Kalimah—Concise Islamic creed.

Kanganies—Middlemen who recruited indentured laborers.

Kattanars—Pastors and priests in Syro-Malabar Christian communities.

Khadi—Homespun cloth, advocated in Gandhi's anticolonial campaign.

Kothi—Imperial mansion.

Kuravanci—Dance drama employing a classical Tamil literary form.

Madrasa—School for Qur'anic instruction.

Mahachakra—Great wheel, representing a righteous political order.

Mahdi—Apocalyptic, messianic figure in Shi'i tradition.

Mandala—Literally, "circle," in some cases representing a realm of spiritual order.

Maths (also "mutts")—Schools for Hindu religious instruction.

Metran—Metropolitan of the Syrian Orthodox Church.

Mlecchas—Barbarians; uncultured foreigners or persons far removed from or ungoverned by Vedic orthodoxy.

Moksha (also "mukti")—Liberation from the cycle of birth and death.

Moors—Iberian designation for Muslims.

Muhajirs—Migrants (Arabic); the designation for Muslim migrants to Pakistan.

Mullah—Muslim scholar, teacher, or religious leader.

Munazara—Classical tradition of debate in Islam.

Munshi—Language teacher, amanuensis, or clerk.

Naturais—Portuguese designation for Indian converts to Catholicism.

Nestorian—Theology associated with Eastern, non-Roman, or non-Chalcedonian Christology.

Oru olai—Notion of "one pot" developed in the theology of Theophilus Appavoo.

Padroado Real—Papal patronage extended to the Portuguese state in ecclesiastical affairs.

Palem—Separate spaces where Dalits reside.

Pandita—Learned female teacher or pandit.

Paraiyar—Particular community of Dalits in South India, mostly landless laborers.

Parangi (farangi) kulam—Kinship group of foreigners.

Paraparan—Sanskrit word for the supreme or transcendent God.

Pariah—Untouchable (now considered offensive).

Pattangattis—Caste leaders of the Paravas, a fisherman caste of South India.

Pazhayakur—Syrian Catholics.

Pirs—Muslim cult saints.

Poonal—Sacred thread worn over the shoulder by men.

Prasad—Food devotionally offered to a divinity.

Propaganda Fide—Missionary establishment commissioned directly by the pope.

Prosopon—"Person" (Greek); the notion that Christ's two natures were united in one person.

Puja—Hindu devotional ceremony offered on behalf of a divinity.

Puranas—Genre of Sanskrit literature.

Puranika—Reciter or teacher of the Puranas.

Purdah—Seclusion of women.

Putirs—Village priests in Ao Naga society.

Reconquista—Reconquest of the Iberian Peninsula, involving the expulsion of Moors and Jews.

Reinois—European-born Portuguese.

Sadhu—Ascetic, often tied to a particular religious order.

Salaf—Early, "golden age" of Islam.

Samasthanam—Little or minor kingdom.

Sannyasi—World renouncer.

Sati—Immolation of widows.

Shastras—Sacred Hindu scriptures.

Sheristadar—High-ranking clerk.

Shirk—Polytheism or idolatry.

Shraddha—Ritual offering for the deceased; Hindu funeral rites.

Shuddhi—Purification rite.

Sola scriptura—Protestant belief in the authority of the Bible alone for Christian faith and practice.

Swadeshi—Of one's own country, or indigenous.

Swaraj—Home rule.

Tat tvam asi—"That art thou"; an assertion of the soul's identity with the divine or impersonal; absolute, found in the Upanishads.

Tevan—Tamil term derived from the Sanskrit word referring to various deities of the Hindu pantheon (singular, *tevar*).

Theotokos—Mother of God.

Tirtha (also "theertham")—Holy water.

Tsungrem—Spirit in Naga cosmology.

Ulema—Muslim scholars of law and theology.

Upanayana—Ritual of caste initiation for Brahmins in particular.

Varna—"Color" or "rank"; any of the four main orders or rankings of the caste system.

Varnashrama dharma—Fourfold caste order of Hinduism and the Hindu stages of life.

Verenigde Oost-Indische Compagnie—Dutch East India Company or VOC.

Zenana—Separate living quarters for women.

Bibliography

Adcock, Cassie, *The Limits of Tolerance: Indian Secularism and the Politics of Religious Freedom* (Oxford: Oxford University Press, 2014).

Address by Quaid-i-Azam Mohammad Ali Jinnah at Lahore Session of Muslim League, March, 1940 (Islamabad: Directorate of Films and Publishing, Ministry of Information and Broadcasting, Government of Pakistan, 1983).

Agmon, Danna, "Conflicts in the Context of Conversion: French Jesuits and Tamil Religious Intermediaries in Madurai, India" in Anand Amaldass and Ines Županov (eds.), *Intercultural Encounter and the Jesuit Mission in South Asia (16th–18th Centuries)* (Bangalore: Asian Trading Corporation, 2014), pp. 179–98.

Agmon, Danna, "Striking Pondicherry: Religious Disputes and French Authority in an Indian Colony of the Ancien Regime," *French Historical Studies*, Vol. 37, No. 3 (2014), pp. 437–67.

Ahmed, Rafiuddin, "Muslim–Christian Polemics and Religious Reform in Nineteenth-Century Bengal: Munshi Meheru'llah of Jessore" in Kenneth Jones (ed.), *Religious Controversy in British India: Dialogues in South Asian Languages* (Albany: State University of New York Press, 1992), pp. 93–122.

Ali, Halimah Mohamed, "The Story of Caste: Old and New," *Journal of Social Sciences*, Vol. 5, No. 4 (2016), pp. 444–59.

Ambedkar, *Why Go for Conversion?* (New Delhi: Dalit Sahitya Academy, 1981).

Ambedkar, *Writings and Speeches. Volume 5* (Bombay: Education Department, Government of Maharashtra, 1989).

Amrith, Sunil, *Crossing the Bay of Bengal: The Furies of Nature and the Fortunes of Migrants* (Cambridge, MA: Harvard University Press, 2013).

Anderson, Allan, "Pandita Ramabai, the Mukti Revival and Global Pentecostalism," *Transformation*, Vol. 23, No. 1 (2006), pp. 37–48.

Anderson, Allan, *From the Ends of the Earth: Pentecostalism and the Transformation of World Christianity* (New York: Oxford University Press, 2013).

Anderson, Benedict, *Imagined Communities: Reflections on the Origin and Spread of Nationalism* (London: Verso, 1983).

Anderson, Gerald (ed.), *Biographical Dictionary of Christian Missions* (Grand Rapids: Eerdmans, 1997).

Anjam, Faraz, "Islam and Hinduism in the Eyes of Early European Travellers to India," *Journal of the Research Society of Pakistan*, Vol. 44, No. 2 (2007), pp. 55–70.

Appasamy, A. J., *Sundar Singh: A Biography* (Cambridge: Lutterworth Press, 1958).

Aprem, Mar, *Nestorian Missions* (Trichur: Mar Narsai Press, 1976).

Arasaratnam, S., "Christians of Ceylon and Nationalist Politics" in G. A. Oddie (ed.), *Religion in South Asia* (New Delhi: Manohar, 1991), pp. 163–82.

Arasaratnam, S., *Ceylon and the Dutch, 1600–1800: External Influences and Internal Change in Early Modern Sri Lanka* (Aldershot: Variorum, 1996).

Arshad, Mehak and John, Youshib Matthew, "Pakistan" in Kenneth Ross, Daniel Jeyaraj, and Todd Johnson (eds.), *Christianity in South and Central Asia* (Peabody, MA: Hendrickson, 2019), pp. 107–18.

Asad, Talal, *Genealogies of Religion: Discipline and Reasons of Power in Christianity and Islam* (Baltimore: Johns Hopkins University Press, 1993).

Asad, Talal, "Comments on Conversion" in Peter van der Veer (ed.), *Conversion to Modernities: The Globalization of Christianity* (New York: Routledge, 1996), pp. 263–73.

Asher, Catherine B. and Cynthia Talbot, *India Before Europe* (Cambridge: Cambridge University Press, 2006).

Assayag, Jackie, *At the Confluence of Two Rivers: Muslims and Hindus in South India* (New Delhi: Manohar, 2004).

Azariah, "The Indian Church and the Depressed Classes," *Guardian*, May 21, 1936, p. 325.

Badauni, *Muntakhab-ut-Tawarikh. Volume II*, translated by W. H. Lowe (Calcutta: J. W. Thomas Baptist Mission Press, 1884).

Bailey, Gauvin Alexander, *The Jesuits and the Grand Mogul: Renaissance Art and the Imperial Court of India, 1580–1630* (Washington, DC: Smithsonian Institute, 1998).

Balkenhol, Markus, "Silence and the Politics of Compassion: Commemorating Slavery in the Netherlands," *Social Anthropology*, Vol. 24, No. 3 (2016), pp. 278–93.

Ballhatchet, Kenneth, *Caste, Class and Catholicism in India, 1789–1914* (Richmond: Curzon Press, 1998).

Bama, *Karukku*, translated by Lakshmi Holmstrom (New York: Oxford University Press, 2012).

Banchoff, Thomas and José Casanova, *The Jesuits and Globalization: Historical Legacies and Contemporary Challenges* (Washington, DC: Georgetown University Press, 2016).

Banerjee, Mou, "The Tale of the Tailor: Munshi Mohammed Meherullah and Muslim–Christian Apologetics in Bengal, 1885–1907," *South Asian Studies*, Vol. 33, No. 2 (2017), pp. 122–36.

Banerjee, Mou, "Questions of Faith: Christianity, Conversion and the Ideological Origins of Political Theology in Colonial India, 1813–1907," PhD thesis, Harvard University, 2018.

Bangash, Yaqoob Khan, "Eyewitness to Perils of Partition," *The News on Sunday*, October 28, 2018, https://www.thenews.com.pk/tns/detail/566571-eyewitness-perils-partition

Bashir, Hassan, *Europe and the Eastern Other: Comparative Perspectives on Politics, Religion and Culture Before the Enlightenment* (Lanham: Lexington Books, 2013).

Bauman, Chad, "Global Megachurch Studies: The State, Evolution, and Maturation of a Field," *The Journal of World Christianity*, Vol. 12, No. 1 (2022), pp. 113–79.

Bauman, Chad, *Pentecostals, Proselytization, and Anti-Christian Violence in Contemporary India* (New York: Oxford University Press, 2015).

Bauman, Chad, "Pentecostals and Interreligious Conflict in India: Proselytization, Marginalization, and Anti-Christian Violence," *PentecoStudies*, Vol. 16, No. 1 (2017), pp. 8–34.

Bauman, Chad, *Anti-Christian Violence in India* (Ithaca: Cornell University Press, 2020).

Bauman, Zygmut, *Legislators and Interpreters: On Modernity, Post-Modernity, and Intellectuals* (Ithaca: Cornell University Press, 1987).

Bayly, C. A., *Empire and Information: Intelligence Gathering and Social Communication in India 1780–1870* (Cambridge: Cambridge University Press, 1996).

Bayly, Susan, "Hindu Kingship and the Origin of Community: Religion, State and Society in Kerala, 1750–1850," *Modern Asian Studies*, Vol. 18, No. 2 (1984), pp. 177–213.

Bayly, Susan, *Saints, Goddesses and Kings: Muslims and Christians in South Indian Society, 1700–1900* (Cambridge: Cambridge University Press, 1989).
Bays, Daniel, *A New History of Christianity in China* (Chichester: Wiley-Blackwell, 2012).
Bebbington, David, *Evangelicalism in Modern Britain: A History from the 1730s to the 1980s* (London: Routledge, 1989).
Beckert, Sven, *Empire of Cotton: A Global History* (New York: Alfred Knopf, 2014).
Berger, Peter, "Pluralism, Protestantization, and the Voluntary Principle" in Thomas Banchoff (ed.), *Democracy and the New Religious Pluralism* (Oxford: Oxford University Press, 2007), pp. 19–30.
Bergunder, Michael, *The South Indian Pentecostal Movement in the Twentieth Century* (Grand Rapids: Eerdmans, 2008).
Beteille, "Hinduism in Danger?," *The Hindu*, January 3, 2003, http://www.thehindu.com/thehindu/2003/01/03/stories/2003010300101000.htm
Beveridge, H. (translator), *The Akbar Nama of Abu-l-Fazl* (New Delhi: Asiatic Society of Bengal, 1972).
Bloomer, Kristin, *Possessed by the Virgin: Hinduism, Roman Catholicism, and Marian Possession in South India* (New York: Oxford University Press, 2018).
Blumhofer, Edith, "Consuming Fire: Pandita Ramabai and the Global Pentecostal Impulse" in Ogbu Kalu (ed.), *Interpreting Contemporary Christianity: Global Processes and Local Identities* (Grand Rapids: Eerdmans, 2008), pp. 207–37.
Blumhofer, Edith, "Pandita Ramabai and Indian Christianity: A North American Perspective" (unpublished manuscript, n.d.), p. 7.
Bonk, Jon, *Missions and Money: Affluence as a Missionary Problem—Revisited* (Maryknoll, NY: Orbis, 2006).
Boyd, Robin, *India and the Latin Captivity of the Church: The Cultural Context of the Gospel* (Cambridge: Cambridge University Press, 1974).
Brouwer, Steve, Paul Gifford, and Susan Rose, *Exporting the American Gospel: Global Christian Fundamentalism* (New York: Routledge, 1996).
Brown, Leslie, *The Indian Christians of St. Thomas* (Cambridge: Cambridge University Press, 1956).
Buchanan, Claudius, *Memoir of the Expediency of an Ecclesiastical Establishment for British India; Both as the Means of Perpetuating the Christian Religion Among our Own Countrymen; and as a Foundation for the Ultimate Civilization of the Natives* (London: T. Cadell and W. Davies, 1805).
Buchanan, Claudius, *An Apology for Promoting Christianity in India* (London: Nathaniel Willis, 1812).
Buchanan, Claudius, *Memoir of the Expediency of an Ecclesiastical Establishment for British India* (Oxford: Oxford University Press, 1813).
Bugge, Henriette, *Mission and Tamil Society: Social and Religious Change in South India, 1840–1900* (Richmond: Curzon Press, 1994).
Burton, Antoinette, "Colonial Encounters in Late Victorian England: Pandita Ramabai at Cheltenham and Wantage, 1883–6," *Feminist Review*, Vol. 49 (1995), pp. 29–49.
Butalia, Urvashi, *The Other Side of Silence: Voices from the Partition of India* (Durham, NC: Duke University Press, 2000).
Cabrita, Joel, David Maxwell, and Emma Wild-Wood (eds.), *Relocating World Christianity: Interdisciplinary Studies in Universal and Local Expressions of the Christian Faith* (Leiden: Brill, 2017).

Cagle, Hugh, *Assembling the Tropics: Science and Medicine in Portugal's Empire, 1450–1700* (Cambridge: Cambridge University Press, 2018).

Caldwell, Robert, *Records of the Early History of the Tinnevelly Mission* (Madras: Higginbotham and Co., 1881).

Camps, Arnulf, *An Unpublished Letter of Father Christoval de Vega, SJ: Its Importance for the History of the Second Mission to the Mughal Court and for the Knowledge of the Religion of Akbar* (Cairo: Franciscan Centre for Christian Oriental Studies, 1956).

Carey, William, *An Inquiry into the Obligations of Christians to Use Means for the Conversion of the Heathen* (London: Hodder and Stoughton, 1891).

Carman, John and Chilkuri Vasantha Rao, *Christians in South Indian Villages, 1959–2009: Decline and Revival in Telangana* (Grand Rapids: Eerdmans, 2014).

Carson, Penelope, *The East India Company and Religion, 1698–1858* (Woodbridge: Boydell Press, 2012).

Casanova, José, "The Jesuits Through the Prism of Globalization: Globalization Through a Jesuit Prism" in Thomas Banchoff and José Casanova (eds.), *The Jesuits and Globalization: Historical Legacies and Contemporary Challenges* (Washington, DC: Georgetown University Press, 2016), pp. 261–85.

The Catholic Directory of India for the Year of Our Lord 1969 (New Delhi: St. Paul Publishers, 1969).

The Catholic Laymen's Directory of India (Mangalore: C. J. Varkey, 1933).

Chakkarai, Vengal, *Jesus the Avatar* (Madras: Christian Literature Society, 1926).

Chakrabarty, Uma, *Rewriting History: The Life and Times of Pandita Ramabai* (New Delhi: Zubaan, 2013).

Chakravarti, Ananya, "The Many Faces of Baltasar da Costa: *Imitatio* and *Accommodatio* in the Seventeenth Century Madurai Mission," *Etnografica*, Vol. 18, No. 1 (2014), pp. 135–58.

Chakravarti, Ananya, *Empire of the Apostles: Religion, Accommodatio, and the Imagination of Empire in Early Modern Brazil and India* (New Delhi: Oxford University Press, 2018).

Chandra, Sudhir, "Hindu Conservatism in the Nineteenth Century," *Economic and Political Weekly*, Vol. 5, No. 50 (1970), pp. 2003–7.

Chandra, Uday, "Liberalism and Its Other: The Politics of Primitivism in Colonial and Postcolonial Indian Law," *Law and History Review*, Vol. 47, No. 1 (2013), pp. 135–68.

Chatterjee, Nandini, *The Making of Indian Secularism: Empire, Law and Christianity, 1830–1960* (London and New York: Palgrave Macmillan, 2011).

Chatterjee, Partha, *The Nation and Its Fragments: Colonial and Postcolonial Histories* (Princeton: Princeton University Press, 1994).

Chatterji, Joya, *Bengal Divided: Hindu Communalism and Partition, 1932–1947* (Cambridge: Cambridge University Press, 1994).

Chatterji, Joya, *Partition's Legacies* (Ranikhet: Permanent Black, 2019).

Chinnaiah, Jangam, "Desecrating the Sacred Taste: The Making of Gurram Joshua—the Father of Dalit Literature in Telugu," *Indian Economic and Social History Review*, Vol. 51, No. 2 (2014), pp. 177–98.

Christopher, K. W., "Between Two Worlds: The Predicament of Dalit Christians in Bama's Works," *Journal of Commonwealth Literature*, Vol. 47, No. 1 (2012), pp. 7–25.

Clark, Mary Mead, *A Corner in India* (Philadelphia: American Baptist Publication Society, 1907).

Clarke, Sathianathan, *Dalits and Christianity: Subaltern Religion and Liberation Theology in India* (New Delhi: Oxford University Press, 1998).

Clooney, Francis, *Western Jesuit Scholars in India: Tracing Their Paths: Reassessing Their Goals* (Leiden: Brill, 2020).

Clough, John E., *Social Christianity in the Orient: The Story of a Man, a Mission and a Movement* (New York: Macmillan, 1914).

Cohn, Bernard, *Colonialism and Its Forms of Knowledge: The British in India* (Princeton: Princeton University Press, 1996).

Coleridge, Henry James, *The Life and Letters of Francis Xavier. Volume I* (London: Burns and Oates, 1872).

Comaroff, John L. and Jean Comaroff, *Of Revelation and Revolution: The Dialectics of Modernity on a South African Frontier* (Chicago: University of Chicago Press, 1997).

Cone, James, *The Cross and the Lynching Tree* (Maryknoll, NY: Orbis, 2011).

Converts from the Government and Missionary Colleges and Schools (Calcutta: Baptist Mission Press, 1852).

Copland, Ian, "The Limits of Hegemony: Elite Responses to Nineteenth-Century Imperial and Missionary Acculturation Strategies in India," *Comparative Studies in Society and History*, Vol. 49, No. 3 (2007), pp. 637–65.

Correia-Afonso, John (ed.), *Letters from the Mughal Court: The First Jesuit Mission to Akbar, 1580–83* (St. Louis: Institute of Jesuit Sources, 1981).

Cox, Jeffrey, *Imperial Fault Lines: Christianity and Colonial Power in India, 1818–1940* (Stanford: Stanford University Press, 2002).

Dahlberg, John Thor, "Two Pakistani Christians to Hang for Blasphemy," *Washington Post*, February 21, 1995, https://www.washingtonpost.com/archive/politics/1995/02/21/2-pakistani-christians-to-hang-for-blasphemy/9a88f707-b28f-4c12-9651-26a701347edf/

Dale, Stephen, "Communal Relations in Pre-Modern India: 16th-Century Kerala," *Journal of the Social and Economic History of the Orient*, Vol. 16, Nos. 2–3 (1973), pp. 319–27.

Dale, Stephen, *Islamic Society on the South Asian Frontier: The Māppiḷas of Malabar, 1498–1922* (Oxford: Clarendon Press, 1980).

Dalrymple, William, *White Mughals: Love and Betrayal in Eighteenth-Century India* (New York: Penguin, 2003).

Dalrymple, William, *The Last Mughal: The Fall of a Dynasty: Delhi, 1857* (New York: Alfred A. Knopf, 2007).

Dalrymple, William, *The Anarchy: The East India Company, Corporate Violence, and the Pillage of an Empire* (New York: Bloomsbury, 2019).

Dandekar, Deepra, *The Subhedar's Son: A Narrative of Brahmin–Christian Conversion from Nineteenth-Century Maharashtra* (New York: Oxford University Press, 2019).

Dandekar, Deepra, *Baba Padmanji: Pioneering Vernacular Christianity in Colonial India* (London: Routledge, 2020).

Daughrity, Dyron and Jesudas Athyal, *Understanding World Christianity: India* (Minneapolis: Fortress Press, 2016).

Deb, Siddhartha, "'They Are Manufacturing Foreigners': How India Disenfranchises Muslims," *New York Times*, September 15, 2021, https://www.nytimes.com/2021/09/15/magazine/india-assam-muslims.html

Delhi Historians' Group, *Communalisation of Education: The History Textbooks Controversy* (New Delhi: Delhi Historians' Group, 2001).

Dirks, Nicolas, *Castes of Mind: Colonialism and the Making of Modern India* (Princeton: Princeton University Press, 2002).

Djadi, Youcef, "Max Weber, Islam and Modernity," *Max Weber Studies*, Vol. 11, No. 1 (2011), pp. 35–47.

Doss, M. Christu, "Repainting Religious Landscape: Economics of Conversion and Making Rice Christians in Colonial South India (1781–1880)," *Studies in History*, Vol. 30, No. 2 (2014), pp. 179–200.

Downs, Frederick, "Christianity as a Tribal Response to Change in Northeast India," *Missiology*, Vol. 8, No. 4 (1980), pp. 407–16.

Downs, Frederick, *The History of Christianity in India. Volume V, Part 5: North East India in the Nineteenth and Twentieth Centuries* (Bangalore: Church History Association of India, 1992).

Downs, Frederick, *Essays on Christianity in Northeast India* (New Delhi: Indus, 1994).

Dubois, J. A., *Description of the Character, Manners and Customs of the People of India and of Their Institutions, Religious and Civil* [translation from the French] (London: Longman, Hurst, Rees, Orme, and Brown, 1817).

Dubois, J. A., *Letters on the State of Christianity in India, in Which the Conversion of the Hindus is Considered as Impracticable* (London: London: A. R. Spottiswoode, 1823).

Dubois, J. A., *Hindu Manners, Customs and Ceremonies* (Oxford: Clarendon Press, 1906).

Eaton, Richard, *The Rise of Islam and the Bengal Frontier, 1204–1760* (Berkeley: University of California Press, 1993).

Eaton, Richard, "Comparative History as World History: Religious Conversion in Modern India" in Richard Eaton (ed.), *Essays on Islam and Indian History* (New Delhi: Oxford University Press, 2000), pp. 243–71.

Eaton, Richard, "Rethinking Religious Divides," *Journal of Asian Studies*, Vol. 73, No. 2 (2014), pp. 305–8.

Eaton, Richard, *India in the Persianate Age, 1000–1765* (Berkeley: University of California Press, 2019).

Ebeling, Sascha and Margherita Trento, "From Jesuit Missionary to Tamil *Pulavar*: Constanzo Gioseffo Beschi SJ (1680–1747), 'The Great Heroic Sage'" in Tiziana Leucci, Claude Markovits, and Marie Fourcade (eds.), *L'Inde et l'Italie: Rencontres Intellectuelles, Politiques et Artistiques* (Paris: Éditions de l'École des Hautes Études en Sciences Sociales, 2018), pp. 53–90.

Embree, Ainslee, *Utopias in Conflict: Religion and Nationalism in Modern India* (Berkeley: University of California Press, 1990).

Fernandez, Jason Keith, *Citizenship in a Caste Polity: Religion, Language and Belonging in Goa* (Hyderabad: Orient Black Swan, 2020).

Fischer-Tiné, Harald, "Third Stream Orientalism? J. N. Farquhar, the Indian YMCA's Literature Department and the Representation of South Asian Cultures and Religions (c.1910–1940)," *Journal of Asian Studies*, Vol. 79, No. 3 (2020), pp. 659–83.

Fisher, Michael, *Indirect Rule in India: Residents and the Residency System, 1764–1858* (New Delhi: Oxford University Press, 1991).

Fisher, Michael, *The Inordinately Strange Life of Dyce Sombre, Victorian Anglo-Indian MP and Chancery "Lunatic"* (London: Hurst and Co., 2010).

Flores, Jorge, *Unwanted Neighbors: The Mughals, the Portuguese, and Their Frontier Zones* (New Delhi: Oxford University Press, 2018).

Forrester, Duncan B., *Caste and Christianity: Attitudes and Policies on Caste of Anglo-Saxon Protestant Missions in India* (London: Curzon Press, 1980).

Foster, William, "The East India Company, 1600–1740" in H. H. Dodwell (ed.), *The Cambridge History of India. Volume V, British India* (Cambridge: Cambridge University Press, 1929), pp. 76–116.

Fraser, Hastings, *Memoir and Correspondence of General James Stuart Fraser of the Madras Army* (London: Whiting and Co., 1885).

Freire, Paulo *Pedagogy of the Oppressed*, translated by Myrna Bergman Ramos (New York: Continuum, 2005).

Frykenberg, Robert Eric, "Religion, Nationalism and Hindu Fundamentalism: The Challenge to Indian Unity," *Ethnic Studies Report*, Vol. 11, No. 2 (1993), pp. 125–42.

Frykenberg, Robert Eric (ed.), *Pandita Ramabai's America: Conditions of Life in the United States*, translated by Kshitija Gomes (Grand Rapids: Eerdmans, 2003).

Frykenberg, Robert Eric, "Avarna and Adivasi Christians and Missions: A Paradigm for Understanding Christian Movements in India," *International Bulletin of Missionary Research*, Vol. 32, No. 1 (2008), pp. 14–20.

Frykenberg, Robert Eric, *Christianity in India: From Beginnings to the Present* (Oxford and New York: Oxford University Press, 2008).

Fuller, C. J., "Kerala Christians and the Caste System," *Man*, Vol. 11, No. 1 (1976), pp. 53–70.

Gabriel, Reuben Louis, "Migration, Human Dislocation and the Good News: The Case of the Parsees in Nineteenth-Century Western India," *Mission Studies*, Vol. 31 (2014), pp. 206–26.

Gabriel, Theodore, *Christian Citizens in an Islamic State: The Pakistan Experience* (Burlington, VT: Ashgate, 2007).

Gandhi, M. K., *Christian Missions: Their Place in India* [*CMPI*], edited by Bharatan Kumarappa (Ahmedabad: Navajivan Publishing House, 1957).

Gandhi, M. K., "With an American Clergyman," *Harijan*, March 6, 1937. *CMPI*, p. 113.

Gandhi, M. K., "The Cow and the Harijan," *Harijan*, March 13, 1937. *CMPI*, p. 58.

Gandhi, M. K., "Conversions for Convenience," *Harijan*, June 12, 1937.

Gandhi, M. K., "Four Questions," *Harijan*, September 25, 1937. *CMPI*, p. 84.

Gandhi, M. K., "Missionary Methods," *Harijan*, December 5, 1937. *CMPI*, p. 147.

Gandhi, M. K., *An Autobiography: The Story of My Experiments With Truth* (London: Jonathan Cape, 1966).

Gascoigne, Bamber, *The Great Moghuls* (London: Jonathan Cape, 1987).

Gauhar, Altaf, "A Short Course on Blasphemy," *Index on Censorship*, Vol. 24, No. 3 (1995), pp. 99–106.

George, Thomas and K. R. Rajani, "Origin and Development of Pentecostalism in India with Special Reference to the Indian Pentecostal Church (IPC): An Expression of Indigenous Spirituality," *International Journal of Humanities and Social Science Research*, Vol. 4, No. 6 (2018), pp. 115–21.

Gerbner, Katharine, *Christian Slavery: Conversion and Race in the Protestant Atlantic World* (Philadelphia: University of Pennsylvania Press, 2018).

Gettleman, Jeffrey, Kai Schultz, and Suhasini Raj, "In India, Coronavirus Fans Religious Hatred," *New York Times*, April 12, 2020, https://www.nytimes.com/2020/04/12/world/asia/india-coronavirus-muslims-bigotry.html

Ghosh, Amitav, *The Nutmeg's Curse: Parables for a Planet in Crisis* (Chicago: University of Chicago Press, 2021).

Gidla, Sujatha, *Ants Among Elephants: An Untouchable Family and the Making of Modern India* (New York: Farrar, Straus and Giroux, 2017).

Gill, Navyug, "Limits of Conversion: Caste, Labor and the Question of Emancipation," *Journal of Asian Studies*, Vol. 78, No. 1 (2019), pp. 3–22.

Gilmartin, David and Bruce Lawrence (eds.), *Beyond Turk and Hindu: Rethinking Religious Identities in Islamicate South Asia* (Gainsville: University Press of Florida, 2000).

Goh, Robbie, *Protestant Christianity in the Indian Diaspora: Abjected Identities, Evangelical Relations, and Pentecostal Visions* (Albany: SUNY Press, 2018).

Goldie, Osuri, *Religious Freedom in India: Sovereignty and (Anti)Conversion* (London: Routledge, 2013).

Goldie, Osuri, "Foreign Swadeshi," *Frontline*, December 24, 2014, https://frontline.thehindu.com/the-nation/foreign-swadeshi/article6715524.ece

Gordon, Stewart, *Robes of Honor: Khilat in Pre-Colonial and Colonial India* (Delhi: Oxford University Press, 2003).

Government of India, *The Collected Works of Mahatma Gandhi. Volume 64* (New Delhi: Publications Division, 1969).

Grafe, Hugald, *History of Christianity in India. Volume IV, Part 2: Tamilnadu in the Nineteenth and Twentieth Centuries* (Bangalore: Church History Association of India, 1990).

Green, Nile, *Bombay Islam: The Religious Economy of the West Indian Ocean, 1840–1915* (Cambridge: Cambridge University Press, 2011).

Green, Nile, *Sufism: A Global History* (Chichester: Wiley-Blackwell, 2012).

Green, Nile, *Terrains of Exchange: Religious Economies of Global Islam* (New York: Oxford University Press, 2015).

Gregory, Brad, *The Unintended Reformation* (Cambridge, MA: Harvard University Press, 2012).

Guha, Ramachandra, *India After Gandhi: History of the World's Largest Democracy* (London: Picador, 2007).

Guha, Ramachandra, "The Rise and Fall of the Term 'Harijan,'" *The Telegraph*, June 10, 2017.

Guru, Gopal, "Rejection of Rejection: Foregrounding Self Respect" in Gopal Guru (ed.), *Humiliation: Claims and Context* (New Delhi: Oxford University Press, 2009), pp. 209–25.

Guyot-Rechard, Berenice, *Shadow States: India, China and the Himalayas, 1910–1962* (Cambridge: Cambridge University Press, 2017).

Hardgrave, Robert, "The Breast-Cloth Controversy: Caste Consciousness and Social Change in Southern Travancore," *Indian Social and Economic History Review*, Vol. 5, No. 2 (1968), pp. 171–87.

Hardgrave, Robert, *The Nadars of Tamilnad: The Political Culture of a Community in Change* (Berkeley: University of California Press, 1969).

Hardiman, David, "Purifying the Nation: The Arya Samaj in Gujarat, 1895–1930," *Indian Economic and Social History Review*, Vol. 44, No. 1 (2007), pp. 41–65.

Harding, Christopher, *Religious Transformation in South Asia: The Meanings of Conversion in Colonial Punjab* (New York: Oxford University Press, 2008).

Harper, Susan Billington, "Azariah, Vedanayagam Samuel (1874–1945)" in Gerald H. Anderson (ed.), *Biographical Dictionary of Christian Missions* (Grand Rapids: Eerdmans, 1999), pp. 35–6.

Harper, Susan Billington, *In the Shadow of the Mahatma: Bishop V. S. Azariah and the Travails of Christianity in British India* (Grand Rapids and Richmond: Eerdmans and Curzon Press, 2000).

Harris, Paul William, "The Social Dimensions of Foreign Missions: Emma Rauschenbusch Clough and Social Gospel Ideology" in Wendy J. Deichmann Edwards and Carolyn De Swarte Gifford (eds.), *Gender and the Social Gospel* (Urbana: University of Illinois Press, 2003), pp. 87–102.

Hasan, Zoya, *Politics of Inclusion: Castes, Minorities, and Affirmative Action* (Delhi: Oxford University Press, 2009).

Hastie, William, *Hindu Idolatry and English Enlightenment: Six Letters Addressed to Educated Hindus Containing a Practical Discussion of Hinduism* (Calcutta: Thacker, Spink and C., 1883).

Hatch, Nathan, *The Democratization of American Christianity* (New Haven: Yale University Press, 1989).

Hedlund, Roger, *Christianity Is Indian: The Emergence of an Indigenous Community* (Mylapore: MIIS, 2000).

Hedlund, Roger, *Christianity Made in India: From Apostle Thomas to Mother Theresa* (unpublished draft, n.d.).

Henn, Alexander, *Hindu–Catholic Encounters in Goa: Religion, Colonialism and Modernity* (Bloomington: Indiana University Press, 2014).

Heredia, Rudolph, "No Entry, No Exit: Savarna Aversion Towards Dalit Conversions," *Economic and Political Weekly*, October 9, 2004, pp. 4543–55.

Horton, Robin, "African Conversion" in Brendon Carmody, *Religious Conversion: An African Perspective* (Lusaka: Gadsden, 2015), pp. 45–54.

Hough, James, *History of Christianity in India. Volume II* (London: Seeley and Burnside, 1839).

Hoyland, J. S. (translator), *The Commentary of Father Monserrate on His Journey to the Court of Akbar* (London: Oxford University Press, 1922).

Hudson, Dennis, "Tamil Hindu Responses to Protestants: Nineteenth Century Literati in Jaffna and Tinnevelly," in Steven Kaplan (ed.), *Indigenous Responses to Western Christianity* (New York: New York University Press, 1995), pp. 95–123.

Hudson, Dennis, *Protestant Origins in India: Tamil Evangelical Christians, 1706–1835* (Grand Rapids and Richmond: Eerdmans and Curzon Press, 2000).

Hughes, T. P., "The Wahhabis of Najd and India" in *Church Missionary Intelligencer and Record: A Monthly Journal of Missionary Record* (London: Seeley, Jackson, and Halliday, 1878), p. 98, 160.

Hutton, John Henry, *The Sema Nagas* (London: Macmillan and Co., 1921).

Ilaiah, Kancha, *Why I Am Not a Hindu* (Calcutta: Samya, 1996).

Inden, Ronald, "Orientalist Constructions of India," *Modern Asian Studies*, Vol. 20, No. 3 (1986), pp. 401–46.

Israel, Hephzibah, *Religious Transactions in Colonial South India: Language, Translation, and the Making of Protestant Identity* (New York: Palgrave Macmillan, 2011).

Jaffrelot, Christophe, *Dr. Ambedkar and Untouchability: Analyzing and Fighting Caste* (New Delhi: Permanent Black, 2005).

Jaffrelot, Christophe, *Hindu Nationalism: A Reader* (Princeton: Princeton University Press, 2007).

Jaffrelot, Christophe and Laurence Louer, *The Islamic Connection: South Asia and the Gulf* (New Delhi: Penguin Random House, 2017).

Jain, Rupam and Tom Lasseter, "By Rewriting History, Hindu Nationalists Aim to Assert their Dominance Over India," Reuters, March 6, 2018, https://www.reuters.com/investigates/special-report/india-modi-culture/

Jalal, Ayesha, *The Sole Spokesman: Jinnah, the Muslim League, and the Demand for Pakistan* (Cambridge: Cambridge University Press, 1985).

James, Jonathan, *McDonaldization, Masala McGospel and Om Economics* (New Delhi: Sage, 2010).

Jarric, Pierre, *Akbar and the Jesuits: An Account of the Jesuit Missions to Akbar's Court*, translated by C. H. Payne (New Delhi and New York: Asian Educational Services and Harper and Brothers, 1996 [1926]).

Jeffrey, Robin, *The Decline of Nair Dominance: Society and Politics in Travancore, 1847–1908* (New Delhi: Manohar, 1994).

Jenkins, Laura, *Identity and Identification in India: Defining the Disadvantaged* (New York: Routledge, 2003).

Jenkins, Laura, *Religious Freedom and Mass Conversion in India* (Philadelphia: University of Pennsylvania Press, 2019).

Jenkins, Philip, *The Next Christendom: The Coming of Global Christianity* (New York: Oxford University Press, 2002).

Jeyaraj, Daniel, *Inkulturation in Tranquebar: der Beitrag der frühen dänisch-halleschen Mission zum Werden einer indisch-einheimischen Kirche (1706–1730)* (Erlangen: Verlag der Ev.-Luth. Mission Erlangen, 1996).

Jeyaraj, Daniel, *Bartholomaeus Ziegenbalg, The Father of Modern Protestant Missions: An Indian Assessment* (New Delhi and Chennai: ISPCK and Gurukal Theological College and Research Institute, 2006).

Jeyaraj, Daniel, *A German Exploration of Indian Society: Ziegenbalg's "Malabarian Heathenism." An Annotated English Translation with an Introduction and a Glossary* (New Delhi and Chennai: Mylapore Institute for Indigenous Studies and ISPCK, 2006).

John, Stanley, *Transnational Religious Organization and Practice: A Contextual Analysis of Kerala Pentecostal Churches in Kuwait* (Leiden: Brill, 2018).

Jones, Arun, "Faces of Pentecostalism in North India Today," *Society*, Vol. 46 (2009), pp. 504–9.

Jones, Arun, *Missionary Christianity and Local Religion: American Evangelicalism in North India, 1836–1870* (Waco, TX: Baylor University Press, 2017).

Jones, Kenneth (ed.), *Religious Controversy in British India: Dialogues in South Asian Languages* (Albany: State University of New York Press, 1992).

Jones, Kenneth, *Socio-Religious Reform Movements in British India* (Cambridge: Cambridge University Press, 1994).

Joseph, Clara, *Christianity in India: An Anti-Colonial Turn* (London: Routledge, 2019).

Kananaikil, Jose, *Scheduled Caste Converts in Search of Justice: Constitution (Scheduled Castes) Orders (Amendment) Bill, 1990, Part III* (New Delhi: Indian Social Institute, 1993).

Kent, Eliza, *Converting Women: Gender and Protestant Christianity in Colonial South India* (New York: Oxford University Press, 2004).

Kent, Eliza, "'Mass Movements' in South India, 1877–1936" in Dennis Washburn and Kevin Reinhart (eds.), *Converting Cultures: Religion, Ideology and Transformations of Modernity* (Leiden: Brill, 2007), pp. 367–94.

Kesavan, B. S., *History of Printing and Publishing in India* (National Book Trust, 1988).

Keune, Jon, "The Intra- and Inter-Religious Conversions of Nilakantha Goreh," *Journal of Hindu-Christian Studies*, Vol. 17 (2004), pp. 45–54.

Khan, Sayyid Ahmad, *The Causes of the Indian Revolt* (Benares: Medical Hall Press, 1873).

Kim, Sebastian, *In Search of Identity: Debates on Religious Conversion in India* (New Delhi: Oxford University Press, 2003).

Klijn, Albertus F. J., *The Acts of Thomas: Introduction, Text and Commentary* (Leiden: Brill, 2003).

Kling, David, *A History of Christian Conversion* (New York: Oxford University Press, 2020).

Kolsky, Elizabeth, "The Colonial Rule of Law and the Legal Regime of Exception: Frontier 'Fanaticism' and State Violence in British India," *American Historical Review*, Vol. 120, No. 4 (2015), pp. 1218–46.

Kopf, David, *British Orientalism and the Bengal Renaissance: Dynamics of Indian Modernization, 1773–1835* (Calcutta: Firma K. L. Mukhopadyay, 1969).

Kopf, David, *The Brahmo Samaj and the Shaping of Modern India* (Princeton: Princeton University Press, 1979).

Kosambi, Meera (translator), *Pandita Ramabai Through Her Own Words* (New Delhi: Oxford University Press, 2000).

Kosambi, Meera (translator), *Pandita Ramabai's American Encounter: The Peoples of the United States* (Bloomington: Indiana University Press, 2003).

Kosambi, Meera (translator), *Returning the American Gaze: Situating Pandita Ramabai's American Encounter* (Bloomington: Indiana University Press, 2003).

Koschorke, Klaus, "Polycentric Structures in the History of World Christianity" in Klaus Koschorke and Adrian Hermann (eds.), *Polycentric Structures in the History of World Christianity* (Wiesbaden: Harrassowitz, 2014), pp. 435–56.

Koschorke, Klaus, *Polycentric Structures in the History of World Christianity* (Wiesbaden: Harrassowitz, 2014).

Koschorke, Klaus, *Owned and Conducted Entirely by the Native Christian Community: Der "christian Patriot" und die Indigen-Christliche Presse im Kolonialen Indien Um 1900* (Wiesbaden: Harrassowitz, 2019).

Kramer, Stephanie, "Religious Composition of India," Pew Research Center, September 21, 2021, p. 15, https://www.pewresearch.org/religion/2021/09/21/population-gro wth-and-religious-composition/

Kuczkiewicz-Fraś, Agnieszka, "Akbar the Great (1542–1605) and Christianity: Between Religion and Politics," *Orientalia Christiana Cracoviensia*, Vol. 3 (2011), pp. 75–89.

Kuczkiewicz-Fraś, Agnieszka (ed.), *Islamicate Traditions in South Asia: Themes from Culture and History* (New Delhi: Manohar, 2013).

Kulke, Hermann and Deitmar Rothermund, *A History of India*, 4th edition (London: Routledge, 2004).

Kumarappa, Bharatan (ed.), *Christian Missions: Their Place in India* (Ahmedabad: Navajivan Publishing House, 1957).

Kuruvilla, K. P., *The Word Became Flesh: A Christological Paradigm for Doing Theology in India* (New Delhi: ISPCK, 2002).

Lalitha, Jayachitra, "Jesus and Ambedkar: Exploring Common Loci for Dalit Theology and Dalit Movements" in Sathianathan Clarke, Deenabandhu Manchala, and Philip Vinod Peacock (eds.), *Dalit Theology in the Twenty-First Century: Discordant Voices, Discerning Pathways* (New Delhi: Oxford University Press, 2010), pp. 124–47.

Larson, Gerald, "Partition: 'The Pulsing Heart that Grieved,'" *Journal of Asian Studies*, Vol. 73, No. 1 (2014), pp. 5–8.

Lee, Joel, "Lal Beg Underground: The Passing of an 'Untouchable' God" in Knut Jacobsen et al. (eds.), *Objects of Worship in South Asian Religion: Forms, Practices and Meanings* (New York: Routledge, 2014), pp. 143–62.

Lee, Joel, *Deceptive Majority: Dalits, Hinduism, and Underground Religion* (Cambridge: Cambridge University Press, 2021).

Lepore, Jill, *These Truths: A History of the United States* (New York: W. W. Norton and Co., 2019).

Lindenfeld, David, *World Christianity and Indigenous Experience: A Global History, 1500–2000* (Cambridge: Cambridge University Press, 2021).

Lipner, Julius, *Brahmabandhab Upadhyay: The Life and Thought of a Revolutionary* (New York: Oxford University Press, 1999).

Longkumer, Arkotong, "Along Kingdom's Highway: The Proliferation of Christianity, Education, and Print Amongst the Nagas in Northeast India," *Contemporary South Asia*, Vol. 27, No. 2 (2019), pp. 160–78.

Luke, P. Y. and John B. Carman, *Village Christians and Hindu Culture: A Study of a Rural Church in Andhra Pradesh South India* (Cambridge: Lutterworth Press, 1969).

Macfarlane, Iris, "Akbar and the Jesuits," *History Today*, Vol. 20, No. 7 (1970), p. 466.

Maclagan, Edward, *The Jesuits and the Great Mogul* (London: Burns Oates and Washbourne, 1932).

Madhaviah, A., *Clarinda: A Historical Novel*, 2nd edition (Tirunelveli: Nambar Vattam, 1992 [1915]).

Mahaprashasta, Ajoy Ashirwad, "Wahhabi Impact," *Frontline*, November 29, 2013, https://www.frontline.in/cover-story/wahhabi-impact/article5338336.ece

Makdisi, Ussama, *Artillery of Heaven: American Missionaries and the Failed Conversion of the Middle East* (Ithaca: Cornell University Press, 2008).

Maleikal, Jose, *Standstill Utopias: Dalits Encountering Christianity* (New Delhi: ISPCK, 2017).

Malekandathil, Pius, "St. Thomas Christians: A Historical Analysis of their Origins and Development up to the 9th Century AD" in Bosco Puthur (ed.), *St. Thomas Christians and Nambudiris, Jews and Sangam Literature: A Historical Appraisal* (Kochi: LRC Publications, 2003), pp. 1–48

Malekandathil, Pius, "Religious Rhetoric, Mercantile Strategies and a Revolting Community: A Study on the Conflicts Between the St. Thomas Christians and the Portuguese *Padroado*" in Rameshwar Prasad Bahuguna (ed.), *Negotiating Religion: Perspectives from Indian History* (New Delhi: Manohar, 2012), pp. 1–48.

Malekandathil, Pius, "Debate the Apostolate of St. Thomas in Kerala: A Response," *Journal of St. Thomas Christians*, Vol. 29, No. 2 (2018), pp. 32–58.

Malhotra, Rajiv and Aravindan Neelakandan, *Breaking India: Western Interventions in Dravidian and Dalit Faultlines* (Princeton: Infinity Foundation, 2011).

Mallampalli, Chandra, *Christians and Public Life in Colonial South India, 1863–1937: Contending with Marginality* (London: Routledge Curzon, 2004).

Mallampalli, Chandra, *Race, Religion and Law in Colonial India: Trials of an Interracial Family* (Cambridge: Cambridge University Press, 2011).

Mallampalli, Chandra, "Dalit Christian Reservations: Colonial Moorings of a Live Debate," *International Journal of Asian Christianity*, Vol. 1 (2018), pp. 25–44.

Mang, Pum Za, "Counteracting Resurgent Buddhist Nationalism and Fostering Interreligious Collaboration in Contemporary Burma" in Richard Fox Young (ed.),

World Christianity and Interfaith Relations (Minneapolis: Fortress Press, 2022), pp. 13-33.

Mani, Lata, *Contentious Traditions: The Debate on Sati in Colonial India* (New Delhi: Oxford University Press, 1998).

Massey, James, *Roots: A Concise History of Dalits* (New Delhi: ISPCK, 1994).

Masuzawa, Tomoko, *The Invention of World Religions: Or, How European Universalism Was Preserved in the Language of Pluralism* (Chicago: University of Chicago Press, 2005).

Maxwell, David, *African Gifts of the Spirit: Pentecostalism and the Rise of Zimbabwean Transnational Religious Movement* (Athens: Ohio University Press, 2006).

McGoldrick, Sylvester, *Bellary Mission* (Buckingham: Franciscan Missionary Union, 1960).

McKee, Gary B., "Latter Rain Falling in the East: Early Twentieth Century Pentecostalism in India and the Debate over Speaking in Tongues," *Church History*, Vol. 68, No. 3 (1999), pp. 648-65.

McPhee, Arthur, *The Road to Delhi: J. Waskom Pickett Remembered* (Bangalore: SAIACS Press, 2005).

Mendiratta, Sidh Daniel Losa, "Framing Identity: Bombay's East Indian Community and Its Indo-Portuguese Historical Background, 1737-1928," *Anais de Historia de Alem-Mar*, Vol. 18 (2017), pp. 207-48.

Menon, Sunil. "The Pastors of the Punjab," *India Today*, November 14, 2022. https://www.indiatoday.in/magazine/14-11-2022.

Metcalf, Thomas R., *Ideologies of the Raj* (Cambridge: Cambridge University Press, 1995).

Miller, Donald, "2006 SSSR Presidential Address—Progressive Pentecostals: The New Face of Christian Social Engagement," *Journal for the Scientific Study of Religion*, Vol. 46, No. 4 (2007), pp. 435-45.

Miller, Roland, "The Dynamics of Religious Coexistence in Kerala: Muslims, Christians, and Hindus" in Yvonne Haddad and Wadi Haddad (eds.), *Christian-Muslim Encounters* (Gainesville: University Press of Florida, 1995), pp. 263-84.

Minault, Gail, *The Khilafat Movement: Religious Symbolism and Political Mobilization in India* (New York: Columbia University Press, 1982).

Mishra, Justice Ranganath, *Report of the National Commission for Linguistic and Religious Minorities* (New Delhi: Government of India, 2007).

Misra, Sangamitra, "The Nature of Colonial Intervention in the Naga Hills, 1840-80," *Economic and Political Weekly*, Vol. 33, No. 51 (1998), pp. 3273-9.

Mocherla, Ashok Kumar, "We Called Her Peddamma: Caste, Gender, and Missionary Medicine in Guntur, 1880-1930," *International Journal of Asian Christianity*, Vol. 3 (2020), pp. 69-84.

Moffett, Samuel Hugh, *A History of Christianity in Asia. Volume I: Beginnings to 1500* (Maryknoll, NY: Orbis, 2004).

Moffett, Samuel Hugh, *A History of Christianity in Asia. Volume II: 1500-1900* (Maryknoll, NY: Orbis, 2005).

Mohan, Jyoti, *Claiming India: French Scholars and the Preoccupation with India During the Nineteenth Century* (New Delhi: Sage, 2018).

Moin, Azfar, *The Millennial Sovereign: Sacred Kingship and Sainthood in Islam* (New York: Columbia University Press, 2014).

Monier-Williams, Monier, *The Study of Sanskrit in Relation to Missionary Work in India* (London: Williams and Norgate, 1861).

Mosse, David, *The Saint in the Banyan Tree: Christianity and Caste Society in India* (Berkeley: University of California Press, 2012).

Mullen, Roderick, *The Expansion of Christianity: A Gazetteer of Its First Three Centuries* (Leiden: Brill, 2003).

Muralidharan, Sukumar, "Patriotism Without People, Milestones in the Evolution of the Hindu Nationalist Ideology," *Social Scientist*, Vol. 21, No. 7 (1993), p. 32.

Myint-U, Thant, *The Making of Modern Burma* (Cambridge: Cambridge University Press, 2004).

Nair, Neeti, *Changing Homelands: Hindu Politics and the Partition of India* (Cambridge, MA: Harvard University Press, 2011).

Nandy, Ashis, "The Politics of Secularism and the Recovery of Tolerance," *Alternatives*, Vol. 13, No. 2 (1988), pp. 177–94.

Neill, Stephen, *Colonialism and Christian Missions* (New York: McGraw Hill, 1966).

Neill, Stephen, *A History of Christianity in India: Beginnings to AD 1707* (Cambridge: Cambridge University Press, 1984).

Nirmal, Arvind P. (ed.), *A Reader in Dalit Theology* (Madras: Gurukul Lutheran Theological College and Research Institute, 1990).

Noll, Mark, *The New Shape of World Christianity: How American Experience Reflects Global Faith* (Downers Grove, IL: Intervarsity Press, 2009).

Numark, Mitch, "Translating *Dharma*: Scottish Missionary Orientalists and the Politics of Religious Understanding in Nineteenth Century Bombay," *Journal of Asian Studies*, Vol. 7, No. 2 (2011), pp. 471–500.

Numark, Mitch, "Hebrew School in 19th Century Bombay: Protestant Missionaries, Cochin Jews, and the Hebraization of India's Bene Israel Community," *Modern Asian Studies*, Vol. 46, No. 6 (2012), pp. 1765–8.

Nussbaum, Martha, *The Clash Within: Democracy, Religious Violence, and India's Future* (Cambridge, MA: Harvard University Press, 2007).

Oberoi, Harjot, *The Construction of Religious Boundaries: Culture, Identity and Diversity in the Sikh Tradition* (New Delhi: Oxford University Press, 1997).

O'Brien, John, *The Unconquered People: The Liberation Journey of an Oppressed Caste* (Oxford: Oxford University Press, 2012).

Oddie, Geoffrey, *Hindu and Christian in South-East India* (London: Curzon Press, 1991).

Oddie, Geoffrey, "Orientalism and British Protestant Missionary Constructions of India in the Nineteenth Century," *South Asia*, New Series, Vol. 18, No. 2 (1994), pp. 27–42.

Oddie, Geoffrey, "Constructing 'Hinduism': The Impact of the Protestant Missionary Movement on Hindu Self-Understanding" in Robert Eric Frykenberg (ed.), *Christians and Missionaries in India: Cross-cultural Communication Since 1500* (Grand Rapids and London: Eerdmans and Routledge, 2003), pp. 166–93.

Oddie, Geoffrey, *Imagined Hinduism: British Protestant Missionary Constructions of Hinduism, 1793–1900* (New Delhi: Sage, 2006).

Omvedt, Gail, "Adivasis, Culture and Modes of Production in India," *Critical Asian Studies*, Vol. 12, No. 1 (1980), pp. 15–22.

Osella, Filipo and Caroline Osella, "Islamism and Social Reform in Kerala, South India," *Modern Asian Studies*, Vol. 42, Nos. 2–3 (2008), pp. 317–19.

Osuri, Goldie, *Religious Freedom in India: Sovereignty and (Anti)Conversion* (London: Routledge, 2013).

Pachuau, Joy, *Being Mizo: Identity and Belonging in Northeast India* (New Delhi: Oxford University Press, 2014).

Pachuau, Joy, "Christianity in Mizoram: An Ethnography" in Pius Malekandathil, Joy Pachuau, and Tanika Sarkar (eds.), *Christianity in Indian History: Issues of Culture, Power and Knowledge* (New Delhi: Primus Books, 2016), pp. 46–57.

Pachuau, Lalsangkima, "Mizo Sakhua in Transition: Change and Continuity from Primal Religion to Christianity," *Missiology: An International Review*, Vol. 34, No. 1 (2006), pp. 41–57.

Pachuau, Lalsangkima, "'Assistants' or 'Leaders'? The Contributions of Early Native Christian Converts in North-East India" in Pius Malekandathil, Joy Pachuau, and Tanika Sarkar (eds.), *Christianity in Indian History: Issues of Culture, Power and Knowledge* (New Delhi: Primus Books, 2016), pp. 102–18.

Pampackal, Joseph, "Vincentian Congregation of the Syro-Malabar Church in Kerala (India)," *Vincentiana*, November–December 2011, pp. 417–27.

Pandey, Gyanendra, *The Construction of Communalism in Colonial North India* (New Delhi: Oxford University Press, 1990).

Pandian, M. S. S., "Nation as Nostalgia: Ambiguous Spiritual Journeys of Vengal Chakkarai," *Economic and Political Weekly*, Vol. 38, Nos. 51–2 (2003–4), pp. 5357–65.

Pandian, M. S. S., "Caste in Tamil Nadu: A History of Nadar Censorship," *Economic and Political Weekly*, Vol. 48, No. 3 (2013), pp. 12–14.

Panicker, P. L. John, *Gandhi on Pluralism and Communalism* (New Delhi: ISPCK, 2006).

Parel, Anthony (ed.), *Gandhi: Hind Swaraj and Other Writings* (Cambridge: Cambridge University Press, 2009).

Pati, Biswamoy, *Identity, Hegemony, Resistance: Towards a Social History of Conversions in Orissa, 1800–2000* (New Delhi: Three Essays, 2003).

Paul, Vinil Baby, "In His Radiance I Would be Cleared of My Black Color: Life and Songs of Dalit Christians in Colonial Kerala," *Nidan*, Vol. 4, No. 1 (2019), pp. 141–58.

Payne, C. H. (translator), *Akbar and the Jesuits: An account of the Jesuit Missions to the Court of Akbar by Father Pierre du Jarric* (New York: Harper and Brothers, 1926).

Peacock, Philip Vinod, "Now We Will Have the Dalit Perspective," *Ecumenical Review*, Vol. 72, No. 1 (2020), pp. 116–27.

Pearson, Harlan, *Islamic Reform and Revival in Nineteenth-Century India: The Tariqah-i-Muhammadiyah* (New Delhi: Yoda Press, 2008).

Pearson, M. N., *The Portuguese in India* (Cambridge: Cambridge University Press, 1987).

Pearson, M. N., *The Indian Ocean* (London: Routledge, 2003).

Pechilis, Karen and Selva Raj (eds.), *South Asian Religions: Tradition and Today* (London: Routledge, 2013).

Pennington, Brian, *Was Hinduism Invented? Britons, Indians and the Colonial Construction of Religion* (New York: Oxford University Press, 2005).

Peterson, Derek, *The Invention of Religion: Rethinking Belief in Politics and History* (New Brunswick: Rutgers University Press, 2002).

Peterson, Indira, "*Bethlehem Kuṟavañci* of Vedanayaka Sastri of Tanjore: The Cultural Discourses of an Early Nineteenth-Century Tamil Christian Poem" in Judith Brown and Robert Frykenberg (eds.), *Christians, Cultural Interactions, and India's Religious Traditions* (London and Grand Rapids: Routledge and Curzon Press, 2002), pp. 9–36.

Pickett, J. Waskom, *Christian Mass Movements in India: A Study With Recommendations* (New York: Abingdon Press, 1933).

Pitts, Jennifer, *A Turn to Empire: The Rise of Imperial Liberalism in Britain and France* (Princeton: Princeton University Press, 2006).

Podipara, Placid, "Hindu in Culture, Christian in Religion, Oriental in Worship" in George Menachery (ed.), *The St. Thomas Christian Encyclopedia of India. Volume 2* (Madras: P. N. K. Press, 1973).

Podipara, Placid, *The Thomas Christians and Their Syriac Treasures* (Alleppey, India: Prakasam Publications, 1974).

Pollock, Sheldon, "The Cosmopolitan Vernacular," *Journal of Asian Studies*, Vol. 57, No. 1 (1998), pp. 6–37.

Pollock, Sheldon, *Language of Gods in the World of Men: Sanskrit, Culture and Power in Premodern India* (Berkeley: University of California Press, 2006).

Powell, Avril, "Maulana Rahmat Allah Kairanawi and Muslim-Christian Controversy in India in the Mid-19th Century," *Journal of the Royal Asiatic Society of Great Britain and Ireland*, Vol. 108, No. 1 (1976), pp. 42–63.

Powell, Avril, *Muslims and Missionaries in Pre-Mutiny India* (Richmond: Curzon Press, 1993).

Powell, Avril, "Creating Christian Community in Early Nineteenth-Century Agra" in Richard Young (ed.), *India and the Indianness of Christianity: Essays on Understanding—Historical, Theological, and Bibliographical—In Honor of Robert Frykenberg* (Grand Rapids: Eerdmans, 2009), pp. 82–107.

Price, Pamela, *Kingship and Political Practice in Colonial India* (Cambridge: Cambridge University Press, 1996).

Puckle, Frederick, "The Gandhi-Jinnah Conversations," *Foreign Affairs*, Vol. 23, No. 2 (1945), pp. 318–23.

Raichaudhuri, Tapan, *Europe Reconsidered: Perceptions of the West in Nineteenth-Century Bengal* (Oxford: Oxford University Press, 1988).

Raj, Ebenezer Sunder, *The Confusion Called Conversion* (New Delhi: TRACI, 1988).

Raj, Selva, "The Quest for a Balanced Representation of South Asian Religions in World Religions Textbooks," *Religious Studies Review*, Vol. 31, Nos. 1–2 (2005), pp. 14–16.

Rajkumar, Peniel, *Dalit Theology and Dalit Liberation: Problems, Paradigms and Possibilities* (London: Ashgate, 2010).

Ramabai, Pandita, *A Testimony of Our Inexhaustible Treasure*, 12th edition (Kendgoan: Mukti Mission, 2001).

Ramaswamy, Sumathy, *Passions of the Tongue: Language Devotion in Tamil India, 1891–1970* (Berkeley: University of California Press, 1997).

Rappaport, Erica, *A Thirst for Empire: How Tea Shaped the Modern World* (Princeton: Princeton University Press, 2017).

Ravenstein, Ernest George (translator), Alvaro Velho, and Joao de Sa, *A Journal of the First Voyage of Vasco da Gama, 1497–1499* (London: Hakluyt Society, 1898).

Reddy, Srinivas, *Raya: Krishnadevaraya of Vijayanagara* (New Delhi: Juggernaut Books, 2020).

Ricci, Ronit, *Islam Translated: Literature, Conversion and the Arabic Cosmopolis in South and Southeast Asia* (Chicago: University of Chicago Press, 2011).

Richard, H. L., *Following Jesus in the Hindu Context: The Intriguing Implications of N. V. Tilak's Life and Thought* (Pasadena: William Carey Library, 1998).

Robbins, Joel, "On the Paradoxes of Global Pentecostalism and the Perils of Continuity Thinking," *Religion*, Vol. 33 (2003), pp. 221–31.

Robbins, Joel, "Continuity Thinking and the Problem of Christian Culture," *Current Anthropology*, Vol. 48, No. 1 (2007), pp. 5–17.

Robert, Dana, "Shifting Southward: Global Christianity Since 1945," *International Bulletin of Missionary Research*, Vol. 24, No. 2 (2000), pp. 50–8.

Robert, Dana, *Christian Mission: How Christianity Became a World Religion* (Malden, MA: Wiley-Blackwell, 2009).

Roberts, Joseph (ed.), *Caste, in Its Religious and Civil Character, Opposed to Christianity* (London: Longman, Brown, Green, and Longmans, 1847).

Roberts, Nathaniel, "Is Conversion a 'Colonization of Consciousness'?," *Anthropological Theory*, Vol. 12, No. 3 (2012), pp. 271–94.

Roberts, Nathaniel, *To Be Cared For: The Power of Conversion and the Foreignness of Belonging in an Indian Slum* (Oakland: University of California Press, 2016).

Robinson, Rowena, *Christians of India* (New Delhi: Sage, 2003).

Rosa, Susan, "Seventeenth-Century Catholic Polemic and the Rise of Cultural Rationalism: An Example from the Empire," *Journal of the History of Ideas*, Vol. 57, No. 1 (1996), pp. 87–107.

Roy, Arundati, "The Doctor and the Saint" in S. Anand (ed.), *The Annihilation of Caste: The Annotated Critical Edition* (New Delhi: Navayana, 2014), pp. 15–169.

Roychaudhury, Adrija, "When Mughal Rulers Borrowed from Christianity to Produce Exquisite Artwork," *Indian Express*, December 23, 2016, https://indianexpress.com/article/research/when-mughal-rulers-borrowed-from-christianity-to-produce-exquisite-art-works-4440469/

Rubiés, Joan-Pau, *Travel and Ethnology in the Renaissance: South India through European Eyes, 1250–1625* (Cambridge: Cambridge University Press, 2000).

Rubiés, Joan-Pau, "From Antiquarianism to Philosophical History: India, China, and the World History of Religion in European Thought" in Peter Miller and François Louis (eds.), *Antiquarianism and Intellectual Life in Europe and China, 1500–1800* (Ann Arbor: University of Michigan Press, 2012), pp. 313–67.

Rubiés, Joan-Pau, "Ethnography and Cultural Translation in the Early Modern Missions," *Studies in Church History*, Vol. 53 (2017), pp. 272–310.

Ryrie, Alec, "Protestantism as a Historical Category," *Transactions of the Royal Historical Society*, Vol. 26 (2016), pp. 59–77.

Ryrie, Alec, *Protestants: The Faith that Made the Modern World* (New York: Viking Press, 2017).

Sahoo, Sarbeswar, *Pentecostalism and the Politics of Conversion in India* (Cambridge: Cambridge University Press, 2018).

Said, Edward, *Orientalism* (New York: Random House, 1978).

Sanneh, Lamin, *Whose Religion is Christianity? The Gospel Beyond the West* (Grand Rapids: Eerdmans, 2003).

Sanneh, Lamin, *Translating the Message: The Missionary Impact on Culture*, 2nd edition revised and expanded (Maryknoll, NY: Orbis, 2009).

Sargant, N. S., *The Dispersion of the Tamil Church* (New Delhi: ISPCK, 1940).

Sarkar, Sumit, *The Swadeshi Movement in Bengal, 1903–1908* (New Delhi: People's Publishing, 1973).

Satyanarayana, Y. B., *My Father Baliah* (Noida: HarperCollins, 2011).

Schouten, Jan Peter, *Jesus as Guru: The Image of Christ Among Hindus and Christians of India* (New York: Rodopi, 2008).

Schouten, Jan Peter, *The European Encounter with Hinduism in India*, translated by Henry Jansen (Leiden: Brill, 2020).

Scott, J. Barton, "Luther in the Tropics: Karsandas Mulji and the Colonial 'Reformation' of Hinduism," *Journal of the American Academy of Religion*, Vol. 83, No. 1 (2015), pp. 181–209.

Sekhar, Chakali Chandra, "In Search of a Touchable Body: Christian Mission and Dalit Conversions," *Religions*, Vol. 10, No. 12 (2019), p. 644.

Sekhar, Chakali Chandra, "Dalit Women and Colonial Christianity: First Telugu Bible Women as Teachers of Wisdom," *Economic and Political Weekly*, Vol. 56, No. 11 (2021), pp. 57–63.

Sen, Amartya, *The Argumentative Indian: Writings on Indian History, Culture and Identity* (London: Penguin, 2006).

Sengupta, Parna, *Pedagogy for Religion: Missionary Education and the Fashioning of Hindus and Muslims in Bengal* (Berkeley: University of California Press, 2011).

Shah, A. B. (ed.), *Letters and Correspondence of Pandita Ramabai* (Bombay: Maharashtra State Board for Literature and Culture, 1977).

Sharafi, Mitra, *Law and Identity in Colonial South Asia: Parsi Legal Culture, 1772–1947* (Cambridge: Cambridge University Press, 2014).

Sharif, Ja'Far, *Islam in India or the Qanum-i-Islam: The Customs of the Musalmans of India*, translated by G. A. Herklots (London: Oxford University Press, 1921).

Sharkey, Heather, *A History of Muslims, Christians, and Jews in the Middle East* (Cambridge: Cambridge University Press, 2017).

Sharma, Bal Krishna, "Nepal" in Kenneth Ross, Daniel Jeyaraj, and Todd Johnson (eds.), *Christianity in South and Central Asia* (Peabody, MA: Hendrickson, 2019), pp. 168–79.

Sharma, Jyoti Pandey, "Architectural Adventurism in Nineteenth-Century Colonial India: Begum Samru and Her Sardhana Church," *International Journal of Islamic Architecture*, Vol. 9, No. 1 (2020), pp. 61–89.

Sharpe, Eric J., *Not to Destroy but to Fulfill: The Contribution of J. N. Farquhar to Protestant Missionary Thought in India Before 1914* (Lund: C. W. K. Gleerup, 1965).

Shellnut, Kate, "Nepal Criminalizes Christian Conversion and Evangelism," *Christianity Today*, October 25, 2017, https://www.christianitytoday.com/news/2017/october/nepal-criminalizes-conversion-christianity-evangelism-hindu.html

Sherinian, Zoe, *Tamil Folk Music as Dalit Liberation Theology* (Bloomington: Indiana University Press, 2014).

Shobhana, Nidhin, "Caste in the Name of Christ: An Angry Note on the Syrian Christian Caste," *Round Table India: For an Informed Ambedkar Age*, March 21, 2014, https://roundtableindia.co.in/index.php?option=com_content&view=article&id=7301:caste-in-the-name-of-christ-caste-in-the-name-of-christ-an-angry-note-on-the-syrian-christian-caste&catid=119&Itemid=132

Shore, Paul, "Contact, Confrontation, Accommodation: Jesuits and Islam, 1540–1770," *Al-Qantara*, Vol. 36, No. 2 (2015), pp. 429–41.

Siddiqui, Zeba, Krishna N. Das, Tommy Wilkes, and Tom Lasseter, "Emboldened by Modi's Ascent, India's Cow Vigilantes Deny Muslims Their Livelihood," Reuters, November 6, 2017, https://www.reuters.com/investigates/special-report/india-politics-religion-cows/#:~:text=Separately%2C%20Reuters%20surveyed%20110%20cow,after%20Modi's%202014%20election%20win.&text=But%20of%20the%20110%20cattle,from%20the%20Hindu%20vigilante%20groups

Singh, Brijraj, *The First Protestant Missionary to India: Bartholomaeus Ziegenbalg, 1683–1719* (New Delhi: Oxford University Press, 1999).

Soneji, Davesh, *Unfinished Gestures: Devadasis, Memory and Modernity in South India* (Chicago: Chicago University Press, 2012).

Spear, Percival, *The Nabobs: A Study of the Social Life of the English in Eighteenth Century India* (London: Oxford University Press, 1963).

Srinivas, M. N., "A Note on Sanskritization and Westernization," *Far Eastern Quarterly*, Vol. 15, No. 4 (1956), pp. 481–96.

Srinivas, M. N., *Caste in Modern India: And Other Essays* (Bombay: Asia Publishing House, 1962).

Stack, Liam, "Amsterdam Considers Apology for Slavery in Former Colony," *New York Times*, February 10, 2020, https://www.nytimes.com/2020/02/10/world/europe/amsterdam-considers-apology-for-slavery-in-former-colony.html

Stang, Charles, *Our Divine Double* (Cambridge, MA: Harvard University Press, 2016).

Stanley, Brian, "Church, State and the Hierarchy of Civilization" in Andrew Neil Porter (ed.), *The Imperial Horizons of Protestant Missions, 1880–1914* (Grand Rapids: Eerdmans, 2003), pp. 58–84.

Stanley, Brian, *Christianity in the Twentieth Century: A World History* (Princeton: Princeton University Press, 2018).

Stern, Philip J., *The Company State: Corporate Sovereignty and the Early Modern Foundations of the British Empire in India* (Oxford: Oxford University Press, 2011).

Stewart, Charles and Rosalind Shaw (eds.), *Syncretism/Anti-Syncretism: The Politics of Religious Synthesis* (London: Routledge, 1994).

Stokes, Eric, *The English Utilitarians and India* (Oxford: Oxford University Press, 1989).

Subrahmanyam, Sanjay, *The Career and Legend of Vasco da Gama* (Cambridge: Cambridge University Press, 1997).

Subrahmanyam, Sanjay, *Penumbral Visions: Making Polities in Early Modern South Asia* (New Delhi: Oxford University Press, 2001).

Subrahmanyam, Sanjay, "The Birth-Pangs of Portuguese Asia: Revisiting the Fateful 'Long Decade', 1498–1509," *Journal of Global History*, Vol. 2, No. 3 (2007), p. 262.

Subrahmanyam, Sanjay, *Europe's India: Words, People, Empires, 1500–1800* (Cambridge, MA: Harvard University Press, 2017).

Sugirtharajah, R. S., *The Bible and Empire: Postcolonial Explorations* (Cambridge: Cambridge University Press, 2005).

Sugirtharajah, R. S. and Cecil Hargreaves (eds.), *Readings in Indian Christian Theology* (New Delhi: ISPCK, 1995).

Sweetman, Will (ed.), *A Discovery of the Banian Religion and the Religion of the Persees: A Critical Edition of Two Early English Works on Indian Religions* (Lewiston: Edwin Mellen Press, 1999).

Tavernier, Jean-Baptiste, *Travels in India: Volume II*, translated by V. Ball (London: Macmillan and Co., 1889).

Tennent, James Emerson, *Christianity in Ceylon: Its Introduction and Progress Under the Portuguese, the Dutch, the British and American Missions with an Historical Sketch of the Brahmanical and Buddhist Superstitions* (Cambridge: Cambridge University Press, 2018 [1850]).

Thapar, Romila, *A History of India. Volume I* (New Delhi: Penguin, 1990).

Thomas, M. M., *The Church's Mission and Post-Modern Humanism* (New Delhi: CSS and ISPCK, 1996).

Thomas, Sonja, *Privileged Minorities: Syrian Christians, Gender, and Minority Rights in Postcolonial India* (Seattle: University of Washington Press, 2018).

Thomas, V. V., *Dalit Pentecostalism: Spirituality of the Empowered Poor* (Bangalore: Asian Trading Corporation, 2008).
Thomaskutty, Johnson, *Saint Thomas the Apostle: New Testament, Apocrypha and Historical Traditions* (London: Bloomsbury, 2018).
Thompson, John, *Evangelizing the Nation: Religion and the Formation of Naga Political Identity* (New York: Routledge, 2016).
Trautmann, Thomas, *The Aryans of British India* (Berkeley: University of California Press, 1997).
Trautmann, Thomas, *Languages and Nations: The Dravidian Proof in Colonial Madras* (Berkeley: University of California Press, 2006).
Trautmann, Thomas, *The Madras School of Orientalism: Producing Knowledge in Colonial South India* (Delhi: Oxford University Press, 2009).
Trento, Margherita, *Writing Tamil Catholicism: Literature, Persuasion, and Devotion in the Eighteenth Century* (Leiden: Brill, 2022).
Truschke, Audre, *The Language of History: Sanskrit Narratives of Indo-Muslim Rule* (New York: Columbia University Press, 2021).
Venkatachalapathy, A. R., *The Province of the Book: Scholars, Scribes, and Scribblers in Colonial Tamilnadu* (Ranikhet: Permanent Black, 2012).
Verghese, Anila, "Deities, Cults and Kings at Vijayanagara," *World Archeology*, Vol. 36, No. 3 (2004), pp. 416–31.
Vishwanathan, Gauri, *Outside the Fold: Conversion, Modernity and Belief* (Princeton: Princeton University Press, 1998).
Vishwanathan, Gauri, *Masks of Conquest: Literary Study and British Rule in India* (New York: Columbia University Press, 2015).
Visvanathan, Susan, *The Christians of Kerala: History, Belief and Ritual Among the Yakoba* (New Delhi: Oxford University Press, 1999).
Viswanath, Rupa, "The Emergence of Authenticity Talk and the Giving of Accounts: Conversion as Movement of the South in South India, ca. 1900," *Comparative Studies in Society and History*, Vol. 55, No. 1 (2013), pp. 120–41.
Viswanath, Rupa, *The Pariah Problem: Caste, Religion and the Social in Modern India* (New York: Columbia University Press, 2014).
Viswanathan, Susan, "Memorable Mission," *Frontline*, July 28, 2006, https://frontline.thehindu.com/arts-and-culture/article30210267.ece
Wagner, Kim, *Thuggee: Banditry and the British in Early Nineteenth-Century India* (New York: Palgrave Macmillan, 2007).
Waha, Kristen Bergmen, "Synthesizing Hindu and Christian Ethics in Madhaviah's English Novel, *Clarinda*," *Victorian Literature and Culture*, Vol. 46 (2018), pp. 237–55.
Walbridge, Linda, *The Christians of Pakistan: The Passion of Bishop John Joseph* (London: Routledge Curzon, 2004).
Walls, Andrew, *The Missionary Movement in Christian History: Studies in the Transmission of Faith* (Maryknoll, NY: Orbis, 1996).
Walls, Andrew, *The Cross Cultural Process in Christian History* (Maryknoll, NY: Orbis, 2002).
Walls, Andrew, "Converts or Proselytes? The Crisis over Conversion in the Early Church," *International Bulletin of Missionary Research*, Vol. 28, No. 1 (2004), pp. 2–6.
Ward, Kerry, *Networks of Empire: Forced Migration in the Dutch East India Company* (Cambridge: Cambridge University Press, 2009).
Washbrook, David, "Migration, Cultural Pluralism and Intellectual Innovation in Early Modern South India" (unpublished paper used with permission, n.d.).

Webster, John C. B., *A Social History of Christianity: Northwest India Since 1800* (New Delhi: Oxford University Press, 2007).
Webster, John C. B., "Writing a Social History of Christianity in India," *International Bulletin of Missionary Research*, Vol. 32, No. 1 (2008), pp. 10–12.
Webster, John C. B., *The Dalit Christians: A History*, 2nd edition (Delhi: ISPCK, 2009).
Wilfred, Felix, *Christians for a Better India* (New Delhi: ISPCK, 2014).
Wilson, Dorothy Clark, "The Legacy of Ida S. Scudder," *International Bulletin of Missionary Research*, Vol. 11, No. 1 (1987), pp. 24–5.
Wilson, John, *The Parsi Religion as Contained in the Zand Avasta* (Bombay: American Mission Press, 1843).
Wilson, Jon, *India Conquered: Britain's Raj and the Chaos of Empire* (New York: Perseus Books, 2016).
Wink, Andre, *Akbar* (Oxford: One World, 2009).
Wink, Andre, *Al-Hind: The Making of the Indo-Islamic World. Volume III* (New Delhi: Primus Books, 2015).
Wuthnow, Robert, *Boundless Faith: The Global Outreach of American Churches* (Berkeley: University of California Press, 2009).
Yelle, Robert, *The Language of Disenchantment: Protestant Literalism and Colonial Discourse in British India* (New York: Oxford University Press, 2013).
Young, Richard Fox (ed.), *Resistant Hinduism: Sanskrit Sources of Anti-Christian Apologetics* (Leiden: Brill, 1981).
Young, Richard Fox, *India and the Indianness of Christianity* (Grand Rapids, MI: Eerdmans, 2009).
Young, Richard Fox, *World Christianity and Interfaith Relations* (Minneapolis: Fortress Press, 2022).
Yule, Henry, *Hobson-Jobson: A Glossary of Colloquial Anglo-Indian Words and Phrases* (London: Murray, 1903).
Zastoupil, Lynn, "Defining Christians, Making Britons: Rammohun Roy and the Unitarians," *Victorian Studies*, Vol. 44, No. 2 (2002), pp. 215–43.
Zelliot, Eleanor, *From Untouchable to Dalit: Essays on the Ambedkar Movement* (New Delhi: Manohar, 1996).
Ziegenbalg, Bartholomaeus, *An Account of the Religion, and Government, Learning, and Oeconomy, &c. of the Malabarians* (London: Joseph Downing, 1717).
Ziegenbalg, Bartholomaeus, *Thirty-Four Conferences Between the Danish Missionaries and the Malabarian Brahmins (or Heathen Priests) in the East Indies* (London: H. Clemens, 1719).
Županov, Ines G., *Disputed Mission: Jesuit Experiments and Brahminical Knowledge in Seventeenth Century India* (New Delhi: Oxford University Press, 1999).
Županov, Ines G., "Twisting a Pagan Tongue: Portuguese and Tamil in Sixteenth Century Jesuit Translations" in Kenneth Mills and Anthony Grafton (eds.), *Conversion: Old Worlds and New* (Rochester: University of Rochester Press, 2003), pp. 109–39.
Županov, Ines G., "The Historiography of the Jesuit Missions in India (1500–1800)," *Jesuit Historiography Online* (first published 2016), http://dx.doi.org/10.1163/2468-7723_jho_COM_192579
Županov, Ines G., "*Antiquissime Christianita*: Indian Religion or Idolatry?," *Journal of Early Modern History*, Vol. 24 (2020), pp. 471–98.
Županov, Ines and Will Sweetman, "Rival Mission, Rival Science? Jesuits and Pietists in Seventeenth- and Eighteenth-Century South India," *Comparative Studies in Society and History*, Vol. 61, No. 3 (2019), pp. 624–53.

Index

For the benefit of digital users, indexed terms that span two pages (e.g., 52–53) may, on occasion, appear on only one of those pages.

Tables and figures are indicated by *t* and *f* following the page number

Abbasids (750–1258 CE), 28
Abdul Hamid II, 193
Abhishekananthan, Samuel, 114–15
Abraham, K. E., 248
Abu'l-fazl, 41–42, 49, 50, 56
accommodatio, 65–66, 73, 75, 76, 78, 87
Acquaviva, Rudolf, 43–44, 46–47, 48, 55, 57, 58
The Acts of Thomas, 7, 19–24, 36–37
AD 2000, 256
adiaphora, 74
adivasis, 165. *See also* tribals
African Americans, 232
Agmon, Danna, 81–82, 281n.80
Agmudaiyars, 78
Agra Mission Press, 133–34
Akbar, Jalal al-Din Muhammad (1542–1605), 8, 40
  and Christianity, 40–61
  conversation with representatives of other religions, 41*f*
  court painters of, 59
  dialogues with Jesuits, 50–56
  Din-i-Ilahi, 40, 42, 45, 46, 58
  Ibadat-khana, 40
  imperial persona, 44–47
  introduced to moral and theological tenets of Bible, 52–53
  receiveing deputation of Jesuits, 52*f*
  visit to Jesuits, 44*f*
Akbarnama, 46, 50, 273n.1
Alapuram, 79
Ali, Rahmat, 199
All India Christian Association, 203
Ambedkar, B. R., 152–53, 190, 197, 208, 221, 225–26, 227, 238
  annihilating caste, 222–23
  attacked Brahminical laws of purity, 233–34
  on conversion, 222–25
  convert to Buddhism, 224–25
  criticized Gandhi, 222–23
  and Dalit Christian theology, 214
  at Yeola Conference in 1935, 224

American Baptist missionaries, 174, 176, 177, 211–12
American Evangelical Lutherans, 166
ammans (goddess), 70
Anand, Javed, 37–38
Anderson, Benedict, 160–61
Anglican Church hierarchy, 153
Anglican missionaries, 90–91, 185
annihilating caste, 222–23
anti-Christian sentiments, 142
anti-Christian violence, 255–58
  Kandhamal riots 2008, 257
  murdered of Graham Staines, 255–56
anti-conversion sentiments, 215–16
Anti-Muslim rhetoric, during Covid-19 pandemic, 258
Ants Among Elephants (Gidla), 162
The Apostolic Faith, 158–59
Appavoo, J. Theophilus, 229–31
Arasaratnam, S., 101
argumentative heritage, 262–63
argumentative Protestants
  and Christian education, 126–27
  and defending Hindu *Dharma,* 127–29
  and 1857 Rebellion, 134–36
  encounters with Jews and Parsis, 129–31
  encounters with Muslims, 131–34
  missionary rhetoric and Indian responses, 123–36
  nabobs and orientalism, 120–21
  new cultural policy, 120–23
  overview, 117–20
  pious tensions, 121–23
  Protestantization, 140–42
  Scotsman *vs.* Bengali, 136–40
  Serampore Trio, 123–25
Arthington Aborigines mission, 178–79
Arya Mahila Sabha, 152
Arya Samaj, 187, 259
Asad, Talal, 141, 147
ashram, 160
Asia Bibi, 207

INDEX

Asiatic Society of Bengal, 120
Assayag, Jackie, 268n.11
Athanasian Creed, 134, 155, 156
avarnas, 165, 218–19, 225
avatars (incarnations), 109
Ayyankali (1863–1941), 249–51
Azariah, V. S., 168–70
   defended mass conversions, 169
Azusa Street Revival, 249, 260

Badauni (Akbar's courtier), 56
Bailey, Benjamin, 35
Bajrang Dal, 255–56, 259
Baldaeus, Philippus, 100
Banerjee, Krishna Mohan, 126–27
Banians, 102, 103
baptism, 186–87
Baptist Missionary Society, 121, 123
Barbosa, Duarte, 94
Barelvi, Syed Ahmad, 133
Basel mission, 133–34
Bauman, Chad, 242, 255
Bayly, Chris, 11, 117–18
Bayly, Susan, 65, 71, 88
Beale, Dorothea, 156
Beckert, Sven, 91–92
Belgian Capuchins, 185–86
Benade, James and Miriam, 203, 204
Bengal, 304–5n.10
   Brahmo Samaj in, 147–48
   conversion in, 126–27
   Hindu nationalists, 147
   Jesuits in, 43
   Mughal officers in, 45
   pandits from, 128
   during partition, 196–97, 198, 199, 201–2
   Serampore Trio and, 123
Bentinck, William, 298n.42
Berg, George, 248
Bergunder, Michael, 243, 246–47, 252–53
Bernard, Jean-Frederic, 101
Beschi, Constanzo Giuseppe, 65, 78–79
Bethlehem Kuravanci, 111
Beyond Movement, 256
bhadralok, 137
Bhagavad Gita, 117–18, 123
bhakti, 117–18, 149, 158, 181–82, 194, 245–46
   devotional poems and literature, 148
   hymns, 148
   movements, 5, 181
   tradition, 148
Bharatiya Janata Party (BJP), 241–42, 255–56

Bharatnatyam dance, 231
Bible, 51
   King James, 128–29
   moral and theological tenets of, 52–53
   "popery," 117
   translated into Malayalam, 35
   translated into Sanskrit, 9
   translated into Tamil, 90–91, 113–14, 116
   trials of translation, 112–14
Bikram, Tribhuvan Bir, 209
Black Americans, 232
Bloomer, Kristin, 87–88
Book of One Thousand Questions, (Ibn Salam), 267n.5
Bouchet, Jean Venant, 82, 98, 262–63
brahmacharya (celibacy), 22
Brahmin Christian community, 145–46
Brahmins, 17, 68–69, 80. *See also* Hinduism
   Carey challenged, 123–24
   conversion in Maharashtra, 147–50
   converted to Christianity, 145
   Dubois views on, 80–81
   of Goa, 86–87
   Kerala, conversion of, 24
   Kulin caste, 137
   of Madurai, 62–63, 73–76
   Nambudiri, 24, 30
   ritual services of, 70–71
   sanyasi, 76
   Saraswat Brahmin, 86–87
   strategies of cooption and assimilation, 227
Brahmo Samaj, 141, 147–48
Breast Cloth Movement, 36
British, 37
   arrival in Travancore, 34
   reforms, 33–36
British Evangelicals, 18–19
British Raj, 190, 192, 196–97
Buchanan, Claudius, 34, 121
Buddhism, 212, 237–38
   Ambedkar convert to, 224–25
   Buddhists and Rohingya conflict, 212
   "fulfillment theology," 139–40
Buntain, Mark, 241
Burma, 211–12

Carey, William, 9, 121, 123, 124–25, 127
   Bengali translation of New Testament, 125*f*
   challenged Brahmin devotee, 123–24
Carman, John, 227–28, 247
caste, 165–66
catechists, 81–82

Catholic Association of South India, 195
Catholic Church
   in Asia, 42–43
   congregations, 87
   in India, 71, 196
   Inquisition, 30–31
Catholicism, 51, 59, 60, 117
   affinity with Hindus, 81
   conversion of low-ranking fishermen to, 69
   in Goa, 71–73
   Indian, 77–78, 79–80, 86
   interactions, 8
   introduced in south India, 71
   in Pondicherry, 82–85
   South Asian, 88
   spiritual *vs.* colonial conversion enterprises, 65–73
   tombs of Catholic saints, 71
Catholic missionaries, 63–64
   approaches in India, 80
Catholic–Muslim conflict, 97
Catholic–Protestant differences, 117
Catholics, 8, 32–33, 79–81, 153, 180, 225, 274n.9
   adopt Hindu rituals, 80, 87–88
   of Bombay, 84–85
   jurisdiction, race, and class, 82–87
   Konkani-speaking, 86–87
   and nationalism, 195–96
   of Pondicherry, 82–85
   worship, 81
Catholic Truth Propagation League, 195
Catholic Truth Society, 195
Catholic Union of India, 204
CBCNEI. *See* Council of Baptist Churches in North East India
Ceylon Pentecostal Mission (CPM), 246–47
Chakkarai, Vengal, 160, 194
Chakravarty, Uma, 150–51
Chamars, 164, 183, 200
Chanda Saheb (*nawab* of the Carnatic), 78
Chandra Sekhar, Chakali, 166–67
Chapman, Mary, 248
Chatterjee, Bankim Chandra, 138–39
Chelladurai, Sam, 253
Cherian, K. C., 248
Child, Josiah, 103–4
Christian Ashram Movement, 160
Christian conversions, 6–7
   anti-conversion laws, 3, 14
   of Brahmins, 9, 24
   of Dalit and tribal experience, 9–10
   of illiterate masses, 11–12
   of Japanese peasantry, 62
   of low-ranking fishermen, 69
   of marginal to Hindu and Muslim communities, 7
   opposition to, 3
Christian education, 126–27
Christianity, 237–38, 262–63
   classical languages, influence of, 5
   growth in Global South, 3
   Indianizing, 10, 15, 225
   local or regional expressions of, 16
   Marathi vernacular, 146
   in Nepal, 209–10
   in Sri Lanka, 210–11
   Tamil expression of, 110–11
Christian missionaries
   Gandhi's encounters with, 219–20
Christian Missionary Activities Enquiry Committee, 209
Christian Patriot, 160
Christian pluralism, 13–14
Christians, 261
   acts of violence against, 257–58
   beliefs and practices, 164
   in Ceylon, 100–1
   demographic shift in, 2–3
   Indianness of, 194
   in Jaffna, 100, 101
   location between Hindu and Muslim, 262
   in South Asia, 4t
   and South Asian history, 10–12
Christian slavery, 216, 238
Christo Samaj, 160
Chuhras, 163, 182–84, 200–1, 217
   Christian identity of, 202f
   mass movement, 184–85
   migrants, 201
Church of North India (CNI), 247
Church of South India (CSI), 247
Citizenship Amendment Bill, 257–58
Clark, Edward Winter, 175
Clarke, Sathianathan, 229–30
Clough, John, 166–67, 171, 188, 217
CMS missionaries, 185–86
Coleridge, Henry, 69–70
communion, 186–87
Community of St. Mary the Virgin (CSMV), 153–54
Compagnie des Indes Orientales, 83
Cone, James, 232
Congress Party, 191–92

Constitutional (SC) Order of 1950, 234–36, 237
Controversial Tracts on Christianity and Mohammedanism, 9
conversion(s), 146–50
  Ambedkar on, 222–25
  of Brahmins in Kerala, 24
  of Brahmins in Maharashtra, 147–50
  caste identity after, 236
  of Dalits, 9–10, 11–12, 87
  Gandhi on, 218–21
  and missionaries, 6–7
  of tribes, 9–10
Cook, Robert, 248
Council of Baptist Churches in North East India (CBCNEI), 180
Council of Islamic Ideology, 205
Counter-Reformation, 42
cultural accommodation, in South Indian Catholicism
  accommodation on trial, 73–75
  Catholics, 79–81
  critics of, 75–87
  overview, 62–65
  priests *vs.* catechists, 81–82
cultural policy
  nabobs and orientalism, 120–21
  pious clause, 121–22
  pious tensions, 122–23

da Costa, Baltasar, 76
da Gama, Vasco, 93–94
Dalit-Bahujans, 226. *See also* Dalits
  identity, 227
Dalit Christians, 10, 215, 233–34, 239
  affirmative action for, 234–38
  consciousness, 231–32
  cultural resources of, 229–31
  dual identities, 227–28
  in Indian society, 238
  inspired by Ambedkar, 233–34
  of Kerala, 12
  as scheduled castes, 234–35
Dalit Christian theology, 225–34
  asserting difference from Hinduism, 225–27
  Dalit culture and experiences, 229–31
  Jesus as Dalit in, 232–33
  multiple identities, 227–28
  for Paraiyars, 229
Dalits, 3, 6–7, 145, 160–61, 214–39
  competing religions and, 264–65
  conversion of, 9–10, 11–12
  Gandhi on conversion of, 218–21
  identities, 11–12, 217, 227

  laborers, 216
  Malas and Madigas, 168–69
  mass conversion, 16, 165–71
  overview, 214–15
  servitude, 216
  slavery, 216
  social liberation and missionary legacy, 215–18
  transformative aspect of Christianity among, 217
Dalrymple, William, 120, 289n.19
Dandekar, Deepra, 145–46, 149
Danish East India Company, 107
Danish Halle missionaries, 109–10, 111
Das, Shri Kalka, 308n.82
Day, Lal Behari, 126–27, 142–43
De Britto, John, 78
de Fontenelle, Bernard Le Bovier, 97–98
de Goes, Benedict, 58–59
devadasis, 307n.62
de Vega, Christoval, 58
dharma, 68, 75–76, 127, 128, 246
Dharma Jagran Manch, 259–60
Dharmashastras, 123
Dhinakaran, D. G. S., 253
Din-i-Ilahi (Religion of God), 40, 42, 46, 58
Dnyanodaya, 148
Dongre, Anant Shastri, 151
Dongre, Ramabai. *See* Ramabai, Pandita
Donohugh, Thomas S., 224
Dubois, Jean-Antoine, 63–64, 80–81
  association with *Hindu Manners, Customs and Ceremonies*, 281n.74
  work on orientation of Brahmins, 281n.75
Duff, Alexander, 9, 126, 129, 142, 143, 260, 264
Dundas, Henry, 121
Dutch East India Company, 99
Dutch predikants (pastors), 100
Dutch Reformed Church, 99, 100
Dutt, Michael Madhusudan, 126–27

Eastern Christians
  as "Nestorian," 26–27
  of Persia, 18
East India Company, 86, 122, 128
  Danish, 107
  Dutch, 99
  English, 84, 91–92, 102, 103–4, 111, 114, 134–35
  French, 83
Eaton, Richard, 174, 275n.20
Ellaiyamman, 229
Estado da India, 42–43, 69, 94

European encounters with Hindus and
    Muslims, 89–116
  early Protestants, 98–104
  imperial ambitions, 91–98
  overview, 89–91
  Prester John, finding, 92
  Tavernier's experience, 89–90
  Tranquebar mission, 104–10
  translatability and Tamil, 110–15
European imperialism, 17–18, 90–91
European liberalism, 147
European Orientalism, 74
Eusebius, 25
Evangelicalism, 107, 288n.13
Ezhavas, 249–51

farangi kulam, 73
farangi(s), 69, 70, 73, 74, 76–77, 82, 116
Farquhar, J. N., 139–40
Farzana Zeb al- Nissa Begum Sombre (r.1778–1836), 59
Fernandes, Goncalo, 76–77
Ferreira, Christovao, 62
Findlay, W. H., 142
Fischer-Tine, Harald, 139–40
Forman, Charles, 203
Francke, August Hermann, 285n.50
Fredrick IV (king of Denmark), 105
Freire, Paulo, 231
Frykenberg, Robert, 150–51, 158, 178

Gandhi, M. K., 188, 189–90, 201–2, 204–5, 214
  campaigned against untouchability, 219
  on conversion, 218–21
  dismissed Pickett's findings, 220
  encounters with Christian
    missionaries, 219–20
  Harijan Sevak Sangh, 218–19
  principle of *swadeshi*, 204, 212
  prioritization of Muslims, 192–93
  relationship with Jinnah, 190
  Scudder with, 190*f*
  talks with Jinnah, 197–99, 198*f*
Ganesh *utsav*, 191–92
Gentiles, 12, 82, 89, 95, 151
  non- Abrahamic religions as, 97
  reinventing, 97–98
Gerbner, Katharine, 215–16
German Pietists, 90–91, 109–10, 285n.50
Ghar Wapsi (reconversion), 14, 187, 258–60
Ghosh, Mahesh Chandra, 126–27
Gidla, Sujatha, 162
Gifford, Paul, 253–54

Gomes, W. H., 115
Gond tribes, 14
Goreh, Nehemiah (formerly Nilakantha), 128, 142–43, 145–46, 149, 153–54
Grant, Charles, 121
Green, Nile, 135–36, 149, 288n.8, 292n.75
Griswold, Hervey De Witt, 186
Gulamgiri (Phule), 157
Guru, Gopal, 235–36
Guru Gobind Singh, 295–96n.6
Guru Nanak, 295–96n.6
Gutierrez, Gustavo, 231–32

Hardgrave, Robert, 188
Harijan Sevak Sangh, 218–19
Harper, Susan Billington, 170
Hasan, Zoya, 235–36
Hassius, Johan Sigismund, 107
Hastie, William, 126–27, 137–39, 142–43
  campaign against "Hindu idolatry," 137
  exchange between Bankim and, 138–39
Hastings, Warren, 120
Henriques, Francis, 43–44, 46–47, 52
high caste conversion, 145
hijras, 48
Hinduism, 60–61, 88, 119, 137–38, 141–42, 144, 219, 221
  avatars in, 109
  by Bankim, 292n.69
  Brahminical, 163
  caste in, 223
  defending, 127–29
  European scholars of, 137–38
  "reformation" of, 142
  social reform, 147–48
  Ziegenbalg's criticism of, 90
Hindu Mahasabha, 191–92
Hindu revivalism, 192
Hindu(s), 137, 262–63
  apologists, 127
  Brahmins, 17, 24
  conversion of, 81
  dharmic order, 117–18
  Dubois views on, 80–81
  early European encounters with, 89–116
  identity, 139
  nationalism, 3, 14, 18, 37–38, 144–45, 159, 195–96, 243
  Orthodox, 157
  participate in Catholic festivals, 87–88
  of Pondicherry, 84–85
  Rath Yatras, 77–78
  reform-minded, 219

Hindu(s) (cont.)
  Tamil, 105–6, 113
  temples in Goa, destruction of, 65–66
  of Tranquebar, 105–8
  worship of Shiva, 70
  Ziegenbalg's exchanges with, 109
Hindutva, 3, 4–5, 14, 191–92, 241–42, 260–61
  activists, rhetoric of, 146–47
  agenda in India, 256
  and anti-Christian violence, 255–58
Hindutva: Who Is a Hindu? (Savarkar), 191–92
  movement, 12
  Pentecostalism and, 243
  rise of, 242
Holy Spirit, 158–59, 243, 246, 249, 251
Huntington, Samuel, 143
Hutton, J. H., 176

Ibadat-khana, 40
identity, 9
  of Brahmins, 29
  caste (after conversion), 68, 164, 165–66, 236
  of Catholics, 63–64, 80, 88, 195
  Christian, 13, 26, 66, 67, 76–77, 110, 164, 173, 181, 186, 188, 194, 216, 227–28, 235
  of Chuhra and Chamar, 182–84
  collective, 141
  complex, 147, 164
  confessional, 143
  crises, 145–46, 202f
  cultural, 177
  Dalit-Bahujans, 227
  of Dalits, 6–7, 10, 11–12, 217, 226, 268n.8
  dual, 227–28
  farangi, 76–77
  group, 165–66
  Hindu, 80, 139, 227
  Jewish, 130
  layering of, 100–1
  multiple, 227–28
  Muslim, 198
  Naga Christian, 177–78
  regional-vernacular, 115
  religious, 119, 140, 143, 192, 234–36
  social, 163, 165
  of Syrian Christians, 27, 30
  of Tamil Christians, 112
  of Thomas Christians, 27, 32–33
  tribal, 172
  unitary, 89
Ilaiah, Kancha, 226–27
Ilbert Bill controversy, 137
Immaculate Conception, 109

India
  competing ideas of, 191–96
  partition of, 190–91, 196–204
Indian National Congress, 137, 196–97
Indian Ocean, 42–43
  map of, 91f
  trade and political expansion, 8–9, 90
  trading opportunities in, 91
Indian Pentecostal Church (IPC), 246–47
Iqbal, Muhammad, 199
Iqbal, Tahir, 207–8
Islam, 28–29, 90, 101, 237–38, 262–63
  Christian attacks on, 133
  "golden age" of, 37–38
  introduced in south India, 71
  revivalist, 37–38
  syncretic variety of, 71–73
  Ziegenbalg's criticism of, 90, 107
Islamization, 28–29, 205–6
Israel, Hephzibah, 112–13

Jaffna
  Christians in, 100, 101
  lower caste converts in, 101
  Tamil Saivites, 128–29
jagir (land grant), 59
Jahan (Shah), 89, 119–20
jatis, 68, 129, 165, 267–68n.6
Jawaharlal Nehru University (JNU), 257–58
Jesuits, 8, 11, 47
  Akbar's visit to, 44f
  arrival in India, 42
  cultural adaptation, legacy of, 62–63
  debates with Lutheran theologians, 276n.52
  dialogues with Akbar and mullahs, 50–56
  earning Akbar's trust, 47–50
  expending influence Mughals, 47–50
  final mission to Akbar's court (1595-1605), 58–59
  Madurai mission, 81–82
  mission to Akbar's court, 42–61
  during Mughal Empire, 40–42
  practice of accommodatio, 75
  universal salvation of "souls," 280n.72
The Jesuits and the Great Mogul, 273n.1
Jesuit Orientalism, 284n.26
Jesus Calls Ministries, 253
Jesus Christ, 13–14, 58, 60
Jesus the Avatar (Chakkarai), 194
Jesus the Dalit Man of Sorrows (Jyoti Sahi), 233f
Jews, 101–2
  Bene Israel community, 129–30, 131
  intolerance toward, 103–4

Protestant missionary encounters
   with, 129–31
 toleration of, 103–4
Jeyaraj, Daniel, 109, 116
Jinnah, Muhammad Ali, 190, 203, 212
 and Christians in Pakistan, 204–5
 death of, 205
 talks with Gandhi, 197–99, 198f
Jones, Arun, 181–82, 246
Joseph, John, 207
Joshi, Anandibai, 157
Joshua, Gurram, 228
Joshua Project, 256
Judaism, 101–30, 262–63
Judeo-Christian framework, 102, 103

kafala system, 38
Kairanawi, Maulana Rahmat Allah, 133–34, 135–36
kanganies, 114
Kanshi Ram, 226
Karunanidhi, M., 104
Katju, Kailas Nath, 208–9
kattanars (pastors or priests), 34
Kent, Eliza, 170–71, 296n.7
Kerala, 18–19, 270n.2
 communism, 37
 conversion of Brahmins, 24
 geographical access to Arab societies, 37–38
 migrants to Arab states, 38–39
 Pentecostal churches in, 38, 248
 Syrian Christians of, 2, 7
khadi, 189
Khan, Liaquat Ali, 204–5
Khan, Syed Ahmed, Sir, 135
Khasi, 179
Kosambi, Meera, 150–51, 153, 157
Koschorke, Klaus, 15–16, 160
kothi (imperial mansion), 60
kuravanci, 111

Labbai, 107
La Crequiniere, 101–2
Lajja (Nasreen), 208
Lalitha, Jayachitra, 233–34
Leitao, Duarte, 58
The Letters of Prester John, 92
London Missionary Society, 121
Lord, Henry, 102–3
Lorrain, James Herbert, 178–79
Lutheran Pietist missionaries, 225

Madigas, 166–67, 168–69, 188, 217. See also Dalits
Madras, 22, 86, 103, 194
 Catholic leaders from, 204
 Christian voices of, 159–60
 Lutheran church in, 109–10
 missionaries in, 217
 public consciousness arising in, 146
 Rethinking Christianity in, 160
Madras Presidency, 34
Mahabharata, 5, 194
Mahdi movement, 45–46
Malayali Pentecostals, 114–15
Malekandathil, Pius, 270n.1, 272n.48
Mancias, Francis, 67
Mandal Commission, 234
Mani, Lata, 122
Mappilas, 28–29
Maraikkayar Muslims, 107
Marathas, 84, 145, 147–48
Marathi Christian, 148, 149
Maravas, 78
Marshman, Joshua, 123
Mar Thoma Syrian Church, 17
Martin, Francois, 84
Martyn, Henry, 9, 51, 131–32, 260
Masih, Abdul, 132, 142–43
mass conversion, of Dalits and tribals, 16
 among Nagas and Mizos, 172–80
 of Chamars and Chuhras in Punjab, 164
 in Northwest India, 181–87
 overview, 162–64
 in South India, 165–71
Matapariksha, 128
Max Muller, Friedrich, 153–54
Meherullah, Munshi Mohammad, 136
Methodist Church of South India, 247
Methodist missionaries, 181
millennial messianism, 50–51, 58
Mirza Muhammad Hakim, 45
Mishra Commission, 236–38
Missions Etrangeres de Paris (MEP), 83
Mitchell, John Murray, 126–27
Mizos, mass conversions of, 178–80
mlecchas, 128
Modi, Narendra, 256–57
moksha (liberation), 22
Monier-Williams, Monier, 144–45, 146, 159
Moody, Dwight, 158
Mosse, David, 79–80
Mott, John R., 139–40, 220
Mountbatten, Lord, 199
Mudaliars, 100
Mughal-Catholic fusion, 59–60

Mughal Empire, 5, 40, 42–44, 47–50, 59, 284n.25
Muhajirs, 200–1
Muhammad. *See* Prophet Muhammad
"Muhammadan Controversy," 133
Muir, John, 126–27, 128
Mukkavars, 67, 70
　conversions of, 87
mullahs (Muslim teachers), 40–41, 47, 50–51, 53–56, 57, 60, 204–5
Multa Praeclare, 85
munazaras, 131–32
Munro, John, 34–35
　Murr, Sylvia, 281n.74
Muslim League, 190, 191–92, 203–4
　demands of, 199
　emergence of, 192
　"two nation theory," 197
Muslims, 28–29, 194, 261
　acts of violence against, 257–58
　apologists, 127
　beliefs and practices, 107–8
　conflict with Portuguese, 67
　criticized New Testament, 108
　early European encounters with, 89–116
　elite society (*ashraf* class), 132
　Gandhi's prioritization of, 192–93
　ignorance of sacred texts, 118, 123–24
　interaction with Gulf countries, 37–38
　intolerance toward, 103–4
　Labbai, 107
　migrants to Malabar Coast, 28–29
　munshis, 132, 134
　orthodox, 59
　Pangals of Manipur, 172
　Paravas' rivalry with, 67
　of Pondicherry, 84–85
　reformers, 133
　revivalism, 37–38
　Rohingya, 212
　Salafis, 37–38
　Sufi, 70
　Tamil-speaking Maraikkayar, 107
　in Tranquebar, 107–9
　upper caste elites, 15
　Wahhabis, 37–38, 88
My Father Baliah (Satyanarayana), 162

nabobs, 120–21
Nadars, 35
Nagas, of northeast India
　Ao Nagas, 174, 175–76
　Christian identity, 177–78
　Horton's model to, 174
　mass conversions of, 174–78
　origins of, 298n.43
　Sema Nagas, 176
Naicker, E. V. Ramaswamy, 227
Namboodiripad, E. M. S., 37
Nambudiri Brahmins, 24, 30, 35–36
Nandi, Gopinath, 126–27
Naqshbandi Sufi Shaykh Ahmad Sirhindi (1564–1624), 45–46
Nasreen, Taslima, 208
National Christian Council of India, 203
National Church, 160
National Commission for Minorities, 237–38
nationalism
　Catholics and, 195–96
　Hindu, 3, 18, 37–38, 144–45
　Protestants and, 193–94
　swadeshi, 212–13
Navalar, Arumuga, 128–29
Nayaka rule, 75–76
Nayars, 30, 35–36
Nehru, Jawaharlal, 203–4, 208
Nepal
　Christianity in, 209–10
　democracy in, 209–10
　Hindu kingdom, 209
New Testament, 17, 59, 148, 214
　Carey's Bengali translation of, 125*f*
　Jew–Gentile distinctions of, 112
　Muslims criticized, 108
　theology of "twinning" in, 270n.2
　vision of Pentecost, 249
Nirmal, Arvind, 231–32
Niyogi Report, 209
Nobili, Roberto de, 8, 62–63, 65, 73–75, 225, 262–63
　accusers of, 77
　critics of, 76
　and *farangi* identity, 76–77
　gained access to Brahminical society, 74–75
　learned Tamil, 74
　lifestyle of Brahmins, 76–78
　and Madurai Brahmins, 73–76
　missionary project, 73
　missionary strategy, 74, 77–78
　portrayed Jesus as divine guru, 74
　strategy of cultural accommodation, 73
Northwest India, mass conversions in, 181–87
　Chuhra mass movement, 184–85
　sincerity, communion, and reconversion, 185–87
　urban conversions, 181–82

Numark, Mitch, 129

Oddie, Geoffrey, 127, 128
Old Testament, 98, 102, 103, 128–29
orientalism, 120–21
oru olai, 230–31
Osella, Caroline and Filipo, 278n.13
other backward castes (OBCs), 234

Pachuau, Joy, 180
Padmanji, Baba, 145–46, 148–49
Padroado, 73, 77–78, 85–86, 87, 100
Padroado Real (royal patronage), 65, 84, 99
pagan society, 78–79, 80, 87
Pahlavi (archaic Persian), 18
Pakistan, 197
  blasphemy laws in, 204, 205–8
  Christians in, 204–6, 208
  postcolonial minoritization, 204–8
  Sunni religious clerics, 205
Pal, Krishna, 142–43
palm leaves *(cadjan),* 106
Pantaenus, 25
pantaram, 76
paraiyar, 165
Paraiyars, 229
Paramhansa Mandali, 148
paraparan, 113
Paravas, 66–69, 70, 71, 79
  Christians, 75, 76, 77–78
  conversions of, 87
Parham, Charles, 243, 249
Parsis, 102, 103
  Protestant missionary encounters with, 129–31
parsopa, 26–27
partition of India, 190–91, 196–204
  Christian responses, 200–4
  Gandhi–Jinnah talks, 197–99, 198*f*
  Hindu–Muslim violence, 196–97, 201–2
  Indian National Congress, 196–97
  map showing, 200*f*
  massive migration, 199
  Muslim League, 196–97
  Radcliffe Line, announcement of, 199
Pathian, 179
pattangattis, 68, 70
Paul, Kanakarayan Tiruselvam, 194
Pentecostals/Pentecostalism, 180, 241, 260
  address needs of poor and oppressed, 252
  among Thomas Christians, 248–49
  appeal of, 246–52
  appeal to Dalits, 249–51

arrival of, 245–46
attacked in India, 242
congregations, 247
definition of, 243
democratic and inclusive message, 251
early revivals and publicity, 244–45
expansion in India, 240
growth in South Asia, 260–61
growth rates in India, 250*t*
and *Hindutva,* 243
Hindutva and anti-Christian violence, 255–58
inclusive vision, 247, 249–52
inroads into Mizoram, 180
in Kerala and in South Asia, 248, 251
legacy, 240–41
Malayali, 114–15
mapping, 243–46
methods and beliefs of, 242
Nathaniel Roberts' study of, 254
oppose aspects of Hinduism, 253
overview, 240–43
prosperity gospel, prevalence of, 253–54
reception of, 245–46
relationship with Hindu beliefs and practices, 252–58
role of women in, 254–55
South Asian, 252–53
worldwide movement, 251–52
The Peoples of the United States, 157
Perozy, Fulgence, 86
Persian Christians, 7, 26
  hierarchy, 28
  orthodoxy of, 26–27
peshwas, 147–48
Pfander, Karl Gottlieb, 51, 133–34
Phule, Jyotirao, 157, 227
Picart, Bernard, 101–2
Pickett, J. Waskom, 220, 224
Pietism, 105
Pietist Christianity, 110–11
Pillai, Arumuga, 128–29
Pillai, Vedanayagam, 109–10
Pinheiro, Emmanuel, 58–59
pious clause, 121–22
Plutschau, Heinrich, 105
polycentrism, 15–16
Pondicherry mission, 80, 82–85
Poona Pact, 221
Popley, Herbert Arthur, 169
Portuguese, 37
  arrival on India, 30, 96*f*
  capturing Bombay, 282n.91

Portuguese (cont.)
  conflict with seafaring Muslims, 67
  hostility towards local religions, 94
  meet Mughals, 42–44
  relationship with local population, 30–31
  views on Islam, 263
Portuguese Catholics, 18–19
postcolonial minoritization, 204–12
  India and Nepal, 208–10
  Pakistan and Bangladesh, 204–8
  Sri Lanka and Burma, 210–12
Powell, Avril, 131–32
Prarthana Samaj, 147–48
Presbyterian Church of India, 180
Prester John, 30, 92, 94, 115–16, 262
  Ethiopia, 92, 93*f*
  "Gentiles," 97
  search for the similar, 93–95
Propaganda Fide, 83, 84, 85–86
Prophet Muhammad, 28, 45–46, 50–51, 108, 133
  blasphemy of, 206–7
  centrality of, 45–46
  Jesuits criticized, 8, 40–41, 51, 55–56
  propagation of faith, 108
  prophethood of, 131–32, 133–34
Protestantism/Protestants, 51, 99, 103, 114, 128, 140–42, 143
  Dutch, 98–102
  and education, 100
  English, 102–4
  and indentured servants, 114–15
  and India's argumentative tradition, 118
  interactions, 8–9
  missionaries, 11, 63–64, 80, 118, 133, 253, 263
  orientalism, 115–16
  and slavery, 216–18
  supremacy, 215–16, 238
Protestantization, 140–42
Protestant Reformation, 117, 143, 149
Pulayas, 220–21, 249–51
Punjab
  Capuchins arrival in, 185
  Chamars and Chuhras, 182–84
  growing Christian numbers in, 187
  jatis of, 183
  low-ranking groups in, 182–83
puranikas, 151, 157

Qaid-i-Azam, 197
Qur'an, 40–41, 50–51, 59, 108, 118–19, 141
  idjtihad, 117–18
  ignorance about, 123–24
  teachings of, 133
  unitary identity, 89
  validity of, 133–34

Radcliffe, Cyril, 199
Radcliffe Line, 199
Rajagopalachari, C., 238
Ramabai, Pandita, 9–10, 16, 142–43, 145–46, 149–59, 160–61
  and American Christianity, 157–58
  and Athanasian Creed, 155
  in Calcutta, 151–52
  at Community of St. Mary the Virgin, 153–54
  conversion of, 153, 157
  critique of Hindu family, 152–53
  early life and family of, 151
  with gifted daughter Manoramabai, 154*f*
  life of, 151
  move to Cheltenham, 156
  Mukti mission, 158–59, 246
  Ramabai Association, 157–58
  received titles "Pandita" and "Sarasvati," 151–52
  and Sister Geraldine at Wantage, 155
Ramayana, 1, 5, 117–18, 184, 194
Ramnad, 78, 79
Rao, Chilkuri Vasantha, 247
Rath Yatras (chariot processions), 77–78
Rauschenbusch, Walter, 171
Rauschenbusch-Clough, Emma, 171
Raychaudhuri, Tapan, 139
Rebellion of 1857, 134–36, 289n.19
Reconquista, 30–31, 95
reinois, 85
Rethinking Christianity, 160–61, 194
Rhenius, C. T. E., 112–13
Ricci, Matteo, 77
rice Christians/conversions, 145, 167–68, 176, 296n.8
Robbins, Joel, 164
Roberts, Nathaniel, 147, 254
Rogerius, Abraham, 8–9
Rohingya Muslims, 212
Roy, Arundhati, 162
Roy, Rammohan, 123, 126, 128
Rubies, Joan-Pau, 282n.2, 282–83n.3
Rushdie, Salman, 207, 208
Ruthnaswamy, M., 204
Ryrie, Alec, 117

Sabat, Nathaniel, 132
Sabatean Proofs of the Truth of Islamism and the Falsehood of Christianity, 132

INDEX 349

The Sacred Books of the East (Max Muller), 153–54
Saheb, Chanda, 78
Sahi, Jyoti, 230f
Sahoo, Sarbeswar, 254–55
Salaam, Qari Muhammad, 207
Salafis, 37–38
samasthanams, 70–71
Sangh Parivar, 3, 241–42, 257–58
Sanneh, Lamin, 13–14, 15, 176
Sanskrit, 144
  Bible translated into, 9
  Monier-Williams' views about, 144
Sanskritization, 144–45, 297–98n.35
Sanskritizing Christianity, 160–61
Santal tribes, 14
sanyasis, 73, 76, 78
Sarasvati, Dayananda, 187
Saraswati, Laxmanananda, 257
Sastri, Vedanayagam, 90–91, 111–12, 113–14, 116
Satanic Verses (Rushdie), 207, 208
sati, 48, 119–20, 121–23, 246
Satyanarayana, Y. B., 162
Saunders, Kenneth, 139
Savarkar, Vinayak Damodar, 191–92
savarnas, 218–19
Savidge, Frederick William, 178–79
Sawarkar, Dinkar Shankar, 149
scheduled castes (SC), 215, 234–35, 236. *See also* Dalits
Schultze, Benjamin, 109–10
Schwartz, Christian Friedrich, 109–10, 111, 115
Scottish Enlightenment, 264
Scottish missionaries, 140
Scudder, Ida, 189, 190f
Second Great Awakening, 121
Sen, Amartya, 117–18, 131
Sen, Keshab Chandra, 151–52
Serampore Trio, 123–25
Seymour, James, 249
Shaiva Orthodoxy, 128
Shaiva Siddhanta, 128
Shanars, 35–36, 217
Sherinian, Zoe, 229–30
sheristadar, 135
shraddha, 137
shuddhi, 187, 259–60
Sikhs
  conversion of, 182
  Kabirpanthi and Mazhabi communities, 182
  residing on Pakistan side, 199
Singh, Brijraj, 116, 285n.54

Singh, Dara, 255–56
Singh, Sadhu Sundar, 160, 194
Singha, S. P., 203
SIUC. *See* South Indian United Church
Society for the Propagation of the Gospel in Foreign Parts (SPG), 111
sola scriptura, 118–19
South Asia
  Christianity roots in, 6
  Christian populations in, 4t
  decolonization in, 204
  definition, 3
  European expansion in, 91–92
  European involvement in, 90
  history of, Christians and, 10–12
  Sanskritic influence in, diffusion of, 267n.4
  and World Christianity, 12–16
South Asia Christians, 2, 265–66
  locating, 5–10
  population of, 4t
  transnational religion, 265
South Asian Pentecostalism, 246–47, 260
South India, mass conversion Dalits in, 165–71
  caste and untouchability, 165–66
  indigenous preachers with villagers in Medapalli, 169f
  motives and outcomes, 166–67
  rice Christians, 167–68
  Vedanayagam Samuel Azariah and, 168–70
  women and mass converts, 170–71
South Indian United Church (SIUC), 247
Spener, Philipp Jakob, 285n.50
Sri Lanka
  Christianity in, 210–11
  National Christian Evangelical Alliance, 211
  Tamil-Sinhala division, 211
Staines, Graham, 255–56
Subrahmanyam, Sanjay, 93–94, 101–2
Sufi Muslims, 70
Sufi *pirs,* 70, 71–73, 77–78, 107
Sunder Raj, Ebenezer, 225–26, 268n.7
Sunni. *See also* Muslims
  ashraf class, 135–36
  merchants, 107
swadeshi, 189, 191–92, 204, 212, 218
  limitations of, 212
  nationalism, 212–13
  religion, 265–66
Swami Vivekananda, 156
syncretism, 79–80
Syrian Catholics *(Pazhayakur),* 249
Syrian Christians, 17–39, 145, 225
  The Acts of Thomas, 19–24

Syrian Christians (*cont.*)
  adopted Brahminical customs, 29
  and British reforms, 33–36
  communities, 2
  and co-participation, 11
  Discriminatory practices of, 249–51
  high caste status, 29
  identity of, 27
  Indianness of, 18
  of Kerala, 2, 12
  origin of arrival of Europeans, 17–18
  Pentecostalism among, 248–49
  and Persian Christianity, 7, 24–28
  ties to West Asia, 10–11
  westernization, 31–36

Tablighi Jamaat, 258
Tamil Bible, 112, 113–14
Tamil Christians, 110–15, 229–30
  diaspora, 116
  identity, 112
  made inroads into lives of laborers, 114–15
  poet, 109–10, 111–12
  regional-vernacular identities, 115
  social distinctions by, 112
  of Tanjore and Tranquebar, 111
Tamil Hindus, 113
Tamil laborers, 114
Tamil Protestants, 113
Tariqah-i-Muhammadiyah, 133, 141
Tavernier, Jean-Baptiste, 89–90
Telugu Christian community, 227–28
Thoburn, James, 158
St. Thomas, 18–19, 71
  Brahmins converted by, 29
  community traces its origins to, 24
  cross of, 23–24
Thomas, Shine, 240, 241, 248
Thomas, Sonja, 212–13
Thomas, V. V., 249–51
Thomas Christians. *See* Syrian Christians
Thomas of Cana, 27
Tilak, Bal Gangadhar, 191–92
Tilak, Narayan Vaman, 145–46, 148, 149
Tipu Sultan, 80
Tranquebar, 90, 104–10
  Hindus of, 105–8
  Muslims in, 107–9
  New Jerusalem Church in, 107–8
  Tamil Christians of, 111
Tranquebar mission, 8–9, 104–10
Tribals, 9–10, 172, 209, 235–36, 242, 258, 297–98n.35, *See also* Nagas and Mizos),
tsungrem, 175, 179

Tuhfat al-Mujahidin, 96–97
Tukaram (1608–50), 148
twashta kasar caste, 148
"two nation theory," 197

ulama (religious scholars), 46, 131–32
Ummayads (661–750 CE), 28
Underwood, G. W., 115
United Christian Forum for Human Rights, 256
untouchability, 3, 162–63, 165–66, 222, 267–68n.6
  Gandhi campaigned against, 219
Upadhyay, Brahmabandhab, 301n.13
upper caste conversion, to Protestantism
  Baba Padmanji, 148–49
  conversion of Brahmin in Maharashtra, 147–48
  Narayan Vaman Tilak, 148
  overview, 144–46
  Pandita Ramabai, 149–59
  Viswanathan's son, 149–50
urban conversions, 181–82

Valignano, Alessandro, 77, 280n.55
van Dale, Anthony, 97–98
van Linschoten, Jan Huygen, 98–99
Varkey, C. J., 204
varnas/varnashrama dharma, 165, 222
Vatican Council (1962–5), 249
Vedas, 144, 187
Velho, Alvaro, 93–94
Verenigde Oost-Indische Compagnie (VOC), 99
Verghese, T. M., 248
Virgin Mary, 36, 43, 51, 59, 77–78, 79, 87–88, 93*f*
Vishwa Hindu Parishad (VHP), 257, 259
Viswanath, Rupa, 218
Viswanathan, Gauri, 149–50
Voltaire, 98
vyakaran, 123–24

Wahhabis, 37–38
Walls, Andrew, 13–14, 143, 151, 245–46
Walter, H. A., 139
Ward, William, 123
Weber, Max, 140
Wesleyan Methodists, 121, 160
Why I Am Not a Hindu (Ilaiah), 226
Wilberforce, William, 171
Wilson, John, 9, 126–27, 129, 130–31, 260, 264
Wodeyar dynasty, 280n.73
World Christianity, 2–3, 160–61, 242, 263–64
  paradigm, 13–14

paradigm, critics of, 14–16
South Asia and, 12–16

Xavier, Francis, 58–59, 65, 67f, 188, 262–63
   converted Parava caste leaders, 70
   early months in Goa, 66
   involvement with Paravas, 67–69
   objects of devotion, 71
   observations about Hindus of south India, 68–69
   relations with Portuguese authorities, 69–70
   shrine to, 72f
Xavier, Jerome, 58–59

Yardi, Appaji Bapuji, 149
Yohannan, K. P., 253

Zenana missions, 170–71

Zend Avesta, 130
Ziegenbalg, Bartholomaeus, 8–9, 51, 90–91, 104–10, 115, 124–25, 260
   attitude toward Muslims, 108–9
   criticisms of Islam, 107
   exchanges with Hindus, 109
   New Jerusalem Church in Tranquebar, 107–8
   and Protestant Orientalism, 116
   relationship with Danish authorities, 107
   and religiosity of Tamil Hindus, 105–6
   south Indian caste practices, 105
   study of south Indian society, 104–5
   study of Tamil language, 104
   Tamil people, views on, 106–7
Zoroastrianism, 23, 130
Zupanov, Ines, 69, 77